WITHDRAWN

Critical Essays on
SHAKESPEARE'S
HAMLET

CRITICAL ESSAYS
ON
BRITISH LITERATURE

Zack Bowen, General Editor
University of Miami

Critical Essays on

SHAKESPEARE'S
HAMLET

edited by

DAVID SCOTT KASTAN

G. K. Hall & Co.
An Imprint of Simon & Schuster Macmillan
New York

Prentice Hall International
London   Mexico City   New Delhi   Singapore   Sydney   Toronto

G. K. Hall & Co.
An Imprint of Simon & Schuster Macmillan
866 Third Avenue
New York, New York 10022

Library of Congress Cataloging-in-Publication Data

Critical essays on Shakespeare's Hamlet / edited by David Scott Kastan.
        p.   cm. —(Critical essays on British literature)
    Includes bibliographical references and index.
    ISBN 0-7838-0001-0
    1. Shakespeare, William, 1564–1616.   Hamlet.   2. Tragedy.
I. Title.   II. Series.
PR2807.K33   1995
822.3'3—dc20   94-46650
                                                                              CIP

The paper used in this publication meets the minimum requirements of
American National Standard for Information Sciences—Permanence of
Paper for Printed Library Materials, ANSI Z39.48-1984. ⊗™

10   9   8   7   6   5   4   3   2   1

Printed in the United States of America

Contents

♦

General Editor's Note

◆

The Critical Essays on British Literature series provides a variety of approaches to both classical and contemporary writers of Britain and Ireland. The formats of the volumes in the series vary with the thematic designs of individual editors and with the amount and nature of existing reviews and criticism, augmented, where appropriate, by original essays by recognized authorities. It is hoped that each volume will be unique in developing a new overall perspective on its particular subject.

Kastan's introduction and selection of essays stress the variations on *Hamlet* that have appeared on the stage over 400 years of theatrical history and in the criticism, which posits highly individualistic versions of the meaning of the play. The introduction begins with Kastan outlining the differences among the early published texts, and the conflations of those versions in later texts, right through the twentieth century. The textual inconsistency is compounded by the variety of staged interpretations, which also selectively used and changed textual material, sometimes influencing later texts. Finally, the critics themselves reflect a plurality of responses to the action of the play and the motivation of its protagonist.

ZACK BOWEN
University of Miami

Publisher's Note

◆

Producing a volume that contains both newly commissioned and reprinted material presents the publisher with the challenge of balancing the desire to achieve stylistic consistency with the need to preserve the integrity of works first published elsewhere. In the Critical Essays series, essays commissioned especially for a particular volume are edited to be consistent with G. K. Hall's house style; reprinted essays appear in the style in which they were first published, with only typographical errors corrected. Consequently, shifts in style from one essay to another are the result of our efforts to be faithful to each text as it was originally published.

Introduction: "Very like a Whale"

◆

DAVID SCOTT KASTAN

Though, famously, T. S. Eliot thought *Hamlet* "most certainly an artistic failure,"[1] it nonetheless stands as Shakespeare's best-known and most often discussed play, arguably the play upon which Shakespeare's literary reputation most securely rests. If *King Lear* is Shakespeare's most emotionally rending tragedy, *Hamlet* is his most intellectually engaging and elusive, "the most problematic play ever written by Shakespeare or by any other playwright," as Harry Levin has written.[2] Critics and actors come to it again and again to confront its mysteries, possibly succeeding only in confirming the play's inexhaustible richness in the very inadequacy of their efforts fully or finally to capture it. Yet the play endlessly provokes response. If, as Michael Goldman has written, "an actor is a man who wants to play Hamlet,"[3] a literary critic could be defined as someone who wants to explicate the play that bears Hamlet's name.

The history of its criticism has been itself extraordinarily well chronicled, receiving almost as much attention as have most literary works. Paul Conklin traces the early commentary in his *History of "Hamlet" Criticism 1601–1821*.[4] A. A. Raven's *"Hamlet" Bibliography and Reference Guide, 1877–1935* provides a valuable catalogue of the post-Romantic responses to the play.[5] Paul Gottschalk, Morris Weitz, and, most recently, Michael Hattaway offer interesting accounts of later twentieth-century approaches.[6] Similarly, the production history (and certainly performance must be understood as a form of interpretation) has been fully documented, most significantly in Raymond Mander and Joe Mitchenson's *"Hamlet" through the Ages: A Pictorial Record from 1709*, J. C. Trewin's *Five and Eighty Hamlets*, and Bernice Kliman's *"Hamlet": Film, Television, and Audio Performance*.[7] And, of course, there have been earlier collections of *Hamlet* criticism, notably David Bevington's selection of essays in the "Twentieth Century Interpretations" series and Martin Coyle's recent anthology for Macmillan's "New Casebooks."[8]

1

All this testifies to the unrivaled attention the play has received from its critics. More has been written about *Hamlet* than about any other literary work. As early as 1908, one eminent Shakespearean was already dismayed by the quantity of published commentary *Hamlet* had engendered. "In the catalogue of a library which is very dear to me," wrote H. H. Furness, "there are about four hundred titles of separate editions, essays, commentaries, lectures, and criticisms on this sole tragedy, and I know this is only the vanguard of the coming years. . . . I am convinced that were I told that my closest friend was lying at the point of death, and that his life could be saved by permitting him to divulge his theory of Hamlet, I would instantly say, 'let him die! let him die! let him die!' "[9]

Furness was, of course, right about the future of *Hamlet* criticism (if not about his idea of friendship). His "four hundred titles" were indeed only the "vanguard of the coming years." The number of titles of *Hamlet* criticism has since grown to many thousands. For 1992 alone, according to the *Shakespeare Quarterly* bibliography, 479 items on *Hamlet* are listed, in one year more than the total number that horrified Furness. Critics continue to "divulge" their various theories of *Hamlet*, perhaps not getting any closer to plucking the heart of its mystery but their efforts offering indisputable evidence of the play's continuing claim on our imagination.

Ironically, however, the *Hamlet* that students read, that critics write about, that actors perform, and that audiences see is a play that Shakespeare never wrote. It is a conflated text, or rather *they* (for *Hamlet* is insistently plural) are conflated *texts*, combining materials from the early printed versions but in fact *differently* conflating these materials so no two modern editions are themselves exactly the same. Indeed it is possible, as Paul Werstine has argued,[10] that some of the complexity regularly celebrated by critics of *Hamlet* belongs less to the play Shakespeare wrote than to these modern editions, which produce contradiction through the unwarranted conflation of discrete and incompatable versions rather than register complexity legitimately residing in the play's provocative densities.

Usually the so-called Second Quarto (Q2) serves as the basis for modern editions. Published late in 1604 by James Roberts and Nicholas Ling, this edition claims to be printed "according to the true and perfect Coppie," and indeed it does seem to have been printed from Shakespeare's manuscript (though clearly it contains material meant—and possibly marked—for deletion).[11] No modern editor, however, relies exclusively upon Q2. Inevitably material from the *Hamlet* of the 1623 Folio, itself printed, as its editors say, "according to the True Originall Copies," is included, added to or substituted for the text of Q2. There are about 230 lines in Q2 that do not appear in the Folio *Hamlet* (including the "vicious mole of nature" speech and Hamlet's "How all occasions do inform against me" soliloquy) and about 70 lines in the Folio *Hamlet* that are not in Q2 (including the description of Denmark as a "prison" and the reference to the "little eyases" and the so-called War of the Theaters). Editors usually select from both versions to produce a conflation that has no independent bibliographic authority. In modern editions, for example, Hamlet, to his critics' delight, compares himself to both of the play's avenging sons, but it is only in the Folio text that he sees "the image of [his own] cause" in Laertes's situation and only in Q2 that he takes the resolute Fortinbras as an "example" for himself. Modern editorial practice has apparently produced a design unintended by Shakespeare or at least one unrealized in the play's substantive texts.

Further complicating the picture of the "text" of *Hamlet* is the existence of the enigmatic First Quarto (Q1). Printed in 1603 by Valentine Simmes for Nicholas Ling and John Trundell, Q1 was almost certainly an unauthorized printing, and it has usually been denigrated by scholars as a "bad" quarto (that is, one not deriving from the author's own papers). "The Revenge of Hamlett Prince [of] Denmarke" had been entered by James Roberts in the Stationers' Register in July of 1602, apparently indicating his intention soon to print the play, but Ling and Trundell beat him to the punch. Their version, of some 2,200 lines (compared to the approximately 3,800 of Q2), claims on its title page to be the play "as it hath beene diuerse times acted by his Highnesse seruants in the Cittie of London: as also in the two Vniuersities of Cambridge and Oxford, and elsewhere," and while it does give evidence of abridgement possibly for a touring company, it is in many places manifestly corrupt. Hamlet's most famous soliloquy in Q1 begins:

> "To be, or not to be, I there's the point,
> To die, to sleepe, is that all? I all:
> No, to sleepe, to dreame, I mary there it goes . . .
> (sig. D4v)

In Q1 Hamlet rants not like a "scullion," as in F, or even like Q2's "stalyon," but like a "scalion"; the Ghost of Q1 ambitiously usurps "the state" instead of the more modest object in Q2 of "this time of night"; and the elderly Norway, appropriately "impotent" in Q2, is in Q1 improbably "impudent."

The text of Q1 was apparently reconstructed for the printshop from the recollection of some of the actors who had performed it (primarily that of the actor who played Marcellus),[12] and the marks of its origins are evident in its numerous paraphrases, transpositions, omissions, and garblings. Thus, though Q1 was the first version of the play to be printed, it seems not to be the first version of the play, as has been sometimes argued.[13] Nonetheless, even if it is a text "put together . . . from memory without recourse or access to an authoritative manuscript,"[14] as a recent editor has stated, it remains of consequence (and traces of it find their way into modern editions and modern productions), for at very least it must tell us something of how Shakespeare's play fared in the playhouse. If it does in places mangle the text, it seemingly registers the abridgment made by the players and possibly records some of its original staging. It is Q1 alone that has the Ghost appear in the Queen's bedchamber dressed "in his night gowne," Q1 alone that has Ophelia enter "playing on a lute, and her haire downe singing," and Q1 alone in which "Hamlet leapes in[to Ophelia's grave] after Leartes" [*sic*].

That *Hamlet* existed in multiple versions cannot be surprising; perhaps what is surprising is only that these versions have survived. Such textual instability was almost certainly the norm of Renaissance play texts, which had no privileged literary status and inevitably must have been regularly revised for performance. But the textual instability of *Hamlet* is perhaps particularly appropriate for a play everywhere about the uncomfortable prolif- eration of possibility in the face of the desperate desire for singularity and certainty. The text is "out of joint" no less than the "time" that Hamlet is unable to "set right" (1.7.196–97).[15] Hamlet, who believes that "a man's life is no more than to say 'one' " (5.2.74; "one" here possibly celebrating the first touch in a fencing bout and certainly referring to the brevity of life and the need to seize the moment but inevitably also voicing his search for integrity and coherence), is frustrated by the doubleness and duplicity that confront him.[16]

"One" he never finds. Rather, everywhere he is faced with two: two kings—the Ghost, "King, father, royal Dane" (1.4.45), and Claudius, Ham- let's stepfather and "uncle [who] is King of Denmark" (2.2.359–60); two moral claims: a "commandment" (1.5.102) from beyond the grave to revenge his father's murder and yet that other commandment that says "Thou shalt not kill"; two cultures: an aristocratic culture of honor, represented by the Ghost, and Hamlet's Humanist academic culture, lived and learned at Wittenberg; Hamlet himself is both "scourge and minister" (3.4.176), prompted to revenge by both "heaven and hell" (2.2 580); even within the obligation to revenge, there is further doubleness: Hamlet is to enact his revenge against Claudius but is to leave Gertrude "to heaven" (1.5.86); and there are Rosencrantz and Guildenstern, Cornelius and Voltemand, and, of course, that defining binary: "To be, or not to be" (3.1.56). *Hamlet*, as Anna Nardo has written, is a play of contradiction and paradox, and Hamlet himself is "a true victim of double binds."[17] The only "union" literally offered by the play is not the marriage of Hamlet and Ophelia, which might have renewed the unweeded garden that is Denmark, but the poisoning pearl that Claudius throws into the wine for Hamlet to drink (5.2.269); and even that "union," symptom and symbol of Denmark's diseased society, is multiple and unstable. Q2 prints not "union" but "Vnice" in some copies and "Onixe" in others.

Hamlet, of course, relentlessly seeks a certainty that the play world denies him, and critical responses to the play usually vary according to what is blamed for his failure to find it. One response has been to take Hamlet at his word, or at least at one of his words, condemning him for allowing his "resolution" to be "sicklied o'er with the pale cast of thought" (3.1.84–85). This is the sensitive Hamlet that 19th-century intellectuals discovered—and discovered themselves in. "It is *we* who are Hamlet," said Hazlitt, defining the prince as a man "whose powers of action have been eaten up by thought."[18] Coleridge's Hamlet was similar: "a man living in meditation . . . continually resolving to do, yet doing nothing but resolve"; and Coleridge confessed: "I have a smack of Hamlet myself, if I may say so."[19] This is the Hamlet who delays, whose tragedy is, as the voice-over to Oliver's film (1947) has it, "the story of a man who could not make up his mind."

A second critical tack has been to take Hamlet at another of his words, to see him as a "proud, revengeful, ambitious" man (3.1.125), who has arrogated to himself the vengence that is properly God's (Romans 12:19) and who, as a result, ends up reenacting rather than revenging Claudius's crime. This Hamlet fails not because he thinks "too precisely on th'event" (4.4.41) but not precisely enough. Faced with an ambiguous ghost, he knows not if it be "a spirit of health or a goblin damn'd" (1.4.40), but here, knowing only "seems," he quickly accepts the vision and ultimately its charge: "I'll call thee Hamlet,/ King, Father, Royal Dane" (1.4.44–45), and vows to "sweep to [his] revenge" (1.5.31). This Hamlet is the Hamlet of "rash and bloody" deeds (3.4.27), who cruelly and arrogantly seeks vengeance, ignoring the condemnations of private revenge spoken by virtually all Renaissance thinkers.[20] This is the Hamlet who evades moral responsibility in his monomaniacal commitment to the Ghost's command. His mind has been "tainted" (1.5.85) as he pursues his revenge. No remorse accompanies Polonius's murder: "Thou wretched, rash, intruding fool, farewell./ I took thee for thy better" (3.4.31–32). And none follows once his friends "Guildenstern and Rosencrantz go to't": "they are not near my conscience, their defeat/ Does by their own insinuation grow" (5.2.56–59). This is the diminished (if not demonic) Hamlet. Once a "noble mind," a courtier, soldier, *and* scholar (3.1.152–53), he becomes only the soldier of his private revenge, and in his death he is fittingly borne "like a soldier to the stage" (5.2.401). "For his passage," says Fortinbras, "The soldier's music and the rite of war/ Speak loudly for him" (5.2.403–5), the exclusively martial frame of reference revealing not only the limited vision of the man who now rules Denmark but also the tragic reduction that Hamlet has undergone.

Each of these approaches centers on the command of the Ghost. Why does Hamlet listen to the voice urging revenge or why does he delay in fulfilling it? And while they are exact opposites in their understanding of Hamlet's failure, they identically define his tragedy in terms of a moral obligation that he fails to meet. A third approach, however, has been not to find fault with Hamlet, either for his rashness or for his indecision, but with the rotten state of Denmark. A murderous uncle on the throne, a "seeming-virtuous queen" (1.5.46), a nation of "drunkards" (1.4.19), disloyal friends and dysfunctional families, inadequate public institutions (not least the fact of no national university for its young adults and no resident theater[21]), all conspire against Hamlet and make his failure inevitable. Denmark is an "unweeded garden," possessed only by "things rank and gross in nature" (1.2.135–36); and if Hamlet in his efforts to restore it to wholesome growth fails and even becomes "a little soil'd i'th' working" (2.1.41) we cannot be surprised. Indeed we may admire him for his willingness to attempt a translation of the Ghost's intention into moral action. No doubt as he tries to weed the overgrown garden that is Denmark he uproots healthy stalks, but we must remember that he is not the one responsible for the garden's diseased condition and that the burden of its weeding has been, unasked for and unwanted, placed upon him.

An indecisive Hamlet, a rash Hamlet, an unsuccessful if sympathetic Hamlet all can be found in the play (or, perhaps better, *plays*) that bears his name. And, of course, so can other Hamlets. But whatever the nature of the Hamlet critics find, it is Hamlet they search for. He dominates the play more than any other titular hero. Even the most vulgar calculus makes this clear: Hamlet speaks about 1,400 lines in the play, some 300 more than any other Shakespearean character. But more consequential than the literal measure of how much Hamlet dominates the stage is the way Hamlet dominates the critical imagination, finally emerging less as a dramatic character than as some psychologically complex and complete human being, one even inviting analytic attention. (As Norman Holland remarks, "Psychoanalysts seem to take to Hamlet like kittens to a ball of yarn."[22]) Even the remarkable feminist response to the play that has restored Ophelia and Gertrude to critical notice tends to focus largely on Hamlet, not merely on his destructive relations with the women of the play but on his disgust with female sexuality itself.[23]

In the essays collected below various Hamlets and various *Hamlet*s appear. Like each of the early texts, these individual readings cannot claim to be definitive or authentic. No more than Horatio can a critic report Hamlet and his cause "aright" (5.2.344). As with Horatio's tale "of carnal, bloody, and unnatural acts,/ Of accidental judgments, casual slaughters,/ of deaths put on by cunning and forc'd cause,/ And, in this upshot, purposes mistook/ Fall'n on th' inventors' heads" (5.2.386–90), the truth of the play remains in excess of any telling. But each of the essays below is, if necessarily partial in both of its senses, a compelling and consequential engagement with this most enigmatic of Shakespeare's plays, discovering Hamlet's tragic experience in the specificities of the play world and discovering its meaning in relation to specificities of our own.[24]

Notes

1. T. S. Eliot, "Hamlet" (1919), in *Selected Essays* (London: Faber and Faber, 1951), p. 143.

2. *The Question of Hamlet* (New York: Viking Press, 1959), p. 131.

3. Goldman, *Shakespeare and the Energies of Drama* (Princeton: Princeton University Press, 1972), p. 74. See below.

4. Conklin, *History of "Hamlet" Criticism 1601–1821* (New York: King's Crown Press, 1947).

5. Raven, *"Hamlet" Bibliography and Reference Guide* (New York: Russell & Russell, 1966).

6. Weitz, *"Hamlet" and the Philosophy of Literary Criticism* (Chicago: University of Chicago Press, 1964); Gottschalk, *The Meanings of Hamlet: Modes of Literary Interpretation since Bradley* (Albuquerque: University of New Mexico Press, 1972); Hattaway, *Hamlet* (London: Macmillan, 1987).

7. Mander and Mitchenson, *"Hamlet" through the Ages* (London: Barrie and Rockliff, 1952); Trewin, *Five and Eighty Hamlets* (London: Hutchison, 1987); Kliman, *"Hamlet": Film, Television, and Audio Performance* (Rutherford, N.J.: Fairleigh Dickinson University Press, 1988).

8. Bevington, ed. *Twentieth Century Interpretations of "Hamlet"* (Englewood Cliffs, N.J.: Prentice-Hall, 1968; and Coyle, *"Hamlet"* (London: Macmillan, 1992).

9. "On Shakespeare, or, What You Will," Phi Beta Kappa Address, Harvard College, 25 June 1908, quoted in James M. Gibson, *The Philadelphia Shakespeare Story: Horace Howard Furness and the New Variorum Shakespeare* (New York: AMS, 1990), p. 220.

10. Werstine, "The Textual Mystery of *Hamlet*," *Shakespeare Quarterly* 39 (1988): 1–26 and reprinted below.

11. See J. Dover Wilson, *The Manuscript of Shakespeare's "Hamlet" and the Problems of its Transmission*, 2 vols., (Cambridge: Cambridge University Press, 1934). On the issue of the survival in Q2 of rejected material, consider one example given by Jenkins in his Arden *Hamlet* (p. 41): "For women feare too much, euen as they loue,/ And womens feare and loue hold quantitie,/ Eyther none, in neither ought, or in extremitie . . ." (sig. H2r). The first line seems clearly a draft of the second and meant to be replaced by it, as shown by the rhyme; and the hyper-metrical and redundant "Eyther none" in the third line seems similarly intended to be omitted.

12. See Kathleen Irace's "Origins and Agents of Q1 *Hamlet*," in *The "Hamlet" First Published (Q1, 1603): Origins, Form, Intertextuality*, ed. Thomas Clayton (Newark, Delaware: University of Delaware Press, 1992), pp. 90–122.

13. But see, for example, Steven Urkowitz, " 'Well-sayd olde Mole': Burying Three *Hamlets* in Modern Editions," in *Shakespeare Studies Today*, ed. Georgianna Ziegler (New York, AMS Press, 1986), pp. 37–70.

14. *Hamlet, Prince of Denmark*, ed. Philip Edwards (Cambridge: Cambridge University Press, 1985), p. 24.

15. All quotations from the play, not clearly indicated as being from one of the early printings, are cited by act, scene, and line from Harold Jenkins's Arden edition of *Hamlet* (London and New York: Methuen, 1982).

16. See Ralph Berry's " 'To Say One': An Essay on *Hamlet*," *Shakespeare Survey* 28 (1975): 107–15; rpt. in *The Shakespearean Metaphor: Studies in Language and Form* (Totowa, N. J., 1978). See also Barbara Everett's suggestive remarks on the word "one" in *Young Hamlet: Essays on Shakespeare's Tragedies* (Oxford: Clarendon Press, 1989), pp. 133–36.

17. Anna K. Nardo, "Hamlet, 'A Man to Double Business Bound,' " *Shakespeare Quarterly* 34 (1983): 181–99. See also Frank Kermode, "Cornelius and Voltemand: Doubles in *Hamlet*," in *Forms of Attention* (Chicago: University of Chicago Press, 1985), pp. 34–63; and George T. Wright's rhetorical analysis, "Hendiadys and *Hamlet*," *PMLA* 96 (1981): 168–93 and reprinted below.

18. William Hazlitt, *Characters of Shakespeare's Plays*, in *The Complete Works of William Hazlitt*, ed. P. P. Howe (London: J. M. Dent, 1930), 4, 232.

19. Samuel Taylor Coleridge, *Lectures 1808–1819: On Literature*, ed. R. A. Foakes (Princeton: Princeton University Press, 1987), 1, 390; and *Table-Talk*, June 24, 1827, in *The Complete Works of Samuel Taylor Coleridge*, ed. W. G. J. Shedd (New York: Harper and Brothers, 1853), 6, 285.

20. See Fredson Bowers, *Elizabethan Revenge Tragedy, 1587–1642* (Princeton: Princeton University Press, 1940), esp. pp. 3–40; and Eleanor Prosser, *Hamlet and Revenge*, 2nd ed., (Stanford: Stanford University Press, 1971).

21. For this fine and witty insight, and much else in my understanding of *Hamlet*, I am indebted to Richard Corum.

22. Norman N. Holland, *Psychoanalysis and Shakespeare* (New York: McGraw Hill, 1964), p. 163.

23. See Jacqueline Rose's "*Hamlet*—the 'Mona Lisa' of Literature," in *Sexuality in the Field of Vision* (London: Verso, 1986), pp. 123–40 and reprinted below; and Janet Adelman's chapter on the play in her *Suffocating Mothers: Fantasies of Maternal Origin in Shakespeare, from "Hamlet" to "The Tempest"* (New York: Routledge, 1992), pp. 11–37. Two pointed exceptions to the generalization about feminist focus on Hamlet are Elaine Showalter's "Representing Ophelia: Women, Madness, and the Responsibility of Feminist Criticism," in *Shakespeare and the Question of Theory*, eds. Patricia Parker and Geoffrey Hartman (London: Routledge, 1985), pp. 77–94; and Lisa Jardine's " 'No offence i' th' world': *Hamlet* and Unlawful Marriage," in *The Uses of History: Marxism, Postmodernism and the Renaissance*, ed. Francis Barker, Peter Hulme, and Margaret Iverson (Manchester: Manchester University Press, 1991), pp. 123–39 and reprinted below.

24. I would like to thank Jesse Lander for his extraordinary help in thinking about and producing this volume.

Shakespeare in the Bush

Laura Bohannan

Just before I left Oxford for the Tiv in West Africa, conversation turned to the season at Stratford. "You Americans," said a friend, "often have difficulty with Shakespeare. He was, after all, a very English poet, and one can easily misinterpret the universal by misunderstanding the particular."

I protested that human nature is pretty much the same the whole world over; at least the general plot and motivation of the greater tragedies would always be clear—everywhere—although some details of custom might have to be explained and difficulties of translation might produce other slight changes. To end an argument we could not conclude, my friend gave me a copy of *Hamlet* to study in the African bush: it would, he hoped, lift my mind above its primitive surroundings, and possibly I might, by prolonged meditation, achieve the grace of correct interpretation.

It was my second field trip to that African tribe, and I thought myself ready to live in one of its remote sections—an area difficult to cross even on foot. I eventually settled on the hillock of a very knowledgeable old man, the head of a homestead of some hundred and forty people, all of whom were either his close relatives or their wives and children. Like the other elders of the vicinity, the old man spent most of his time performing ceremonies seldom seen these days in the more accessible parts of the tribe. I was delighted. Soon there would be three months of enforced isolation and leisure, between the harvest that takes place just before the rising of the swamps and the clearing of new farms when the water goes down. Then, I thought, they would have even more time to perform ceremonies and explain them to me.

I was quite mistaken. Most of the ceremonies demanded the presence of elders from several homesteads. As the swamps rose, the old men found it too difficult to walk from one homestead to the next, and the ceremonies gradually ceased. As the swamps rose even higher, all activities but one came to an end. The women brewed beer from maize and millet. Men, women, and children sat on their hillocks and drank it.

People began to drink at dawn. By midmorning the whole homestead

*Reprinted from *Natural History*, 75 (1966):28–33. Used by permission of the author.

was singing, dancing, and drumming. When it rained, people had to sit inside their huts: there they drank and sang or they drank and told stories. In any case, by noon or before. I either had to join the party or retire to my own hut and my books. "One does not discuss serious matters when there is beer. Come, drink with us." Since I lacked their capacity for the thick native beer, I spent more and more time with *Hamlet*. Before the end of the second month, grace descended on me. I was quite sure that *Hamlet* had only one possible interpretation, and that one universally obvious.

Early every morning, in the hope of having some serious talk before the beer party, I used to call on the old man at his reception hut—a circle of posts supporting a thatched roof above a low mud wall to keep out wind and rain. One day I crawled through the low doorway and found most of the men of the homestead sitting huddled in their ragged cloths on stools, low plank beds, and reclining chairs, warming themselves against the chill of the rain around a smoky fire. In the center were three pots of beer. The party had started.

The old man greeted me cordially. "Sit down and drink." I accepted a large calabash full of beer, poured some into a small drinking gourd, and tossed it down. Then I poured some more into the same gourd for the man second in seniority to my host before I handed my calabash over to a young man for further distribution. Important people shouldn't ladle beer themselves.

"It is better like this," the old man said, looking at me approvingly and plucking at the thatch that had caught in my hair. "You should sit and drink with us more often. Your servants tell me that when you are not with us, you sit inside your hut looking at a paper."

The old man was acquainted with four kinds of "papers": tax receipts, bride price receipts, court fee receipts, and letters. The messenger who brought him letters from the chief used them mainly as a badge of office, for he always knew what was in them and told the old man. Personal letters for the few who had relatives in the government or mission stations were kept until someone went to a large market where there was a letter writer and reader. Since my arrival, letters were brought to me to be read. A few men also brought me bride price receipts, privately, with requests to change the figures to a higher sum. I found moral arguments were of no avail, since in-laws are fair game, and the technical hazards of forgery difficult to explain to an illiterate people. I did not wish them to think me silly enough to look at any such papers for days on end, and I hastily explained that my "paper" was one of the "things of long ago" of my country.

"Ah," said the old man. "Tell us."

I protested that I was not a storyteller. Storytelling is a skilled art among them; their standards are high, and the audiences critical—and vocal in their criticism. I protested in vain. This morning they wanted to hear a story while they drank. They threatened to tell me no more stories until I told them one of mine. Finally, the old man promised that no one would criticize my style "for we know you are struggling with our language." "But," put in one of the elders, "you must explain what we do not understand, as we do when we tell you our stories." Realizing that here was my chance to prove *Hamlet* universally intelligible, I agreed.

The old man handed me some more beer to help me on with my storytelling. Men filled their long wooden pipes and knocked coals from the fire to place in the pipe bowls; then, puffing contentedly, they sat back to listen. I began in the proper style, "Not yesterday, not yesterday, but long ago, a thing occurred. One night three men were keeping watch outside the homestead of the great chief, when suddenly they saw the former chief approach them."

"Why was he no longer their chief?"

"He was dead," I explained. "That is why they were troubled and afraid when they saw him."

"Impossible," began one of the elders, handing his pipe on to his neighbor, who interrupted, "Of course it wasn't the dead chief. It was an omen sent by a witch. Go on."

Slightly shaken, I continued. "One of these three was a man who knew things"—the closest translation for scholar, but unfortunately it also meant witch. The second elder looked triumphantly at the first. "So he spoke to the dead chief saying, 'Tell us what we must do so you may rest in your grave,' but the dead chief did not answer. He vanished, and they could see him no more. Then the man who knew things—his name was Horatio—said this event was the affair of the dead chief's son, Hamlet."

There was a general shaking of heads round the circle. "Had the dead chief no living brothers? Or was this son the chief?"

"No," I replied. "That is, he had one living brother who became the chief when the elder brother died."

The old men muttered: such omens were matters for chiefs and elders, not for youngsters; no good could come of going behind a chief's back; clearly Horatio was not a man who knew things.

"Yes, he was," I insisted, shooing a chicken away from my beer. "In our country the son is next to the father. The dead chief's younger brother had become the great chief. He had also married his elder brother's widow only about a month after the funeral."

"He did well," the old man beamed and announced to the others, "I told you that if we knew more about Europeans, we would find they really were very like us. In our country also," he added to me, "the younger brother marries the elder brother's widow and becomes the father of his children. Now, if your uncle, who married your widowed mother, is your father's full brother, then he will be a real father to you. Did Hamlet's father and uncle have one mother?"

*   *   *

His question barely penetrated my mind; I was too upset and thrown too far off balance by having one of the most important elements of *Hamlet* knocked straight out of the picture. Rather uncertainly I said that I thought they had the same mother, but I wasn't sure—the story didn't say. The old man told me severely that these genealogical details made all the difference and that when I got home I must ask the elders about it. He shouted out the door to one of his younger wives to bring his goatskin bag.

Determined to save what I could of the mother motif, I took a deep breath and began again. "The son Hamlet was very sad because his mother had married again so quickly. There was no need for her to do so, and it is our custom for a widow not to go to her next husband until she has mourned for two years."

"Two years is too long," objected the wife, who had appeared with the old man's battered goatskin bag. "Who will hoe your farms for you while you have no husband?"

"Hamlet," I retorted without thinking, "was old enough to hoe his mother's farms himself. There was no need for her to remarry." No one looked convinced. I gave up. "His mother and the great chief told Hamlet not to be sad, for the great chief himself would be a father to Hamlet. Furthermore, Hamlet would be the next chief: therefore he must stay to learn the things of a chief. Hamlet agreed to remain, and all the rest went off to drink beer."

While I paused, perplexed at how to render Hamlet's disgusted soliloquy to an audience convinced that Claudius and Gertrude had behaved in the best possible manner, one of the younger men asked me who had married the other wives of the dead chief.

"He had no other wives," I told him.

"But a chief must have many wives! How else can he brew beer and prepare food for all his guests?"

I said firmly that in our country even chiefs had only one wife, that they had servants to do their work, and that they paid them from tax money.

It was better, they returned, for a chief to have many wives and sons who would help him hoe his farms and feed his people; then everyone loved the chief who gave much and took nothing—taxes were a bad thing.

I agreed with the last comment, but for the rest fell back on their favorite way of fobbing off my questions: "That is the way it is done, so that is how we do it."

I decided to skip the soliloquy. Even if Claudius was here thought quite right to marry his brother's widow, there remained the poison motif, and I knew they would disapprove of fratricide. More hopefully I resumed, "That night Hamlet kept watch with the three who had seen his dead father. The dead chief again appeared, and although the others were afraid, Hamlet followed his dead father off to one side. When they were alone, Hamlet's dead father spoke."

"Omens can't talk!" The old man was emphatic.

"Hamlet's dead father wasn't an omen. Seeing him might have been an omen, but he was not." My audience looked as confused as I sounded. "It *was* Hamlet's dead father. It was a thing we call a 'ghost.' " I had to use the English word, for unlike many of the neighboring tribes, these people didn't believe in the survival after death of any individuating part of the personality.

"What is a 'ghost?' An omen?"

"No, a 'ghost' is someone who is dead but who walks around and can talk, and people can hear him and see him but not touch him."

They objected. "One can touch zombis."

"No, no! It was not a dead body the witches had animated to sacrifice and eat. No one else made Hamlet's dead father walk. He did it himself."

"Dead men can't walk," protested my audience as one man.

I was quite willing to compromise. "A 'ghost' is the dead man's shadow."

But again they objected. "Dead men cast no shadows."

"They do in my country," I snapped.

The old man quelled the babble of disbelief that arose immediately and told me with that insincere, but courteous, agreement one extends to the fancies of the young, ignorant, and superstitious, "No doubt in your country the dead can also walk without being zombis." From the depths of his bag he produced a withered fragment of kola nut, bit off one end to show it wasn't poisoned, and handed me the rest as a peace offering.

"Anyhow," I resumed, "Hamlet's dead father said that his own brother, the one who became chief, had poisoned him. He wanted Hamlet to avenge him. Hamlet believed this in his heart, for he did not like his father's brother." I took another swallow of beer. "In the country of the great chief, living in the same homestead, for it was a very large one, was an important elder who was often with the chief to advise and help him. His name was Polonius. Hamlet was courting his daughter, but her father and her brother . . . [I cast hastily about for some tribal analogy] warned her not to let Hamlet visit her when she was alone on her farm, for he would be a great chief and so could not marry her."

"Why not?" asked the wife, who had settled down on the edge of the old man's chair. He frowned at her for asking stupid questions and growled, "They lived in the same homestead."

"That was not the reason," I informed them. "Polonius was a stranger who lived in the homestead because he helped the chief, not because he was a relative."

"Then why couldn't Hamlet marry her?"

"He could have," I explained, "but Polonius didn't think he would. After all, Hamlet was a man of great importance who ought to marry a chief's daughter, for in his country a man could have only one wife. Polonius was afraid that if Hamlet made love to his daughter, then no one else would give a high price for her."

"That might be true," remarked one of the shrewder elders, "but a chief's son would give his mistress's father enough presents and patronage to more than make up the difference. Polonius sounds like a fool to me."

"Many people think he was," I agreed. "Meanwhile Polonius sent his son Laertes off to Paris to learn the things of that country, for it was the homestead of a very great chief indeed. Because he was afraid that Laertes might waste a lot of money on beer and women and gambling, or get into trouble by fighting, he sent one of his servants to Paris secretly, to spy out what Laertes was doing. One day Hamlet came upon Polonius's daughter Ophelia. He behaved so oddly he frightened her. Indeed"—I was fumbling for words to express the dubious quality of Hamlet's madness—"the chief and many others had also noticed that when Hamlet talked one could understand the words but not what they meant. Many people thought that he had become mad." My audience suddenly became much more attentive. "The great chief wanted to know what was wrong with Hamlet, so he sent for two of Hamlet's age mates [school friends would have taken long explanation] to talk to Hamlet and find out what troubled his heart. Hamlet, seeing that they had been bribed by the chief to betray him, told them nothing. Polonius, however, insisted that Hamlet was mad because he had been forbidden to see Ophelia, whom he loved."

"Why," inquired a bewildered voice, "should anyone bewitch Hamlet on that account?"

"Bewitch him?"

"Yes, only witchcraft can make anyone mad, unless, of course, one sees the beings that lurk in the forest."

I stopped being a storyteller, took out my notebook and demanded to be told more about these two causes of madness. Even while they spoke and I jotted notes, I tried to calculate the effect of this new factor on the plot. Hamlet had not been exposed to the beings that lurk in the forests. Only his relatives in the male line could bewitch him. Barring relatives not mentioned by Shakespeare, it had to be Claudius who was attempting to harm him. And, of course, it was.

For the moment I staved off questions by saying that the great chief also refused to believe that Hamlet was mad for the love of Ophelia and nothing else. "He was sure that something much more important was troubling Hamlet's heart.

"Now Hamlet's age mates," I continued, "had brought with them a famous storyteller. Hamlet decided to have this man tell the chief and all his homestead a story about a man who had poisoned his brother because he desired his brother's wife and wished to be chief himself. Hamlet was sure the great chief could not hear the story without making a sign if he was indeed guilty, and then he would discover whether his dead father had told him the truth."

The old man interrupted, with deep cunning, "Why should a father lie to his son?" he asked.

I hedged: "Hamlet wasn't sure that it really was his dead father." It was impossible to say anything, in that language, about devil-inspired visions.

"You mean," he said, "it actually was an omen, and he knew witches sometimes send false ones. Hamlet was a fool not to go to one skilled in reading omens and divining the truth in the first place. A man-who-sees-the-truth could have told him how his father died, if he really had been poisoned, and if there was witchcraft in it; then Hamlet could have called the elders to settle the matter."

The shrewd elder ventured to disagree. "Because his father's brother was a great chief, one-who-sees-the-truth might therefore have been afraid to tell it. I think it was for that reason that a friend of Hamlet's father—a witch and an elder—sent an omen so his friend's son would know. Was the omen true?"

"Yes," I said, abandoning ghosts and the devil; a witch-sent omen it would have to be. "It was true, for when the storyteller was telling his tale before all the homestead, the great chief rose in fear. Afraid that Hamlet knew his secret he planned to have him killed."

The stage set of the next bit presented some difficulties of translation. I began cautiously. "The great chief told Hamlet's mother to find out from her son what he knew. But because a woman's children are always first in her heart, he had the important elder Polonius hide behind a cloth that hung against the wall of Hamlet's mother's sleeping hut. Hamlet started to scold his mother for what she had done."

There was a shocked murmur from everyone. A man should never scold his mother.

"She called out in fear, and Polonius moved behind the cloth. Shouting, 'A rat!' Hamlet took his machete and slashed through the cloth." I paused for dramatic effect. "He had killed Polonius!"

The old men looked at each other in supreme disgust. "That Polonius truly was a fool and a man who knew nothing! What child would not know enough to shout, 'It's me!'" With a pang, I remembered that these people are ardent hunters, always armed with bow, arrow, and machete; at the first rustle in the grass an arrow is aimed and ready, and the hunter shouts "Game!" If no human voice answers immediately, the arrow speeds on its way. Like a good hunter Hamlet had shouted, "A rat!"

I rushed in to save Polonius's reputation. "Polonius did speak. Hamlet heard him. But he thought it was the chief and wished to kill him to avenge his father. He had meant to kill him earlier that evening. . . ." I broke down, unable to describe to these pagans, who had no belief in individual afterlife, the difference between dying at one's prayers and dying "unhousell'd, disappointed, unaneled."

This time I had shocked my audience seriously. "For a man to raise his hand against his father's brother and the one who has become his father— that is a terrible thing. The elders ought to let such a man be bewitched."

I nibbled at my kola nut in some perplexity, then pointed out that after all the man had killed Hamlet's father.

"No," pronounced the old man, speaking less to me than to the young men sitting behind the elders. "If your father's brother has killed your father, you must appeal to your father's age mates; *they* may avenge him. No man may use violence against his senior relatives." Another thought struck him. "But if his father's brother had indeed been wicked enough to bewitch Hamlet and make him mad that would be a good story indeed, for it would be his fault that Hamlet, being mad, no longer had any sense and thus was ready to kill his father's brother."

There was a murmur of applause. *Hamlet* was again a good story to them, but it no longer seemed quite the same story to me. As I thought over the coming complications of plot and motive, I lost courage and decided to skim over dangerous ground quickly.

"The great chief," I went on, "was not sorry that Hamlet had killed Polonius. It gave him a reason to send Hamlet away, with his two treacherous age mates, with letters to a chief of a far country, saying that Hamlet should be killed. But Hamlet changed the writing on their papers, so that the chief killed his age mates instead." I encountered a reproachful glare from one of the men whom I had told undetectable forgery was not merely immoral but beyond human skill. I looked the other way.

"Before Hamlet could return, Laertes came back for his father's funeral. The great chief told him Hamlet had killed Polonius. Laertes swore to kill Hamlet because of this, and because his sister Ophelia, hearing her father had been killed by the man she loved, went mad and drowned in the river."

"Have you already forgotten what we told you?" The old man was reproachful. "One cannot take vengeance on a madman; Hamlet killed Polonius in his madness. As for the girl, she not only went mad, she was drowned. Only witches can make people drown. Water itself can't hurt anything. It is merely something one drinks and bathes in."

I began to get cross. "If you don't like the story, I'll stop."

The old man made soothing noises and himself poured me some more beer. "You tell the story well, and we are listening. But it is clear that the elders of your country have never told you what the story really means. No, don't interrupt! We believe you when you say your marriage customs are different, or your clothes and weapons. But people are the same everywhere; therefore, there are always witches and it is we, the elders, who know how witches work. We told you it was the great chief who wished to kill Hamlet, and now your own words have proved us right. Who were Ophelia's male relatives?"

"There were only her father and her brother." Hamlet was clearly out of my hands.

"There must have been many more; this also you must ask of your elders when you get back to your country. From what you tell us, since Polonius was dead, it must have been Laertes who killed Ophelia, although I do not see the reason for it."

We had emptied one pot of beer, and the old men argued the point with slightly tipsy interest. Finally one of them demanded of me, "What did the servant of Polonius say on his return?"

With difficulty I recollected Reynaldo and his mission. "I don't think he did return before Polonius was killed."

"Listen," said the elder, "and I will tell you how it was and how your story will go, then you may tell me if I am right. Polonius knew his son would get into trouble, and so he did. He had many fines to pay for fighting, and debts from gambling. But he had only two ways of getting money quickly. One was to marry off his sister at once, but it is difficult to find a man who will marry a woman desired by the son of a chief. For if the chief's heir commits adultery with your wife, what can you do? Only a fool calls a case against a man who will someday be his judge. Therefore Laertes had to take the second way: he killed his sister by witchcraft, drowning her so he could secretly sell her body to the witches."

I raised an objection. "They found her body and buried it. Indeed Laertes jumped into the grave to see his sister once more—so, you see, the body was truly there. Hamlet, who had just come back, jumped in after him."

"What did I tell you?" The elder appealed to the others. "Laertes was up to no good with his sister's body. Hamlet prevented him, because the chief's heir, like a chief, does not wish any other man to grow rich and powerful. Laertes would be angry, because he would have killed his sister without benefit to himself. In our country he would try to kill Hamlet for that reason. Is this not what happened?"

"More or less," I admitted. "When the great chief found Hamlet was still alive, he encouraged Laertes to try to kill Hamlet and arranged a fight with machetes between them. In the fight both the young men were wounded to death. Hamlet's mother drank the poisoned beer that the chief meant for Hamlet in case he won the fight. When he saw his mother die of poison, Hamlet, dying, managed to kill his father's brother with his machete."

"You see, I was right!" exclaimed the elder.

"That was a very good story," added the old man, "and you told it with very few mistakes. There was just one more error, at the very end. The poison Hamlet's mother drank was obviously meant for the survivor of the fight, whichever it was. If Laertes had won, the great chief would have poisoned him, for no one would know that he arranged Hamlet's death. Then, too, he need not fear Laertes' witchcraft; it takes a strong heart to kill one's only sister by witchcraft.

"Sometime," concluded the old man, gathering his ragged toga about him, "you must tell us some more stories of your country. We, who are elders, will instruct you in their true meaning, so that when you return to your own land your elders will see that you have not been sitting in the bush, but among those who know things and who have taught you wisdom."

On the Value of *Hamlet*

Stephen Booth

It is a truth universally acknowledged that *Hamlet* as we have it—usually in a conservative conflation of the second quarto and first folio texts—is not really *Hamlet*. The very fact that the *Hamlet* we know is an editor-made text has furnished an illusion of firm ground for leaping conclusions that discrepancies between the probable and actual actions, statements, tone, and diction of *Hamlet* are accidents of its transmission. Thus, in much the spirit of editors correcting printer's errors, critics have proposed stage directions by which, for example, Hamlet can overhear the plot to test Polonius' diagnosis of Hamlet's affliction, or by which Hamlet can glimpse Polonius and Claudius actually spying on his interview with Ophelia. Either of these will make sense of Hamlet's improbable raging at Ophelia in III.i. The difficulty with such presumably corrective emendation is not only in knowing where to stop, but also in knowing whether to start. I hope to demonstrate that almost everything else in the play has, in its particular kind and scale, an improbability comparable to the improbability of the discrepancy between Hamlet's real and expected behavior to Ophelia; for the moment, I mean only to suggest that those of the elements of the text of *Hamlet* that are incontrovertibly accidental may by their presence have led critics to overestimate the distance between the *Hamlet* we have and the prelapsarian *Hamlet* to which they long to return.

I think also that the history of criticism shows us too ready to indulge a not wholly explicable fancy that in *Hamlet* we behold the frustrated and inarticulate Shakespeare furiously wagging his tail in an effort to tell us something, but, as I said before, the accidents of our texts of *Hamlet* and the alluring analogies they father render *Hamlet* more liable to interpretive assistance than even the other plays of Shakespeare. Moreover, *Hamlet* was of course born into the culture of Western Europe, our culture, whose every thought—literary or nonliterary—is shaped by the Platonic presumption that the reality of anything is other than its apparent self. In such a culture it is no wonder that critics prefer the word *meaning* (which implies effort rather than success) to *saying*, and that in turn they would rather talk about

*From *Reinterpretations of Elizabethan Drama*, ed. Norman Rabkin, (1969): 74–93. Reprinted by permission of Columbia University Press.

what a work *says* or *shows* (both of which suggest the hidden essence bared of the dross of physicality) than talk about what it *does*. Even stylistic critics are most comfortable and acceptable when they reveal that rhythm, syntax, diction, or (and above all) imagery are vehicles for meaning. Among people to whom "It means a lot to me" says "I value it," in a language where *significant* and *valuable* are synonyms, it was all but inevitable that a work with the peculiarities of *Hamlet* should have been treated as a distinguished and yearning failure.

Perhaps the value of *Hamlet* is where it is most measurable, in the degree to which it fulfills one or another of the fixable identities it suggests for itself or that are suggested for it, but I think that before we choose and argue for one of the ideal forms toward which *Hamlet* seems to be moving, and before we attribute its value to an exaggeration of the degree to which it gets there, it is reasonable to talk about what the play *does* do, and to test the suggestion that in a valued play what it does do is what we value. I propose to look at *Hamlet* for what it undeniably is: a succession of actions upon the understanding of an audience. I set my hypothetical audience to watch *Hamlet* in the text edited by Willard Farnham in The Pelican *Shakespeare* (Baltimore, 1957), a text presumably too long to have fitted into the daylight available to a two o'clock performance, but still an approximation of what Shakespeare's company played.

I

The action that the first scene of *Hamlet* takes upon the understanding of its audience is like the action of the whole, and most of the individual actions that make up the whole. The first scene is insistently incoherent and just as insistently coherent. It frustrates and fulfills expectations simultaneously. The challenge and response in the first lines are perfectly predictable sentry-talk, but—as has been well and often observed—the challenger is the wrong man, the relieving sentry and not the one on duty. A similarly faint intellectual uneasiness is provoked when the first personal note in the play sets up expectations that the play then ignores. Francisco says, "For this relief much thanks. 'Tis bitter cold,/ And I am sick at heart" (i.i.8–9). We want to know why he is sick at heart. Several lines later Francisco leaves the stage and is forgotten. The scene continues smoothly as if the audience had never focused on Francisco's heartsickness. Twice in the space of less than a minute the audience has an opportunity to concern itself with a trouble that vanishes from consciousness almost before it is there. The wrong sentry challenges, and the other corrects the oddity instantly. Francisco is sick at heart, but neither he nor Bernardo gives any sign that further comment might be in order. The routine of sentry-go, its special diction, and its commonplaces continue across the audience's momentary tangential journey; the audience returns as if *it* and not the play had wandered. The audience's sensation of being unexpectedly and very slightly out of step is repeated regularly in *Hamlet*.

The first thing an audience in a theater wants to know is why it is in the theater. Even one that, like Shakespeare's audiences for *Richard II* or *Julius Caesar* or *Hamlet*, knows the story being dramatized wants to hear out the familiar terms of the situation and the terms of the particular new dramatization. Audiences want their bearings and expect them to be given. The first thing we see in *Hamlet* is a pair of sentries. The sight of sentries in real life is insignificant, but, when a work of art focuses on sentries, it is usually a sign that what they are guarding is going to be attacked. Thus, the first answer we have to the question "what is this play about?" is "military threat to a castle and a king," and that leads to our first specific question: "what is that threat?" Horatio's first question ("What, has this thing appeared again to-night?" I.i.21) is to some extent an answer to the audience's question; its terms are not military, but their implications are appropriately threatening. Bernardo then begins elaborate preparations to tell Horatio what the audience must hear if it is ever to be intellectually comfortable in the play. The audience has slightly adjusted its expectations to accord with a threat that is vaguely supernatural rather than military, but the metaphor of assault in which Bernardo prepares to carry the audience further along its new path of inquiry is pertinent to the one from which it has just deviated:

> Sit down awhile,
> And let us once again assail your ears,
> That are so fortified against our story,
> What we two nights have seen.
> (I.i.30–33)

We are led toward increased knowledge of the new object—the ghost—in terms appropriate to the one we assumed and have just abandoned—military assault. Bernardo's metaphor is obviously pertinent to his occupation as sentinel, but in the metaphor he is not the defender but the assailant of ears fortified against his story. As the audience listens, its understanding shifts from one system of pertinence to another; but each perceptible change in the direction of our concern or the terms of our thinking is balanced by the repetition of some continuing factor in the scene; the mind of the audience is in constant but gentle flux, always shifting but never completely leaving familiar ground.

Everyone onstage sits down to hear Bernardo speak of the events of the past two nights. The audience is invited to settle its mind for a long and desired explanation. The construction of Bernardo's speech suggests that it will go on for a long time; he takes three lines (I.i.35–38) to arrive at the grammatical subject of his sentence, and then, as he begins another parenthetical delay in his long journey toward a verb, "the bell then beating one," *Enter Ghost*. The interrupting action is not a simple interruption. The description is interrupted by a repetition of the action described. The entrance of the ghost duplicates on a larger scale the kind of mental experience we have had before. It both fulfills and frustrates our expectations: it is what we expect and desire, an action to account for our attention to sentinels; it is unexpected and unwanted, an interruption in the syntactical routine of the exposition that was on its way to fulfilling the same function. While the ghost is on the stage and during the speculation that immediately follows its departure, the futile efforts of Horatio and the sentries (who, as watchers and waiters, have resembled the audience from the start) are like those of the audience in its quest for information. Marcellus' statement about the ghost is a fair comment on the whole scene: " 'Tis gone and will not answer" (I.i.52), and Horatio's "In what particular thought to work I know not" (I.i.67) describes the mental condition evoked in an audience by this particular dramatic presentation of events as well as it does that evoked in the character by the events of the fiction.

Horatio continues from there into the first statement in the play that is responsive to an audience's requirement of an opening scene, an indication of the nature and direction of the play to follow: "But, in the gross and scope of my opinion,/ This bodes some strange eruption to our state" (I.i.68–69). That vague summary of the significance of the ghost is political, but only incidentally so because the audience, which was earlier attuned to political/military considerations, has now given its attention to the ghost. Then, with only the casual preamble of the word *state*, Marcellus asks a question irrelevant to the audience's newly primary concerns, precisely the question that no one asked when the audience first wanted to know why it was watching the sentries, the question about the fictional situation whose answer would have satisfied the audience's earlier question about its own situation: Marcellus asks "Why this same strict and most observant watch/ So nightly toils the subject of the land" (I.i.71–72). Again what we are given is and is not pertinent to our concerns and expectations. This particular variety among the manifestations of simultaneous and equal propriety and impropriety in *Hamlet* occurs over and over again. Throughout the play, the audience gets information or sees action it once wanted only after a new interest has superseded the old. For one example, when Horatio, Bernardo, and Marcellus arrive in the second scene (I.ii.159), they come to do what they promise to do at the end of scene one, where they tell the audience that the way to information about the ghost is through young Hamlet. By the time they arrive "where we shall find him most conveniently," the audience has a new concern—the relation of Claudius to Gertrude and of Hamlet to both. Of course interruptions of one train of thought by the introduction of another are not only common in *Hamlet* but a commonplace of literature in general. However, although the audience's frustrations and the celerity with which it transfers its concern are similar to those of audiences of, say, Dickens, there is the important difference in *Hamlet* that there are no sharp lines of demarcation. In *Hamlet* the audience does not so much shift its focus as come to find its focus shifted.

Again the first scene provides a type of the whole. When Marcellus asks why the guard is so strict, his question is rather more violent than not in its divergence from our concern for the boding of the ghost. The answer to Marcellus' question, however, quickly pertains to the subject of ours: Horatio's explanation of the political situation depends from actions of "Our last king,/ Whose image even but now appeared to us" (I.i.80–81), and his description of the activities of young Fortinbras as "The source of this our watch" is harnessed to our concern about the ghost by Bernardo, who says directly, if vaguely, that the political situation is pertinent to the walking of the ghost:

> I think it be no other but e'en so.
> Well may it sort that this portentous figure
> Comes armed through our watch so like the king
> That was and is the question of these wars.
>
> (I.i.108–11)

Horatio reinforces the relevance of politics to ghosts in a long speech about supernatural events on the eve of Julius Caesar's murder. Both these speeches establishing pertinence are good examples of the sort of thing I mean: both seem impertinent digressions, sufficiently so to have been omitted from the folios.

Now for the second time, *Enter Ghost.* The reentrance after a long and wandering digression is in itself an assertion of the continuity, constancy, and unity of the scene. Moreover, the situation into which the ghost reenters is a careful echo of the one into which it first entered, with the difference that the promised length of the earlier exposition is fulfilled in the second. These are the lines surrounding the first entrance; the italics are mine and indicate words, sounds, and substance echoed later:

HORATIO: *Well, sit we down,*
      And let us hear Bernardo speak of this.

BERNARDO: Last night of all,
      When yond same star that's *westward* from the pole
      Had made his course t' illume that part of heaven
      Where now it burns, Marcellus and myself,
      The bell then beating one—

                                        Enter Ghost.

MARCELLUS: *Peace, break thee off. Look where it comes again.*

                                         (I.i.33–40)

Two or three minutes later a similar situation takes shape in words that
echo, and in some cases repeat, those at the earlier entrance:

MARCELLUS: *Good now*, *sit down*, and tell me he that knows,
          Why this same strict and most observant watch,
          So nightly toils the subject of the land . . .

                    . . . .

                                                  Enter Ghost

          But soft, behold, lo where it comes again!

                                      (I.i.70–72, 126)

After the ghost departs on the crowing of the cock, the conversation, already
extravagant and erring before the second apparition when it ranged from
Danish history into Roman, meanders into a seemingly gratuitous preoccupation with the demonology of cocks (I.i. 148–65). Then—into a scene that
has from the irregularly regular entrance of the two sentinels been a succession
of simultaneously expected and unexpected entrances—enters "the morn in
russet mantle clad," bringing a great change from darkness to light, from
the unknown and unnatural to the known and natural, but also presenting
itself personified as another walker, one obviously relevant to the situation
and to the discussion of crowing cocks, and one described in subdued but
manifold echoes of the two entrances of the ghost. Notice particularly the
multitude of different kinds of relationship in which "yon high eastward
hill" echoes "yond same star that's westward from the pole":

          But look, the morn in russet mantle clad
          Walks o'er the dew of *yon high eastward* hill.
          Break we our watch up . . .
                      (I.i. 166–68)

The three speeches (I.i. 148–73—Horatio's on the behavior of ghosts at
cockcrow, Marcellus' on cocks at Christmas time, and Horatio's on the dawn)
have four major elements running through them: cocks, spirits, sunrise, and
the presence or absence of speech. All four are not present all the time, but
the speeches have a sound of interconnection and relevance to one another.
This at the same time that the substance of Marcellus' speech on Christmas
is just as urgently irrelevant to the concerns of the scene. As a gratuitous
discussion of Christianity, apparently linked to its context only by an accident
of poulterer's lore, it is particularly irrelevant to the moral limits usual to
revenge tragedy. The sequence of these last speeches is like the whole scene
and the play in being both coherent and incoherent. Watching and comprehending the scene is an intellectual triumph for its audience. From sentence to
sentence, from event to event, as the scene goes on it makes the mind of its
audience capable of containing materials that seem always about to fly apart.

The scene gives its audience a temporary and modest but real experience of being a superhumanly capable mental athlete. The whole play is like that.

During the first scene of *Hamlet* two things are threatened, one in the play, and one by the play. Throughout the scene the characters look at all threats as threats to the state, and specifically to the reigning king. As the king is threatened *in* scene one, so is the audience's understanding threatened *by* scene one. The audience wants some solid information about what is going on in this play. Scene one is set in the dark, and it leaves the audience in the dark. The first things the play teaches us to value are the order embodied in the king and the rational sureness, purpose, and order that the play as a play lacks in its first scene. Scene two presents both the desired orders at once and in one—the king, whose name even in scene one was not only synonymous with order but was the regular sign by which order was reasserted: the first confusion—who should challenge whom—was resolved in line three by "Long live the king"; and at the entrance of Horatio and Marcellus, rightness and regularity were vouched for by "Friends to this ground. And liegemen to the Dane." As scene two begins it is everything the audience wanted most in scene one. Here it is daylight, everything is clear, everything is systematic. Unlike scene one, this scene is physically orderly; it begins with a royal procession, businesslike and unmistakable in its identity. Unlike the first scene, the second gives the audience all the information it could desire, and gives it neatly. The direct source of both information and orderliness is Claudius, who addresses himself one by one to the groups on the stage and to the problems of the realm, punctuating the units both with little statements of conclusion like "For all, our thanks" and "So much for him" (I.ii.16, 25), and with the word "now" (I.ii.17, 26, 42, 64), by which he signals each remove to a new listener and topic. Denmark and the play are both now orderly, and are so because of the king. In its specifics, scene two is the opposite of scene one. Moreover, where scene one presented an incoherent surface whose underlying coherence is only faintly felt, this scene is the opposite. In scene one the action taken *by* the scene—it makes its audience perceive diffusion and fusion, division and unification, difference and likeness at once—is only an incidental element in the action taken or discussed *in* the scene—the guards have trouble recognizing each other; the defense preparation "does not divide the Sunday from the week," and makes "the night joint-laborer with the day" (I.i.76, 78). In scene two the first subject taken up by Claudius, and the subject of first importance to Hamlet, is itself an instance of improbable unification—the unnatural natural union of Claudius and Gertrude. Where scene one brought its audience to feel coherence in incoherence by response to systems of organization other than those of logical or narrative sequence, scene two brings its audience to think of actions and characters alternately and sometimes nearly simultaneously in systems of value whose contradictory judgments rarely collide in the mind of an audience. From an uneasiness prompted by a sense of lack of order, unity, coherence, and continuity, we have progressed to an uneasiness prompted by a sense of their excess.

Claudius is everything the audience most valued in scene one, but he is also and at once contemptible. His first sentences are unifications in which his discretion overwhelms things whose natures are oppugnant. The simple but contorted statement, "therefore our . . . sister . . . have we . . . taken to wife," takes Claudius more than six lines to say; it is plastered together with a succession of subordinate unnatural unions made smooth by rhythm, alliteration, assonance, and syntactical balance:

> Therefore our sometime sister, now our queen,
> Th' imperial jointress to this warlike state,
> Have we, as 'twere with a defeated joy,
> With an auspicious and a dropping eye,
> With mirth in funeral and with dirge in marriage,
> In equal scale weighing delight and dole,
> Taken to wife.
>
> (i.ii.8–14)

What he says is overly orderly. The rhythms and rhetoric by which he connects any contraries, moral or otherwise, are too smooth. Look at the complex phonetic equation that gives a sound of decorousness to the moral indecorum of "With mirth in funeral and with dirge in marriage." Claudius uses syntactical and rhetorical devices for equation by balance—as one would a particularly heavy and greasy cosmetic—to smooth over any inconsistencies whatsoever. Even his incidental diction is of joining: "jointress," "disjoint," "Colleagued" (i.ii.9, 20, 21). The excessively lubricated rhetoric by which Claudius makes unnatural connections between moral contraries is as gross and sweaty as the incestuous marriage itself. The audience has double and contrary responses to Claudius, the unifier of contraries.

Scene two presents still another kind of double understanding in double frames of reference. Claudius is the primary figure in the hierarchy depicted— he is the king; he is also the character upon whom all the other characters focus their attention; he does most of the talking. An audience focuses its attention on him. On the other hand, one of the members of the royal procession was dressed all in black—a revenger to go with the presumably vengeful ghost in scene one. Moreover, the man in black is probably also the most famous actor in England (or at least of the company). The particulars of the scene make Claudius the focal figure, the genre and the particulars of a given performance focus the audience's attention on Hamlet.

When the two focuses come together ("But now, my cousin Hamlet, and my son—") Hamlet's reply (i.ii.65) is spoken not to the king but to the audience. "A little more than kin, and less than kind" is the first thing spoken by Hamlet and the first thing spoken aside to the audience. With that line Hamlet takes the audience for his own, and gives himself to the audience as its agent on the stage. Hamlet and the audience are from this point in the play more firmly united than any other such pair in Shakespeare, and perhaps in dramatic literature.

Claudius' "my cousin Hamlet, and my son" is typical of his stylistic unifications of mutually exclusive contrary ideas (cousin, son). Hamlet's reply does not unify ideas, but disunifies them (more than kin, less than kind). However, the style in which Hamlet distinguishes is a caricature of Claudius' equations by rhetorical balance; here again, what interrupts the order, threatens coherence, and is strikingly at odds with its preamble is also a continuation by echo of what went before. Hamlet's parody of Claudius and his refusal to be folded into Claudius' rhetorical blanket is satisfying to an audience in need of assurance that it is not alone in its uneasiness at Claudius' rhetoric. On the other hand, the orderliness that the audience valued in scene two is abruptly destroyed by Hamlet's reply. At the moment Hamlet speaks his first line, the audience finds itself the champion of order in Denmark and in the play, and at the same time irrevocably allied to Hamlet—the one present threat to the order of both.

II

The play persists in taking its audience to the brink of intellectual terror. The mind of the audience is rarely far from the intellectual desperation of Claudius in the prayer scene when the systems in which he values his crown and queen collide with those in which he values his soul and peace of mind. For the duration of *Hamlet* the mind of the audience is as it might be if it could take on, or dared to try to take on, its experience whole, if it dared drop the humanly necessary intellectual crutches of compartmentalization, point of view, definition, and the idea of relevance, if it dared admit any subject for evaluation into any and all the systems of value to which at different times one human mind subscribes. The constant occupation of a sane mind is to choose, establish, and maintain frames of reference for the things of its experience; as the high value placed on artistic unity attests, one of the attractions of art is that it offers a degree of holiday from that occupation. As the creation of a human mind, art comes to its audience ready-fitted to the human mind; it has physical limits or limits of duration; its details are subordinated to one another in a hierarchy of importance. A play guarantees us that we will not have to select a direction for our attention; it offers us isolation from matter and considerations irrelevant to a particular focus or a particular subject. *Hamlet* is more nearly an exception to those rules than other satisfying and bearable works of art. That, perhaps, is the reason so much effort has gone into interpretations that presume that *Hamlet*, as it is, is not and was not satisfying and bearable. The subject of literature is often conflict, often conflict of values; but, though the agonies of decision, knowing, and valuing are often the objects of an audience's concern, an audience rarely undergoes or even approaches such agonies itself. That it should enjoy doing so seems unlikely, but in *Hamlet* the problems the audience thinks about and the intellectual action of thinking about them are very similar. *Hamlet* is the tragedy of an audience that cannot make up its mind.

One of the most efficient, reliable, and usual guarantees of isolation is genre. The appearance of a ghost in scene one suggests that the play will be a revenge tragedy. *Hamlet* does indeed turn out to be a revenge tragedy, but here genre does not provide the limited frame of reference that the revenge genre and genres in general usually establish. The archetypal revenge play is *The Spanish Tragedy*. In the first scene of that, a ghost and a personification, Revenge, walk out on the stage and spend a whole scene saying who they are, where they are, why they are there, what has happened, and what will happen. The ghost in *The Spanish Tragedy* gives more information in the first five lines of the play than there is in the whole first scene of *Hamlet*. In *The Spanish Tragedy* the ghost and Revenge act as a chorus for the play. They keep the doubt and turmoil of the characters from ever transferring themselves to the audience. They keep the audience safe from doubt, safely outside the action, looking on. In *The Spanish Tragedy* the act of revenge is presented as a moral necessity, just as, say, shooting the villain may be in a Western. Revenge plays were written by Christians and played to Christian audiences. Similarly, traditional American Westerns were written by and for believers faithful to the principles of the Constitution of the United States. The possibility that an audience's Christian belief that vengeance belongs only to God will color its understanding of revenge in *The Spanish Tragedy* is as unlikely as a modern film audience's consideration of a villain's civil rights when somebody shouts, "Head him off at the pass." The tension between revenge morality and the audience's own Christian morality was a source of vitality always *available* to Kyd and his followers, but one that they did not avail themselves of. Where they did not ignore moralities foreign to the vaguely Senecan ethic of the genre, they took steps to take the life out of conflicts between contrary systems of value.

When Christian morality invades a revenge play, as it does in III.xiii of *The Spanish Tragedy* when Hieronimo says *Vindicta Mihi* and then further echoes St. Paul's "Vengeance is mine; I will repay, saith the Lord," the quickly watered-down Christian position and the contrary position for which Hieronimo rejects it are presented as isolated categories between which the *character* must and does choose. The conflict is restricted to the stage and removed from the mind of the audience. The effect is not to make the contrariety of values a part of the audience's experience but to dispel the value system foreign to the genre, to file it away as, for the duration of the play, a dead issue. In its operations upon an audience of *The Spanish Tragedy*, the introduction and rejection of the Christian view of vengeance is roughly comparable to the hundreds of exchanges in hundreds of Westerns where the new schoolmarm says that the hero should go to the sheriff rather than try to outdraw the villain. The hero rarely gives an intellectually satisfying reason for taking the law into his own hands, but the mere fact that the pertinent moral alternative has been mentioned and rejected is ordinarily sufficient to allow the audience to join the hero in his morality without fear of further interruption from its own.

The audience of *Hamlet* is not allowed the intellectual comfort of isolation in the one system of values appropriate to the genre. In *Hamlet* the Christian context for valuing is persistently present. In i.v the ghost makes a standard revenge-tragedy statement of Hamlet's moral obligation to kill Claudius. The audience is quite ready to think in that frame of reference and does so. The ghost then—in the same breath—opens the audience's mind to the frame of reference least compatible with the genre. When he forbids vengeance upon Gertrude, he does so in specifically Christian terms: "Taint not thy mind, nor let thy soul contrive/ Against thy mother aught. Leave her to heaven . . ." (i.v.85–86). Moreover, this ghost is at least as concerned that he lost the chance to confess before he died as he is that he lost his life at all.

Most of the time contradictory values do not collide in the audience's consciousness, but the topic of revenge is far from the only instance in which they live anxiously close to one another, so close to one another that, although the audience is not shaken in its faith in either of a pair of conflicting values, its mind remains in the uneasy state common in nonartistic experience but unusual for audiences of plays. The best example is the audience's thinking about suicide during *Hamlet*. The first mention of suicide comes already set into a Christian frame of reference by the clause in which self-slaughter is mentioned: "Or that the Everlasting had not fixed/ His canon 'gainst self-slaughter" (i.ii.131–32). In the course of the play, however, an audience evaluates suicide in all the different systems available to minds outside the comfortable limitations of art; from time to time in the play the audience thinks of suicide variously as (1) cause for damnation, (2) a heroic and generous action, (3) a cowardly action, and (4) a last sure way to peace. The audience moves from one to another system of values with a rapidity that human faith in the rational constancy of the human mind makes seem impossible. Look, for example, at the travels of the mind that listens to and understands what goes on between the specifically Christian death of Laertes (LAERTES: ". . . Mine and my father's death come not upon thee,/ Nor thine on me."—HAMLET: "Heaven make thee free of it" v.ii.319–21) and the specifically Christian death of Hamlet (HORATIO: ". . . Good night, sweet prince,/ And flights of angels sing thee to thy rest . . ." v.ii.348–49). During the intervening thirty lines the audience and the characters move from the Christian context in which Laertes' soul departs, into the familiar literary context where they can take Horatio's attempted suicide as the generous and heroic act it is (v.ii.324–31). Audience and characters have likewise no difficulty at all in understanding and accepting the label "felicity" for the destination of the suicide—even though Hamlet, the speaker of "Absent thee from felicity awhile" (v.ii.336), prefaces the statement with an incidental "By heaven" (v.ii.332), and even though Hamlet and the audience have spent a lot of time during the preceding three hours actively considering the extent to which a suicide's journey to "the undiscovered country" can be called "felicity" or predicted at all. When "Good night, sweet prince" is spoken by the antique Roman of twenty lines before, both he and the audience return to thinking in a Christian frame of reference, as if they had never been away.

The audience is undisturbed by a nearly endless supply of similar inconstancies in itself and the play; these are a few instances:

The same audience that scorned pretense when Hamlet knew not "seems" in I.ii admires his skill at pretense and detection in the next two acts.

The audience joins Hamlet both in admiration for the self-control by which the player "could force his soul so to his own conceit" that he could cry for Hecuba (II.ii.537), and in admiration for the very different self-control of Horatio (III.ii.51–71).

The audience, which presumably could not bear to see a literary hero stab an unarmed man at prayer, sees the justice of Hamlet's self-accusations of delay. The audience also agrees with the ghost when both have a full view of the corpse of Polonius, and when the ghost's diction is an active reminder of the weapon by which Hamlet has just attempted the acting of the dread command: "Do not forget. This visitation/ Is but to whet thy almost blunted purpose" (III.iv.111–12).

The audience that sees the ghost and hears about its prison house in I.v. also accepts the just as obvious truth of "the undiscovered country from whose bourn no traveller returns. . . ."

What have come to be recognized as the problems of *Hamlet* arise at points where an audience's contrary responses come to consciousness. They are made bearable in performance (though not in recollection) by means similar to those by which the audience is carried across the quieter crises of scene one. In performance, at least, the play gives its audience strength and courage not only to flirt with the frailty of its own understanding but actually to survive conscious experiences of the Polonian foolishness of faith that things will follow only the rules of the particular logic in which we expect to see them. The best example of the audience's endurance of self-knowledge is its experiences of Hamlet's madness. In the last moments of Act I Hamlet makes Horatio, Marcellus, and the audience privy to his intention to pretend madness: ". . . How strange or odd some'er I bear myself/ (As I perchance hereafter shall think meet/ To put an antic disposition on) . . ." (I.v.170–73). The audience sets out into Act II knowing what Hamlet knows, knowing Hamlet's plans, and secure in its superiority to the characters who do not. (Usually an audience is superior to the central characters: it knows that Desdemona is innocent, Othello does not; it knows what it would do when Lear foolishly divides his kingdom; it knows how Birnam Wood came to come to Dunsinane. In *Hamlet*, however, the audience never knows what it would have done in Hamlet's situation; in fact, since the King's successful plot in the duel with Laertes changes Hamlet's situation so that he becomes as much the avenger of his own death as of his father's, the audience never knows what Hamlet would have done. Except for brief periods near the end of the play, the audience never has insight or knowledge superior to Hamlet's or, indeed, different from Hamlet's. Instead of having superiority *to* Hamlet, the audience goes into the second act to share the superiority *of* Hamlet.) The audience knows that Hamlet will play mad, and its expectations are quickly confirmed. Just seventy-five lines into Act II, Ophelia comes in and describes a kind of behavior in Hamlet that sounds like the behavior of a young man of limited theatrical ability who is pretending to be mad (II.i.77–84). Our confidence that this behavior so puzzling to others is well within our grasp is strengthened by the reminder of the ghost, the immediate cause of the promised pretense, in Ophelia's comparison of Hamlet to a creature "loosèd out of hell/ To speak of horrors."

Before Ophelia's entrance, II.i has presented an example of the baseness and foolishness of Polonius, the character upon whom both the audience and Hamlet exercise their superiority throughout Act II. Polonius seems base because he is arranging to spy on Laertes. He instructs his spy in ways to use the "bait of falsehood"—to find out directions by indirections (II.i.1–74). He is so sure that he knows everything, and so sure that his petty scheme is not only foolproof but brilliant, that he is as contemptible mentally as he is morally. The audience laughs at him because he loses his train of thought in pompous byways, so that, eventually, he forgets what he set out to say: "What was I about to say? . . . I was about to say something! Where did I leave?" (II.i.50–51). When Ophelia reports Hamlet's behavior, Polonius takes what is apparently Hamlet's bait: "Mad for thy love?" (II.i.85). He also thinks of (and then spends the rest of the act finding evidence for) a specific cause for Hamlet's madness: he is mad for love of Ophelia. The audience knows (1) Hamlet will pretend madness, (2) Polonius is a fool, and (3) what is actually bothering Hamlet. Through the rest of the act, the audience laughs at Polonius for being fooled by Hamlet. It continues to laugh at Polonius' inability to keep his mind on a track (II.ii.85–130); it also laughs at him for the opposite fault—he has a one-track mind and sees anything and everything as evidence that Hamlet is mad for love

(II.ii.173–212; 394–402). Hamlet, whom the audience knows and understands, spends a good part of the rest of the scene making Polonius demonstrate his foolishness.

Then, in Act III, scene one, the wise audience and the foolish Polonius both become lawful espials of Hamlet's meeting with Ophelia. Ophelia says that Hamlet made her believe he loved her. Hamlet's reply might just as well be delivered by the play to the audience: "You should not have believed me . . ." (III.i.117). In his next speech Hamlet appears suddenly, inexplicably, violently, and really mad—this before an audience whose chief identity for the last hour has consisted in its knowledge that Hamlet is only pretending. The audience finds itself guilty of Polonius' foolish confidence in predictable trains of events. It is presented with evidence for thinking just what it has considered other minds foolish for thinking—that Hamlet is mad, mad for love of an inconstant girl who has betrayed him. Polonius and the audience are the self-conscious and prideful knowers and understanders in the play. They both overestimate the degree of safety they have as innocent onlookers.

When Hamlet seems suddenly mad, the audience is likely for a minute to think that it is mad or that the play is mad. That happens several times in the course of the play; and the play helps audiences toward the decision that the trouble is in themselves. Each time the play seems insane, it also is obviously ordered, orderly, all of a piece. For example, in the case of Hamlet's truly odd behavior with Ophelia in III.i some of the stuff of his speeches to her has been otherwise applied but nonetheless present in the play before (fickleness, cosmetics). Furthermore, after the fact, the play often tells us how we should have reacted; here the King sums up the results of the Ophelia experiment as if they were exactly what the audience expected they would be (which is exactly what they were not): "Love? his affections do not that way tend,/ . . . what he spoke . . . / Was not like madness" (III.i.162–64). In the next scene, Hamlet enters perfectly sane, and lecturing, oddly enough, on what a play should be (III.ii.1–42). Whenever the play seems mad it drifts back into focus as if nothing odd had happened. The audience is encouraged to agree with the play that nothing did, to assume (as perhaps for other reasons it should) that its own intellect is inadequate. The audience pulls itself together, and goes on to another crisis of its understanding. Indeed, it had to do so in order to arrive at the crisis of the nunnery speech. At exactly the point where the audience receives the information that makes it so vulnerable to Hamlet's inexplicable behavior in the nunnery scene, the lines about the antic disposition (I.v.170–73) act as a much needed explanation—*after the fact of the audience's discomfort*—of jocular behavior by Hamlet ("Art thou there, true-penny?" "You hear this fellow in the cellarage," "Well said, old mole!" I.v.150–51, 162) that is foreign to his tone and attitude earlier in the scene, and that jars with the expectations aroused by the manner in which he and the play have been treating the ghost. For a moment, the play seems to be the work of a madman. Then Hamlet explains what he *will* do, and the audience is invited to feel lonely in foolishly failing to understand that that was what he was doing before.

III

The kind of experience an audience has of *Hamlet* in its large movements is duplicated—and more easily demonstrated—in the microcosm of its responses to brief passages. For example, the act of following the exchange initiated by Polonius' "What do you read, my Lord?" in II.ii is similar to the larger experience of coping with the whole career of Hamlet's madness:

POLONIUS: . . . What do you read, my Lord?

HAMLET: Words, words, words.

POLONIUS: What is the matter, my lord?

HAMLET: Between who?

POLONIUS: I mean the matter that you read, my lord.

HAMLET: Slanders, sir, for the satirical rogue says here that old men have grey beards, that their faces are wrinkled, their eyes purging thick amber and plum-tree gum, and that they have a plentiful lack of wit, together with most weak hams. All which, sir, though I most powerfully and potently believe, yet I hold it not honesty to have it thus set down, for you yourself, sir, should be old as I am if, like a crab, you could go backward.

POLONIUS: [aside] Though this be madness, yet there is method in't . . .

(II.ii.190–204)

The audience is full partner in the first two of Hamlet's comically absolute answers. The first answer is not what the questioner expects, and we laugh at the mental inflexibility that makes Polonius prey to frustration in an answer that takes the question literally rather than as it is customarily meant in similar contexts. In his first question Polonius assumes that what he says will have meaning only within the range appropriate to the context in which he speaks. In his second he acts to limit the frame of reference of the first question, but, because "What is the matter?" is a standard idiom in another context, it further widens the range of reasonable but unexpected understanding. On his third try Polonius achieves a question whose range is as limited as his meaning. The audience—composed of smug initiates in Hamlet's masquerade and companions in his cleverness—expects to revel further in the comic revelation of Polonius' limitations. Hamlet's answer begins by letting us laugh at the discomfiture inherent for Polonius in a list of "slanders" of old men. Because of its usual applications, the word "slander" suggests that what is so labeled is not only painful but untrue. Part of the joke here is that these slanders are true. When Hamlet finishes his list, he seems about to continue in the same vein and to demonstrate his madness by saying something like "All which, sir, though . . ., yet are lies." Instead, a syntactical machine ("though . . . yet"), rhetorical emphasis ("powerfully and potently"), and diction ("believe") suitable for the expected denial are used to admit the truth of the slanders: "All which, sir, though I most powerfully and potently believe, yet I hold it not honesty to have it thus set down, for you yourself, sir. . . ." The speech seems to have given up comic play on objection to slanders on grounds of untruth, and to be about to play from an understanding of "slander" as injurious whether true or not. The syntax of "I hold it not honesty . . ., for" signals that a reason for Hamlet's objections will follow, and—in a context where the relevance of the slanders to Polonius gives pain enough to justify suppression of geriatric commonplaces—"for you yourself, sir" signals the probable general direction of the explanation. So far the audience has followed Hamlet's wit without difficulty from one focus to another, but now the bottom falls out from under the audience's own Polonian assumption, in this case the assumption that Hamlet will pretend madness according to pattern: "for you yourself, sir, should be old as I am if, like a crab, you could go backward." This last is exactly the opposite of what Polonius calls it, this is madness without method.

The audience finds itself trying to hear sense in madness; it suddenly undergoes experience of the fact that Polonius' assumptions about cause and effect in life and language are no more arbitrary and vulnerable than its own. The audience has been where it has known that the idea of sanity is insane, but it is there very briefly; it feels momentarily lonely and lost—as it feels when it has failed to get a joke or when a joke has failed to be funny. The play continues blandly across the gulf. Polonius' comment reflects comically on the effects on him of the general subject of old age; the banter between Hamlet and Polonius picks up again; and Polonius continues his self-confident diagnostic asides to the audience. Moreover, the discussion of Hamlet's reading is enclosed by two passages that have strong nonlogical, nonsignificant likeness to one another in the incidental materials they share— breeding, childbearing, death, and walking:

HAMLET: For if the sun breed maggots in a dead dog, being a good kissing carrion—Have you a daughter?

POLONIUS: I have, my lord.

HAMLET: Let her not walk i' th' sun. Conception is a blessing, but as your daughter may conceive, friend, look to't.

POLONIUS: [aside] How say you by that? Still harping on my daughter. Yet he

knew me not at first. 'A said I was a fishmonger. 'A is far gone, far
gone. And truly in my youth I suffered much extremity for love,
very near this. I'll speak to him again.—What do you read, my
lord?

(II.ii.181–90)

POLONIUS: [aside] Though this be madness, yet there is method in't.—Will
you walk out of the air, my lord?

HAMLET: Into my grave?

POLONIUS: Indeed, that's out of the air. [aside] How pregnant sometimes his
replies are! a happiness that often madness hits on, which reason and
sanity could not so prosperously be delivered of. . . .

(II.ii.203–9)

From beginning to end, in all sizes and kinds of materials, the play offers
its audience an actual and continuing experience of perceiving a multitude of
intense relationships in an equal multitude of different systems of coherence,
systems not subordinated to one another in a hierarchy of relative power.
The way to an answer to "What is so good about *Hamlet?*" may be in an
answer to the same question about its most famous part, the "To be or not
to be" soliloquy.

The soliloquy sets out with ostentatious deliberation, rationality, and
precision. Hamlet fixes and limits his subject with authority and—considering that his carefully defined subject takes in everything humanly conceiv-
able—with remarkable confidence: "To be, or not to be—that is the
question." He then restates and further defines the question in four lines
that echo the physical proportions of "To be or not to be" (two lines on
the positive, two on the negative) and also echo the previous grammatical
construction ("to suffer . . . or to take arms"):

> Whether 'tis nobler in the mind to suffer
> The slings and arrows of outrageous fortune
> Or to take arms against a sea of troubles
> And by opposing end them.
>
> (III.i.57–60)

The speech is determinedly methodical about defining a pair of alternatives
that should be as easily distinguishable as any pair imaginable; surely being
and not being are distinct from one another. The next sentence continues
the pattern of infinitives, but it develops the idea of "not to be" instead of
continuing the positive-negative alternation followed before:

> To die, to sleep—
> No more—and by a sleep to say we end

> The heartache, and the thousand natural shocks
> That flesh is heir to. 'Tis a consummation
> Devoutly to be wished.
>
> (III.i.60–64)

As an audience listens to and comprehends the three units "To die," "to sleep," and "No more," some intellectual uneasiness should impinge upon it. "To sleep" is in apposition to "to die," and their equation is usual and perfectly reasonable. However, death and sleep are also a traditional type of unlikeness; they could as well restate "to be or not to be" (to sleep or to die) as "not to be" alone. Moreover, since to die is to sleep, and is also to sleep no more, no vocal emphasis or no amount of editorial punctuation will limit the relationship between "to sleep" and "no more." Thus, when "and by a sleep to say we end . . ." reasserts the metaphoric equation of death and sleep, the listener feels a sudden and belated need to have heard "no more" as the isolated summary statement attempted by the punctuation of modern texts. What is happening here is that the apparently sure distinction between "to be" and "not to be" is becoming less and less easy to maintain. The process began even in the methodically precise first sentence where passivity to death-dealing slings and arrows described "to be," and the positive aggressive action of taking arms described the negative state, "not to be." Even earlier, the listener experienced a substantially irrelevant instability of relationship when "in the mind" attached first to "nobler," indicating the sphere of the nobility, and then to "suffer," indicating the sphere of the suffering: "nobler in the mind to suffer."

"The thousand natural shocks/ That flesh is heir to" further denies the simplicity of the initial alternatives by opening the mind of the listener to considerations excluded by the isolated question whether it is more pleasant to live or to die; the substance of the phrase is a summary of the pains of life, but its particulars introduce the idea of duty. "Heir" is particularly relevant to the relationship and duty of Hamlet to his father; it also implies a continuation of conditions from generation to generation that is generally antithetical to any assumption of finality in death. The diction of the phrase also carries with it a suggestion of the Christian context in which flesh is heir to the punishment of Adam; the specifically religious word "devoutly" in the next sentence opens the idea of suicide to the Christian ethic from which the narrowed limits of the first sentences had briefly freed it.

While the logical limits and controls of the speech are falling away, its illogical patterns are giving it their own coherence. For example, the constancy of the infinitive construction maintains an impression that the speech is proceeding as methodically as it began; the word "to," in its infinitive use and otherwise, appears thirteen times among the eighty-five words in the first ten lines of the soliloquy. At the same time that the listener is having trouble comprehending the successive contradictions of

"To die, to sleep—/ No more—and by a sleep to say we end . . .," he also hears at the moment of crisis a confirming echo of the first three syllables and the word "end" from "*and by o*pposing *end* them" in the first three syllables and word "end" in "*and by a* sleep to say we *end*." As the speech goes on, as it loses more and more of its rational precision, and as "to be" and "not to be" become less and less distinguishable, rhetorical coherence continues in force. The next movement of the speech begins with a direct repetition, in the same metrical position in the line, of the words with which the previous movement began: "To die, to sleep." The new movement seems, as each new movement has seemed, to introduce a restatement of what has gone before; the rhetorical construction of the speech insists that all the speech does is make the distinct natures of "to be" and "not to be" clearer and clearer:

> To die, to sleep—
> To sleep—perchance to dream: ay, there's the rub,
> For in that sleep of death what dreams may come
> When we have shuffled off this mortal coil,
> Must give us pause. There's the respect
> That makes calamity of so long life.
>
> (III.i.64–69)

As Hamlet describes his increasing difficulty in seeing death as the simple opposite of life, the manner of his description gives his listener an actual experience of that difficulty; "shuffled off this mortal coil" says "cast off the turmoil of this life," but "shuffled off" and "coil" both suggest the rejuvenation of a snake which, having once thrown her enamell'd skin, reveals another just like it underneath. The listener also continues to have difficulty with the simple action of understanding; like the nature of the things discussed, the natures of the sentences change as they are perceived: "what dreams may come" is a common construction for a question, and the line that follows sounds like a subordinate continuation of the question; it is not until we hear "must give us pause" that we discover that "what dreams may come" is a noun phrase, the subject of a declarative sentence that only comes into being with the late appearance of an unexpected verb. In the next sentence ("There's the respect/ That makes calamity of so long life"), logic requires that we understand "makes calamity so long-lived," but our habitual understanding of *makes . . . of* constructions and our recent indoctrination in the pains of life make us likely to hear the contradictory, illogical, and yet appropriate "makes a long life a calamity."

Again, however, the lines sound ordered and reasonable. The rejected first impressions I have just described are immediately followed by a real question, and one that is largely an insistently long list of things that make life a monotonously painful series of calamities. Moreover, nonlogical coherence is provided by the quiet and intricate harmony of "to dream," "of death," and "shuffled off" in the metrical centers of three successive lines; by the echo of the solidly metaphoric "there's the rub" in the vague "there's the respect"; and by the repetition of "for" from "For in that sleep" to begin the next section of the speech.

> For who would bear the whips and scorns of time,
> Th' oppressor's wrong, the proud man's contumely,
> The pangs of despised love, the law's delay,
> The insolence of office, and the spurns
> That patient merit of th' unworthy takes,
> When he himself might his quietus make
> With a bare bodkin? Who would fardels bear,
> To grunt and sweat under a weary life,
> But that the dread of something after death,
> The undiscovered country, from whose bourn
> No traveller returns, puzzles the will,
> And makes us rather bear those ills we have
> Than fly to others that we know not of?
>
> (III.i.70–82)

Although the list in the first question is disjointed and rhythmically frantic, the impression of disorder is countered by the regularity of the definite article, and by the inherently conjunctive action of six possessives. The possessives in *'s*, the possessives in *of*, and the several nonpossessive *of* constructions are themselves an underlying pattern of simultaneous likeness and difference. So is the illogical pattern present in the idea of burdens, the word "bear," and the word "bare." The line in which the first of these questions ends and the second begins is an epitome of the construction and action of the speech: "With a bare bodkin? Who would fardels bear,. . . ." The two precisely equal halves of a single rhythmic unit hold together two separate syntactical units. The beginning of the new sentence, "Who would fardels bear," echoes both the beginning, "For who would bear," and the sound of one word, "bare," from the end of the old. Moreover, "bare" and "bear," two words that are both the same and different, participate here in statements of the two undistinguishable alternatives: "to be, or not to be"— to bear fardels, or to kill oneself with a bare bodkin.

The end of the speech sounds like the rationally achieved conclusion of just such a rational investigation as Hamlet began. It begins with *thus*, the sign of logical conclusion, and it gains a sound of inevitable truth and triumphant clarity from the incremental repetition of *and* at the beginning of every other line. The last lines are relevant to Hamlet's behavior in the play at large and therefore have an additional sound of rightness here. Not only are the lines broadly appropriate to the play, the audience's understanding of them is typical of its understanding throughout the play and of its understanding of the previous particulars of this speech: Hamlet has hesitated to kill Claudius. Consideration of suicide has seemed a symptom of that hesitancy. Here the particular from which Hamlet's conclusions about his inability to act derive is his hesitancy to commit suicide. The audience hears those conclusions in the context of his failure to take the action that suicide would avoid.

> Thus conscience does make cowards of us all,
> And thus the native hue of resolution
> Is sicklied o'er with the pale cast of thought,
> And enterprises of great pitch and moment
> With this regard their currents turn awry
> And lose the name of action.
>
> (III.i.83–88)

These last lines are accidentally a compendium of phrases descriptive of the action of the speech and the process of hearing it. The speech puzzles the will, but it makes us capable of facing and bearing puzzlement. The "To be or not to be" soliloquy is a type of the over-all action of *Hamlet*. In addition, a soliloquy in which being and its opposite are indistinguishable is peculiarly appropriate to a play otherwise full of easily distinguishable pairs that are not easily distinguished from one another by characters or audience or both: Rosencrantz and Guildenstern; the pictures of Gertrude's two husbands (III.iv.54–68); the hawk and the handsaw (II.ii.370); and father and mother who are one flesh and so undistinguished in Hamlet's farewell to Claudius (IV.iii.48–51). The soliloquy is above all typical of a play whose last moments enable its audience to look unblinking upon a situation in which Hamlet, the finally successful revenger, is the object of Laertes' revenge; a situation in which Laertes, Hamlet's victim, victimizes Hamlet; a situation in which Fortinbras, the threat to Denmark's future in scene one, is its hope for political salvation; in short, a situation in which any identity can be indistinguishable from its opposite. The soliloquy, the last scene, the first scene, the play—each and together—make an impossible coherence of truths that are both undeniably incompatible and undeniably coexistent.

IV

The kind of criticism I am doing here may be offensive to readers conditioned to think of revelation as the value of literature and the purpose of criticism. The things I have said about *Hamlet* may be made more easily palatable by the memory that illogical coherence—coherent madness—is a regular topic of various characters who listen to Hamlet and Ophelia. In the Reynaldo scene (II.i) and Hamlet's first talk with Rosencrantz and Guildenstern the power of rhetoric and context to make a particular either good or bad at will is also a topic in the play. So too is the perception of clouds which may in a moment look "like a camel indeed," and "like a weasel" and be "very like a whale" (III.ii.361–67).

What I am doing may seem antipoetical; it should not. On the contrary, the effects I have described in *Hamlet* are of the same general kind as the nonsignificant coherences made by rhythm, rhyme, alliteration, and others of the standard devices of prosody. For example, the physics of the relationship among Hamlet, Laertes, Fortinbras, and Pyrrhus, the four avenging sons in *Hamlet*, are in their own scale and substance the same as those of the relationship among *cat*, *rat*, *bat*, and *chat*. The theme of suicide, for all the inconstancy of its fluid moral and emotional value, is a constant and unifying factor in the play. So too is the theme of appearance and reality, deceit, pretense, disguise, acting, seeming, and cosmetics which gives the play coherence even though its values are as many as its guises and labels. The analogy of rhyme or of a pair of like-metered lines applies profitably to the nonsignifying relationship between Hamlet's two interviews with women. Both the nunnery scene with Ophelia and the closet scene with Gertrude are stage-managed and overlooked by Polonius; neither lady understands Hamlet; both are amazed by his intensity; in both scenes Hamlet makes a series of abortive departures before his final exit. There is a similar kind of insignificant likeness in numerous repeated patterns of scenes and situations like that of Hamlet's entrance reading in II.ii and its echo in Ophelia's show of devotional reading in III.i. Indeed, the same sort of thing can be said about any of the themes and images whose value critics have tried to convert to significance.

The tools of prosody and the phenomena I have talked about show their similarity well when they cooperate in Hamlet's little poem on perception and truth, a poem that is a model of the experience of the whole play. Polonius reads it to the king and queen:

> Doubt thou the stars are fire;
> Doubt that the sun doth move;
> Doubt truth to be a liar;
> But never doubt I love.
>
> (II.ii.116–19)

I suggest that the pleasure of intellectual possession evoked by perception of the likeness and difference of "fire" and "liar" and of "move" and "love," or among the four metrically like and unlike lines, or between the three positive clauses and the one negative one, or between "stars" and "sun" or "truth" and "liar" is of the same kind as the greater achievement of intellectual mastery of the greater challenge presented by "doubt" in the first three lines. The first two *doubts* demand disbelief of two things that common sense cannot but believe. The third, whose likeness to the first two is insisted upon by anaphora, is made unlike them by the words that follow it: disbelief that truth is a liar is a logical necessity; therefore, "doubt" here must mean "believe" or "incline to believe" as it does earlier in this scene (l. 56) and several other times in the play. To be consistent with the pair of hyperbolic impossibilities to which it is coupled, and to fit the standard rhetorical formula (Doubt what cannot be doubted, but do not doubt . . .) in which it appears, "Doubt truth to be a liar" must be understood in a way inconsistent with another pattern of the poem, the previously established meaning of "doubt." Even the first two lines, which seem to fit the hyperbolic formula so well, may make the poem additionally dizzying because their subject matter could remind a Renaissance listener (once disturbed by the reversal of the meaning of the third "doubt") of doubts cast upon common-sense impressions by still recent astronomical discoveries, notably that the diurnal motion of the sun is an illusion.

The urgent rhetorical coherence of the poem is like that of the play. As the multitude of insistent and overlapping systems of coherence in the poem allows its listener to hold the two contradictory meanings of "doubt" in colloid-like suspension and to experience both the actions "doubt" describes, so in the play at large an alliteration of subjects—a sort of rhythm of ideas whose substance may or may not inform the situation dramatized— gives shape and identity, nonphysical substance, to the play that *contains* the situation. Such a container allows Shakespeare to replace *conclusion* with *inclusion*; it provides a particular and temporary context that overcomes the intellectual terror ordinarily inherent in looking at an action in all the value systems it invades. Such a container provides a sense of order and limitation sufficient to replace the comforting boundaries of carefully isolated frames of reference; it makes its audience capable of contemplating more truth than the mind should be able to bear.

In summary I would say that the thing about *Hamlet* that has put Western man into a panic to explain it is not that the play is incoherent, but that it is coherent. There are plenty of incoherent plays; nobody ever looks at them twice. This one, because it obviously makes sense and because it just as obviously cannot be made sense of, threatens our inevitable working assumption that there are no "more things in earth" than can be understood in one philosophy. People see *Hamlet* and tolerate inconsistencies that it does not seem they could bear. Students of the play have explained that such people do not, in fact, find the play bearable at all. They therefore whittle the play down for us to the size of one of its terms, and deny the others. Truth is bigger than any one system for knowing it, and *Hamlet* is bigger than any of the frames of reference it inhabits. *Hamlet* allows us to comprehend—hold on to—all the contradictions it contains. *Hamlet* refuses to cradle its audience's mind in a closed generic framework, or otherwise limit the ideological context of its actions. In *Hamlet* the mind is cradled in nothing more than the fabric of the play. The superior strength and value of that fabric is in the sense it gives that it is unlimited in its range, and that its audience is not only sufficient to comprehend but is in the act of achieving total comprehension of all the perceptions to which its mind can open. The source of the strength is in a rhetorical economy that allows the audience to perform both of the basic actions of the mind upon almost every conjunction of elements in the course of the play: it perceives strong likeness, and it perceives strong difference. Every intellectual conjunction is also a disjunction, and any two things that pull apart contain qualities that are simultaneously the means of uniting them.

Hamlet and Our Problems

Michael Goldman

Henry V, by virtue of his public role, is forced to be something of an actor—hence his apprenticeship at roleplaying in *Henry IV*. But every private man is an actor too—for our acts are often performances, in the sense that they strive either to express or conceal something that we think of as inside us, our true self. We are all actors, then, to a degree. But in the ordinary, professional sense of the word, what is an actor? An actor is a man who wants to play Hamlet. Playing the role of the Prince proves you are truly an actor and not a clown, an entertainer, a personality, a "type," or a movie star. It is the ultimate validation of an actor's professional status—and yet, curiously enough, it is far from being the hardest of acting tasks. Most men of the theater would probably accept Sir John Gielgud's characterization of the play as "audience-proof"; and certainly Macready's observation remains true today: a total failure in the role is rare.[1] Many other parts are harder to make a success of, and some—like King Lear—demand skills which the successful actor of Hamlet may not possess. But Hamlet strikes us as somehow unique in requiring and displaying the actor's art.

Why should this be so? One answer lies in the variety that Dr. Johnson recognized as a distinguishing excellence of the play. No other role offers so much action of so many different kinds. Hamlet is soldier, scholar, statesman, madman, fencer, critic, magnanimous prince, cunning revenger, aloof noble, witty ironist, man of the people, etc.; and he is regularly required to change from one role to another before our eyes or to maintain several—or a disarming mixture of several—at once. The play abounds in situations that require the principal actor to shift his mood or mode of action because of a change in audience. A number of examples result from Hamlet's having to deceive those around him, but there are many occasions when the shift does not come about as a result of the necessity for self-protection ("Horatio, or I do forget myself," the jokes with the gravedigger, his toying with Osric, the address to the players, the grand apology to Laertes). And there are intermediate stages where we cannot say with any precision whether Hamlet is "acting" or not. These are all occasions on which we are keenly

*From *Shakespeare and the Energies of Drama* (1972): 74–93. Reprinted by permission of Princeton University Press.

aware of the actor's range and of the pleasures it can give us, of the different things the man on the stage is able to do and do well, and of his skill in making something coherent out of this variety.

The problems involved here are in an important sense exemplary of all acting. For as Hamlet suggests in his speech to the players, there is a critical technical and aesthetic difficulty inherent in the variety available to any professional actor. Great acting demands "temperance," "smoothness," moderation, control—and variety tests this control to the full. Lear is required to do just one kind of thing for most of his play, a very momentous and demanding kind of thing to be sure, but his problem as an actor is to find sufficient variety (and reserves of energy) to get through the evening. Hamlet's problem, assuming he is competent to execute the incredibly many separate "bits" the play allows him, is to control them, to focus them, to find an overall conception in which each has its place, and to give a meaningful smoothness to his transitions. Hamlet is not urging any principle of simple realism when he reminds the actors that their art consists in holding the mirror up to nature. The actor's task is to interpret life: "to show virtue her own feature, scorn her own image, and the very age and body of the time his form and pressure" (III, ii, 25–27).

It is Prince Hamlet's task, too, and his problems are very similar to those of the actor who plays him.

Hamlet awakes in its audience a unique concern for the actor's art— and particularly for his interpretive skill, his ability to make satisfying sense out of all the actions he is called upon to perform. It is possible to ask of an actor who portrays King Lear, "How will he get through it?" and the "it"—what Lear undergoes—will be on our minds as much as Lear himself. But with Hamlet we ask as of no other play, "How will he act the part?"

We do not ask, "Will he make any sense of it?" In the theater at least *Hamlet* runs no risk of obscurity. Indeed one of the problems of Hamlet, and one reason why the role is both a supreme challenge and one in which it is very hard to fail utterly, is that even a crude, simplifying, singleminded interpretation—a making one kind of sense but not full sense of the role— can produce solid, effective theater.

Interpretation is one of the necessary questions of *Hamlet*; to an important extent it is something the play is "about." Like its chief character, *Hamlet* draws our attention to varieties of action and to the questions of interpretation they raise. Our experience of *Hamlet* in the theater is primarily an attempt to follow an action so various, intricate, and proliferating that it cries out for interpretation at every turn. The "problems" of the play point, finally, to the subtle means it employs for manipulating one of our most fundamental theatrical appetites: the desire for action that makes sense, especially for action that seems complete and resolved.

As an example, consider III, iii, where Hamlet comes upon the King at prayer. What does the audience see? Two great antagonists who have been maneuvering toward each other throughout the play are alone together at last. They do not look at each other. They do not act. In fact each is frozen in a posture that manifestly suggests an action he does not perform. We see a praying man and his armed opponent. Hamlet has brought his father's murderer to his knees. But the praying man is not praying and the man with the sword is not going to strike. The King, however, wants to pray, just as Hamlet wants to kill the King. The moment we have waited for so patiently arrives and it is not what we meant at all. It is a scene of extraordinary and peculiar tension. The frozen action allows us to register simultaneously an intense impulse to action, an incompleted action, and no action—action whose meaning may be the opposite of what we see. Criticism of this scene has focused on the reasons Hamlet gives for not killing Claudius, but clearly any doubts we may have as to the significance of what Hamlet says at this point are only part of our response to this powerfully engaging stage image, only one of many uncertainties as to action and its interpretation that are being deployed in us. But "doubt" and "uncertainty" tend to suggest speculative states, reflective categories that might be applied to the play in retrospect. Though they are not inaccurate to describe part of our feeling in the theater, they obscure the major source of that feeling and hence its precise quality, which springs from the maneuvering of bodies on the stage and the rhythm of our response to the action as it unfolds.

To understand this more fully, an important technical device must be discussed. III, iii is one of a number of places in *Hamlet*—particularly toward the middle of the play—where what might be called a "stop-action" technique is used, that is, where one or more players is stopped in mid-gesture and the action frozen in a variety of ways. As, for instance, when the First Player describes Pyrrhus stopping in the very act of killing Priam:

> for, lo! his sword,
> Which was declining on the milky head
> Of reverend Priam, seem'd i' th' air to stick.
> So, as a painted tyrant, Pyrrhus stood
> And, like a neutral to his will and matter,
> Did nothing.
>   (II, ii, 499–504)

It helps to visualize the Player performing in a style which marks him off as an "actor" from the other figures on stage, gesturing overemphatically, throwing himself into the part ("Look whe'er he has not turn'd his colour and has tears in's eyes"). We may expect that the player has suited the action to the word and frozen grandly.

The Player continues. Pyrrhus's gesture is started up again, but only after preparatory verbal fanfare that again draws attention to the stopped action:

> But, as we often see, against some storm,
> A silence in the heavens, the rack stand still,
> The bold winds speechless, and the orb below
> As hush as death, anon the dreadful thunder
> Doth rend the region; so, after Pyrrhus' pause,
> Aroused vengeance sets him new a-work;
> And never did the Cyclops' hammers fall
> On Mars his armour forg'd for proof eterne
> With less remorse than Pyrrhus' bleeding sword
> Now falls on Priam.
>
> (505–14)

A few lines later Polonius stops him; he starts up once again, and immediately Hamlet interrupts! (It might be noted that Hamlet in giving the first few lines of the speech interrupts himself twice. The pattern of interruption contributes to the stop-action configuration, though there is probably little gesture or physical action to interrupt.)

Hamlet's soliloquy after the players leave turns on a violent self-interruption, as the Prince catches himself in the full flight of some great melodramatic gesture:

> . . . Bloody, bawdy villain!
> Remorseless, treacherous, lecherous, kindless villain!
> O, vengeance! [too much?]
> Why, what an ass am I . . .
>
> (608–11)

Again the shortened line ("O, vengeance!") orchestrates a stopped action.[2] Here, as at so many points in the play, we are made conscious of the fine line between genuine intensity and pose. Indeed, there is no line—and this is what the stop-action reveals. Hamlet's response is genuine in the sense that it is strongly felt, irresistible, and grows naturally and persuasively out of the situation. There is nothing in the preparation that suggests pretense, nor need there be. Hamlet is throwing himself into the role of revenger. But by interrupting himself at the height of his outburst, by freezing the pose, Hamlet draws our attention to his theatricality of gesture and language. At this moment, sincerity and "acting" are hard to tell apart—and one is not necessarily to be preferred to the other. In fact, Hamlet now is prompted by revulsion at his own playacting to use a much more elaborate piece of theatricality to catch the conscience of the King—the play within the play. The sudden break has allowed action to be revealed as acting, and has also involved us more deeply in doubt as to the ultimate direction or interpretation of any action.[3]

The stop-action tableaus play upon a question that recurs in various forms throughout *Hamlet:* when is an action not an action? It is raised of course in the "To be or not to be" soliloquy, where Hamlet—who has a moment ago appeared ready to catch the conscience of the King—now analyzes the conditions under which action loses its name or falls into non-being. Hamlet sees his situation as paradoxical—action results in not being. To be is not to act. And the question *when is an action not an action?* reappears in a dozen guises, as, for example, when is revenge not revenge? when is a madman not a madman? when is a mother not a mother? when is a funeral not a funeral? when is a suicide not a suicide? when is play in earnest?[4] If there is a "question of Hamlet" it is this. As the role of Hamlet itself directs our attention to the problems of interpreting and making sense out of action, so the play is endlessly varying the motif of doubt as to the significance of action.

The famous problem of whether Hamlet is active or inactive may be understood as a misleading abstraction from this type of effect. The Prince may be described as either active or inactive because in *Hamlet* action is constantly losing its name. Though there is an endless variety of it, we are always aware—as in the stop-action sequences—of our appetite for a certain kind of completeness, a meaningfulness which we as members of the audience demand of action.

The critical approach that focuses on Hamlet's "inaction" typically concerns itself with his speculative capacities. But the familiar distinction that this interpretation turns on—between action and reason—is inappropriate to the play. Hamlet's Renaissance sense of human dignity unites reason and action in a single continuum. Man is a great piece of work because his capacity for both reason and action, for reason in action, is divine. Not only does reason exist to prompt us to action, it is only *used* when we act:

> Sure, He that made us with such large discourse,
> Looking before and after, gave us not
> That capability and god-like reason
> To fust in us unus'd.
>
> (IV, iv, 36–39)

The actions that matter, of course, are the ones that make satisfying sense—full sense, not like Laertes' half-cocked rebellion, say, but like Hamlet's ultimate revenge. The importance of reason in action in *Hamlet*, of action that is meaningful in the face of difficult situations, may be seen if we compare three familiar speeches from the beginning, middle, and end of the play. The "To be or not to be" soliloquy where significant action is inhibited by the fear of death, is a paradoxical reversal of Hamlet's first soliloquy, in which he longs for death because he can no longer attribute significance to action ("How weary, stale, flat, and unprofitable,/ Seems to me all the uses of this world"). But by the end of the play he sees a unifying meaning to all his actions; his life is now a "story" ("And in this harsh world draw thy breath in pain/ To tell my story"). He is only afraid that death will keep it from being apparent to others.

Reason and action are not opposed in *Hamlet*, but for most of the play they fail to coalesce as either we or the characters would like them to. Without intelligible meaning, action is unsatisfying or disturbing, a fact exploited from the opening scene. We feel there not only doubt and interrogation but an immediate pressure to sort out the significances of a peculiarly tense and busy action. (Who's on duty here? Why does the wrong guard challenge? Why are they trying to get rid of Francisco? What does the ghost mean? Why are they on guard?) Our response is natural, as is that of the characters. Action and reason seek their meaning in each other, and nowhere more than in *Hamlet*. This may help to account for the special emphasis the play gives to the theme of speech (e.g. its concern with the way actors speak, the significant use of the word "discourse," the prominence of Osric, Hamlet's emphatic "say" at II, ii, 596, where one would ordinarily expect "do")— for speech is a kind of intermediary step between willing significance and establishing it. It is neither reason nor action, but a reaching out of one toward the other. And it is exactly this effort that the action of *Hamlet* repeatedly highlights and foils.

Most of the characters are engaged in a continuing struggle to find out—and interpret—what the others are doing or have done. Their efforts may be said to come to a head when Hamlet confronts the Queen. His address to the players has contained hints of the stress he will be under in this scene. In the very torrent, tempest, and whirlwind of his passion he will have to be careful, as the Ghost has warned him, not to o'erstep the modesty of nature. It is his toughest acting assignment so far, and when he comes to it he quite literally sets out to hold a mirror up to nature:

> Come, come, and sit you down. You shall not budge.
> You go not till I set you up a glass
> Where you may see the inmost part of you.
>
> (III, iv, 18–20)

Again the difficult relations between action, acting, and the self come to the fore. Gertrude is a striking example of divorce between action and meaning. She has allowed herself to sleep with Claudius and become his queen largely by refusing to think about what she has been doing. She has followed her senses and blocked out the meaning of her actions. "What have I done?" is her revealing cry, and Hamlet proceeds to interpret for her (the italics are, of course, mine):

HAMLET: Such an *act*
That blurs the grace and blush of modesty

> . . . O, such a *deed*
> As from the body of contraction plucks
> The very soul . . .
> Yea, this solidity and compound mass,
> With tristful visage, as against the doom,
> Is thought-sick at the *act*.

QUEEN: Ay me, what *act*,
That roars so loud and thunders in the index?

(40–52)

The fierce and disturbing intensity of their dialogue derives from Hamlet's insistence on the physical actuality of his mother's crime. He wants to make her *see*, to put action and meaning together, just as he has wanted to say what is in his heart and to act on his cue for revenge. But at the very moment Hamlet is trying to make the Queen interpret her own actions, a great tangle of misinterpretation forms around them. Polonius thinks Hamlet will kill the Queen. Hamlet thinks Polonius is the King. On two separate occasions and for different reasons, Gertrude thinks Hamlet is mad. To these we may add the Queen's "What have I done?" and our own curiosity as to why she doesn't see the Ghost. As so often in the play, an increasing pressure toward clarity has carried us into deeper uncertainty and doubt.

To act significantly in these circumstances it is necessary to be an actor—to play a part and hence to use disguise, to be and not to be. One's inmost part may be that which passeth show, and any action may be such as a man might play, but some kind of playacting seems necessary to reveal what ordinary action keeps hidden. After the play-within-the-play Hamlet has announced, in rhetoric that reminds us of the theatricality of the revenger's occupation ("'Tis now the very witching time of night . . . Now could I drink hot blood") that he is ready for violent action—but with his mother he intends only to act the part, "I will speak daggers to her, but use none." Though his appearance will perfectly suit the reality within him, it will be only a pretense. He will act and not act, but the acting will be so effective that it will cause Polonius to cry out from behind the arras and result in a violence Hamlet did not (and did) intend. Hamlet has now been seen twice to attack the King and not to attack him, and he concludes the scene with his mother by saying goodnight five times before he leaves.

The play, then, is full of action, but the action is handled in such a way that our responses perform in effect an analysis of the feelings and appetites we attach to the very notion of action. We are regularly invited to complete an action—to consider what it means, to anticipate where it may lead—only to have our response blocked, distracted, or diverted, compromised in some way. The stop-action sequences; the early air of mystery; the multiple networks of doubt, deceit, and detection; the stress given to nuances and paradoxes of acting technique; the teasing verbal play with reason and action, saying and doing, being and not being, all contribute to this effect.[5]

Considered in this light, many matters which have provoked critical disagreement in the past may be recognized not as problems requiring solutions one way or the other, but as signs of the play's careful management of our response. The first act, for example, ends with Hamlet vowing vengeance and promising some secret course of action toward that end. In II, i, we learn that Hamlet has appeared to Ophelia in marvellous disarray, apparently mad. Is this part of his plan? The answer is that there are simply too many variables for us to be certain. When the Bristol Old Vic presented the play in New York, Hamlet actually appeared in this scene—out of Polonius's line of vision—and with a number of broad winks conveyed to Ophelia—and us—that he was just kidding; it was all part of the antic disposition. This is one way of clearing up the action, but it is not Shakespeare's way, which is not to clear it up. It is Hamlet's absence from the stage that gives the scene its significance. Shakespeare might have introduced him, could have rearranged existing material to do so. But without Hamlet we are forced to guess whether his charade was deliberately intended to mislead, or an expression of the anguish that is also developed in Act I. We only know for sure that Polonius's interpretation is wrong.

Shakespeare could also easily have allowed Hamlet to resolve another problem that has perplexed the critics: whether any significant delay occurs between Acts I and II. This is not simply a matter of the flexible time dimension of the Elizabethan stage. Shakespeare can be very explicit about linear time when it suits him. He can also deliberately follow an impossible sequence, as in *Othello*, and keep us from noticing—and he can simply be careless of time when it doesn't matter. But he does none of these things in this case. He does finally let us know that Hamlet has spent more time than he would have liked between I, V and II, i, but he allows us this information only at the very end of Act II. Thus, here—and elsewhere— the question of whether Hamlet delays unnecessarily is deliberately left opaque. There are good reasons for him to delay, but they are fed to us at the wrong time dramatically and in the wrong way for us to be confident that they are the right ones, or even to be sure the delay has been so egregious as at moments he claims it is.[6] The play of course does not permit us to fall into careful examination of these questions; they exist only as part of the pattern of interrupted action and blocked significance.

The pattern (like the Oedipal pattern) is designed to excite both our deepest interest and our deepest resistance. Unfortunately, because it is so original (and perhaps because it is disturbing) it has often provoked stupid "improvements." Since the "To be or not to be" soliloquy breaks the arc of feeling between Hamlet's appearance in II, ii and III, ii, many companies follow the mutilated First Quarto and place it in the midst of II, ii. It makes more "sense" that way, that is, it makes it easier to interpret Hamlet. For similar reasons, III, iii, which unexpectedly detours Hamlet into the King's closet, was for more than two centuries either omitted or substantially cut in most performances. But in both cases the break in our expectations, the resistance to interpretation, is vital.

Critics concerned with the problem of Hamlet's delay have long concentrated on the scene with Claudius and with reason. But the question to be asked here is not why does Hamlet delay, but why does the play delay—why are *we* delayed? There is more than a grain of truth in the facetious statement that Hamlet delays because there would be no play if he did not. Part of our response to the closet scene depends on our knowledge that the play cannot end here—and not merely because we have paid for an hour's more entertainment. As soon as Hamlet enters we know he will not kill the King. He cannot kill Claudius at prayer, not for theological reasons, sound as they may be, but for aesthetic ones. It is undramatic, too easy. The King's back is to him. There is no source of resistance. The play is going elsewhere. The action, we realize, would not satisfy us, though like Hamlet we have longed for it since the first act. If Shakespeare ever played with an audience, it is here: once again our desire for significant action is drawn upon in a way that also arouses our latent sense of how difficult this appetite is to satisfy.

When two such deeply opposed antagonists have been kept apart for so long by actions of such brilliance and complexity, we come to need an ending that will release all our pent-up energies. We need a spacious ending, a great clarifying release. And this is what we get in the splendid free-for-all that concludes the play, in which the King is hoist on both his petards, and Hamlet, after a display of athletic, military, and moral virtuosity, kills him in full possession of palpably damning evidence and is vindicated before a large audience. To the characters on stage the scene is confusion, an example of the futility of all efforts to force a significance on action, to grasp what Hamlet calls the invisible event. It is a tableau, finally, of "purposes mistook/ Fall'n on the inventors' heads," but for us it is nothing of the sort. If an Elizabethan audience wanted to refer it to a theological principle they might see it as an example of the workings of Providence, but their rhythm of response to the action would be much the same as ours. All through the play we have been reminded, both explicitly and by the imagery and movement of the verse, of the pleasure that attends any great release of energy in ample and unambiguous action:

> . . . in grace whereof,
> No jocund health that Denmark drinks to-day,
> But the great cannon to the clouds shall tell,

> And the King's rouse the heavens shall bruit again,
> Re-speaking earthly thunder.
>
> (I, ii, 124–28)

> But I will delve one yard below their mines,
> And blow them at the moon. O, 'tis most sweet,
> When in one line two crafts directly meet.
>
> (III, iv, 208–10)

> And let the kettle to the trumpets speak,
> The trumpet to the cannoneer without,
> The cannons to the heavens, the heaven to earth.
>
> (V, ii, 286–88)

Even when Claudius uses the opposite figure of a missile missing its target, he does it by way of another beautiful evocation of a sudden, sweeping, clearly aimed discharge

> Whose whisper o'er the world's diameter,
> As level as the cannon to his blank,
> Transports his poisoned shot, may miss our name,
> And hit the woundless air.
>
> (IV, i, 41–44)

Now the final release comes in a scene which rarely fails to produce an overwhelming excitement and satisfaction.

Pressure toward a full physical clash onstage has begun at least as early as Hamlet's failure to kill the King at prayer, and progressed through his taunting of the King and escaping his guards, Laertes' abortive attack on Claudius, and Hamlet's inconclusive struggle with Laertes in the grave. We are also given the details of a wonderful fight at sea and the just deserts of Rosencrantz and Guildenstern (which is also the result of "a kind of fighting"). At last Hamlet is asked to "play" with Laertes, and the fencing match begins. It is an action whose significance keeps shifting: it means different things at different moments for the different players. And simultaneously we are aware of the gratifying opportunities it offers the actors. The court ceremony is elaborate. The fencing must be excellent. Nowhere is the Prince more various. The actors must show the difference between fencing in play and fighting in deadly earnest, with at least one intermediary stage between. But if the bystanders on the stage are confused by the results, we for once are not. All the significances are clear and we watch them explode into action. Every piece of inner villainy leaves its telltale outer mark and is repaid in fully emblematic action. ("The point envenom'd too!/ Then, venom, to thy work!") The purpose of playing is achieved; acting and being are one. In form and moving all is express and admirable.

The play ends with a final unambiguous discharge of energy. Fortinbras, who has a soldier's simple sense of what is appropriate, orders a peal of ordnance shot off. The air has been cleared. We have experienced, in this long heightening and ultimate fulfillment of our basic theatrical desires, the equivalent of Hamlet's tangled meditations on action and human worth. Hamlet has been concerned from the first with the good actor's root problem—sincerity. Any gesture is, after all, such as a man might play, but if this is the case how does one truthfully perform what is within him? In an earlier chapter I pointed out that Hamlet seems to be about eighteen at the play's beginning and thirty near its end. As a factual question the problem is of little importance, and there is nothing that absolutely contradicts the specific figure of thirty given by the gravedigger. But it is interesting that the two ages often mark a great change in a man's understanding of sincerity. At eighteen the imperative is not to live a lie. By thirty, one realizes how hard it is to be certain one isn't.

The problem of sincerity is of interest only in those for whom it is difficult. The obvious sincerity of Fortinbras, Laertes, and the First Player leave Hamlet irritated or envious. There is nothing within them that passes show. But to say "I have that within which passeth show," is really to challenge the whole enterprise of theater; it is to say I have a self which cannot be sounded in action, that any encounter I have with the world must merely be playacting in a derogatory sense. The crisis of young Hamlet's life comes when he is forced to act, forced by the Ghost to find a show that will be true to what is within him and to the world in which he finds himself. As with the actor who plays the role, the greatest strain falls on Hamlet's capacity for expressive coherence, for action that at each moment is true to the delicacy and difficulty of his entire situation. The tragic effect comes because we are made to feel that this achievement is possible for Hamlet only at the cost of great destruction.

A good way to see the nature of Prince Hamlet's difficulty in its relation to tragic emotion is to contrast his play with *Julius Caesar*, the tragedy immediately preceding it in composition. Prince Hamlet strikes us as an intellectual for much the same reasons Brutus does; we see them deliberating certain problems of action and attempting to formulate them in abstract terms. But Brutus's problem is that he would like to separate significance from the agents that produce significance. Though he cannot kill Caesar's spirit without killing Caesar, he tries to limit the significance of his act to the spiritual, to treat the "genius" as if it were independent of its "mortal instruments." Hamlet's problem, on the other hand, is to *attach* significance to action, to overcome his initial sense that all the uses of the world are flat and unprofitable, to fully unite action and reason, to find a revenge which is both internally and externally satisfying, an action that like all good acting holds the mirror up to nature.

But the achievement of clarity and full expressiveness in action is immensely difficult for Hamlet and immensely expensive. The destructive or demonic force that we are accustomed to encounter in tragedy seems in *Julius Caesar* to rise from the body of Caesar itself and is exemplified first in the blood that floods the stage and later in Caesar's ghost. The source of the energy that destroys Brutus, then, is the very element of the problem he has tried to overcome—Caesar's inescapable physicality, the mortal instruments that become genius only by virtue of their mortality. In the same way, Hamlet is finally destroyed and fulfilled by an action whose source is beyond his control. It is only when he has agreed not to force a significance upon his actions, not to look before and after but to let be, that he is swept to his revenge. The revenge kills him as it has also killed Gertrude, Ophelia, and Polonius. The destructive element turns out to be the very element in his situation which he has struggled in his mind to root out and overcome— whatever there is in the self that the mind cannot grasp and control in thought and adequately express in action.

We are thus brought back to the dubieties of the great central soliloquy. There are more things in heaven and earth than any man's philosophy can unravel. A taint of death lies not only in every action but in discourse of reason itself. Being and not being, playacting and sincerity, action and letting be, the pressure to clarity and the proliferation of doubt are inextricably intertwined in mortal experience. Shakespeare's tragic heroes are men who insist on the self-destruction proper to their genius; sooner or later they seek out that death which allows their capacities most fully to illuminate the world for the audience that watches them die. The destruction Hamlet seeks allows him to take as far as possible and to test to the full an impulse we all to some extent share, and to which the art of the theater is dedicated— through action to make sense of life.

Notes

1. Rosamond Gilder, *John Gielgud's Hamlet* (New York, 1937), p. 50; *Macready's Reminiscences and Selections from His Diaries and Letters*, ed. Sir Frederick Pollock (New York, 1875), p. 37.

2. The authenticity of this line has been questioned. But if Harold Jenkins is right, and it represents a playhouse interpolation, it still casts light on the way the speech was performed, and very likely on its intended effect. The actor felt the need or opportunity for marking the punctuation, for heightening the frozen posture with a posturing phrase. In any case, the stop-action is plain even without "O vengeance!" (See "Playhouse Interpolations in the Folio Text of *Hamlet*." *Studies in Bibliography*, XIII [1960], 31–47.)

3. Two or three other moments of stop-action deserve mention. The action of the play scene itself is stopped in a number of ways. The dumb show allows us to preview the murder of Gonzago in the slow-motion of pantomime, and later the performance is broken off sharply before the climax. The entrance of the Ghost in III, iv provides yet another example. Hamlet breaks off in the midst of his attack on the Queen to bend his eye on vacancy, and they are fixed in this tableau for several lines.

Robert Hapgood discusses a number of "arrested actions" in his "Hamlet Nearly Absurd: The Dramaturgy of Delay," *Tulane Drama Review* (Summer, 1965), pp. 132–45; several of his examples strike me as contributing to the effects described above. I should add, however, that Hapgood's understanding of these moments (which he treats primarily as instances of delay) seems to be very different from mine.

4.   Cf. Maynard Mack's superb essay, "The World of *Hamlet*," *Yale Review*, 41 (1952), 513–14. My concern is less with the authenticity of "acts," as Professor Mack's is, than with the problems posed by our appetite for significant "action."

5.   There are a number of attractive minor examples of action losing its name. When the Ghost speaks up from the cellarage and Hamlet calls upon his friends to swear secrecy, the same action is repeated three or four times to the accompaniment of the Ghost's "Swear . . . Swear . . . Swear by his sword . . . Swear" [following Q₂]. The repetition tends to leach the solemnity out of the action, to blur its clarity in the very act of insisting on it— to detach the significant gesture from the felt significance.

Similarly, when Horatio brings his great news to Hamlet in the first act, they are so incapable of interpreting each other correctly they are forced to repeat themselves:

HAMLET: My father!—methinks I see my father.

HORATIO: Oh, where, my lord?

HAMLET: In my mind's eye, Horatio. . . .

HORATIO: My lord, I think I saw him yesternight.

HAMLET: Saw? Who?

HORATIO: My lord, the King your father.

HAMLET: The King my father!

(ii, 184–91)

Actions are frequently repeated, allowing us to note the effect of different interpretations. Hamlet and the First Player recite the same speech; Claudius's treason is narrated by the Ghost, acted in dumb show and then again with words. Osric plays the fop and Hamlet imitates him. And there is a very funny and intricate variation on the theme of sincerity when Hamlet insists on welcoming Rosencrantz and Guildenstern *a second time* before welcoming the players. He insists that he must overact this second reception, so that when he acts less sincerely (he claims) for the players it will not falsify the meaning of his welcome to his old school friends:

GUILDENSTERN: There are the players.

HAMLET: Gentlemen, you are welcome to Elsinore. Your hands, come. The appurtenance of welcome is fashion and ceremony. Let me comply with you in the garb, lest my extent to the players, which, I tell you, must show fairly outward, should more appear like entertainment than yours. You are welcome.

(II, ii, 386–93)

He probably repeats his gestures of welcome two or three times during the speech.

6.   "How all occasions do inform against me" (IV, iv, 32ff) gives us our strongest sense that Hamlet delays, and is the source for most critical speculation as to his reasons. But it should be observed that the soliloquy occurs at the only point in the play where Hamlet, under guard and on his way to England, has absolutely no opportunity for revenge.

Hamlet and the Power of Words

Inga-Stina Ewbank

If the first law of literary and dramatic criticism is that the approach to a work should be determined by the nature of that work, then I take courage from the fact that *Hamlet* is a play in which, in scene after scene, fools tend to rush in where angels fear to tread. That such fools also tend to come to a bad end—to be stabbed behind the arras or summarily executed in England, "not shriving-time allowed"—I prefer at this point not to consider.

The area into which I propose to rush is the language of *Hamlet*. The method of entry is eclectic. If there is any timeliness about the rush it is that—just as ten years or so ago King Lear was Our Contemporary—Hamlet is now coming to the fore as one of the inhabitants of No Man's Land. A recent book on Shakespeare's *Tragic Alphabet* speaks of the play being about "a world where words and gestures have become largely meaningless," and even as long as twenty-five years ago an article on "The Word in *Hamlet*" began by drawing attention to "the intensely critical, almost disillusionist, attitude of the play towards language itself."[1] Against these, I must confess a firm (and perhaps old-fashioned) belief that *Hamlet*, the play, belongs not so much in No Man's as in Everyman's Land: that it is a vision of the human condition realized in the whole visual and verbal language of the theatre with such intensity and gusto that from any point of view it becomes meaningless to call that language meaningless; and that in the play as a whole speech is something far more complex, with powers for good and ill, than the "words, words, words" of Hamlet's disillusionment. My aim is to explore the part which speech plays in the life of this play *and* the function of speech as part of Shakespeare's vision in the play. I must start with an example.

At the opening of act IV—or, as some would prefer to describe it, at the close of the closet scene—Claudius pleads with Gertrude, whom he has found in considerable distress: "There's matter in these sighs, these profound heaves,/You must translate; 'tis fit we understand them." Of course he thinks he knows what the "matter" is, for he also immediately adds "Where is your son?" Gertrude has just been through the most harrowing[2] experience:

*From *Shakespeare Survey*, 30 (1977):85–102. Copyright © 1977 by Cambridge University Press. Reprinted with the permission of Cambridge University Press.

Hamlet's words to her have "like daggers" entered into her "ears" and turned her "eyes into [her] very soul" where she has gained such unspeakable knowledge of her "black and grained spot" as might well have made her feel unable to comply with Claudius's request for a "translation." Indeed, in a modern play, where husbands and wives tend to find that on the whole they don't speak the same language, the shock of insight might well have led her to make some statement of noncommunication—some version of the reply by Ibsen's Nora (that early noncommunicating wife) to her husband's wish to "understand" her reactions: "You don't understand me. Nor have I ever understood you."[3] In fact, of course, Gertrude does the opposite. She provides a translation of the preceding scene which manages to avoid saying anything about herself but to describe Hamlet's madness, his killing of Polonius, and his treatment of the body. As so often in this play,[4] we have a retelling of an episode which we have already witnessed. And so we can see at once that Gertrude's translation is a mixture of three kinds of components: first, of what really happened and was said (including a direct quotation of Hamlet's cry "a rat," though she doubles it and changes it from a question to an exclamation);[5] secondly, of what she thinks, or would like to think, happened and was said. She is prepared to read into Hamlet's behaviour such motivations, and to add such details, as she would have liked to find— as Polonius suspected when he appointed himself "some more audience than a mother, / Since nature makes them partial" (III, iii, 31–2), though even he could not have foreseen that her partiality would come to extend to a fictitious description of Hamlet mourning over his corpse.[6] Thirdly, but most importantly, as it most controls both what she says and how she says it, her translation consists of what she wants the king to think did happen: that the scene demonstrated what Hamlet in a doubly ironic figure of speech had told her not to say, i.e., that he is "essentially" mad and not "mad in craft." Her emotion is released, and her verbal energy spends itself, not on the part of the recent experience which concerns herself most radically, but on convincing her husband that her son is "Mad as the sea and wind, when both contend/Which is the mightier."

Claudius may end the scene "full of discord and dismay," but—and this seems usually to be the most Gertrude can hope for—things are not as bad as they might have been. She has in a manner protected her son by sticking to her assurance to him that "if words be made of breath/And breath of life, I have no life to breathe/What thou hast said to me"; she has at least not added to Claudius's suspicions of Hamlet's "antic disposition"; and she has paid some tribute to the victim of the game between the two, the murderer and the revenger: "the unseen good old man." I do not think that Gertrude's design is as conscious as this analysis may have suggested, but her translation has worked.

In so far as anything in this play, so full of surprises at every corner, is typical of the whole, the scene seems to me a model for how language functions within much of the play: communicating by adapting words to thought and feeling, in a process which involves strong awareness in the speaker of who is being spoken to. Of course there has not been much truth spoken and on that score, no doubt, the scene is a thematic illustration of that dreaded pair of abstracts, Appearance and Reality; and the author's attitude is "disillusionist" enough. And of course the scene in one sense speaks of noncommunication between husband and wife. Gertrude has drawn apart, with her unspeakable knowledge and suspicion, much as Macbeth has when he bids his wife "Be innocent of the knowledge, dearest chuck" (*Macbeth*, III, ii, 45). But, in its dramatic context, the language does a great deal more than that. There is, as Polonius has said, "some more audience" in the theatre, and to them—to us—the language speaks eloquently of the strange complexities of human life, of motives and responses and the realignment of relationships under stress. It speaks of Gertrude's desperate attempt to remain loyal to her son but also (however misguidedly) to her husband and to his chief councillor. Ultimately the power of the words is Shakespeare's, not Gertrude's, and it operates even through the total muteness of Rosencrantz and Guildenstern who, like parcels, are, most Stoppard-like, sent out and in and out again in the course of the scene.

Claudius's verb for what he asks Gertrude to do is apter than he knew himself: "You must translate." Presumably (and editors do not seem to feel that annotation is needed) he simply wants her to interpret her signs of emotion in words, to change a visual language into a verbal. But, as anyone knows who has attempted translation in its now most commonly accepted sense, the processes involved in finding equivalents in one language for the signs of another are far from simple. There is a troublesome tension—indeed often an insoluble contradiction—between the demands of "interpretation" and those of "change," between original meaning and meaningfulness in another language. That Shakespeare was aware of this—although, unlike many of his fellow poets and dramatists, he was apparently not an interlingual translator—is suggested, in the first place, by the various ways in which he uses the word "translate" in his plays. Alexander Schmidt's *Shakespeare-Lexicon* separates three clearly defined meanings: 1. to transform or to change, as Bottom is "translated," or as beauty is *not* translated into honesty in the nunnery scene; 2. "to render into another language (or rather to change by rendering into another language)," as Falstaff translates Mistress Ford's inclinations "out of honesty into English," or as the Archbishop of York translates his whole being "Out of the speech of peace . . . Into the harsh and boist'rous tongue of war" (both these examples being rather demanding in the way of dictionaries); and 3. to interpret or explain, as in the Claudius line I have been discussing, or as Aeneas has translated Troilus to Ulysses.[7] Not only do Schmidt and the *OED* disagree over these definitions,[8] but, as the examples I have given indicate, meanings seem to overlap within Shakespeare's uses of the word—so that all three hover around the following lines from Sonnet 96: "So are those errors that in thee are seen/ To truths translated and for true things deem'd." That sonnet is in a sense about the problem of finding a language for the "grace and faults" of the beloved—a problem which haunts many of the Sonnets and can be solved, the poems show, only by fusing change and interpretation into a single poetic act. In much the same way, *Hamlet* is dominated by the hero's search for a way to translate (though Shakespeare does not use the word here) the contradictory demands of the Ghost:

> If thou hast nature in thee, bear it not;
> . . . .
> But, howsomever thou pursuest this act,
> Taint not thy mind . . .
> (I, v, 81, 84–5)

Claudius, we are going to see, finds that his position translates best into oxymorons; and Troilus feels the need to be bilingual—"this is, and is not, Cressid"—or simply silent: "Hector is dead; there is no more to say."

If, then, to translate means both to interpret and to change, it also usually means being particularly conscious of the words used in the process. All of us, surely, are prepared to claim with Coleridge that we have "a smack of Hamlet" in us; but those of us who have approached the English language from the outside may perhaps claim a special kind of smack. For lack of sophistication we may share that alertness to a rich, hybrid language, to latent metaphors and multiple meanings waiting to be activated, which Hamlet has by an excess of sophistication. With still fresh memories of looking up a word in the English dictionary and finding a bewildering row of possible meanings, or an equally bewildering row of words for a supposedly given meaning, we are also peculiarly prepared to give more than local significance to Claudius's line: "You must translate; 'tis fit we understand."

I would not indulge in these speculations if I did not believe that they applied directly to *Hamlet*. George Steiner, in *After Babel*, maintains that *"inside or between languages, human communication equals translation."*[9] *Hamlet*, I think, bears out the truth of this. Hamlet himself is throughout the play trying to find a language to express himself through, as well as languages to speak to others in; and round him—against him and for him—the members of the court of Elsinore are engaging in acts of translation. The first meeting with Rosencrantz and Guildenstern, in II, ii, would be a specific example of this general statement. Hamlet's speech on how he has of late lost all his mirth—mounting to the much-quoted "What a piece of work is man! . . . / And yet, to me, what is this quintessence of dust?"— is only partly, if at all, a spontaneous overflow of his mythical sorrows (let alone of Shakespeare's). Partly, even mainly, it is his translation, in such terms of *fin-de-siècle* disillusionment as clever young men will appreciate, of just as much of his frame of mind as he wants Rosencrantz and Guildenstern to understand. And the verbal hide-and-seek of the whole episode turns what might have been a simple spy / counterspy scene into a complex study of people trying to control each other by words. Here, and elsewhere in the play, the mystery of human intercourse is enacted and the power of words demonstrated: what we say, and by saying do, to each other, creating and destroying as we go along.

No one in the play seems to regret that it is words they "gotta use" when they speak to each other. Hamlet, unlike Coriolanus, never holds his mother "by the hand, silent"; and his only major speechless moment is that which Ophelia describes to Polonius, when "with a look so piteous in purport / As if he had been loosed out of hell / To speak of horrors—he comes before me" (II, i, 81–4).

The Ghost does indeed hint at unspeakable horrors—"I could a tale unfold"—but he is very explicit about the effects its "lightest word" would have, and the only reason he does not speak those words is a purgatorial prohibition on telling "the secrets of my prison-house" to "ears of flesh and blood" (I, v, 13 ff.). Words govern the action of the play, from the ironical watchword—"Long live the King!"—which allays Fransisco's fears at the opening, to Hamlet's "dying voice" which gives the throne of Denmark to Fortinbras at the end; and, beyond, to the speech which will be given by Horatio when it is all over, explaining "to th'yet unknowing world / How these things came about." Words control the fates and the development of the characters, and not only when they are spoken by the Ghost to Hamlet and turned by him into a principle of action ("Now to my word": I, v, 110). Words can open Gertrude's eyes, help to drive Ophelia mad, unpack Hamlet's heart (however much he regrets it); and if Claudius finds that "words without thoughts never to heaven go" (III, iii, 98), this merely validates those words which have thoughts. Sometimes the words deceive, sometimes they say what is felt and meant, sometimes they are inadequate— but the inadequacy reflects on the speaker rather than the language. In the study, where the play so readily presents itself spatially and thematically, it may be easy to speak of it as demonstrating the inadequacy of words. In the theatre, the words have to get us through the four-and-a-half hours traffic of the stage, and (when they have not been cut or played about with) they give us a play of relationships, of "comutual" (as the Player King would call them) interactions and dialogues—a world where it is natural to ask not only "What's Hecuba to him?" but also "or he to Hecuba?" *Hamlet*, for all its soliloquies, may well be the Shakespeare play which most confirms Ben Jonson's statement, in *Discoveries*, that language "is the instrument of society"; and in exploring the function of speech in the play we may do well to listen to Henry James's words to the graduating class at Bryn Mawr College in June 1905: "All life therefore comes back to the question of our speech, the medium through which we communicate with each other; for all life comes back to the question of our relations with each other. . . . the way we say a thing, or fail to say it, fail to learn to say it, has an importance in life that is impossible to overstate—a far-reaching importance, as the very hinge of the relation of man to man."[10]

Looking at the world of "relations" in *Hamlet* from the outside, we can have no doubt that its hinges are well oiled, by the sheer size of its vocabulary. Long ago now, the patient industry of Alfred Hart demonstrated that *Hamlet* has "the largest and most expressive vocabulary" of all Shakespeare's plays, and that it abounds in new words—new to Shakespeare and also, in many cases, apparently new to English literature—a considerable number of which do not recur in any later Shakespeare plays.[11] And a new language for new and unique experiences is suggested not only by the single words but by the new structures, images and figures into which they are combined—as indeed by the new uses of old syntactical patterns and rhetorical figures. (It is worth remembering that, seen through the eyes of T. W. Baldwin and Sister Miriam Joseph, Hamlet's forerunners are Holofernes and Sir Nathaniel.[12]) Language is being stretched and reshaped to show the form and pressure of the *Hamlet* world. The extraordinary variety of language modes is important, too: we move, between scenes or within a scene or even within a speech, from moments of high elaboration and formality to moments of what Yeats would have called "walking naked,"[13] where speech is what the Sonnets call "true and plain" and we call "naturalistic."

If we view the world of *Hamlet* from the inside, we find that what the still small voices in the play have in common with the loud and eloquent ones is a general belief in the importance of speaking. The play begins with three men repeatedly imploring a ghost to speak and ends with Hamlet's concern for what Horatio is going to "speak to th'yet unknowing world," and in between characters are always urging each other to speak. It is as natural for Laertes to part from Ophelia with a "let me hear from you" (I, iii, 4) as it is for Polonius to react to Ophelia's "affrighted" description of Hamlet's appearance with "What said he?" (II, i, 86). In this particular instance there is no speech to report, but the keynote of most of the character confrontations in the play could, again, have been taken from the *Discoveries:* "Language most shews a man: Speak, that I may see thee."[14] In *Hamlet*, unlike *King Lear*, seeing is rarely enough. Ophelia's lament at the end of the nunnery scene—"O, woe is me/ T' have seen what I have seen, see what I see!"—follows upon an unusually (for her) eloquent analysis of both what she has seen and what she is seeing ("O, what a noble mind is here o'er-thrown!"); and Gertrude, we know, soon finds words to translate into words her exclamation, "Ah, mine own lord, what have I seen tonight!" Often seeing has to be achieved through hearing. "You go not till I set you up a glass," Hamlet tells his mother, but that "glass" is not so much "the counterfeit presentment of two brothers" as Hamlet's speech on Gertrude's lack of "eyes." Unlike Edgar, Horatio is left with the exact and exacting task of speaking not what he feels, but what he ought to say. One begins to feel that the ear is the main sense organ in *Hamlet*, and concordances confirm that the word "ear" occurs in this play more times than in any other of Shakespeare's.[15] Through the ear—"attent," or "knowing"—comes the understanding which Claudius asks Gertrude for in IV, i; but through the "too credent" or "foolish" ear come deception and corruption. Claudius seems obsessed with a sense of Laertes's ear being infected "with pestilent speeches" while he himself is being arraigned "in ear and ear" (IV, v, 87–91). Well he might be, for in the Ghost's speech all of Denmark had, as in a Bosch vision, been contracted into a single ear: "so the whole ear of Denmark/Is by a forged process of my death/Rankly abus'd" (I, v, 36–8); and the ironic source and sounding-board of all these images is of course the literal poisoning by ear on which the plot of the play rests.

So the characters not only speak, they listen. Not only do we, the audience, marvel at the variety of idioms heard, from Gravedigger to Player King, from Osric, who has "only got the tune of the time and the outward habit of encounter" (V, ii, 185), to Ophelia whose real fluency comes only in madness. But the characters themselves take a conscious and delighted interest in the idiosyncrasies of individual and national idioms, in how people speak, as Polonius says, "according to the phrase and the addition / Of man and country" (II, i, 47–8). Hamlet's parodies of spoken and written styles are outstanding, but Polonius—in instructing Reynaldo—is just as good at imitating potential conversations. Seen from our point of view or the characters', the play is alive with interest in how people react to each other and to each other's language.

Like Claudius, in the scene from which I began, the characters, when they urge each other to speak, expect to understand the "matter," or meaning, of what is said. Hence they are particularly disturbed by the apparent meaninglessness of "antic" speech—"I have nothing with this answer, Hamlet; these words are not mine," is Claudius's sharpest and most direct rebuke to his nephew / son (III, ii, 93–4)—and by the dim apprehension, again expressed by Claudius, after overhearing the nunnery scene, that the lack of "form" in such speech may conceal "something" (III, i, 162 ff.) Laertes does recognize that mad speech may reach beyond rational discourse—"This nothing's more than matter"—and be more effectively moving (IV, v, 171 and 165–6). But the first we hear of Ophelia's madness is Gertrude's abrupt opening line in IV, v: "I will not speak with her," followed by the Gentleman's long account of her language:

> Her speech is nothing,
> Yet the unshaped use of it doth move
> The hearers to collection; they yawn at it,
> And botch the words up fit to their own thoughts.
>
> (ll. 7–10)

Yielding to Horatio's cautiously applied pressure—" 'Twere good she were spoken with"—Gertrude can attempt a dialogue only through the usual request for *meaning:* "Alas, sweet lady, what imports this song?"; and even Ophelia knows through her madness the kind of question that will be asked about her: "when they ask you what it means, say you this: . . ."

We have returned to the idea of translation, for in their intercourse the characters seem unusually aware of their interlocutors' tendency to "botch the words up fit to their own thoughts." One main aspect of this is the belief, demonstrated throughout the play, in the importance of finding the right language for the right person. The opening scene is a model of this. Horatio had been brought in as a translator ("Thou art a scholar; speak to it, Horatio")[16] but, though the Ghost's first appearance turns him from scepticism to "fear and wonder," he is unsure of his language. His vocabulary is wrong: "What art thou that usurp'st [a particularly unfortunate verb in the circumstances] this time of night . . .?" and so is his tone: "By heaven I charge thee, speak!" On the Ghost's second appearance, Horatio's litany of appeals—"If . . . Speak to me"—more nearly approaches the ceremony which befits a king. The second "If," with its sense of "comutual" purpose, gets very warm—"If there be any good thing to be done, / That may to thee do ease and grace to me"—but Horatio then loses himself in the motivations of generalized ghost lore; and, in any case, Time in the form of a cock's crow interrupts any possible interchange. A "show of violence" signals the hopeless defeat of verbal communication. Horatio now knows that none but Hamlet can find the language needed, and so the scene ends with the decision to "impart what we have seen tonight / Unto young Hamlet," for: "This spirit, dumb to us, will speak to him."

But the gap between speakers which—they are aware—must be bridged by translation is not always as wide as the grave. The king appeals to Rosencrantz and Guildenstern as being on the same side of the generation gap as Hamlet—"being of so young days brought up with him, / And sith so neighboured to his youth and haviour" (II, ii, 11–12)—which should give them a language "to gather,/So much as from occasion you may glean"; and Hamlet conjures them to tell the truth "by the consonancy of our youth" (II, ii, 283). When the opening of the closet scene has demonstrated that Gertrude's language and her son's are in diametrical opposition—"Hamlet, thou hast thy father much offended." "Mother, you have my father much offended."—and that he will not adopt the language of a son to a mother ("Have you forgot me?") but insists on a vocabulary and syntax which ram home the confusion in the state of Denmark—

> No, by the rood, not so:
> You are the Queen, your husband's brother's wife,
> And—would it were not so!—you are my mother—

Then Gertrude can see no other way out of the deadlock but to call for translators: "Nay then, I'll set those to you that can speak." Hamlet's refusal to be thus translated is what leads to Polonius's death. Polonius spends much energy, in his last few days of life, on finding a language for a madman, trying—as in II, ii—at the same time to humour and to analyse Hamlet. But Rosencrantz and Guildenstern are perhaps even more supremely aware of the necessity of different languages for different persons. They take their colour, their style, tone and imagery, from their interlocutors, whether it is a question of speaking the snappy, quibbling dialogue of clever young students with Hamlet on first meeting him, or enlarging before Claudius on the idea of "the cease of majesty" so that it becomes an extended image of "a massy wheel,/Fixed on the summit of the highest mount" (III, iii, 10 ff.). They are in the end chameleons rather than caterpillars, and it is naturally to them that Hamlet speaks the words in which the play's interest in suiting language to persons is taken to the extreme of parody: "Besides, to be demanded of a sponge—what replication should be made by the son of a king?" (IV, ii, 12). It is natural, too, that when the programming has gone wrong in their language laboratory they are helpless and can say nothing but "What should we say, my lord?" (II, ii, 275).

The characters of the play, then, are on the whole very self-conscious speakers, in a way which involves consciousness of others: they believe in the word and its powers, but they are also aware of the necessity so to translate intentions and experiences into words as to make them meaningful to the interlocutor. And not only vaguely meaningful: they know the effect they want to produce and take careful steps to achieve it. Perhaps the Reynaldo scene is the best model of this. Polonius, in a dialogue of superb naturalism, with its stops and starts, doublings back and forgettings what he was about to say, gives Reynaldo a lesson in translation which is much closer to the heart of the play than any mere plot function might suggest. Anyone who thinks Polonius just a fool ought to look again at the almost Jamesian subtlety with which Reynaldo is instructed to control the *tone* of his indirect enquiries into Laertes's Parisian life, to "breathe his faults so quaintly / That they may seem the taints of liberty" (II, i, 31–2), and, in case he has not got the point, to lay "these slight sullies on my son,/As 'twere a thing a little soil'd wi' th' working" (ll. 39–40). This is a situation less Machiavellian than the Revenge *genre* might seem to demand, and more like the instruction of Strether where, as here, facts tend to refract into opaque impressions rather than moral certainties.

Perhaps I am now being seduced by the power of words—and Polonius's of all people. Not that Shakespeare allows this to happen for very long: the moment that Reynaldo exits, Ophelia bursts in, and the contrast is blatant between the urbanity of the preceding scene and the raw experience of her account—acted out as much as spoken—of Hamlet's speechless visit to her. Clearly, when the characters in *Hamlet* use their language, or languages, for purposes of persuasion and diplomacy, they are generally engaging in duplicity and deception. In the end, the evil underneath is (as James also knew) made more, not less, pernicious by the bland surface of the dialogue. An outstanding example of this is the "witchcraft of his wits" (as the Ghost is to describe the usurper's "power/So to seduce") practised by Claudius in the second scene of the play. His opening speech establishes him as a very clever chairman of the board. First he gets the minutes of past proceedings accepted without query, by a carefully arranged structure of oxymorons:[17]

> Therefore our sometime sister, now our queen,
> Th'imperial jointress to this warlike state,
> Have we, as 'twere with a defeated joy,
> With an auspicious and a dropping eye,
> With mirth in funeral, and with dirge in marriage,
> In equal scale weighing delight and dole,
> Taken to wife.
>
> (I, ii, 8–14)

The oxymorons, in a relentless series of pairings, operate to cancel each other out, smoothing over the embarrassment (or worse) involved in "our sometime sister, now our queen," stilling criticism and enforcing acceptance of the apparent logic of the argument, so that by the time we finally get to the verb ("Taken to wife") the "Therefore" seems legitimate. Then he justifies chairman's action by suggesting that there have been consultations all along, spiking the guns of any potential rebel by thanking him in advance for his agreement:

> nor have we herein barr'd
> Your better wisdoms, which have freely gone
> With this affair along. For all, our thanks.
>
> (ll. 14–16)

Having dealt with the minutes, he then proceeds to the agenda and polishes off, in turn, the foreign policy problems with Norway, the home and domestic issue of Laertes, and finally the awkward business with Hamlet which—who knows—might be both personal and national, psychological and political. He intends to deal with Hamlet, too, through the technique of dissolving contradictions—"But now, my cousin Hamlet, and my son" (l. 64)—but his briskness here comes to grief, as Hamlet becomes the first to raise a voice, albeit in an aside, which punctures such use of language: "A little more than kin, and less than kind" (l. 65).

Intrepidly, Claudius continues in an image suggesting the tone of decorous grief which ought to be adopted—"How is it that the clouds still hang on you?"—but this again founders on Hamlet's pun on sun/son. The pun, according to Sigurd Burckhardt in *Shakespearean Meanings*, "gives the lie direct to the social convention which is language. . . . It denies the meaningfulness of words."[18] But in their dramatic context here, Hamlet's puns do no such thing: they deny the logic and sincerity and meaningfulness of Claudius's words but suggest that there is a language elsewhere.

The rest of the scene, until it closes on Hamlet's decision to "hold my tongue," is a series of contrasts and clashes between different languages. Hamlet's "common" is not the queen's and implies a far-reaching criticism of hers. Gertrude's reply suggests that she is not aware of the difference, Claudius's that he is trying to pretend that he is not, as he follows Hamlet's terrible outburst against seeming with an, in its way, equally terrible refusal to acknowledge any jar: "'Tis sweet and commendable in your nature, Hamlet,/ To give these mourning duties to your father" (ll. 87–88).

Hamlet has no reply to Claudius's appeal to the "common theme" of death of fathers, nor to the request that he give up Wittenberg for "the cheer and comfort of our eye;" his reply, promising to "obey," is made to his mother. But it is Claudius who comments on it as "loving" and "fair," and it is he who sums up the conversation, translating the tense scene just past into an image of domestic and national harmony—"This gentle and unforc'd account of Hamlet / Sits smiling to my heart" (ll. 123–24)—and an excuse for a "wassail." The incongruity is as if a satire and a masque by Jonson were being simultaneously performed on the same stage. The ultimate clash comes as, immediately upon Claudius's summing-up, Hamlet breaks into his first soliloquy, giving *his* version of himself and of "all the uses of this world," particularly those involving his mother and uncle.

The different languages spoken in a scene like this clearly add up to a kind of moral map. That is, the adding up is clear, the map itself not necessarily so. It is not just a matter of Hamlet's words being sincere and Claudius's not. In the dialogue Hamlet is striving for effect in his way just as much as Claudius in his. And Claudius is soon going to be sincere enough, when we learn from his own mouth, in an image that could well have been used by Hamlet, that he is aware of the ugliness of his deed as against his "most painted word" (III, i, 50–4) and that his words are unable to rise in prayer (III, iii, 36 ff.). Morality and sensitivity to language are peculiarly tied up with each other in this play; and in trying to think how they are related I, at least, am driven back to James and "The Question of Our Speech": to the importance of "the way we say a thing, or fail to say it, fail to learn to say it."[19] In a play peopled by translators, it is in the end the range of languages available to each character—those they "fail to learn" as well as those they speak—which measures their moral stature. Both Claudius and Gertrude at various times have their consciences stung, but neither seems able to find a language for his or her own inner self. Even Polonius is able to learn and, up to a point, articulate what he has learnt. "I am sorry," he says about having misunderstood the nature of Hamlet's love for

Ophelia, "that with better heed and judgment/I had not quoted him" (II, i, 111–12). Hamlet himself never has such a moment of recognition in regard to Ophelia. But typically Polonious at once takes the edge off any personal pain of remorse by translating it into a sententious generalization:

> It is as proper to our age
> To cast beyond ourselves in our opinions
> As it is common for the younger sort
> To lack discretion.
>
> (II, i, 114–17)

Claudius similarly lacks a really private language. Even when he is alone and trying to pray, his speech retains the basic characteristics of his public "translations." Images which in content might seem to anticipate Macbeth's, are turned out in carefully balanced phrases—"heart, with strings of steel" against "sinews of the new-born babe";[20] his similes have the considered effect of earlier tragic verse:

> And, like a man to double business bound,
> I stand in pause where I shall first begin,
> And both neglect
>
> (III, iii, 41–43)

and the most trenchant self-analysis is as cleverly antithetical as anything he has to say before the assembled court in I, ii: "My stronger guilt defends my strong intent." Unlike Macbeth, Claudius seems to be talking *about* himself, not from inside himself, and his own evil seems to contain no mystery to him, nothing unspeakable. Gertrude has known less evil, and her moral imagination has an even narrower range. Even after the closet scene, her appearances suggest that, like Claudius and unlike Lady Macbeth, she is able to cancel and pass on. The woman who describes Ophelia's death, and strews flowers on her grave, is harrowed within her limits but not marked and changed by her experience, in language and being. The fact that Hamlet and Ophelia are thus changed (however variously) sets them apart. Each of them receives shocks and undergoes sufferings which are taken into their language; and at the extremest point each speaks—whether in madness or not—a language foreign to the other characters.[21]

And yet Hamlet's own language is in many ways that of Elsinore. As others, notably R. A. Foakes, have pointed out, his speech modes and habits are largely those of the court: wordiness, formality, sententiousness, fondness of puns and other forms of word-play, etc.[22] He too uses language in all the ways practised by Claudius and his entourage: for persuasion, diplomacy, deception, and so on. His sheer range, which is as large almost as that of the play itself, has made it difficult for critics to define his own linguistic and stylistic attributes. As Professor Foakes succinctly puts it, "Hamlet seems master of all styles, but has no distinctive utterance of his own." Up to a point we can explain this, as Professor Foakes does, by seeing Hamlet as "the supreme actor who never reveals himself."[23] But beyond that point we still need a way of talking about Hamlet's language which includes his uncontrolled and (surely) revealing moments, such as the nunnery scene or the leaping into Ophelia's grave, as well as his moments of deliberately antic disposition; and the simple statements in the dialogues with Horatio as well as the tortuous questioning in the monologues. It might be helpful, then, to think of Hamlet as the most sensitive translator in the play: as the one who has the keenest sense both of the expressive and the persuasive powers of words, and also and more radically the keenest sense both of the limitations and the possibilities of words. No one could be more disillusioned with "words, words, words." Even before he appears on stage, his mother's rush "to incestuous sheets" has had an impact which he later describes as having (in contemporary parlance) deprived language of its very credibility: "O, such a deed/ As . . . sweet religion makes/A rhapsody of words" (III, iv, 45–8); and, though a Wittenberg scholar could hardly have lived unaware of the general maxim that "one may smile, and smile, and be a villains," the encounter with the Ghost proves it on his own pulses and leaves him permanently aware that language may be a cloak or masque. Yet no one could use his disillusionment more subtly or positively to fit his words to the action, the interlocutor and his own mood—so far indeed that the disillusionment is swallowed up in excitement at the power of words.

No other Shakespearian hero, tragic or comic, has to face so many situations in which different speakers have different palpable designs on him, and where he so has to get hold of the verbal initiative. No other hero, not even Falstaff or Benedick, is so good at grasping the initiative, leading his interlocutor by the nose while—as with Polonius and Osric—playing with the very shape and temperature of reality. Many of the play's comic effects stem from this activity, and the strange tonal mixture of the graveyard scene has much to do with Hamlet, for once, almost playing the stooge to the indomitable wit of the First Gravedigger. No other Shakespearian hero is so good at running his antagonists right down to their basic premises and striking them dumb, as with Rosencrantz and Guildenstern in the recorder scene. He won't be played upon, and so he listens in order, with lightning speed, to pick up a key-word and turn it into a pun or some other device for playing upon others.

But, unlike many other Shakespearian tragic heroes, Hamlet also listens in a more reflective way—listens and evaluates, as Othello does not (but Hamlet surely would have done) with Iago. In some situations we begin to feel that his linguistic flexibility is founded on a sympathetic imagination. In him, alone in the play, the ability to speak different languages to different people seems to stem from an awareness that, in George Eliot's words, another being may have "an equivalent centre of self, whence the lights and shadows must always fall with a certain difference."[24] Other characters meet to plot or to remonstrate, or they step aside for an odd twitch of conscience. To Hamlet, conversations may become extensions of moral sympathy. Even under the immediate impact of encountering the Ghost he can stop to realize and regret that he has offended Horatio with the "wild and whirling words" which came out of a hysterical absorption in his own experience (I, V, 133 ff.). In retrospect the scene at Ophelia's grave is illuminated by the same sympathy:

> I am very sorry, good Horatio,
> That to Laertes I forgot myself;
> For by the image of my cause I see
> The portraiture of his;
>
> (V, ii, 75–8)

and the courtly apology to Laertes (V, ii, 218 ff.), which some critics have taken to be mere falsehood,[25] is surely a genuine attempt at translating his own "cause" into the language of Laertes. In a case like this, his verbal virtuosity seems to aim at an interchange, a two-way traffic of language between selves. It is worth noting that Hamlet's most explicit tribute to Horatio is to call him "e'en as just a man / As e'er my conversation cop'd withal" (III, ii, 52–3). Two senses of "conversation" merge in that phrase— "the action of consorting or having dealings with others; . . . society; intimacy" (*OED* 2) and "interchange of thoughts and words" (*OED* 7)—and, one feels, in Hamlet's consciousness.

There is a kinship here between Hamlet and Cleopatra, another character who in her language combines intense self-preoccupation with strong awareness of others. In North's Plutarch Shakespeare would have found an emphasis on her verbal powers, even at the expense of her physical beauty which, "as it is reported, was not so passing as unmatchable of other women, nor yet such as upon present view did enamour men with her; but so sweet was her company and conversation that a man could not possibly but be taken." Not the least part of the power of Cleopatra's "conversation" was her ability to speak different languages: "her tongue was an instrument of music to divers sports and pastimes, the which she easily turned to any language that pleased her. She spake unto few barbarous people by interpreter, but made them answer herself."[26] It may not be wholly fanciful to imagine that North's comments on Cleopatra's interlingual dexterity have in Shakespeare been translated into an intralingual flexibility. Cleopatra is able to speak different languages to Emperor and to Clown as well as to forge her own variety of idioms according to situation and mood—and finally to create, through language, her own reality and Antony's ("Methinks I hear/Antony call. . . . Husband I come"). In her case, as in Hamlet's, the vitality which comes from superb handling of language affects us both aesthetically and morally. To measure it we need only turn to Octavia who is "of a holy, cold and still conversation."

Yet by the same measurement there is only a hair's breadth between moral sympathy and callousness, and *Hamlet* shows this too. Hamlet's awareness of others as autonomous beings with "causes," and accordingly with languages, of their own also helps to explain why he despises Rosencrantz and Guildenstern so, and can so unflinchingly let them "go to't," recounting his dealings with them as "not near my conscience" only a few lines before he speaks to Horatio of his regret for what he did and said to Laertes. To him they lack any "centre of self"; they are instruments used to turn others into "unworthy" things (III, iii, 353); they are sponges whose only function is to be "at each ear a hearer" (II, ii, 377). Hamlet's sympathetic imagination falls far short of Stoppard's, and of Christian charity. The killing of Polonius, whom he sees only as an over-hearer and a mouthpiece, affects him no more than a putting-down in verbal repartee: "Take thy fortune; / Thou find'st that to be busy is some danger" (III, iv, 32–3). At this point, his whole sense of "conversation"—of dealings with others—is narrowed onto speaking "daggers" to Gertrude: "Leave wringing of your hands. Peace; sit you down,/ And let me wring your heart" (III, iv, 34–5).

Everyone knows that Hamlet speaks rather than acts, and therefore delays; but it is worth pointing out that his peculiar involvement with words can be at the expense of humanity as well as of deeds. It is worth remembering, when we speak of Hamlet as an actor (who can "act" but not act), that what he remembers from plays are great speeches; and that his own acting—as against his advice to the actors and his full admiration of their art—is almost entirely a matter of handling language: of the ability to control other people's reaction to his words. His self-reproach after the Hecuba speech is not that he can do nothing but that "I . . . unpregnant of my cause/ . . . can say nothing" (II, ii, 562–3).

Yet, less than twenty lines later he is reproaching himself for saying too much, "That I, the son of a dear father murder'd,/ Prompted to my revenge by heaven and hell,/ Must, like a whore, unpack my heart with words" (II, ii, 579–81). There is no contradiction here for, while the words with which he unpacks his heart are merely therapeutic, even an anodyne, directed at no object and no audience, the "saying" which he admires in the First Player is the absorption of the self in a purposeful act of communication, "his whole function suiting / With forms to his conceit." The language needed for his own "conceit" is nonverbal, the act of revenge to which he is "prompted." Yet in the logic of this soliloquy, transferring his own "motive" and "cue for passion" to the Player and imagining the result, the act is translated into a theatrical declamation:

> He would drown the stage with tears,
> And cleave the general ear with horrid speech;
> Make mad the guilty, and appal the free,
> Confound the ignorant, and amaze indeed
> The very faculties of eyes and ears.
>
> (II, ii, 555–9)

It is natural for him to translate intention into language—into verbal rather than physical violence—hence the apparent relief as he finds gruesome reasons not to murder the praying Claudius, or as the "bitter business" of the "witching time" can, for the moment, be allowed to be resolved into a matter of words: "I will speak daggers to her, but use none". Hence, too, the play to be put on excites him beyond its detective purpose. It is going to speak for him, or he through it—and at least at the outset of II, ii his hopes of the effect of the play seem to hinge on the speech "of some dozen or sixteen lines" which he has composed himself—to Claudius, to form a translation fully and terribly meaningful only to Claudius. If, besides, it means different things to the rest of the court,[27] all the better a translation. Murder speaks metaphorically in much Elizabethan-Jacobean tragedy, but rarely is the speaking so completely *heard* by the imagination as in Hamlet's plan for the effect of "The Murder of Gonzago": "For murder, though it have no tongue, will speak/ With most miraculous organ" (II, ii, 589–90). Hamlet's excitement with speech as translation of deeds would help to explain, too, why in the graveyard scene it is Laertes's rhetoric which becomes the centre of Hamlet's grievance and object of his aggression. The leaping into the grave is a kind of act fitted to the word, a rhetorical flourish:

> Dost come here to whine?
> To outface me with leaping in her grave?
> . . . Nay, an thou'lt mouth,
> I'll rant as well as thou.
>
> (v, i, 271–2, 277–8)

We return here to the notion of human sympathy, as well as positive action, being absorbed and lost in speech. For it is in his dealings with Ophelia—which is as much as to say his language to Ophelia—that Hamlet most shows the destructive powers of speech. His vision of the world as "an unweeded garden" ultimately drives Ophelia to her death, wearing the "coronet weeds" of her madness. I do not wish to turn the play into a *Hamlet and Ophelia:* the love story is played down in the structure as a whole, its pre-play course known only by the odd flashback and inference, and it disappears altogether after the graveyard scene. All the responsibility that Laertes can remember to remove from Hamlet with his dying breath is "mine and my father's death." But I still believe that the Hamlet–Ophelia relationship reveals something essential to Hamlet's and his creator's vision of the power of words; and also that it illuminates the way in which Hamlet contracts what Kenneth Muir has called "the occupational disease of avengers"[28]—how he is tainted by the world in which he is trying to take revenge.

The poisoning of that relationship within the play is full of searing ironies. Hamlet never says "I love you" except in the past tense and to unsay it at once. By the time he tells the world "I loved Ophelia," she is dead. The first time he refers to her it is antically, as the daughter of Polonius, the fishmonger. From Hamlet's love-letter—which we are surely meant to take more seriously than Polonius does—we learn that in his wooing he was both as exalted and as tongue-tied as any lover who hesitates to sully the uniqueness of his love by common speech. When he tries to write a love sonnet, the attempt to look in his heart and write turns into a touching version of the conventional idea that the beloved is inexpressible: "O dear Ophelia, I am ill at these numbers. I have not art to reckon my groans; but that I love thee best, O most best, believe it" (II, ii, 119–21). When, his world shattered, he came to her in the scene she recounts to Polonius, he was speechless and, though he frightened her, he also, as her mode of telling shows, drew out all her sympathy. But when he actually confronts her on stage, he has translated her into a whore, like Gertrude, and he is only too articulate, in a language which is meaningless and yet desperately hurtful to her—one to which she might well have responded in Desdemona's words: "I understand a fury in your words,/ But not the words"[29] (*Othello*, IV, ii, 32–3).

Hamlet's vision of Ophelia has changed with his vision of the world. The language to be spoken to her is that current in a world where frailty is the name of woman, love equals appetite, vows are "as false as dicers' oaths" (III, iv, 45), and nothing is constant. It is a terrible coincidence, and a masterly dramatic stroke, that before Hamlet and Ophelia meet within this vision, Laertes and Polonius have been speaking the same language to her, articulating out of their worldly wisdom much the same view of their love as the one Hamlet has arrived at through his shock of revulsion from the world. In I, iii, while Hamlet offstage goes to meet the Ghost, Ophelia meets with equally shattering (to her world) commands from her father, attacking her past, present and future relations with Hamlet.

Laertes is made to open the attack, all the more insidiously since it is by way of well-meaning brotherly advice, and since it is phrased in the idiom of the courtly "songs" to which he is reducing Hamlet's love:

> For Hamlet, and the trifling of his favour,
> Hold it a fashion and a toy in the blood,
> A violet in the youth of primy nature,
> Forward not permanent, sweet not lasting,
> The perfume and suppliance of a minute.
>
> (I, iii, 5–9)

On highly reasonable social grounds he argues that Hamlet's language must
be translated:

> Then if he says he loves you,
> It fits your wisdom so far to believe it
> As he in his particular act and place
> May give his saying deed.
>
> (ll. 24–7)

I need not point out how deeply rooted this is in the language assumptions
of the play as a whole. Laertes's tone is not unkind in its knowingness;
his final thrust has some of the ineluctable sadness of the Sonnets when
contemplating examples of the precariousness of youth and beauty—

> Virtue itself scapes not calumnious strokes;
> The canker galls the infants of the spring
> Too oft before their buttons be disclos'd;
> And in the morn and liquid dew of youth
> Contagious blastments are most imminent—
>
> (ll. 38–42)

and Ophelia, as her spirited reply suggests, is on the whole able to cope
with both the matter and the manner of his preaching. But when Polonius
picks up the attack, it is different. His technique is far more devastating:
an interrogation where each answer is rapidly demolished. Ophelia does not
have the speech-habits of most of the other characters; she is brief, simple
and direct—and therefore particularly vulnerable. In a play where rhetorical
units of measurement may be "forty thousand brothers," there is a moving
literalness about her statement that Hamlet has "given countenance to his
speech . . . /With *almost* all the holy vows of heaven." She does not have
the worldly wisdom to produce translations which protect her feelings and
hide her thoughts. So to Polonius's opening question—"What is't, Ophelia,
he hath said to you?"—she simply, and vainly, tries to be nonspecific: "So
please you, something touching the Lord Hamlet" (l. 89). Some fifteen lines
later her confidence is already undermined: "I do not know, my lord, what
I should think."

Polonius's method is particularly undermining in that he lets Ophelia
provide the key-words which he then picks up and translates by devaluing
them—painfully literally so when Ophelia's "many tenders/Of his affection"
provokes: ". . . think yourself a baby/That you have ta'en these tenders for
true pay/Which are not sterling" (ll. 105–7). His translation is partly a
matter of devaluation by direct sneer ("think" and "fashion" are thus dealt
with), partly a matter of using the ambiguities of the English language to
shift the meanings of words (thus "tender" is translated into the language

of finance and "entreatment" into that of diplomacy); and partly a dizzifying matter of making one meaning slide into another by a pun. In this last way Hamlet's vows are translated, first into finance, then into religion—

> Do not believe his vows; for they are brokers,
> Not of that dye which their investments show,
> But mere implorators of unholy suits,
> Breathing like sanctified and pious bonds—
> (11. 127–30)

but always in proof of their falsehood: "The better to beguile." "What supplies the power of Polonius's words is also a logic which, like Iago's, strikes at the root of the victim's hold on reality: "You do not understand yourself so clearly / As it behoves my daughter and your honour" (ll. 96–7); and which has a kind of general empirical truth—such as in the comedies might have been spoken by a sensible and normative heroine: "I do know, / When the blood burns, how prodigal the soul / Lends the tongue vows" (ll. 115–17).

By the end of the scene, Polonius's words have left Ophelia with no hold on her love and with nothing to say but "I shall obey, my lord."[30] When there is no one left even to obey, she will go to pieces. But before then she has to be pushed to the limit by Hamlet's verbal brutality which doubly frightens and hurts her because it seems to prove both that Hamlet is mad and that Polonius was right. A first and last intimation of the intimacy and tenderness which might once have prevailed in their dialogues rings out of her greeting to Hamlet in the nunnery scene—"Good my lord, / How does your honour for this many a day?"—but by the end of that scene there is not even a dialogue. The two of them are speaking *about* each other, Hamlet's stream-of-consciousness circling around nuns and painted harlots and Ophelia appealing, twice, to an invisible and silent audience: "O, help him, you sweet heavens!" and "O heavenly powers, restore him!" She is left to speak her only soliloquy over the ruins of what used to be her reality, and to lament the most terrible translation of all: "the honey of his music vows" is now "like sweet bells jangled, out of time and harsh."

Hamlet and Ophelia no longer speak the same language. I dwelt at some length on the Polonius–Ophelia scene because it brings out, ironically and indirectly, an important aspect of the "tainting" of Hamlet. Though he does not know it, and would hate to be told so, his language has moved away from Ophelia's and towards Polonius's. It is a language based on the general idea of "woman" rather than a specific awareness of Ophelia (to whom he now listens only to score verbal points off her, usually bawdy ones, too). Even his technique is like Polonius's as he picks up words only to demolish them, and her. Thus, in perhaps the cruellest stretch of dialogue in the whole play, Ophelia is allowed, briefly, to think that she knows what Hamlet means, only to have this understanding taken from her:

HAMLET: . . . I did love you once.

OPHELIA: Indeed, my lord, you made me believe so.

HAMLET: You should not have believ'd me; for virtue cannot so inoculate our old stock but we shall relish of it. I loved you not.

OPHELIA: I was the more deceived.

(III, i, 115–20)

Polonius turned her into an object, an instrument, by "loosing" her to Hamlet in the nunnery scene; Hamlet turns her into a thing—as "unworthy a thing" as he ever may accuse Rosencrantz and Guildenstern of attempting to make out of him—in the play scene where, in public and listening to a play which from her point of view must seem to be mainly about women's inconstancy and sexual promiscuity, she is all but sexually assaulted by Hamlet's language.[31] We have no evidence that Hamlet ever thinks of her again before he discovers that the grave he has watched being dug is that of "the fair Ophelia," and no redeeming recognition that the power of his own words has helped to drive her into that grave. In their story speech functions, in the end, as part of a vision of man's proneness to kill the thing he loves.

So we seem in the end to be left with a long row of contradictions: Hamlet's use of language is sensitive and brutal; he listens and he does not listen; his speech is built on sympathy and on total disregard of other selves; his relationship with words is his greatest strength and his greatest strength and his greatest weakness. Only a Claudius could pretend that these are not contradictions and only he could translate them into a simple unity. Hamlet's soliloquies are not much help to this end. Even they speak different languages and add up, if anything, to a representation of a man searching for a language for the experiences which are forcing themselves upon him, finding it now in the free flow of I-centered exclamations of "O, that this too too solid flesh would melt," now in the formally structured and altogether generalized questions and statements of "To be, or not to be." It is tempting to hear in Hamlet's self-analytical speeches a progression towards clarity, reaching its goal in the fusion of the individual and the general, of simple form and complex thought, in the speech about defying augury—"If it be now, 'tis not to come; if it be not to come, it will be now; if it be not now, yet it will come—the readiness is all"—and coming to rest on "Let bes." It is tempting because many Jacobean tragic heroes and heroines were to go through such a progression, through tortured and verbally elaborate attempts at definition of their vision of life to simple statements of—as in Herbert's poem "Prayer"— "something understood." But to me this seems too smooth a curve, too cathartic a movement, more indicative of critics' need to experience the peace which Hamlet himself happily appears to gain at the end than of the true impact of the language of the play as a whole. That impact is surely much closer to the sense that for a complex personality in an impossible situation— and in "situation" I include a number of difficult human relationships—there is no single language. This does not mean that the play ultimately sees speech as meaningless, or that Shakespeare (or even Hamlet) is finally trapped in a disillusionist attitude to language. It means that we are given a very wide demonstration of the power of words to express and communicate— it is, after all, words which tell Horatio and us even that "the rest is silence"—but also, and at the same time, an intimation that there is something inexpressible and incommunicable at the heart of the play.

Shakespeare—whatever the true facts of the *Ur-Hamlet*—must have seen himself as producing a new "translation" of what the title page of the second Quarto describes as "The Tragicall History of Hamlet, Prince of Denmark." Like Gertrude's translation, in IV, i, it meant both changing and interpreting his raw material. Like Gertrude, he concentrated on the speech and deeds of the prince, and their ramifications, merging any personal pressure of experience in a concern for communicating with an audience. The analogy ends here, for Gertrude was, even like Hamlet himself, only part of his translation—a translation which T. S. Eliot criticized for trying to "express the inexpressibly horrible."[32] To me the final greatness of the play lies just there: in its power to express so much and yet also to call a halt on the edge of the inexpressible where, to misquote Claudius, we must learn to say "'Tis fit we do not understand." This, I think, is the hallmark of Shakespeare as a translator, into tragedy, of the human condition.

Notes

1. Lawrence Danson, *Tragic Alphabet: Shakespeare's Drama of Language* (New Haven and London, 1974), p. 48; John Paterson, "The Word in *Hamlet*," *Shakespeare Quarterly*, II (1951), 47.

2. Though Gertrude herself does not use the verb "harrow," I use it advisedly, as it seems to be a *Hamlet* word. It occurs once in *Coriolanus*, in its literal sense, but Shakespeare's only two metaphorical uses of it are in *Hamlet*: by the Ghost (I, v, 16) and by Horatio describing the impact of the Ghost (I, i, 44).

3. *A Doll's House*, act III (*Et dukkehjem*, in *Henrik Ibsens Samlede Verker*, Oslo, 1960, II, 474).

4. Some other examples of "translated" versions of an episode we have already seen are: Rosencrantz and Guildenstern's slanted report, in III, i, 4 ff., of their meeting with Hamlet in II, ii; Polonius's to Claudius and Gertrude, in II, iii; 130 ff., of how he admonished Ophelia in I, iii; and Polonius's attempt to bolster up Claudius, in III, iii, 30 ff., by attributing to him his own plan hatched at III, i, 184–5. Significantly, at the end of the

nunnery scene Polonius and Claudius specifically do not want a report from Ophelia: "We heard it all" (III, i, 180).

5. That is, in the punctuation of modern editors (e.g. Alexander and Dover Wilson). In Q 2 Hamlet says "a Rat," and Gertrude "a Rat, a Rat,"; in F I the readings are, respectively, "a Rat?" and "a Rat, a Rat."

6. As Dover Wilson points out in his note on "a weeps for what is done," "the falsehood testifies to her fidelity" (New Cambridge Shakespeare, *Hamlet*, 1934, p. 218).

7. See *A Midsummer Night's Dream*, III, i, 109; *Hamlet*, III, i, 113; *The Merry Wives*, I, iii, 47; *2 Henry IV*, IV, i, 46–8; *Troilus and Cressida*, IV, v, 112.

8. The *OED*, for example, uses both Claudius's line and the one from *The Merry Wives* to illustrate the meaning "to interpret, explain" ("Translate" II.3. *fig.*)

9. *After Babel: Aspects of Language and Translation* (1975), p. 47 (Dr Steiner's italics).

10. See *Discoveries* CXXVIII, and Henry James, *The Question of Our Speech* (Boston and New York, 1905), p. 10 and p. 21.

11. Alfred Hart, "Vocabularies of Shakespeare's Play," *Review of English Studies* XIX (1943), 128–40, and "The Growth of Shakespeare's Vocabulary," *ibid.*, 242–3. The subject was freshly illuminated in the paper on "New Words between *Henry IV* and *Hamlet*" given by Professor Marvin Spevack at the Seventeenth International Shakespeare Conference in Stratford-upon-Avon, August 1976, and by the booklet of word lists which he distributed in connection with his paper.

12. T. W. Baldwin, *William Shakespeare's Small Latine and Lesse Greeke*, 2 vols. (Urbana, Ill., 1944), *passim*; and Sister Miriam Joseph, *Shakespeare's Use of the Arts of Language* (New York, 1947), esp. p. 12.

13. W. B. Yeats, "A Coat." (*Collected Poems*, 1933, p. 142).

14. *Discoveries* CXXXII (*Oratio imago animi*).

15. "Ear" and "ears" occur, together, 24 (16+ 8) times. The second largest figure is for *Coriolanus:* 17 (3 + 14) times. The different lengths, in lines, make comparisons somewhat unreliable; though *Coriolanus* is less than 500 lines shorter than *Hamlet*, and *King Lear*, with 3,205 lines as against *Hamlet's* 3,762, has only 5 (4 + 1) occurrences of "ear" and "ear." (I take my figures for lengths in lines from Hart, "Vocabularies of Shakespeare's Play," and for word frequencies from Marvin Spevack's *Harvard Concordance to Shakespeare*, Cambridge, Mass., 1973).

16. As Professor A. C. Sprague has pointed out to me, G. L. Kittredge exploded the idea (still adhered to by Dover Wilson; see his note on I, i, 42) that this line refers to the fact that exorcisms of spirits were usually performed in Latin. "Horatio, as a scholar, knows how to address the apparition in the right way, so as neither to offend it nor to subject himself to any evil influence." (G. L. Kittredge, ed., *Sixteen Plays of Shakespeare* (Boston, 1939), p. 1021).

17. Danson, *Tragic Alphabet*, p. 26, has some excellent comments on Claudius's use of the oxymoron.

18. Sigurd Burckhardt, *Shakespearean Meanings* (Princeton, N.J., 1968), pp. 24–5, quoted also by Danson, p. 27, n. 2.

19. See note 10.

20. Claudius wonders whether there is not "rain enough in the sweet heavens" to wash his "cursed hand . . . white as snow," and he associates innocence with a "new-born babe."

21. Marvin Spevack has a very interesting discussion of how Hamlet's imagery shows him transforming all he sees, and how he is thus isolated by speaking, as it were, a foreign language; see "Hamlet and Imagery: The Mind's Eye," *Die Neueren Sprachen*, n.s. v (1966), 203–12.

22. R. A. Foakes, "*Hamlet* and the Court of Elsinore," *Shakespeare Survey* 9 (Cambridge, 1956), pp. 35–43.

23. R. A. Foakes, "Character and Speech in *Hamlet*," in *Hamlet: Stratford-upon-Avon Studies* 5 (1963), p. 161.

24. *Middlemarch*, end of chap. 21 (Penguin ed., p. 243).

25. For a conspectus of these, see Dover Wilson's note on v, ii, 230, and the Furness *Variorum* edition of *Hamlet*, I, 440. Dr Johnson wished that Hamlet "had made some other defence; it is unsuitable to the character of a brave or good man to shelter himself in falsehood; and Seymour believed that the passage was an interpolation: "The falsehood contained in it is too ignoble."

26. *Shakespeare's Plutarch*, ed. T. J. B. Spencer in the Penguin Shakespeare Library (Harmondsworth, 1964), p. 203. Cleopatra, it is pointed out, differs from "divers of her progenitors, the Kings of Egypt," who "could scarce learn the Egyptian tongue only."

27. A. C. Bradley, *Shakespearean Tragedy* (paperback ed., 1955, p. 109, note), finds it strange that while everyone at court "sees in the play-scene a gross and menacing insult to the King," no one "shows any sign in perceiving in it also an accusation of murder." Dover Wilson, in his note on III, ii, 243, points out that "Hamlet arranges *two* meanings to the Play, one for the King (and Horatio), the other for the rest of the spectators, who see a king being murdered by his nephew."

28. Kenneth Muir, *Shakespeare's Tragic Sequence* (1972), p. 57.

29. I have discussed some aspects of Ophelia's and Desdemona's language, especially the way in which the hero and the heroine in these tragedies become unable to speak the same language, in a short paper to the Second International Shakespeare Congress, held in Washington, D.C., in April 1976.

30. To "obey" (which is of course also what Hamlet promises his mother in I, ii, 120) is a troublesome matter in Shakespearean tragedy. Cf. *Othello*, I, iii, 180 and *King Lear*, I, i, 97.

31. I have found Nigel Alexander's study of Hamlet, *Poison, Play and Duel* (1971), esp. chap. 5, "The Power of Beauty," the most illuminating analysis of Hamlet's relationship with Ophelia.

32. "Hamlet and His Problems," in *Selected Essays* (New York, 1932), p. 126.

Hendiadys and *Hamlet*

George T. Wright

> A horse and a man
> Is more than one,
> And yet not many.
> —*The Taming of the Shrew*

> What's his weapon?
> Rapier and dagger.
> That's two of his weapons . . .
> —*Hamlet*

Editors of Shakespeare have long been aware that the classical figure *hendiadys*—which, as a schoolboy, I learned to rhyme with *Hyades*—appears now and then in the plays, but no one has ever treated it as more than a technical curiosity. Scholars interested in Shakespeare's use of traditional rhetorical devices are content to mention it briefly as one among dozens of figurative patterns, drawn mainly from the practice of Latin poets and bearing formidable Greek names, that Elizabethan rhetoric books recommended to their readers as effective means of embellishing one's style.[1] But hendiadys deserves more thoughtful attention than it has ever been given, for Shakespeare uses it far more freely and frequently than his scholarly commentators have led us to believe—over three hundred times in all, mainly in the great plays of his middle career and most of all in *Hamlet*. Furthermore, the peculiar structure of hendiadys is native enough to Shakespeare's style, and so apt to his purposes, that any scholar or teacher of the plays may find it helpful to recognize this figure as one characteristic of the Shakespearean manner.

I

The basic pattern of hendiadys is simple enough. The Latin grammarian Servius, writing about A.D. 400, coined the term to describe a common

---

*Reprinted by permission of the Modern Language Association of America from *PMLA*, 96 (1981): 168–93. Copyright © 1981 by the Modern Language Association of America.

figurative device in Vergil's *Aeneid*: the use of two substantives, joined by a conjunction (*et*, *atque*, or *-que*, all signifying "and"), to express a single but complex idea. The most frequently cited example, however, is from the *Georgics* (II.192): *"pateris libamus et auro"* 'we drink from *cups and gold*.'[2] English translators normally suppress the oddity of this phrasing (the phrasing and oddity, we might say) by interpreting one of the nouns as dependent on the other: "we drink from golden cups." Similarly, *"membris et mole valens"* 'powerful in *limbs and weight*' (*Aeneid* v.431) is usually rendered by some such phrase as "mighty in mass of limb" (J. W. Mackail).

Recent scholars of Vergil have questioned this traditional way of interpreting such phrases. It suits the name of the figure (*hendiadys* means, literally, "one through two"), but it does not account for the poet's deliberate stylistic choice of two parallel substantives instead of what we would call a noun phrase (noun and adjective [*golden cups*] or noun and dependent noun [*cups of gold*]). They wonder, indeed, whether there *is* such a thing as hendiadys. For when Vergil, they tell us, describes the ceremonial sacrifice at which the celebrants drink wine from *cups and gold*, he means us to grasp two ideas, not one: such an occasion requires the appropriate sacred vessel and an appropriately rich material. In the same way, to anyone observing the old hero Entellus in action, what is impressive is not simply his mightiness "in mass of limb" but, successively, his powerful limbs—his muscles—and, indeed, his whole massive figure. In both examples, and in many others, Vergil accurately conveys our dual perception of a dual phenomenon. The *et* in each phrase precisely registers the separateness and successiveness of the two distinct segments of the event. The perception may even be a triple one—of each idea in turn and then of their combination or fusion.[3]

When Shakespeare began to write, he had available to him no such subtle accounts of the phenomenology of Vergilian hendiadys. But we know how readily he adopted the rhetorical devices of classical poetry, which it appears he might have learned from three sources: the Latin authors, including Vergil, whom he read at school and later; Continental rhetoricians, from Cicero and Quintilian to Erasmus and Susenbrotus, whose rhetoric books included lists of tropes and schemes; and English rhetoricians especially interested in figures, such as Sherry, Peacham, Puttenham, and Day. In fact, we can be more precise about where Shakespeare learned hendiadys, for it has, among traditional figures, a unique history. It *never* appears in any ancient or medieval list of schemes or tropes or figures. The first Renaissance rhetorician to give a fairly clear account of it is Joannes Susenbrotus, whose *Epitome Troporum ac Schematum* was published in London in 1562 and became, according to T. W. Baldwin, "the new standard grammar school text on the tropes and schemes of *elocutio*."[4] The earliest English rhetorician to mention hendiadys is Henry Peacham, but his first edition of *The Garden of Eloquence* (1577) gets it wrong; the second omits it. Puttenham's *The Arte of English Poesie* (1589) defines it correctly and gives several examples; so does the 1592 edition of Angel Day's *The English Secretorie*, though more briefly and less clearly. Although either or both of these works might have put Shakespeare in mind of Hendiadys, it seems doubtful that his extensive use of the figure could have been based solely on the scanty treatment it is accorded by these two writers. It seems more likely either that he inquired about it and looked again into Vergil or, more probably, that he had studied the figure in school, from Susenbrotus or from a teacher of Vergil who knew Susenbrotus. Perhaps only if he had learned the figure as a schoolboy and practiced making up examples of his own, as the system then required pupils to do for the figures they did learn and as Baldwin shows Shakespeare must have done for other figures, could he have used it with such facility when he became a professional writer.

As we might expect with so *arriviste* a figure, Shakespeare's hendiadys does not follow exactly Vergil's usual pattern, in which, as Charles Gordon Cooper tells us, the second substantive explains or unfolds or augments the first (pp. 128–32). In Shakespeare's practice, the second may unfold the first (*"ponderous and marble"*) or the first the second (*"from cheer and from your former state"*); or one may logically modify the other (*"law and heraldry,"* for "heraldic law"); or, as is most usual, the parallel structure may mask some more complex and less easily describable dependent relation (*"perfume and suppliance"*).[5] Shakespeare's examples are dazzlingly various; the developing playwright appears to have taken this odd figure to his bosom and to have made it entirely his own.

For, much as English poets have imitated Shakespeare, almost no one has followed him in this. Most later writers have wanted to be clear and precise, and hendiadys works to give a poetic passage that "perpetual slight alteration of language" that T. S. Eliot admired in Jacobean playwrights but that most writers of English prose and verse have avoided.[6] The same quest for clarity and precision has kept editors from recognizing hendiadys in all but a few of the passages in which it appears in Shakespeare's plays; hendiadys, far from explaining mysteries, establishes them. Whereas to point out the pattern of other figures is to contribute to a reader's understanding, to say that a phrase is hendiadys may only deepen its mystery. For, except in the simplest instances, hendiadys resists logical analysis: we all *know* that when Hamlet speaks of the soldiers of Fortinbras as going to their deaths "for a *fantasy and trick* of fame" (IV.iv.61) he means something like "for a deceptive dream of fame." But if we take the words one by one, it is hard to make them and their syntax add up to this meaning.

The central word in hendiadys is usually *and*, a word we take as signaling a coordinate structure, a parallelism of thought and meaning. Such coordinations are among our major instruments for ordering the world we live in; in turn, we rely on them for reassurance about the way the world is structured. Normally, when we meet *and* in a sentence, we can count on finding something in what follows it that parallels what led up to it. But in hendiadys, as in some related figures, this normal expectation is not met, or is even deliberately thwarted. In hysteron proteron, for example, the natural narrative order of events is reversed, as in Puttenham's illustration, "When we had climbde the clifs, and were ashore"[7] (and in Shakespeare's line describing how the ships of Antony and Cleopatra "fly and turn the rudder" [*Antony and Cleopatra* III.x.3]). Zeugma and syllepsis frequently use *and* to join phrases that are not exactly balanced: in zeugma one verb, for example, may serve a whole list of nouns; in syllepsis the same arrangement may involve some trivial grammatical incongruity, as in "My Ladie laughs for joy, and I for wo" (Puttenham, p. 138), where, if the verb were repeated in the second clause, it would have to appear without the *s*.

All these figures derive their effect from their slight or ample deviation from normal patterns of coordination, patterns that exert great force on our linguistic lives. We expect small grammatical units joined by *and* to be parallel not only in grammar but also in bearing. They ought, we feel, to face in the same direction; otherwise, they strike us as bad English—or comic. We are amused when Lewis Carroll's Baker describes the correct procedure for hunting a snark: "You may seek it with thimbles—and seek it with care; / You may hunt it with *forks and hope.* . . ." Pope's witty zeugmas ("When *husbands*, *or* when *lapdogs* breathe their last" and "Dost sometimes *counsel* take—*and* sometimes *tea*") similarly exploit our shock at the violation of categories by using misleadingly coordinate nouns. Auden's poems of the 1930s use this technique frequently: "the student of *prose and conduct*," "And *governments and men* are torn to pieces," "An afternoon of *nurses and rumours*," "Abandoned by *his general and his lice*," "And drugs to move the bowels or the heart."[8] These poets are engaging in zeugma, not hendiadys, for each of these phrases binds in a syntactically parallel structure two disparate ideas, not two related ones. The technique is a witty way of recognizing that a linguistic structure can be filled in with blanks of very different sorts; more specifically, that in English, as in many other languages, we expect a conjunction like *and* to join together entities that are not only grammatically but conceptually assimilable. It may seem comic—even when the subject is ghastly, as in some of the examples from Auden—to be disoriented for a moment, but we are reassured by our certainty that the incongruity will not persist, that normally our language will range similar things together—concrete term with concrete term, abstract with abstract, things of one scale or category or context with comparable things. Indeed, our whole intellectual culture and all its achieved distinctions are engraved in our linguistic sense of parallelism, in our awareness of what, in our English speech, can decorously coordinate with what.

The Romans may have felt these structures differently. Even in Latin prose, as Cooper demonstrates, the conjunction is sometimes used to join substantives in the same peculiar way that we have observed is characteristic of hendiadys. The collocation of "a concrete and an abstract term," says

E. Adelaide Hahn in the course of her persuasive disparagement of hendiadys in Vergil, "does not seem to have made upon the Roman mind the anomalous and even ludicrous impression which in English it frequently produces on us" (p. 194). We are at a different stage of history, perhaps; we have more categories and we have grown more anxious about them. Whatever the explanation, hendiadys (if there is such a thing) has always struck English-speaking people as a disturbing and foreign device, and whenever it has turned up in the English language or in our literature, it has seemed an anomaly.

Some scholars claim that hendiadys occurs in English speech, but the claim is not entirely convincing. For one thing, the instances they cite usually join adjectives, or occasionally verbs, whereas hendiadys in Vergil and Shakespeare predominantly involves the linking of nouns. Fowler, in *Modern English Usage*, suggests that phrases like *nice and warm* are adjectival versions of hendiadys, that *try and do better* is a verbal example. [9] The familiar *go and see* is sometimes said to be another (cf. "And they would *go and kiss* dead Caesar's wounds" [*Julius Caesar* III.ii.137]); but this interpretation is doubtful unless the element of intention (go *to* see) is felt to be stronger than the element of temporal sequence (go first, then see); otherwise, any sequence of action verbs (*run and hide, approach and read*) would qualify. More scrupulously, Cooper suggests "Be a good fellow and close the door" (p. 131). Here, as he argues, the second term explains or unfolds the first. We frequently join adjectives on the pattern of *nice and warm, good and loud, big and fat, sick and tired, long and leggy*. Each of these pairs represents a single concept in which the general idea contained in the first adjective is explained or specified or opened up by the second; and, insofar as such expressions may be continually invented, this pattern seems the closest thing to adjectival hendiadys in English. Formulaic phrases such as *nice and* and *good and* may be completed by virtually any adjective (or at least any pithy one) in the language. Being formulaic, however, they lack the element of surprise, of improvisation, and of eccentric coordination that we find in classical hendiadys. Other expressions of a similar kind include *hot and bothered, far and away*, and *still and all* (these last two adverbial in function) and the curious phrases *time and again* and *to hell and gone*.

To what extent such phrases become idiomatic in other languages I do not know, but in English at least they owe something to the gusto with which we collectively form what Logan Pearsall Smith calls "phrasal collocations or doublets, in which two words are habitually used together for the sake of emphasis." [10] He give dozens of examples, including *fits and starts, high and mighty, rack and ruin*. Most of these are either parallel terms or synonyms, but in some pairs one term seems to modify, or lead to, the other: for example, *rough and tumble, fear and trembling, wear and tear*. Indeed, some Shakespearean expressions that are hendiadys (or almost hendiadys) have become familiar and even idiomatic staples of our speech: *sound and fury*, *slings and arrows, lean and hungry.* We know pretty well what they mean, and the doublet form has accustomed us to use, or listen to, similar phrases without asking how, given these words, we arrive at this meaning. How many of us, for example, understand the signification of both terms in *spick and span, part and parcel, null and void, hard and fast,* and *by hook or by crook?*

But the very familiarity of such phrases dissuades us from classifying them as hendiadys. That they have become idiomatic only emphasizes how unusual it is for us to link adjectives, nouns, or verbs *impromptu* in this pattern.[11] Nor is there any evidence that Roman speakers did so. Hendiadys is a literary device, a rhetorical figure that a few writers adopt and use for their individual purposes. Through it Vergil can make penetratingly accurate observations about events that are charged with meaning. Shakespeare's practice is, as we shall see, both different and various; his hendiadys usually elevates the discourse and blurs its logical lines, and this combination of grandeur and confusion is in keeping with the tragic or weighty action of the major plays.

We might expect a figure whose structure expresses the mystery of things to recommend itself especially to Romantic authors, but few of them seem to have been aware of hendiadys. The only examples I have noticed in the prose fiction of any period are Poe's *"ponderous and ebony* jaws" ("The Fall of the House of Usher," penultimate paragraph), which shamelessly copies the *"ponderous and marble* jaws" of Hamlet's father's sepulcher; and perhaps Hawthorne's "the *gnawing and poisonous* tooth of bodily pain" (*The Scarlet Letter,* Ch. xii). As far as I know, the only poet since Milton to use it even occasionally is Dylan Thomas, whose language often aims at an archaic ceremoniousness and welcomes those dislocations of clear sense that hendiadys effectively provides. "In my *craft or sullen art"* is a possible example. We normally take *craft* here as a noun almost identical in meaning with *art,* but why should *sullen* modify one of these words and not the other? To place one adjective before *art* is to suggest that the first noun may have an adjectival force, that the phrase may mean something close to "in my crafty, sullen art." At the end of the poem the phrase is repeated without the adjective: "Who pay no praise or wages / Nor heed my craft or art." If this language seems more straightforward, it is nevertheless here that Thomas seems most closely to echo a Vergilian instance of hendiadys: "res . . . *laudis et artis"* 'a thing of praise and art' (*Georgics* II.174)—that is, a thing that has received praise and was formed by art, a thing praised for its artistry, or, more probably, the theme of an art of praise.

In the same poem we are told:

> I labour by singing light
> Not for ambition or bread
> Or the *strut and trade* of charms
> On the ivory stages . . .

There is zeugma in "Not for ambition or bread"; but *"strut and trade"* surely means something like "parading for money." Thomas uses the device elsewhere, too, notably in "A Refusal to Mourn the Death, by Fire, of a Child in London": I shall not, he says, "mourn / The *majesty and burning* of the child's death." The linked nouns seem related to each other not as parallel objects of the verb but (1) as parallel elements in a phrase whose deep structure is *two* phrases: "the burning of the child" and "the majesty of the death," and (2) as elements in a further implicit phrase: "the majesty of the child's death by burning." Thomas has certainly achieved here something of the complexity of Vergilian hendiadys.[12]

As these examples suggest, hendiadys is often characterized by its elevation above the ordinary tone of conventional English and by a kind of syntactical complexity that seems fathomable only by an intuitional understanding of the way the words interweave their meanings, rather than by painstaking lexical analysis. These qualities perhaps make it easier to understand both why the device has been used so rarely by writers of the last few centuries and why it has been so little attended to by scholars. I have not looked closely at sixteenth- and seventeenth-century verse and prose, or at Jacobean drama, to see how extensively hendiadys is used in these precincts. But Sir Thomas Browne, whose affection for doublets amounts almost to passion, certainly falls into it occasionally: ". . . and therefore in this *Encyclopaedie and round* of knowledge, like the great and exemplary wheeles of heaven, we must observe two Circles"; or "In that obscure *world and wombe* of our mother."[13] Prose after Dryden largely abandoned such flourishes, such baroque mannerisms (for so they must have seemed). In American literature, which preserved so many Elizabethan rhetorical habits, the ceremonious doubling of nouns (not hendiadys usually, but grandiloquent rewording—as it is, mainly, in Browne) continued through the eighteenth century and into the far from chaste prose of some American Romantics. If later poets ever gave a thought to hendiadys, they seem to have disdained it. Even the English Romantics, though they deliberately break up the measured antitheses that structure eighteenth-century verse, adhere, with certain exceptions that do not include hendiadys, to the sensible rules of discursive or descriptive prose. Milton uses hendiadys occasionally—some seventeen times in his three long poems[14]—but its grammatical oddity is not readily apparent in a style everywhere marked by syntactical transformations. Perhaps it is only in the earlier English Renaissance, when the style of prose and verse could tolerate and delight in overstated symmetries and congruities, that hendiadys could so casually take its place in a poetic style, and perhaps it could do so with great ironic effect only at the moment when confidence in those symmetries and congruities was being badly shaken. The wonder is that for all these years it has been so little noticed.

But Shakespeare's style—is it really possible to say it at this late date?—has never been adequately explored. In particular, those stylistic devices that make for elusiveness have not been amenable to study by most of the categorizing techniques with which scholars have approached the analysis of style. Hendiadys is too confusing, too disorderly; it is one strand of that verbal web that made Shakespeare's work seem to its early critics undisciplined and rough. Even in our own day, when the patterns of Shakespeare's imagery and dramatic structure are better understood, the kinds of discourse to be found in his plays still seem bewilderingly various, beyond the wisdom and reach of any single commentator. Critics who deeply analyze the action, structure, character, and imagery of the plays often take little interest in the figurative devices that seem merely decorative. But even those who study the playwright's style are likely to examine his tropes more closely than his figures.[15] We have lists of those figures, and we know how deeply Shakespeare had absorbed these classical patterns. But no one, to my knowledge, has found a way of showing us just how, in the plays from *Hamlet* on, when the school figures are loosened, transformed, adapted to his most complex purposes, the great Shakespearean style performs its work.

Hendiadys is, of course, only a single feature of that style, and only once, so far as I know, has any critic come close to discussing its effect. Granville-Barker, though he does not distinguish hendiadys from other doublets, accurately describes a style in which such word combinations play a prominent role:

> A very common English means of emphasis is what may be called "repetition by complement"; but, again, so common is this, its better-known locutions are so hackneyed, that their value is largely lost. "Flesh and blood," "safe and sound," "hue and cry," "kith and kin," "use and wont"—these are worn currency indeed. Shakespeare, in *Hamlet*, shows an extraordinary fondness for this device, and employs it, one would say, as carelessly as constantly. It may at times betoken the teeming mind—his own or his character's—finding two words as easily as one and too eager to be getting on to choose between them. The use of the conjunction makes smooth going for the verse, the familiar form and the bare addition to the meaning easy listening; and even when this last is negligible, as it is—to take four samples out of Hamlet's mouth alone in a single stretch of a single scene—in "book and volume," "grace and mercy," "strange or odd," "love and friending"—the actor's voice can itself color the second word to a richer implication. But the meaning is often definitely amplified or intensified; amplified in "grunt and sweat"; in "slings and arrows" a sense of piercing is added to a mere blow; and the suggestion in "pitch and moment" carries us upward first and then on. The sense is enlarged in "fit and seasoned" and "mortal and unsure"; its force is modified in "scourge and minister."
>
> The concrete imagery of a noun turned adjective can add weight to the weightiest adjective, as with "ponderous and marble jaws"; or the simple

image may be elaborated and made beautiful, as in "the morn and liquid dew of youth."[16]

Granville-Barker is probably right in thinking Shakespeare's doubling habit at times rather random and casual, even perfunctory (he gives some examples of "how tiresome the trick can be if it is overemployed" [p. 170]). But he does not sufficiently recognize the elevating, dignifying, and even the estranging effect of the device in most of its appearances, nor does he see that in those examples that can properly be called hendiadys there is something more at work—not merely amplification or intensification but an interweaving, indeed sometimes a muddling, of meanings, a deliberate violation of clear sense that is in perfect keeping with Shakespeare's exploration, in this period, of "things supernatural and causeless" (*All's Well That Ends Well* II.iii.3).

II

Phrases that look like hendiadys occur in all but three of Shakespeare's plays. Throughout his career he was fond of using nouns joined by *and* to give a feeling of elevation or complexity, and sometimes the nouns so joined seem unevenly matched in dimension or category. Thus, even as early as *Henry VI, Part II*, Young Clifford is appalled that his father should die violently "in *thy reverence and thy chair days*" (v.ii.48)—that is, in your reverend old age when you ought to be taking your ease in a chair. But only in 1599, in *Henry V*, does Shakespeare begin to use the device with some frequency. The eleven weighty plays he wrote between about 1599 and 1606 (i.e., from *Henry V* through *Macbeth*, but excluding *The Merry Wives of Windsor*) contain about seventy percent of all the hendiadys in the plays. Except for *The Merry Wives of Windsor*, in which there are no examples, the device appears at least eight times in every play Shakespeare wrote in these years, and in perhaps six or eight of these plays it is a fairly prominent stylistic feature.

He uses it most in *Hamlet*, sixty-six times, more than twice as often as in any other play. The other three great tragedies—*Macbeth* (18), *King Lear* (15), and especially *Othello* (28)—provide numerous examples of the figure. So do *Troilus and Cressida* (19), *Measure for Measure* (16), *Henry V* (15), and *Twelfth Night* (13); *As You Like It* (10) and *All's Well That Ends Well* (9) contain somewhat fewer instances, but each has more than any play earlier or later than this period. This list suggests that hendiadys is most congenial to Shakespeare's purposes in those plays that explore the problematical depths of thought and feeling, as opposed to those that survey, from a perspective less intensely or less personally involved, the spectacle of erring human behavior.

In general, it can be said that the device is appropriate to a "high style" and that it normally but not invariably occurs in passages of a certain elevation, dignity, or remoteness from ordinary experience. Goneril's rebuke to Albany, "This *milky gentleness and course* of yours" (*King Lear* I.iv.364), expresses her distant contempt for him; and when Northumberland says that Bolingbroke's company "hath very much beguiled / The *tediousness and process* of my travel" (*Richard II* II.iii.11–12), the fancy figure he uses underscores the unctuousness of his flattery. The occasion on which the Ghost of the elder Hamlet speaks hopefully of his sins being "*burnt and purged away*" (I.v.13) (i.e., purged by burning) is a supernatural one. Polonius instructing Reynaldo, Laertes advising Ophelia, Hamlet questioning the cosmos or defining poetry—all such ceremonies can evoke hendiadys, along with other formal locutions that estrange the diction from ordinary speech. In practice, hendiadys can often be distinguished only with difficulty from the normal use of the syntactical patterns it works through.

Adjectival hendiadys resembles the merely formal separation of adjectives that might easily be joined. In English we do not usually say, "The day was cold, clear," but we may say, "It was a cold, clear day." We make the sentence more deliberate if we separate the two adjectives: "It was a cold and clear day." We go still further toward elaborateness and formality if we say, "It was a cold and a clear day." Shakespeare uses this form often: "Why, 'tis a loving and a fair reply" (*Hamlet* I.ii.121), "It is a nipping and an eager air" (I.iv.2), and "Where a malignant and a turbaned Turk" (*Othello* v.ii.353). Such phrasing, however, risks making it seem as if the speaker is talking about two different things, as indeed Claudius is doing when he says he is conducting his affairs "With an auspicious and a dropping eye" (I.ii.11). But this merely ceremonious separation of double adjectives is distinct from adjectival hendiadys, in which the meanings of the adjectives interweave. When the Duke in *As You Like It* speaks of "This *wide and universal* theatre" (II.vii.137), we understand him to mean something like "this theatre, wide as the universe" or "this wide theatre of the universe" (cf., in the Prologue to Act IV of *Henry V*, "the wide vessel of the universe"). When Horatio says he would not believe in the Ghost "Without the *sensible and true* avouch / Of mine own eyes" (I.i.57–58), he must mean "the sensorily accurate testimony" of his eyes—that is, the first adjective must modify the second—or, if one prefers, "the accurate sensory testimony," with "sensory testimony" taken as a compound unit modified by "accurate." Either way the two elements of the hendiadys, though grammatically parallel, are not semantically parallel, and the most likely paraphrases would change the coordinate structure and make one of the two elements subordinate to the other or to a unit that includes the other. Similarly, when the Queen describes the about-to-be-drowned Ophelia as seeming for a moment to be "a creature *native and indued* / Unto that element" (IV.vii.180–81), most readers will hear in the phrase the undercurrent "natively indued": the adjectives seem not parallel but part of a complex idea: a creature native to that element and hence endowed with the qualities necessary to live in it.[17]

When hendiadys involves nouns, as it does in Shakespeare seventy-eight percent of the time (as compared with nineteen percent for adjectives and three percent for verbs), it must be distinguished from the many commonplace expressions that have the grammatical form *noun a and noun b*, especially those of two types: first, ordinary collocations of related objects, groups, qualities, constituents, titles (*wind and rain*, *women and children*, *pen and ink*, *flesh and blood*, *time and place*); second, mere rewordings of the same idea without any significant increment, usually for an effect of expansion or elevation (*lord and master*, *part and parcel*, from ordinary speech; "*help and vantage*," from *Macbeth* [I.iii.113]; "*chance and hazard*," from *Antony and Cleopatra* [III.vii.48]; and "*mute and dumb*," from *Hamlet* [II.ii.137]). Shakespeare, throughout his work, habitually indulges in this ceremonious parading of synonyms.

These two familiar uses of the form (nouns joined by *and*) compose the norm, the background, against which we measure the oddness of hendiadys. Something like their pattern is what we expect from hendiadys and fail to get. Instead, we feel uneasily that the two words compose an idea more complex and less compound than their grammatical situation implies. Not *sound and sight*, but "*sound and fury*" (*Macbeth* v.v27); not *body and soul*, but "*body and beauty*" (*Othello* IV.i.217); not *intent and purpose*, but "*intent and coming*" (*Measure for Measure* v.i.124). The effect of the figure, therefore, is usually of some meaning blurred, of a relationship inaccurately represented, and represented as more straightforward, more dignified, more grand than it actually is. "I have told you what I have seen and heard, but faintly," Edmund warns Edgar, "nothing like the *image and horror* of it" (*King Lear* I.ii.190–92). Certainly the horror of it is intensified by the hendiadys more than it would have been if Edmund had said, more conventionally, "the horrible image of it." It may be argued that Edmund's mind moves from the image to the horror, from the perception to its emotional quality; but this very movement, this procession of interior events, which deeply justifies the phrase, takes us by surprise and makes us feel, as the best examples of hendiadys tend to do, that some structural situation we had become ready for (our picturing something) has jumped and become a different structural situation (our being horrified at something). Edmund, of course, is lying, and so, it seems, is his syntax.

Like rhyme or slant rhyme in its near but not perfect repetition of an earlier event, hendiadys makes us do a double take, and many instances together may make us feel uneasy. Lady Macbeth challenges her husband "To be the same in thine own *act and valor*" (i.e., in this valorous act of yours) "As thou art in desire" (I.vii.40–41). A moment later she is plotting to befuddle Duncan's officers "with *wine and wassail*" (I.vii.64), which may mean "wine and ale," but since *wassail* often means "carousing, revelry," the phrase has some of the same imbalance as "beer and a party." A few lines later, having overwhelmed Macbeth's weak scruples (or, perhaps, weakness and scruples), she agrees that the grooms will be blamed for the murder:

> Who dares receive it other,
> As we shall make our *griefs and clamor* roar
> Upon his death?   (I.vii.77–79)

Some part of Lady Macbeth's specious persuasiveness may be due to, or reflected in, her use of hendiadys in all these passages: *"griefs and clamor"* means "clamorous griefs" or "wailing sounds," but the separation of the two ideas gives them an oddly empty, discordant, and disconnected feeling, not entirely unrelated to the feeling Macbeth has at the end of the play when he perceives life as "a tale / Told by an idiot, full of *sound and fury*" (v.v.27). As the griefs have been separated from the clamor, so the fury has been abstracted from the sound; nothing is compact, normal unions are disassembled.

In different characters, hendiadys may expose different qualities. In *Measure for Measure* the Duke's aloofness is perhaps partly conveyed by his using hendiadys eight times. In *Henry IV, Part II*, the extravagance of Pistol's language is made vivid through the same figure:

> Thy Doll, and Helen of thy noble thoughts,
> Is in *base durance and contagious prison*,
> Haled thither
> By most *mechanical and dirty* hand.
>   (v.v.35–38)

The first figure's *and* might well be *in*, and the last line means "by the very dirty hand of a workman." A low word like *dirty* in the grandiose setting of hendiadys, of course, produces bathos. But even in less antic characters, such as Polonius and Othello, the use of hendiadys may betray a tendency to orotundity. It may be mere rewording, not hendiadys, for Othello to claim, "I fetch my *life and being* / From men of royal siege" (I.ii.21–22); to record his unwillingness, but for Desdemona's love, to put his "unhoused free condition / . . . into *circumscription and confine*" (I.ii.26–27); and to exculpate his running off with her on the grounds that they have simply been married: "The very *head and front* of my offending / Hath this extent, no more" (I.iii.80–81). But as we hear him speak of *"broil and battle"* (I.iii.87), of "the *flinty and steel* couch of war" (I.iii.231), of *"place and exhibition"* (I.iii.238), of *"accommodation and besort"* (I.iii.239), of *"worldly matters and direction"* (I.iii.300), we may find him excessively disposed to use the doublet theatrically. Certainly this construction contributes to the dramatic irony we feel in a passage like the following:

And Heaven defend your good souls, that you think
I will your *serious and great* business scant
For she is with me. No, when light-winged toys
Of feathered Cupid seel with wanton dullness
My *speculative and officed* instrument,
That my disports *corrupt and taint* my business,
Let housewives make a skillet of my helm,
And all *indign and base* adversities
Make head against my estimation!

(I.iii.267–75)

Not all the italicized phrases are hendiadys, but they all display Othello's carelessness about the precise relations between entities. He rewords for effect, though the second term is sometimes anticlimactic, and he occasionally falls into hendiadys, as when he rebukes his subordinates for quarreling "on the *court and guard* of safety" (II.iii.216)—that is, on the very ground of the court whose function is to guard the safety of the people. Later, incorrigibly extravagant, he compares his constancy to that of "the Pontic Sea, / Whose *icy current and compulsive course* / Ne'er feels retiring ebb" (III.iii.453–55). A duller but more logical phrasing might be "the Pontic Sea, the compulsive course of whose icy current. . . ." At the end of the play, with something of the Macbeths' ghastly disconnecting of related things, he advises Desdemona to pray "to *Heaven and grace*" (V.ii.27).

III

But it is in *Hamlet*, above all, that Shakespeare uses hendiadys both to explore his characters and to probe his themes. The figure occurs here, by my count, sixty-six times, and the examples I list (see App. I, Table 1) seem to me only the fairly certain cases; there are many other phrases one might make a claim for, including one (Laertes' "*leave and favor* to return to France") that many editors routinely classify as hendiadys (see App. I, Table 2). The device is always somewhat mysterious and elusive, and its general appropriateness to the story and setting of *Hamlet* is obvious. All eight major characters speak hendiadys on some occasion, and so do some lesser figures. It appears in both verse and prose. Sometimes an instance occurs in isolation; sometimes we find several examples in a scene or even in a single speech. In the great enigma of *Hamlet*, this perplexing figure serves to remind us, in comic as in tragic moments, how uncertain and treacherous language and behavior can be.

Polonius' fondness for hendiadys appears most prominently in the scene where he shows Reynaldo how to elicit information about Laertes in Paris.

The technique he recommends embraces *"encompassment and drift of question"* (II.i.10)—perhaps two techniques, but not really parallel. Reynaldo's "forgeries" about Laertes are to include only "such *wanton, wild, and usual* slips" (we should ordinarily expect *usual* to appear before the other two adjectives and to modify the compound substantive they compose with the noun— i.e., such usual extravagances) "As are companions *noted and most known"*— that is, recognized as especially familiar—"To *youth and liberty"* (II.i.22–24)—that is, to youth when it is at liberty, or to youthful license. "And thus do we *of wisdom and of reach"* (II.i.64)—that is, "of far-reaching wisdom" (Harrison), or wise enough to see far, though *reach* and *wisdom* may be two distinct faculties—gain our devious ends. This advisory lecture Polonius calls *"lecture and advice"* (II.i.67), and when Ophelia tells him of Hamlet's strange conduct, he says, "I am sorry that with better *heed and judgment"* (II.i.111)—that is, with the kind of close attention that would have permitted me to discern the truth—"I had not quoted him."

Despite his "youth and liberty," Laertes is equally sententious, though he indulges more freely in rodomontade. Especially in his advice to Ophelia, his frequent hendiadys reveals his own uncertain and divided sensibility. It seems harmless enough when he warns his sister, "For *Hamlet, and the trifling of his favor* [See n. 11], / Hold it *a fashion and a toy* in blood . . ." (I.iii.5–6); that is, consider it capricious behavior of a kind we expect in men of spirit— a view consonant with that of Polonius, who three scenes later is plotting surveillance of such trifling in Laertes. Laertes also calls it "The *perfume and suppliance* of a minute" (I.iii.9), a phrase that identifies the minute's nature (aromatic, hence insubstantial) and its evanescence (its being in short supply).

But in the long speech that follows, sometimes noted only for its sententiousness, Laertes goes on to develop a theory of division that reflects both his own furtive style and the dissociations that have often received attention in this play. In doing so he uses hendiadys lavishly, at least seven times in his forty-line sermon. He begins, strangely enough, by echoing Vergil's *"membris et mole,"* "For Nature crescent does not grow alone / In *thews and bulk"* and continues, "but as this temple waxes / The inward service of the mind and soul / Grows wide withal" (I.iii.11–14). Now, as he proceeds, we begin to see that within his ponderous argument on the constraints and dangers of rank his syntax betrays his own baffled and unsteady equilibrium (and that of the play). Through all his graceful shifting from one sphere to another, what remains constant is his perception of doubleness in everything:

> Perhaps he loves you now,
> And now no *soil nor cautel* doth besmirch
> The virtue of his will. But you must fear,
> His greatness weighed, his will is not his own,
> For he himself is subject to his birth.

He may not, as unvalued persons do,
Carve for himself, for on his choice depends
The safety and health of this whole state,
And therefore must his choice be circumscribed
Unto the *voice and yielding* of that body
Whereof he is the head. Then if he says he loves you,
It fits your wisdom so far to believe it
As he in his particular *act and place*
May give his saying deed, which is no further
Than the main voice of Denmark goes withal.
Then weigh what loss your honor may sustain
If with too credent ear you list his songs,
Or lose your heart, or your chaste treasure open
To his unmastered importunity.
Fear it, Ophelia, fear it, my dear sister,
And keep you in the rear of your affection,
Out of the *shot and danger* of desire.
The chariest maid is prodigal enough
If she unmask her beauty to the moon.
Virtue itself 'scapes not calumnious strokes.
The canker galls the infants of the spring
Too oft before their buttons be disclosed,
And in the *morn and liquid dew* of youth
Contagious blastments are most imminent.
Be wary, then, best safety lies in fear.
Youth to itself rebels, though none else near.
                                        (I.iii.14–44)

Body is one thing, the inner life another; the inner life is itself double ("mind and soul"); Hamlet's love may be pure now, but it is subject to corruption, free from neither "*soil nor cautel*," neither "impurity nor deceit"— or are these qualities linked? Is deceit, falseness, a kind of soilure, or will the soilure of lust, when it appears, have to be covered up by deceit? Whatever that case, Hamlet's "will," even if virtuous, "is not his own." As minds (and souls) are subject to the size of bodies ("temples"), Hamlet is "subject to his birth"; as "head," he is subject to the "body" of Denmark, and his "choice . . . circumscribed / Unto the *voice and yielding* of that body"—unto its vote of approval. Hamlet is to the body politic what the mind or soul is to the body—inside it, restricted in movement and choices, unable to act without its acquiescence. Denmark's a prison. Paradoxically, the very grandeur of Hamlet's rank narrows his freedom and, to compound the paradox, makes his possible licentiousness, his "unmastered importunity" (his freedom in another sense), all the more dangerous to Ophelia. She, in her turn, is to become dual if she follows her brother's advice to "keep you in the rear of your affection"; Laertes even addresses her doubly: "Fear it, Ophelia, fear it, my dear sister"; and her double nature is to stay "Out of the *shot and danger* of desire"—that is, out of the range of danger, out of dangershot. Still masked, she may yet be unable to avoid calumny and disease ("canker" and "Contagious blastments") that attack "Virtue" and especially imperil anyone "in the *morn and liquid dew* of youth." Laertes' summary stresses the doubleness of youth that is both danger and guardian: "best safety lies in fear. / Youth to itself rebels, though none else near." The phrases, for all their elegance, betray his nervousness about the divided nature of selves.

That Ophelia has received the message becomes clear from her reply, in which she urges her brother:

> Do not, as some ungracious pastors do,
> Show me the steep and thorny way to Heaven
> Whilst, like a puffed and reckless libertine,
> Himself the primrose path of dalliance treads
> And recks not his own rede.
>
> (I.iii.47–51)

His images of war, of masks, of disease are answered by her more lucid image of climbing; his hendiadys is echoed by her merely linked adjectives ("steep and thorny," "puffed and reckless"); but her phrases are drenched in the same erotic suggestiveness as his; and she, too, is apprehensive of conduct that is at odds with counsel. The little scene unfolds, in turn, a double Hamlet, a double Ophelia, a double Laertes, each threatened by internal "importunity," "affection," "dalliance," against which the strongest defense is "fear." The ironies accumulate, of course, until Laertes, after urging his sister so emphatically to "fear" (using the word four times), puts off her own advice with a shrug: "Oh, fear *me* not" (my italics), as, subsequently, he receives in silence, in boredom perhaps, as if not meant for him, his father's advice to be true to his own self, in order to avoid being false to any other man.

IV

This account of the doublenesses in part of one scene in *Hamlet* could, of course, be much expanded if we were to consider the whole play. Even in this scene the members of the family appear in pairs—Laertes and Ophelia, Polonius and Laertes (with Ophelia silent), Polonius and Ophelia—and the advice they give to each other contains many small ironies and reversals, which brilliantly expose the follies and hypocrisies of advice giving. The context of later developments, however, and even the solemnity and apprehensiveness about human nature that color the advisory speeches confirm the view that the doublenesses we perceive here are characteristic of the whole play and that hendiadys is a stylistic means of underlining the play's themes of anxiety, bafflement, disjunction, and the falsity of appearances.

The doublenesses in the play, the way the situations of the characters echo and recapitulate one another, the mirror imagery have all been treated at length by numerous critics. It may still be useful, however, to review the extraordinary degree to which *Hamlet* shows dualisms of one kind or another to be misleading, unions to be false or unsteady, and conjunctions of persons or events or objects to mask deeper disjunctions. For this kind of deceptive linking is exactly what hendiadys expresses. There are obvious pairs into whose presumed disjunctions we never inquire, but Rosencrantz and Guildenstern, Voltimand and Cornelius, and perhaps the English ambassadors are virtual parodies of human association, related characters into whose differences we need not look because they appear too distant from the center of our concern, almost identical twins, mirror images of each other, agents, double agents, about whom someone else might write a play but whose natures here require no close inspection. We do not know whether in the ceremonious exchange,

KING: Thanks, Rosencrantz and gentle Guildenstern.

QUEEN: Thanks, Guildenstern and gentle Rosencrantz,

(II.ii.33–34)

the Queen, that "imperial jointress," is trying to show the joint monarchs' equal gratitude to the two men or is correcting the King ("Don't you remember? The gentle one is Rosencrantz"). But these pairs mainly serve, like ordinary conjunctions of nouns in sentences, as examples of undifferentiated unions against which other pairs in the play establish by contrast their patterns of eccentricity, of separateness and disjunction, and ultimately their incommensurability.

At the very beginning of the play, for example, when Bernardo and Francisco challenge each other ("Who's there?" "Nay, answer me"), who is on guard? Francisco presumably; yet it is Bernardo who gives the first challenge, though he must know that Francisco is there or thereabouts. We learn in a moment that, although Francisco is "sick at heart," it is not he but Bernardo who has seen a ghost; that another pair, Horatio and Marcellus, are "rivals" of Bernardo's watch; and that a different pair, Bernardo and Marcellus, have seen the Ghost on two previous occasions. In Scene ii, Marcellus and Bernardo mainly answer Hamlet's questions in concert, and when Hamlet appears on the platform to confront the Ghost, Bernardo is absent; Marcellus and Horatio play virtually the same role in trying to restrain Hamlet; and after this scene Marcellus disappears altogether. Such a pattern of developing and dissolving pairs leaves this side of the stage, so to speak, entirely to Hamlet and Horatio, who are united by their initials, their common experience of the university, their friendship, their sympathy, their confidence, by the incorporation, as it were, of one into the other (who "wear[s] him / In my heart's core—aye, in my heart of heart" [III.ii.77–78]), and by their commitment to Hamlet's cause and story. If there exists in the play any image of a true conjunction of spirits, it is surely that of Hamlet and Horatio, though it is not Hamlet *solus* but his anima who chooses his friend ("Since my dear soul was mistress of her choice / And could of men distinguish, her election / Hath sealed thee for herself" [III.ii.68–70]).

But all the other relationships in the play, all the other parallels, are misleading, suspect, corrupt. Mirror relationships are frequent, but they offer no true images. Hamlet and Laertes, sons of murdered advice-giving fathers, destroy each other; Fortinbras, their foreign shadow, acts in his own sphere, waits in theirs; Hamlet's father Hamlet is the ghost of himself, the ghost of his son; Gertrude wavers between two brothers, two portraits; the Polonius family echoes the Hamlet family: two men, one woman, two generations, one parent dead. But in every apparent identity some features are different: Laertes misses the point of everything, Hamlet must experience each event in its profoundest terms; the Ghost is a ghost, not Hamlet's father exactly, and since others see him he is not simply a part of Hamlet; Claudius and the elder Hamlet are utterly different in character, as are their marriages to the same woman; and Polonius and his family are partly victims, partly agents, of the Hamlet family. The doubling in every mirror falsifies. The mirrors of other persons, of the clouds, of ghosts; the glass of fashion; the glass of guilt ("You go not till I set you up a glass / Where you may see the inmost part of you" [III.iv.19–20]); even the mirror of art, the play with its Italian murder mirror—all these, though they expose the truth, fail to give us true reflections.

The unions themselves are extremely tenuous. Polonius and his affectionate family are easily undone, for beneath their intimacy lie contempt, theatricality, and deviousness. Polonius shows no warmth to Ophelia; he offers his son sententious counsel and spies on him. Laertes finds his father tedious and resists even his sister's friendly advice; and the revenge he takes for both, ill-considered and futile, succeeds in completing the destruction of his family, a result that, even in his dying moments, he seems not to notice. The marriage of Gertrude and the elder Hamlet, for all its apparent affection ("Why, she would hang on him . . ."), is easily relinquished; that of Gertrude and Claudius, though neither ever quite repudiates it, is corrupt, resting on murder, adultery, and bad taste. At the heart of the play are Hamlet's uncertain relationships with mother, father, and uncle, the oedipal conflicts and evasions that are clearly a source of his problem. Throughout, Hamlet is tormented by the joinings he sees about him: "I say we will have no more marriages. Those that are married already, all but one, shall live; the rest shall keep as they are" (III.i.154–57). Claudius, similarly, is tormented by his own false relationships: false brother, false king, false husband, false father to Hamlet, false even in contrition, his words false to his thoughts.

In effect, the play calls into question—and hendiadys helps it to do so—all relationships, familial, political, cosmic, and even artistic. As a tragic hero of unprecedented intelligence and awareness, Hamlet doubts not only his own personal relationships and the relations of powers in a state but also the relation of human beings to the whole cosmos in which they live, the unity of one's own personal identity, and even the relations of individuals to one another in conversation, in the dialogue of plays, in aesthetic roles. Almost every conjunction he finds false:

> God hath given you one face and you make yourselves another.
> (III.ii.149–50)

> Look here upon this picture, and on this,
> The counterfeit presentment of two brothers.
> (III.iv.53–54)

> The body is with the King, but the King is not with the body.
> (IV.ii.29–30)

> Wasn't Hamlet wronged Laertes? Never Hamlet.
> If Hamlet from himself be ta'en away,
> And when he's not himself does wrong Laertes,
> Then Hamlet does it not, Hamlet denies it.
> Who does it, then? His madness. If 't be so,
> Hamlet is of the faction that is wronged,
> His madness is poor Hamlet's enemy.
> (v.ii.244–50)

This last speech, however, is spoken by the same young man who earlier rebuked his mother for thinking him mad:

> Mother, for love of grace,
> Lay not that flattering unction to your soul
> That not your trespass but my madness speaks.
> (III.iv.144–46)

Hamlet is full, as we know, of references to mirrors, to paintings, to plays, all of which contribute to the same complex presentation of false parallels and unreliable conjunctions. What has been noted less often is the extent to which characters act *through* others. When at any given moment on the stage two persons appear to be in conference, we are likely to understand them better as one character working through the other—as indeed it is through all the characters together that we see their world, their stage, the age and body of their time pressing its form.

Again, this situation is exactly that of hendiadys. The play is full of agents, and the characters use them lavishly, but most of the time, as it turns out, the agents never really succeed in accomplishing what they set out to accomplish. Claudius works through Laertes, uses him almost as his mask, just as he has earlier used Laertes' father. This father and son are killed as they front for him; to kill Hamlet the father and Hamlet the son, he pours equivalent "leperous distillment[s]" into their ears—poison in one's, Laertes' challenge in the other's. Claudius uses others as well—Gertrude, Rosencrantz and Guildenstern, his ambassadors, England, Osric, and "your better wisdoms" of the court he has won. Polonius works through Ophelia, Reynaldo, the players, and—fatally for him—the Queen. Laertes pleads through Polonius for permission to go to France; he works through the King to avenge his family. The Ghost uses Bernardo, Marcellus, and Horatio to get to Hamlet, who then becomes the Ghost's agent in securing revenge. Bernardo and Marcellus work through Horatio to get to Hamlet. Hamlet himself uses players, pirates, guards, England, his mother, and Horatio to serve all sorts of purposes, from exposing the King to disposing of Rosencrantz and Guildenstern, to reporting his cause aright. In almost all these examples, the chief instigator gives his agents careful instructions about how to proceed; a remarkable proportion of the play consists of just such instructions: do this, don't do that. In the service of one plot or another, these employers of agents use various props—poison, a play, an antic disposition, letters and seals, arras, masks, and rhetoric of many kinds. The problem for everyone who employs agents or props is to know which ones to choose and how to manipulate them, but every tool becomes, sooner or later, another image of oneself, one's mask, one's mirror, one's hands, and all these images may come to seem insubstantial. "These hands are not more like," Horatio says, to verify the Ghost (I.ii.212)—more like each other, he means, than the Ghost is to his memory of Hamlet's father. No one's plot entirely succeeds. The great employers of agents—Claudius, Hamlet, Polonius, Laertes—all see their plans go awry and come to grief.

Such frustration is clearly in the nature of things. However much mirrors, paintings, or plays can show us, the shadows they reflect elude our grasp. Hamlet calls into question every dimension of reality, but all his techniques for probing, for questioning the causes of the world, the cause-effect nature of its processes, end by casting doubt on causality itself and even on motive. Motive and cause, much speculated on in the play, turn out to be deeper than anyone can fathom. (Why do Hamlet and Gertrude especially act as they do? We never know.)

In a sense, madness carries the enigmas only one step further. It is not only Hamlet and Ophelia who bear watching; all the members of the two families behave unaccountably and exhibit signs of disturbance. Claudius' guilt paralyzes him:

> And like a man to double business bound,
> I stand in pause where I shall first begin
> And both neglect.[18]
>
> (III.iii.41–43)

Gertrude's situation is equally appalling:

> Thou turn'st mine eyes into my very soul,
> And there I see such black and grained spots
> As will not leave their tinct.
>
> O Hamlet, thou hast cleft my heart in twain.
>
> (III.iv.89–91, 156)

We see Ophelia pathetically "Divided from herself and her fair judgment" (IV.v.85)—a phrase that, if we do not take it as hendiadys, shows Ophelia now in three segments. Laertes may be, as Claudius suggests, "A face without a heart" (IV.vii.110). Polonius invites the King to "Take this from this, if this be otherwise" (II.ii.156), which it is; in an unexpected fashion, the offer is redeemed. These are all violent or shocking images, and they suggest the extent to which these six main characters are, like the syntax in hendiadys, disjoined, stricken, divided within.

Causality, purpose, persons all askew. But the distinction basic to all these is that between heaven and earth, opposites that need to be in harmony if any other conjunctions are to be trusted. Again and again Hamlet invokes both of them:

> Heaven and earth!
> Must I remember?
> (I.ii.142–43)

> O all you host of Heaven! O earth!
> (I.v.92)

> There are more things in Heaven and earth, Horatio,
> Than are dreamt of in your philosophy.
> (I.v.166–67)

In both the first act and the last, the King's cannon announce his drinking to the heavens, which echo back to earth. Hamlet knows well enough, however, how false such noises are. At one moment he considers the earth "a sterile promontory" and the heavens "a foul and pestilent congregation of vapors" (II.ii.310–15). While Ophelia calls on heaven to restore him (III.i.138, 147), Hamlet cries in self-disgust, "What should such fellows as I do crawling between heaven and earth?" (III.i.129–30). Horatio, early in the play, sees "Heaven and earth" as having "together demonstrated" in Denmark graphic signs of events to come (I.i.124). Laertes also complains that the odd circumstances of his father's death and burial "Cry to be heard, as 'twere from Heaven to earth" (IV.v.216), and so enraged is he at first "That both the worlds I give to negligence" (IV.v.134). If the two worlds he refers to are this one and the next, they represent a conjunction like that between heaven and earth. Heaven and hell are often linked in the play; Ophelia at her death is suspended for a while between air and water; the Ghost inhabits at least two realms. The play and the players move between Denmark and England, the land and the sea, the terrifying heights of the castle and its courtly depths, between formal and personal occasions, between impotence and action, between verse and prose, between "natural" and "unnatural" behavior, between reasoning and rashness, and so on.

What the play suggests, and what hendiadys helps to convey, is that the conjunctions on which life depends, on which this world's customs and institutions are founded, cannot be trusted. The ultimate disjunction that hendiadys and the play express is that between man and the world (family, nation, or cosmos), apparently in union with each other but actually in deep opposition, disequilibrium. Like the "union" that Claudius throws into the cup, "Richer than that which four successive kings / In Denmark's crown have worn" (V.ii.284–85), this one is deadly poison. As madness is a loosening of connections (that mimics murder, fratricide, regicide, or monkeys jumping from rooftops [III.iv.192–96]), so is hendiadys; as mirrors and paintings mock the reality they pretend to reproduce, so hendiadys mocks normal unions of entities. A miniature stylistic play within the play, hendiadys holds its mirror up to *Hamlet* and—like the court scenes, the duel, the arranged performance of the players, and other stage devices and significant turns of language—enforces our awareness of the drama's central action. For in hendiadys, as in the play, we experience an encounter between two mismatched and incommensurable forces, in open and yet obscure relation to each other, joined yet disparate, one pair in the sentence and one in life (or in this representation of life). And as in each the halves cannot fit easily together, so between the two realms, between the linguistic emblem of hendiadys and the situation of Hamlet in the world, there is no simple concord, no clear and easy passage from one to the other. In hendiadys the words are as isolated as the characters, as aloof as Hamlet, and the device itself as ill at ease in the language as Hamlet is in Denmark.

V

Whatever the role of hendiadys as a stylistic emblem of the major meanings of *Hamlet*, our awareness of its extensive use in the play can at least throw light on some important passages. Because phrases involving hendiadys are not often understood as such, their meanings are jumbled, reduced to a stricter logic than the verbal situation can justify, or even entirely misread. *Hamlet* and most of Shakespeare's other plays of this period contain far too many examples of hendiadys to permit discussion of all of them, but it may be helpful to inspect a few famous instances—or, rather, famous phrases not often recognized as instances. Scholarly readers at least ought to understand that such familiar phrases as "sound and fury," "slings and arrows," "whips and scorns," or "scourge and minister" are not ordinary unions of nouns but instances or cousins of this peculiar Latinate figure.

Some phrases are simple enough. When Hamlet promises the Ghost to erase from memory everything "That *youth and observation* copied there" (I.v.101), we understand immediately that these terms are not separate but compound, that he must mean "youthful observation," the habit of observation that he has engaged in up to this moment, which is to say, in his youth.[19] Ophelia's description of Hamlet as "The *expectancy and rose* of the fair state" (III.i.160) is easily translatable as "the rosy expectancy," the man whom everyone has been expecting to become, as king, the fairest flower of our country. The Ghost supposes it likely that, when he tells his tale to his son, Hamlet's "*knotted and combined* locks" will part (I.v.18)—that is, not two different kinds of locks but locks that are combined by being knotted, by growing together. Soon the Ghost must return to "*sulphurous and tormenting* flames" (I.v.3)—that is, to flames that torment *because* they are sulphurous. Hamlet, on seeing the Ghost, wonders why his father's sepulcher "Hath oped his *ponderous and marble* jaws" (I.iv.50)—that is, heavy *because* marble. (The phrasing here, in a question that seeks a cause, obscures a cause.) Gertrude asks Rosencrantz and Guildenstern "To show us so much *gentry and goodwill*"—courtesy and goodwill, but also the goodwill we expect of gentlemen like yourselves—"As to expend your time with us a while / For the *supply and profit* of our hope" (II.ii.22–24)—to supply, to our advantage, the thing we are hoping for. The King suspects that "the *hatch and the disclose*" of whatever Hamlet is brooding over "Will be some danger" (III.i.174–75): the brood, when we know what it is. (*Disclose*, for Shakespeare's audience, would be a pun; the verb meant both "hatch" and "reveal.")

Once we realize that Shakespeare is using hendiadys freely, some passages become clearer, or at least their obscurity grows brighter. The "*slings and arrows* of outrageous fortune" (III.i.58) are not parallel terms: one is an instrument for slinging, the other is the thing slung, but slings do not sling arrows; in speech we might expect "bows and arrows" or "slings and bows" or "slings and stones" or "stones and arrows." If the phrase Hamlet uses is not exactly hendiadys, it is at least more comprehensible in a setting where hendiadys is a prominent figure. The *"whips and scorns* of time" (III.i.70), which Hamlet, in the same soliloquy, doubts we would want to bear if we did not fear death, also come from different categories: one is concrete and metaphorical, the other abstract and immediate, and together they might seem out of focus if we were not so accustomed to the pattern of hendiadys. Time or a satirist's scorn may make us feel whipped, or the two words may express two ways time has of punishing us (wrinkles and disappointment), but the terms seem to interweave their meanings as simple conjoined nouns do not usually do.

Hamlet's remarks on "playing" yield up more of their meaning when we notice their use of hendiadys. The purpose of playing, he tells us, "was and is to hold as 'twere the mirror up to Nature—to show Virtue her own feature, scorn her own image, and the very *age and body of the time* his *form and pressure*" (III.ii.23–27). The last phrase surely means "the imprint, or stamp, of his form," though we may also be justified in hearing a more complex meaning: "his form and the stamp of his form."[20] But whose form? The previous phrase is more puzzling, but I take the two terms it joins to be not *age* and *body* but *age* and *body of the time*. For one thing, "age . . . of the time" is meaningless, as Dr. Johnson noted. On the other hand, *age* and *body of the time* are clearly not parallel, but what happens here is what frequently happens in hendiadys: the second term unfolds the first. The very age—that is to say, the period of time, conceived as a body—will find the imprint of its figure in the mirror of stage representations.

While readings based on hendiadys are sometimes not much at variance with traditional ones, an awareness of this device and its peculiar structure can help us appraise more clearly the meanings of many phrases cast in this pattern that elude our exact understanding. The usual assumption of editors, when confronted with a phrase in the $a + b$ form, is that the linked words are either synonymous or complementary. It might help their readers—*us*— if they realized that Shakespeare frequently uses a third pattern, which, though it works differently in different examples, constitutes a distinct alternative way of organizing compound phrases. The function of this third pattern is evidently not to resolve ambiguities but to assert them, to acknowledge and dramatize the elusiveness of even the simplest relations, and at once to deny and to extend the adequacy of linguistic forms to convey our experience. Instead of retreating in dismay before such phrases, we might, with whatever misgivings, surprise them in their mimetic shadows with Francisco's scholarly cry: "Stand, and unfold yourself."

Notes

1. See, e.g., Sister Miriam Joseph, *Shakespeare's Use of the Arts of Language* (New York: Hafner, 1947), pp. 61–62, 298–99; and Richard A. Lanham, *A Handlist of Rhetorical*

Terms: A Guide for Students of English Literature (Berkeley: Univ. of California Press, 1969), p. 53. Brian Vickers never mentions hendiadys in his otherwise admirable *Classical Rhetoric in English Poetry* (London: Macmillan, 1970) or in his essay "Shakespeare's Use of Rhetoric," in *A New Companion to Shakespeare Studies*, ed. Kenneth Muir and S. Schoenbaum (Cambridge: Cambridge Univ. Press, 1971), pp. 83–98. The linguist Geoffrey N. Leech, impatient with those scholars of rhetoric for whom "the identification, classification, and labelling of specimens of given stylistic devices becomes an end in itself," pounces on hendiadys as an egregiously ridiculous instance of this obsession. He scoffs at "the survival in modern textbooks of figures like *hendiadys*, which we can value only as curiosities. . . . It is so rare that I have found no certain instance of it in English literature" (*A Linguistic Guide to English Poetry* [London: Longmans, 1969], p. 4).

2. Throughout, emphasis has been added in quotations to stress examples of hendiadys.

3. See E. Adelaide Hahn, "Hendiadys: Is There Such a Thing?" *Classical Weekly*, 8 May 1922, pp. 193–97; Charles Gordon Cooper, *Journey to Hesperia* (London: Macmillan, 1959), pp. 128–32; and Kenneth Quinn, *Virgil's Aeneid: A Critical Description* (Ann Arbor: Univ. of Michigan Press, 1969), pp. 423–28. Both Hahn and Cooper call the term hendiadys a "misnomer." Quinn includes the figure among the many devices that show Vergil's preference for coordinating structures over subordinating ones; the poet's conscious purpose is to enforce "the constant assertion" (p. 424) of the narrative, the insistent forward movement of the living past. Wherever possible, therefore, Vergil places the elements of a situation in coordinate syntax and expects his readers to recognize "the differing flavour of his words in the two arms of the parataxis" (p. 426).

4. Baldwin, *William Shakspere's Small Latine and Lesse Greeke* (Urbana: Univ. of Illinois Press, 1944), II, 43. I have relied also on Joseph Xavier Brennan's doctoral dissertation, "The Epitome Troporum ac Schematum of Joannes Susenbrotus: Text, Translation, and Commentary," Diss. Univ. of Illinois 1953.

Susenbrotus cited as sources of his own work the earlier lists of tropes and figures complied by Mancinellus (*Carmen de Floribus*, 1489) and by Mosellanus (*Tabulae de Schematibus et Tropis*, 1529), both of whom briefly mention hendiadys, but his account of hendiadys is fuller and clearer than theirs and indicates that he had evidently also looked closely at Servius. Richard Sherry, who relied largely on Mosellanus (see Baldwin, II, 35–37), omits any mention of hendiadys in his *A Treatise of Schemes and Tropes* (London, 1550). It was Susenbrotus' treatment of hendiadys, available only from 1562 on, that was taught in the schools, that Puttenham and Day must have consulted, and that must have caught Shakespeare's eye.

5. In his single paragraph on the subject, Susenbrotus, evidently puzzled, defines his puzzling figure three times: "an adjective is turned into a noun . . . one idea [*unum*] is explained through two . . . for poetic effect one idea [*res una*] is divided into two by an intervening conjunction, whether the other of those words signifying that idea be an adjective or a noun" (Brennan's trans.). The first two brief phrases are adapted from earlier writers, beginning with Mancinellus in 1489; the last comes directly from Servius (*Servii Grammatici*, ed. Georgius Thilo [Leipzig: B. G. Terbneri, 1878], I, 36), but its crucial concluding clause is original with Susenbrotus: "sive alterum è vocibus rem illam significantibus, adiectivum, sive utrumque substantivum fuerit" 'whether the second of the words signifying that (single) idea be an adjective or a noun.' This comment suggests that there are two patterns: in one a phrase consisting of a noun and adjective (say, *pateris aureis* 'golden cups') is split into two substantives (*pateris et auro* 'cups and gold'); in the other a phrase consisting of a noun and a dependent genitive noun (*molem altorum montium* 'a heap of high mountains') is split into two substantives (*molemque et montes . . . altos* 'a heap and high mountains'). (Servius and Susenbrotus cite both these examples from Vergil.) If Shakespeare worked from Susenbrotus, the playwright's normal procedure may well have been either to break open relatively bland

adjectival phrases like *furious sound* or *horrible image* (both discussed below) into striking coordinate phrases ("*sound and fury,*" "*image and horror*") or to work from genitive constructions, from *law of heraldry* to "*law and heraldry*" (*Hamlet* 1.i.87). In English, the force is largely the same whether the phrasing is "law of heraldry" or "heraldic law," and Shakespeare may have started from either phrase as a base from which to begin his hendiadic transformations. Shakespeare's hendiadys, however, often appears to originate in, and to be translatable by, more complex phrasing: for example, *morning freshness* (or *fresh morning*) seems to be first transformed, by metaphor, into *morning dew* (or *dewy morning*) and thence, by hendiadys (and amplification), into "the *morn and liquid dew* of youth" (*Hamlet* 1.iii.41). By contrast, in Milton, who may also have learned hendiadys at school from Susenbrotus, the figure almost always seems to follow one of the two types described above. (I am grateful to my colleague Calvin B. Kendall for helping me to fix more precisely the perceptions described in this note.)

Almost all quotations and line numbers from Shakespeare are based on G. B. Harrison, ed., *Shakespeare: The Complete Works* (New York: Harcourt, 1968), but numerous other editions have been consulted, including David Bevington, ed., *The Complete Works of Shakespeare*, 3rd ed. (Glenview, Ill.: Scott, Foresman, 1980); Sylvan Barnet, gen. ed., *The Complete Signet Classic Shakespeare* (New York: Harcourt, 1972); G. Blakemore Evans, ed., *The Riverside Shakespeare* (Boston: Houghton, 1974); George Lyman Kittredge, ed. *The Tragedy of Hamlet, Prince of Denmark* (Boston: Ginn, 1939); George Rylands, ed., *Hamlet* (Oxford: Clarendon, 1947); R. C. Bald, ed., *Hamlet* (New York: Appleton-Century-Crofts, 1946); Hardin Craig, ed., *An Introduction to Shakespeare* (New York: Scott, Foresman, 1952); and Horace Howard Furness, ed., *A New Variorum Edition of Shakespeare* (1877; rpt. New York: American Scholar, 1965), esp. the two vols. devoted to *Hamlet*.

6. Eliot, "Philip Massinger," *Selected Essays* (New York: Harcourt, 1932), p. 185.

7. George Puttenham, *The Arte of English Poesie* (Menston, Eng.: Scolar, 1968), p. 142.

8. Carroll, *The Hunting of the Snark and Other Poems and Verses* (New York: Harper, 1903), p. 21; Alexander Pope, *The Rape of the Lock* III.158,8; *The English Auden: Poems, Essays, and Dramatic Writings, 1927–1939*, ed. Edward Mendelson (New York: Random, 1977), pp. 203, 235, 241, 258; and *Collected Poems*, ed. Edward Mendelson (New York: Random, 1976), p. 224.

9. Fowler, *Modern English Usage* (Oxford: Clarendon, 1957), p. 607. Hendiadys is treated under "Technical terms of rhetoric. . . ."

10. Smith, *Words and Idioms: Studies in the English Language* (Boston: Houghton, 1925), p. 173. Smith's lists of doublets are on pp. 173–75.

11. One exception is the familiar construction in which we link a person with something that belongs to the person: "I wanted to talk with you about *Susie and her grades*"— i.e., about Susie's grades. Or: "Do you have any comment on *your opponent and the charges* he has brought against you?"—i.e., your opponent's charges. Not all such constructions are reducible to one noun phrase, but many are. The speech of Laertes that I analyze at length below begins in the same manner: "For *Hamlet, and the trifling of his favor,*" which means "As for the trifling of Hamlet's favor." Having recognized only very late that this construction is sometimes a form of hendiadys (thanks again to my colleague Calvin B. Kendall), I may have missed a few instances of this form in my count of hendiadys in Shakespeare's plays. But examples are often problematical. Brutus is using hendiadys when he says, "You know that I held *Epicurus* strong, / And *his opinion*" (*Julius Caesar* v.i.77–78); but Joan La Pucelle, though she is echoing a phrase of Plutarch's (and possibly of Caesar's), has two distinct ideas in mind when she compares herself to "that proud insulting ship / Which *Caesar and his fortune* bare at once" (*Henry VI, Part 1* 1.ii.138–39).

12. *The Collected Poems of Dylan Thomas* (New York: New Directions, 1971), pp. 142, 112.

13. From *Pseudodoxia Epidemica* (1646) and *Religio Medici* (1642), in *The Prose of Sir Thomas Browne*, ed. Norman Endicott (New York: New York Univ. Press, 1968), pp. 97 and 47. I am grateful to my colleague Gordon W. O'Brien for calling my attention to Browne's use of hendiadys and for helping me read some Shakespearean phrases more accurately.

14. See *Paradise Lost* I.233–34, 771, 786; II.67, 69, 80, 346; III.417; IV.562; V.349; X.345–46, 956; *Paradise Regained* I.457; II.29; IV.439; *Samson Agonistes*, ll. 34, 1654. These seem likely instances, 17 in 14,393 lines, or 1 in every 847 lines.

15. See, e.g., Maurice Charney, *Style in* Hamlet (Princeton: Princeton Univ. Press, 1969). In Renaissance lists of rhetorical schemes, hendiadys is treated as a figure, not as a trope, for its point lies in its peculiar syntax, not in the alteration of meaning that is usually felt to be the mark of a trope, whether the alteration occurs in a single word, as often in metaphor, metonymy, synecdoche, and so on, or proceeds from a governing design, as in allegory or a sustained ironic structure. But to find in the figure such extensive meanings as the present essay proposes is, in effect, to suggest that hendiadys has the force of a trope and helps in some measure to organize the meanings of the play.

16. Harley Granville-Barker, *Prefaces to Shakespeare* (Princeton: Princeton Univ. Press, 1946), I, 169–70.

17. Editors frequently gloss this phrase in a way that confirms my reading of hendiadys. Harrison hears *indued* as "endowed; i.e., a creature whose natural home is the water (*element*)." Other editors offer such readings for *indued* as "adapted by nature" (Kittredge and Bevington), "in harmony with" (Signet),"belonging to" (Rylands), "habituated" (Evans), or "accustomed" (Bald). C. T. Onions' *A Shakespeare Glossary* (Oxford: Clarendon, 1919) suggests "endowed with qualities fitting her for living in water." None of these has any warrant from the *OED*, but that work's fourth meaning for the word ("To lead on; to bring up, educate, instruct") is probably the one Shakespeare had mainly in mind. Ophelia seems a creature native to the water and brought up in it—two distinct ideas and hence not hendiadys, except that, since the historical confusion between *indued* (or *endued*) and *endowed* existed in the Renaissance, Shakespeare and his audience may well have heard not only the meaning just proposed but also, perhaps a little loosely, "natively endowed."

18. Cf. Pyrrhus, in the heroic extract Hamlet begins and the First Player continues: "So as a painted tyrant Pyrrhus stood / And like a neutral to his will and matter, / Did nothing" (II.ii.502–4). That "Did nothing" constitutes the whole of l. 504 emphasizes the blankness of Pyrrhus' stance and state of mind.

19. Cf. *"youth and liberty"* (II.i.24) and *"youth and havior"* or *"humour"* (II.ii.12), which work the same way, and, in *All's Well That Ends Well*, *"youth and ignorance"* (II.iii.171). Such phrases contrast sharply with those that join parallel terms—e.g., "youth and nobleness of birth" (*Two Gentlemen of Verona* I.iii.33).

20. *"In form and moving* how *express and admirable!"* Hamlet has earlier exclaimed about man (II.ii.316–17). Although the two nouns could be taken separately, they seem more effective in combination: "in his form, and in the movements of that form." It would seem more appropriate to describe the movements of the body as "express" than to speak so of the body at rest. The word *moving* sets the idea of *form* in motion.

Most editors have felt some anxiety about *express*. Several gloss it as "exact," one as "well-devised," another as "well-framed(?)." Rylands suggests "active, purposeful, *or* well-modelled (Lat. *exprimere*, to portray)." Kittredge offers "precisely adapted to its purpose—like a delicately adjusted piece of mechanism." (He does not say what mechanism—a Swiss watch? the 3:18 to Stratford?—Shakespeare may have had in mind.) But most of the *OED*'s meanings for *express* emphasize the idea of distinctness: clearly outlined, sharp, definite, explicit. So "how express and admirable" probably means "how admirably distinct, how wonderfully clear and sharp in the articulation of its form."

APPENDIX

Here are the instances of hendiadys I have found in *Hamlet*. In all these the two conjoined terms are not quite parallel, as I hope readers will see. Almost half of them are discussed in the text; for the rest I have proposed brief paraphrases (admittedly too prosaic sometimes) or additional notes and comments.

It is often difficult to be sure which category a phrase belongs to: clearly parallel (but unusual), almost hendiadys, or hendiadys. Editors differ with one another and sometimes with the *OED*; my readings are sometimes at variance with all others.

Line	*Speaker*
1. Without the *sensible and true* avouch (I.i.57)	Horatio
2. But in the *gross and scope* of my opinion (I.i.68) = full breadth	Horatio
3. Well ratified by *law and heraldry* (I.i.87) = heraldic law	Horatio
4. In the dead *vast and middle* of the night (I.ii.198) = desolation of midnight, or the dead and desolate midnight	Horatio
5. For *Hamlet, and the trifling of his favor* (I.iii.5) (see n. 11, above)	Laertes
6. Hold it a *fashion and a toy* in blood (I.iii.6)	Laertes
7. The *perfume and suppliance* of a minute (I.iii.9)	Laertes
8. In *thews and bulk* (I.iii.12) = physical size	Laertes
9. And now no *soil nor cautel* doth besmirch (I.iii.15)	Laertes
10. Unto the *voice and yielding* of that body (I.iii.23)	Laertes
11. Out of the *shot and danger* of desire (I.iii.35)	Laertes
12. And in the *morn and liquid dew* of youth (I.iii.41) = the fresh morning, or morning freshness	Laertes
13. *Angels and ministers of grace* defend us (I.iv.39) = angels who minister grace	Hamlet
14. Hath oped his *ponderous and marble* jaws (I.iv.50)	Hamlet
15. When I to *sulphurous and tormenting* flames (I.v.3)	Ghost
16. Are *burnt and purged* away (I.v.13)	Ghost
17. Thy *knotted and combined* locks to part (I.v.18) (Folios read "*knotty.*")	Ghost
18. The *thin and wholesome* blood (I.v.70) = thin because wholesome (or vice versa?)	Ghost
19. That *youth and observation* copied there (I.v.101)	Hamlet

20. Within the *book and volume* of my brain (i.v.103)   Hamlet
    Two competing senses of *volume* are felt here: (1)
    tome, (2) "Size, bulk, or dimensions (of a book)"
    (*OED*). At first glance, the two words seem nearly
    synonymous, but the phrase also seems to mean
    "within the book and largeness of my brain," i.e.,
    "within the spacious book of my brain."

21. These are but *wild and whirling* words, my lord   Horatio
    (i.v.133)
        = wildly whirling

22. But, sir, such *wanton, wild, and usual* slips (ii.i.22)   Polonius
23. As are companions *noted and most known* (ii.i.23)   Polonius
24. To *youth and liberty* (ii.i.24)   Polonius
25. According to *the phrase or the addition* (ii.i.47)   Polonius
        = form of address
    (Folios read "*the phrase and the addition.*")

26. Of *man and country* (ii.i.48)   Polonius
        = the man's country

27. So, by my former *lecture and advice* (ii.i.67)   Polonius
28. I am sorry that with better *heed and judgment* (ii.i.111)   Polonius
29. And sith so neighbored to his *youth and havior* (ii.ii.12)   King
    (Folios read "*youth and humour.*")

30. To show us so much *gentry and goodwill* (ii.ii.22)   Queen
31. For the *supply and profit* of our hope (ii.ii.24)   Queen
32. On such regards of *safety and allowance* (ii.ii.79)   Voltimand
        = "on such conditions with regard to the public
    safety [or your own safe-conduct] as are (in this
    document) submitted for your approval"
    (Kittredge)

33. In *form and moving* (ii.ii.316–17)   Hamlet
34. how *express and admirable* (ii.ii.317)   Hamlet
35. The appurtenance of welcome is *fashion and ceremony*   Hamlet
    (ii.ii.388–89)
        = "formal ceremony" (Harrison), conventional
    formal greeting

36. That lend a *tyrannous and damned* light (ii.ii.482)   Hamlet
        = damnably pitiless, or the kind of pitiless light
    that shines on the damned

37. But with the *whiff and wind* of his fell sword (ii.ii.495)   First Player
        = whiffing wind, whiff as of wind, the whiff *of*
    wind that his sword makes in striking through the
    air

38. they are the *abstracts*[1] and *brief chronicles* of the time   Hamlet
    (ii.ii.549–50)

39. The *expectancy and rose* of the fair state (III.i.160)   Ophelia
40. And I do doubt *the hatch and the disclose* (III.i.174)   King
41. and the very *age and body of the time* (III.ii.26)   Hamlet
42. his *form and pressure* (III.ii.26–27)   Hamlet
43. So far *from cheer and from your former state* (III.ii.174)   Player Queen
     = from your former cheerfulness
44. That *live and feed* upon your majesty (III.iii.10)   Guildenstern
     = live by feeding
45. But in our *circumstance and course of thought* (III.iii.83)   Hamlet
     = as far as we mere mortals can judge
46. That blurs the *grace and blush* of modesty (III.iv.41)   Hamlet
     = the innocent (blushing) grace of a modest
       young woman
47. Yea, this *solidity and compound mass* (III.iv.49)   Hamlet
     = solid compound mass (the earth)
48. A *combination and a form* indeed (III.iv.60)   Hamlet
     = a form made up by combining the qualities of
       various gods
49. Upon the *heat and flame* of thy distemper (III.iv.123)   Queen
     = hot flame
50. That I must be their *scourge and minister* (III.iv.175)   Hamlet
     = scourging minister
51. No, in despite of *sense and secrecy* (III.iv.192)   Hamlet
     = good sense, which calls for secrecy
52. We must, with all our *majesty and skill* (IV.i.31)   King
     = royal skill
53. If his chief *good and market* of his time (IV.iv.34)   Hamlet
     = "the best use he makes of his time" (Onions)
54. That *capability and godlike reason* (IV.iv.38)   Hamlet
     = godlike capacity of reason
55. That for a *fantasy and trick* of fame (IV.iv.61)   Hamlet
56. Which is not *tomb enough and continent* (IV.iv.64)   Hamlet
     = a large enough tract of land to provide a tomb
57. Divided from *herself and her fair judgment*[2] (IV.v.85)   King
58. Burn out the *sense and virtue* of mine eye (IV.v.155)   Laertes
     = sensory virtue, capacity to see
59. So *crimeful and so capital* in nature (IV.vii.7)   Laertes
     = so capitally criminal, so criminal as to deserve
       to be punished by death
60. That I, in forgery of *shapes and tricks* (IV.vii.90)   King
     = imaginary tricks
61. For *art and exercise* in your defense (IV.vii.98)   King
62. Or like a creature *native and indued* (IV.vii.180)   Queen

63. Of *bell and burial* (v.i.257)   First Priest
     = religious burial
64. Between the *pass and fell incensed points* (v.ii.61)   Hamlet
     = between the thrusting points
65. That might your *nature, honor, and exception* (v.ii.242)   Hamlet
66. I have a *voice and precedent* of peace (v.ii.260)   Laertes
     = an opinion that will serve as a precedent

Appendix Notes

1. The First Folio and First Quarto read "abstracts." Most editors prefer *abstract* and, in failing to gloss it, imply that it is an adjective, although Kittredge (after Clark and Wright) notes, "Always a noun in Shakespeare." The plural form fits better with *chronicles*. The singular form offers the modern reader a pleasing elusiveness—what is an abstract chronicle, exactly? But I take Shakespeare to have meant that the players (in concert, in what they perform together) are abstracts of the time, i.e., they summarize the time, extract its essence, in the form of brief chronicles.

2. The form of example 57 ("Poor Ophelia / Divided from herself and her fair judgment") is not analyzed in my list of deviations; it seems too anomalous. Still, Shakespeare frequently writes phrases that join a self with a part or a possession of the self or that join what seem to be two different kinds or parts of the self. *Antony and Cleopatra* has several such phrases: "I and my sword" (III.xiii.175), "Mine honesty and I" (III.xiii.41), "My resolution and my hands" (IV.xv.49). Cf. Lady Macbeth's "Your constancy / Hath left you unattended" (II.ii.68–69); or "Virtue and she / Is her own dower" (*All's Well That Ends Well* II.iii.150–51). Such phrases show a kind of schizophrenic division in the self that is not unusual in Shakespeare. But if Laertes, in the speech discussed earlier in this essay, sees Ophelia as dual, this phrase of Claudius' seems to divide her into three. What part of her can be "Divided from herself," except another self? And both are to be understood as distinct from her judgment. But this strange situation forced on us by the syntax dissolves if we see that the last five words amount to hendiadys for "her own fair judgment."

Hieronimo, Hamlet and Remembrance

JOHN KERRIGAN

As *The Choephoroe*, the second play in Aeschylus's *Oresteia* (458 B.C.), begins, Orestes stands beside his father's tomb, thinking about the past. He offers Agamemnon a lock of hair and laments that he was not in Argos to mourn at his father's funeral. He seems to be sunk in passive grief. But his contemplation of the past suddenly turns into a cry for vengeance: "O Zeus," he says, "grant that I may avenge the death/of my father, and of your grace fight on my side!"[1] Exactly the same movement of feeling is experienced by Electra when she, in turn, comes to the tomb with the chorus of libation bearers. She recalls the circumstances of Agamemnon's cruel murder, then shifts abruptly from retrospection to revenge: "I pray that one may appear to avenge you, father,/and that the killers may in justice pay with life for life."[2]

Electra's prayer is answered. She finds the hair, and it matches her own; her feet fit into the prints left by her brother; and then Orestes steps forward, persuaded by what she has said of Agamemnon what she will not betray him. In the magnificent sequence which follows, brother, sister and Chorus unite in reminding each other, the dead king and the audience of the bloody deed performed in the first part of the trilogy. Here, even more clearly than in the private prayers, retrospection prompts a desire for revenge: "Remember the bath in which you were murdered, father!" says Orestes; "Remember the new sort of covering they devised!" replies his sister.[3] A torrent of stichomythia begins, and it is only contained when the Chorus says:

> Indeed, there has been no fault in this your lengthy utterance;
> making atonement to the tomb for the lament that was denied it;
> and for the rest, since you are resolved to act, do
> now the deed and make trial of your fortune.[4]

At this point it becomes clear that the relationship between past and future has changed. There is more than a suggestion in the Chorus's words that the retrospection which prompts revenge can also postpone it. Though Ore-

*From *Essays in Criticism*, 31 (1981):105–126. Reprinted by permission of the Editors of *Essays in Criticism*.

stes and Electra are not quite rebuked for delay, they are offered (as the next lines show) barbed praise. The Chorus wants them to use, rather than become obsessed by, the past.

In these first few hundred lines of *The Choephoroe*, Aeschylus dramatises the psychological ambiguity of vengeful retrospection. He shows the past inciting revenge; but he also suggests that retrospection offers its own grim satisfaction, that the past can draw a revenger back from his task instead of pushing him towards it. The two greatest Elizabethan revenge plays, *The Spanish Tragedy* (1587–89) and *Hamlet* (1600), are as preoccupied with the past as is *The Choephoroe*.[5] In the former, Kyd presents a hero inexorably impelled by remembrance towards revenge; in the latter, Shakespeare shows us a hero continually recoiling from revenge into a "remembrance of things past."

Greek retrospection: Elizabethan remembrance. Aeschylus's revengers, like the Orestes and Electra of Sophocles and Euripides, have no private memory of their father; they know about his life and death only because it is public knowledge. They take revenge for equally public reasons: as children of the house of Atreus, they are bound to punish those who have weakened and disgraced their house by shedding the blood of the king. Elizabethan revenge tragedy replaces the vital exteriority of the links between living and dead in the Greek plays by something more private: almost invariably, its revengers cherish vivid, personal memories of their lost friends and kinsmen. These memories are usually, as in *The Spanish Tragedy*, shared with the audience. In Kyd's play, objects held as mementoes combine with a sweepingly explicit rhetoric to publish Hieronimo's private bond with Horatio. But in *Hamlet* the memories disclosed by the hero only suggest more, lying deeper, unspoken. Receding into the privacy of memory, Hamlet excludes the audience from knowledge of 'that within which passes show'; and, in the process, he wins for himself a depth and secrecy of character utterly unlike anything to be found in Greek tragedy.

When Hieronimo finds his son hanging in the arbour, run through with swords, he does not think only of revenge. Dipping Horatio's "handkercher" or "napkin" into his wounds, he declares:

> Seest thou this handkercher besmear'd with blood?
> It shall not from me till I take revenge:
> Seest thou those wounds that yet are bleeding fresh?
> I'll not entomb them till I have reveng'd:
> Then will I joy amidst my discontent,
> Till then my sorrow never shall be spent.
>
> (II.v.51–56)[6]

Hieronimo sets out to secure his revenge by equipping himself with objects charged with remembrance: the corpse, a surrogate ghost to whet his purpose should it ever blunt, and the gory napkin, a memento to be carried near his sorrowing heart. Why did Kyd choose to make a handkercher the portable emblem of Hieronimo's remembrance? In the previous act, after describing the death of Andrea, Horatio had announced to Bel-imperia: "This scarf I pluck'd from off his liveless arm,/And wear it in remembrance of my friend" (I.iv.42–43). Now this scarf, as Bel-imperia had explained, was originally given by her to Andrea as a love token—a token which she in turn grants Horatio. So Kyd introduced the handkercher to help build up a chain of remembrances: Andrea takes a scarf from Bel-imperia; Horatio takes it from him, presumably stained by the "purple" battlefield;[7] and then Hieronimo takes the bloody napkin from his son. Kyd's play has often been criticised for dividing between two centres of interest: Andrea's revenge and Horatio's. But the scarf and handkercher, complementary emblems of remembrance, feed one plot into the other, uniting the play around the relationship between remembrance and revenge.

In the first scene, Andrea tells us that after his body was buried by Horatio, his spirit crossed "the flowing stream of Acheron," pleased Cerberus "with hony'd speech" and presented itself to the three judges of the underworld. Aeacus deemed that the proper place for Andrea was among lovers on the "fields of love," but Rhadamanth objected that "martial fields" better suited the soldier. It was left to Minos, the third judge, "to end the difference," by sending the spirit further into Hades to consult a higher authority. The dialectical nature of Minos's judgement is echoed in the structure of the underworld: Andrea must take "the middle path" of three if he is to reach Pluto's court. Interestingly, Virgil, Kyd's authority for most of the speech, had insisted in Book VI of the *Aeneid* that there were two paths, not three. Kyd clearly had some special purpose in establishing the idea that in the underworld the road to justice leads through and beyond alternatives— and that it leads, in the end, to the Revenge which is Proserpine's "doom." I think that he offers the journey as a paradigm for Hieronimo's movement through the play: although the Knight Marshal inhabits sixteenth-century Spain, he explores the same moral landscape as the spirit of Andrea. In one sense indeed he must travel towards Revenge, for the goddess of the play, Proserpine, has granted Andrea a "doom" (meaning "destiny" as well as "judgement"), and Hieronimo is the instrument of her will. But in another sense he chooses to make the journey, and he does so because of the constant prompting of remembrance.

The Knight Marshal is considering a hellish pilgrimage as early as his III.ii soliloquy. "The ugly fiends do sally forth of hell," he says, "And frame my steps to unfrequented paths." Dreams of remembrance ("direful visions" in which he sees once more the "wounds" of his son) have made him susceptible to such temptation. But at this stage of the play, memory can provoke nothing but frustration, for Hieronimo does not yet know who murdered Horatio. He is caught between desire for action and an intolerable, tormenting patience, and the strain tells on his sanity. He thinks that everything must be caught up in his anguished dilemma. As Empson says in "Let it go," at the border of madness, "The contradictions cover such a range": "Eyes, life, world, heavens, hell, night, and day, / See, search, shew, send, some man, some mean, that may—" [*A letter falleth.*] Seeking a "mean" (both "opportunity" and "middle path"), Hieronimo hunts the kind of path along which Minos sent Andrea to Revenge. He finds it when Bel-imperia's letter falls from the balcony, telling him how to break the deadlock and advance into action: "Me hath my hapless brother hid from thee," it says, "Revenge thyself on Balthazar and him,/For these were they that murdered thy son." "*Red ink*" reads the practical note in the Quarto margin, and the letter tells Hieronimo that it has been written in blood for want of ink. So the paper flutters to the stage looking very like Hieronimo's bloody hand-kercher. It is another link in the chain, another memento inciting revenge.

By the end of the act, his desire for retribution still unsatisfied, ignored by God and kept from the King by the cunning of Lorenzo, Hieronimo has once more become desperate, and he turns back to "unfrequented paths." Standing between the traditional tools of suicide, "*a poniard in one hand, and a rope in the other*," he tries to decide which offers the better path to justice:

> Hieronimo, 'tis time for thee to trudge:
> Down by the dale that flows with purple gore,
> Standeth a fiery tower: there sits a judge
> Upon a seat of steel . . .
> Away, Hieronimo, to him be gone:
> He'll do thee justice for Horatio's death.
> (III.xii.6–9, 12–13)

Dagger and halter become parts of the landscape: "Turn down this path, thou shalt be with him straight,/Or this, and then thou need'st not take thy breath:/This way, or that way?" (14–16). Again, it is the remembrance of his loss that breaks the deadlock: "if I hang or kill myself, let's know/ Who will revenge Horatio's murder then?" The weapons are thrown down, both paths rejected, and what stands between, the man remembering, goes forward to revenge—along "the middle path" of three.

The same dialectic operates at the third and most formidable point of deadlocked uncertainty, represented by the soliloquy "*Vindicta mihi!*" (III.xiii.1–44). The first five lines of this, in which Hieronimo considers the possibility of leaving God to revenge his son, are made the more moving by his choice of *Romans* xii–xiii as text. The biblical passage forbids private revenge, but it allows the "minister of God to take vengeance on him that doeth evil."[8] As a "civil magistrate," Hieronimo would be regarded by the Elizabethan audience as just such a "minister." Cut off from higher authority by the cunning of Lorenzo, and unable to try his son's killers himself (because he could not be an impartial "magistrate" in such a trial, only a father), Hieronimo has been stripped of precisely that power of "vengeance" which, for the original audience, was the most essential adjunct of his public office. It's hardly surprising then that the Knight Marshal goes on from *Romans* to consider contrary advice, taken from Seneca's *Agamemnon*: "*Per scelus semper tutum est sceleribus iter.*"[9] Although it's not clear whether Hieronimo applies this paraphrase of Clytemnestra's decision to kill her husband to himself (who, like her, has a child to revenge) or to Lorenzo (who has a better claim to "*scelus*"), either way the line dictates action: vengeance or a preemptive strike. If he dithers, he reflects, he will simply lose his life: "For he that thinks with patience to contend/To quiet life, his life shall easily end." But here the argument starts to recoil, for the ambiguity of "easily" allows "patience" and "quiet life" to register as attractive positives even while they are being rejected as cowardly and dangerous. The patient man lives and dies in ease.[10] Hieronimo's will is puzzled, and he consoles himself with classical commonplaces. If destiny allows one to be happy, one will be; and if not, then one has the comfort of a tomb. Moreover (thinking now of a famous line from *Pharsalia*), if destiny denies even that, "Heaven covereth him that hath no burial." Suddenly his memory sparks into life: Horatio lies unburied because of his father's delay. "And to conclude," he says (though logically it's no conclusion), "I will revenge his death!" The complicated tangle of impulse and argument is broken through; and nothing more is heard of patience.

With Horatio's memory uppermost in his mind, the magistrate is then offered " 'The humble supplication/Of Don Bazulto for his murder'd son.' " At first he denies that anyone could claim such loss but himself ("No sir, it was my murder'd son"); but he then recognises in Bazulto his "portrait," his uncanny double, and he offers to wipe the old man's tearful cheeks. As he draws out the handkercher, however, he is once more overwhelmed by remembrance, and, through that, by desire for revenge:

> O no, not this: Horatio, this was thine,
> And when I dy'd it in thy dearest blood,
> This was a token 'twixt thy soul and me
> That of thy death revenged I should be.
>   (III.xiii.86–89)

He begins to rave about the journey he must make, down to "the dismal gates of Pluto's court," within the walls of which, "Proserpine may grant/ Revenge on them that murdered my son." Why does he end this account (so reminiscent of Andrea's in the first scene) by tearing up the legal papers of Bazulto and his fellow petitioners? Because of his obsession with remembrance and revenge. Claiming that he has not damaged the documents, the revenger says: "Shew me one drop of blood fall from the same." The papers are no concern of his: they are not the corpses of "Don Lorenzo and the rest"; he cannot therefore have touched them. Moreover, the sheets of paper written with ink, unlike Bel-imperia's letter inscribed with blood, offer no consolation to the memory: yielding no blood, they cannot resemble the handkercher; Hieronimo cannot therefore have consulted them. Not until the performance of "Soliman and Perseda" in the following and final act are the two impulses so crazily at work here fully resolved.

Towards the end of *The Choephoroe*, Orestes displays before the Chorus both the bodies of Aegisthus and Clytemnestra and the robe or net in which Agamemnon was murdered. He summons up the past to justify his revenge: "Did she do the deed or not?," he asks, "This robe/is my witness, as to how Aegisthus' sword dyed it./ And the blood that gushed forth was time's partner/in spoiling the many dyes applied to the embroidery."[11] The most striking Elizabethan parallel to this is Antony's speech to the mob in *Julius Caesar* (1599), where Caesar's mangled and bloodstained robe is used to justify the revenge which the orator is provoking in the minds of the people:

> If you have tears, prepare to shed them now.
> You all do know this mantle. I remember
> The first time ever Caesar put it on;
> 'Twas on a summer's evening, in his tent,
> That day he overcame the Nervii.
> Look, in this place ran Cassius' dagger through;
> See what a rent the envious Casca made;
> Through this the well-beloved Brutus stabb'd,
> And as he pluck'd his cursed steel away,
> Mark how the blood of Caesar followed it.
>
> (III.ii. 169–78)

Yet the rich interplay between public and private here, between "You all do know this mantle" and "I remember" (that shift which, for the Elizabethan audience, authenticates Antony, makes him a revenger rather than a mere murderer), is utterly different from the forceful publicity of the Aeschylean tableau. And when Hieronimo stands among the corpses of his enemies, producing the bloody "napkin" to justify his action to the stage audience, the object of remembrance is even more private in its associations than the "mantle." How can the Spanish court make sense of it? How can they share the Knight Marshal's remembrance?

Oddly enough, in chapter iii of *Le Temps Retrouvé*, Marcel's memory is prompted by the texture of a "napkin": "*la serviette que j'avais prise pour m'essuyer la bouche avait précisément le genre de raideur et d'empesé de celle avec laquelle j'avais eu tant de peine à me sécher devant la fenêtre, le premier jour de mon arrivée á Balbec, et, maintenant, devant cette bibliothèque de l'hôtel de Guermantes, elle déployait, réparti dans ses pans et dans ses cassures, le plumage d'un océan vert et bleu comme la queue d'un paon.*"[12] Again, an enormous shift in sensibility:

for Hieronimo the past is sustained by the continuity of an object; it survives within Marcel as sensation, the feel of a feel. But the connection with Kyd (and even, though distantly, with Aeschylus) is there in the thought which the reverie evokes in Marcel: "*je remarquais qu'il y aurait là, dans l'oeuvre d'art que je me sentais prêt déjà . . . de grandes difficultés.*" Through the work of art which he, by undertaking, becomes, Proust's narrator can make his audience live through the experiences which are so liable, being past, to invade the present. Art can publish the past, even when it is private. Orestes creates a self-justificatory tableau out of the robe-net and the bodies, Antony performs a little play of passion over Caesar's corpse and mantle, and art similarly communicates the significance of the handkercher which Hieronimo shows the court after "Soliman and Perseda."

On reading Pedringano's letter, Hieronimo had said: "Holp he to murder mine Horatio?/And actors in th'accursed tragedy/Wast thou, Lorenzo, Balthazar and thou?" (III.vii.40–42). That drama returns when the "tragedy" supposedly written by Hieronimo in his student days is performed before the court, the equivalent of Orestes' Chorus and Antony's mob. Once more a gentle knight is murdered so that his faithful mistress can be won by a royal lover. Balthazar plays his own part, that of Soliman, and Belimperia hers, the "Italian dame,/Whose beauty ravish'd all that her beheld" (IV.i.111–12). Horatio, however, cannot play the part of the knight Erasto, so Lorenzo does that, leaving Hieronimo to "play the murderer," the bashaw, the character who in the playlet is the equivalent of Lorenzo in "th' accursed tragedy." When Soliman agrees to Erasto's death, reluctantly, as Balthazar did to Horatio's, Hieronimo stabs Lorenzo, the arbour scene returns, the court is invited by the redemption of the past effected through art to comprehend those private memories which cluster around the handkercher that Hieronimo is about to produce, and, in the death of Lorenzo in Horatio's role, revenge is finally clinched in remembrance.

When the ghost exhorts Hamlet to "Revenge his foul and most unnatural murther," the Prince's response is only superficially "apt": "Haste me to know't, that I with wings as swift/As meditation, or the thoughts of love,/May sweep to my revenge" (I.v.25, 29–31). "May" is not "will," and the overtones of "meditation" and "thoughts of love" are distinctly at odds with their apparent sense. But when the ghost leaves his son with the injunction "Adieu, adieu, adieu: remember me!," Hamlet takes his task to heart with all the passion he can muster:

> O all you host of heaven! O earth! What else?
> And shall I couple hell? O fie, hold, hold, my heart.
> And you, my sinews, grow not instant old,
> But bear me stiffly up. Remember thee!
> Ay, thou poor ghost, whiles memory holds a seat

> In this distracted globe. Remember thee!
> Yea, from the table of my memory
> I'll wipe away all trivial fond records,
> All saws of books, all forms, all pressures past
> That youth and observation copied there,
> And thy commandment all alone shall live
> Within the book and volume of my brain,
> Unmix'd with baser matter . . .
>   . . . Now to my word:
> It is "Adieu, adieu: remember me!"
> I have sworn't.
>
>   (92–112)

The contrast with Hieronimo is striking: Hamlet never promises to revenge, only to remember.[13]

The whole play is steeped in remembrance. Hardly has it begun than it pauses for Horatio to celebrate Old Hamlet as a representative of that lost and epic age in which political issues were decided by fierce, single combat, an age in sorry contrast to that in which kings take power by poison and in which combat is no more than a courtly exercise played with bated foils. Again, after the nunnery scene, Ophelia recalls a Hamlet we have never really known:

> O, what a noble mind is here o'erthrown!
> The courtier's, soldier's, scholar's, eye, tongue, sword,
> Th'expectancy and rose of the fair state,
> The glass of fashion and the mould of form,
> Th'observed of all observers, quite, quite, down!
>
>   (III.i.150–54)

In her touchingly Polonian way, Ophelia is celebrating the Prince as Horatio had eulogised Old Hamlet. She recalls her own father, in turn, in the ballads sung during her madness: "He is dead and gone, lady,/He is dead and gone,/At his head a grass-green turf,/At his heels a stone" and "His beard was as white as snow,/All flaxen was his poll,/He is gone, he is gone,/And we cast away moan" (IV.v.29–32, 195–98). It is this persistent sense of engagement with the past which creates the play's distinctive music: plangent and pathetic in the case of Ophelia's ballads, wistful but touched with melancholy humour in Hamlet's reverie over Yorick, or tormented with loss, as in his first soliloquy. And it determines the movement of the tragedy: slow, eddying, as though reluctant to leave the past behind, a movement which can admit an elegiac set speech, like Gertrude's description of Ophelia's death, not reluctantly, as a beautiful irrelevance, but as a necessary question of the play.

In the context of these memories, generously celebrating something lost, others seem very selfish. Claudius admits that "the memory" of his brother is but "green," but he nevertheless insists on "remembrance of ourselves" (I.ii.1–2, 7). The Prince remembers one king, his uncle another. Rosencrantz and Guildenstern mark their betrayal of Hamlet by linking themselves with Claudius's selfish memory: their hire and salary, they are told, will be "such thanks/As fits a king's remembrance" (II.ii.25–26). And Fortinbras, winding things up in his peremptory way, cynically invokes a sense of the past to justify his actions: "I have some rights of memory in this kingdom,/Which now to claim my vantage doth invite me" (V.ii.389–90).[14]

Such true and false remembrances all reflect on the play's most important link with bygone things: Hamlet's memory of his father. Even before he sees the ghost, the Prince remembers. When he first meets Horatio, for example, he almost sees the apparition which his friend has come to announce:

HAMLET: My father—methinks I see my father.

HORATIO: Where, my lord?

HAMLET: In my mind's eye, Horatio.

HORATIO: I saw him once; 'a was a goodly king.

HAMLET: 'A was a man, take him for all in all,
                    I shall not look upon his like again.
                                              (I.ii.184–88)

Hamlet fends off Horatio's recollection of the public man—the shared, "goodly king." His words advertise a privacy which remains his throughout the play. We can show that remembrance haunts him, even to the point of madness. We can call this the heart of his mystery. But that heart can never, as he assures Guildenstern, be plucked out; for it is too secret. Remembering, Hamlet eludes us.

The kind of experience which the Prince has in his first exchange with Horatio is not to be endured without pain. He may be rapt into the past and find comfort there, but that only makes the present seem more desolate, "an unweeded garden/That grows to seed" (I.ii.135–36). In the words of the psychologist John Bowlby: "because of the persistent and insatiable nature of the yearning for the lost figure, pain is inevitable."[15] Hamlet's compulsion to remember must of necessity cause him anguish:

> So excellent a king, that was to this
> Hyperion to a satyr; so loving to my mother
> That he might not beteem the winds of heaven
> Visit her face too roughly. Heaven and earth,
> Must I remember?
>   (I.ii.139–43)

Claudius calls this state of mind "unmanly," accusing the Prince of "obstinate condolement" (ib.93–94). But he is not two months bereaved of a good and noble father. In any case, we know that Hamlet, healthily, is trying to shake off at least part of the burden of his father's memory.

In *Twelfth Night* (usually dated to the same year as *Hamlet*) Olivia clearly does indulge in "obstinate condolement," imposing seven years of isolation on herself to keep her dead brother "fresh/And lasting in her sad remembrance" (I.i.30–31). But we learn very early on that Hamlet is actively seeking the escape which Comedy forces on Olivia in the form of Orsino's handsome page: the "tenders" of "affection" made to Ophelia "of late" (I.iii.99–100)—which can only mean since his return from Wittenberg for the funeral of his father— prove that the Prince is trying hard to replace his dead love-object with a living one. Hamlet's inky cloak is an ambiguous thing: a mark of respect for his lost father, it also indicates his desire eventually to detach himself from him. As Freud put it: "Mourning has a precise psychical task to perform: its function is to detach the survivor's memories and hopes from the dead."[16]

A combination of things prevents Hamlet from effecting this severance. Ophelia's apparent rejection of him is one: by returning his letters and refusing him access she throws his love back onto the father who has never emotionally betrayed him. Another is Claudius's refusal to let him return to school in Wittenberg: this leaves Hamlet surrounded by the people and objects which most remorselessly remind him of the dead king. But most important, of course, is the ghost's injunction: "Remember me!" When the apparition commands Hamlet to remember, he condemns him to an endless, fruitless "yearning for the lost figure." In the nunnery and closet scenes, we see the effect of this sentence on the Prince's sanity.

"My lord," says Ophelia, "I have remembrances of yours/That I have longed long to redeliver./I pray you now receive them" (III.i.92–94). This confirms for Hamlet a suspicion bred of his mother's "o'er-hasty marriage" (II.ii.57), that woman's love is a brief, unworthy thing. It seems that Ophelia, not content with simply ignoring the man who loves her, wants to divest herself of every shred of attachment, even to the extent of forgetting those days when their affair was happier. She wants to shed her remembrances. In this she is no better than Gertrude, glad to forget her first husband in another's bed. This is bad enough, but the girl's gesture, "There, my lord" (III.i.101), recalls an earlier scene: Old Hamlet, like Ophelia, had pressed on the Prince remembrances that were, in any case, too much his already. Through the loss of Ophelia, Hamlet feels that of his father—which is why the hysteria which follows is so much in excess of the apparent object. The sexuality which the Prince denounces is that of his mother as well as Ophelia; Claudius, as well as he, is an "arrant knave" (the echo of the speech to the guard makes the point; 128, cf I.v.124); and there is indeed a sad resonance in the question, "Where's your father?" "Hysterics," wrote Freud, "suffer mainly from reminiscences."[17]

The queen triggers off Hamlet's raving in her bedchamber by calling
Claudius "your father" (III.iv.9). Forced by this to compare one king with
another, Hamlet insists that his mother do the same. As he shows her the
counterfeit presentments, the tormented, idealising remembrance which had
filled his first soliloquy once more overwhelms him:

> See what a grace was seated on this brow:
> Hyperion's curls, the front of Jove himself,
> An eye like Mars, to threaten and command,
> A station like the herald Mercury
> New lighted on a heaven-kissing hill,
> A combination and a form indeed,
> Where every god did seem to set his seal
> To give the world assurance of a man.
>
> (55–62)

" 'A was a man, take him for all in all": we are back with that almost
hallucinatory moment when Old Hamlet drifted into the "mind's eye."
And this time the ghost, fancied even more vividly, appears, suspended
mysteriously between spiritual and imaginative existence. "In melancholy
men," writes Burton of the phantasy, "this faculty is most powerful and
strong, and often hurts, producing many monstrous and prodigious things,
especially if it be stirred up by some terrible object, presented to it from
. . . memory."[18] Hamlet sees a prodigy, but Gertrude, who has forgotten,
does not.

It may seem rash to define Hamlet's madness in terms of remembrance
when we have Polonius's warning that "to define true madness,/What is't but
to be nothing else but mad?" (II.ii.93–94). Yet this should encourage us rather
than otherwise, for by its queer logic there is one character in the play admirably
qualified to offer a definition. Not even R. D. Laing could dispute that Ophelia
goes mad; and when, in a sequence which is in obvious parallel to the nunnery
scene, she gives her brother, like Hamlet before him, remembrances, she says:
"There's rosemary, that's for remembrance; pray you, love, remember. And
there is pansies, that's for thoughts." "A document in madness," translates
Laertes, "thoughts and remembrance fitted" (IV.v.175–79).

What about revenge? In the body of the play, as in the first exchange
with the ghost, it is far less important to Hamlet than remembrance. This
imbalance is dramatised with particular clarity in the use which he makes
of "The Murder of Gonzago." "Soliman and Perseda" was staged to effect
Hieronimo's revenge, but there is never any question of Claudius being
killed in or at "The Mousetrap." Perhaps Hamlet does stage it to test the
ghost. Presumably he is not simply rationalising when he says that it will
"catch the conscience of the King" (II.ii.605). But the crucial motive is
revealed in his speech to Ophelia just before the performance: "O heavens,

die two months ago, and not forgotten yet? Then there's hope a great man's memory may outlive his life half a year, but by'r lady, 'a must build churches then, or else shall 'a suffer not thinking on, with the hobby-horse, whose epitaph is, 'For O, for O, the hobby-horse is forgot' " (III.ii.130–35). Hamlet recovers the orchard as Hieromimo the arbour, but the Prince does so because he wants to see his father alive again and to help the "great man's memory" survive. Revenge is stifled by remembrance. As the Player King says: "Purpose is but the slave to memory." Only the transformation of the stage-murderer from brother to nephew—Claudius to Hamlet—reveals the Prince's guilty sense that if he could but abandon himself, becomes as crude and cruel as "Lucianus, nephew to the king," he could satisfy the ghost.

But Hamlet cannot change his nature and so does not revenge his father. The weapons finally used to kill Claudius (the venomous rapier and poisoned drink) mark Hamlet's attack as spontaneous retaliation not long-delayed retribution: the King dies for the murder of Gertrude and the Prince, not for the murder in the orchard. Old Hamlet is not even mentioned by his son in the last, violent minutes of the play—an omission which seems the more striking when Laertes, who is being hurried off by the fell sergeant death with yet more despatch than the Prince, finds time to refer to Polonius. Hamlet knows that revenge would please the stern, militaristic father whom he loves, and he wants to please him; but he cannot overcome his radical sense of the pointlessness of revenge. Claudius has killed Old Hamlet and whored the Queen. Neither evil can be undone. Revenge cannot bring back what has been lost. Only memory, with all its limitations, can do that.

Nowhere is this lesson brought home more forcefully than in the grave-yard scene (V.1). As they delve in the clay, the gravediggers turn up the past as it really is: earth indistinguishable from earth, skulls, loggat bones. This might be a politician's pate, or a courtier's, says the Prince. And might not this be the skull of a lawyer? "It might, my lord," but, equally, it might not: none of Hamlet's speculations can give life to this refuse. The skulls remain, despite his earnest efforts, terrifying, vacant emblems of death, mouthing the slogan of the *memento mori* tradition: "*Fui non sum, es non eris.*"[19] Only one of them can mean more: when the Prince learns that he holds the skull of Yorick, he is able to give it form and feature: "Alas, poor Yorick! I knew him, Horatio, a fellow of infinite jest, of most excellent fancy. He hath bore me on his back a thousand times." How frail is Yorick's link with life. Only his small fame, lingering in the minds of gravedigger and Prince, dem-onstrates what a piece of work he was. The rest of him, like every other bone in the cemetery, signifies death: "Now get you to my lady's chamber, and tell her, let her paint an inch thick, to this favour she must come."

Alexander came to it, and so did "imperious Caesar." Even now one might be stopping a bung-hole and the other patching a wall. Why does Hamlet consider the fate of these great men so curiously? Certainly because "*Fui non sum*" has struck home: he recognises the inevitability of his own death, as his great speech on the fall of the sparrow shows (V.ii.219–24). But he is also interested in them because they are famous men, men remembered. It does not matter that their mortal remains have come to base ends: they linger in men's minds nonetheless. If the graveyard focuses Hamlet's imagination on his approaching end, it also reminds him of the possibility of survival through memory. As he has cherished his father, so he hopes to be cherished. That is why Horatio is so important to him at the end of the play:

> You that look pale, and tremble at this chance,
> That are but mutes or audience to this act,
> Had I but time—as this fell sergeant, Death,
> Is strict in his arrest—O, I could tell you—
> But let it be. Horatio, I am dead,
> Thou livest. Report me and my cause aright
> To the unsatisfied.
>
> (V.ii.334–40)

But *can* Horatio report either Hamlet or his cause aright? His brief account to Fortinbras, with its "carnal, bloody and unnatural acts . . . accidental judgements, casual slaughters," suggests that he cannot, for everything that seems most essential to Hamlet's tragedy is left out. Honest, compassionate and intelligent though he is, Horatio is simply not equipped by circumstance to inform the yet unknowing world about the nunnery scene, Claudius's words to heaven, "To be or not to be" or, indeed, any of those decisive soliloquies. Only the play can report such things, which is why the dramatic imagery of Hamlet's speech is so interesting.

When John Pickeryng turned to Lydgate's *Troy Book* to find material for the first Elizabethan revenge tragedy, *Horestes* (1567), he found a distinctly gloomy view of fame and memory: "O vnsur trust of al worldly glorie,/ With sodeyn chaunge put oute of memorie!," laments Lydgate at the death of Agamemnon, "O ydel fame, blowe up to the skye,/Ouer-whelmyd with twyncling of an eye!"[20] Pickeryng's attitude could not be more different. For him it is only Agamemnon's fame which makes him worth revenging. Moreover, it is fame which in his version of the story offers the strongest suasion both for and against the murder of Clytemnestra: think what evil Oedipus did in killing his parent, urges Nature, "And eke remember now, what fame of him abrode doth go"; to which Idumeus counters, having encouraged his ward to persist in revenge: "remembar well the same; /In doing thus you shall pourchas to the immortaull fame,/The which I hope you wyll assaye for to atchife in dede."[21] Obviously, Lydgate wrote in the late middle ages and Pickeryng in the renaissance when men became (like the King in *Love's Labour's Lost*) fascinated by the idea that the great could live a life beyond life in their fame. But Pickeryng was also dramatising a story which was merely told in his source. He therefore found himself considering the springs of Horestes' action, his link with the dead man, and, in consequence, Agamemnon's survival in the public memory.

In the event, fame, the subject of a few lines in the *Troy Book*, seemed so important to Pickeryng that he made it into a distinct dramatic character. After the murder of Clytemnestra, Fame comes on stage clutching the gold and iron trumps through which she announces good and bad deeds to eternity:

> Aboue eache thinge kepe well thy fame, what euer y^t thou lose;
> For fame once gone, they memory with fame a way it gose;
> And it once lost thou shalt, in south, accomptyd lyke to be
> A drope of rayne that faulyth in the bosom of the see.
>
> (890–93)

Or, to put it in Hamlet's terms: unless a man is remembered, he is no more after his death than a "pate full of fine dirt" (V.i.107–08). But the most striking link between *Horestes* and *Hamlet* lies in Fame's function as the presenter of Pickeryng's play. She tells us what is happening both in and just outside the action. So the play which Fame presents, dramatises the fame which she personifies. This is one reason why *Horestes*, though it does not link its revenger with the lost object through the private channel of remembrance, could never be taken as a Greek tragedy: Pickeryng is careful to remind us, through the medium of Fame, that what we are seeing is not action but the performance of an action. Aeschylus's actors are Aristotle's, πράττοντες, which John Jones has translated well as "the doers of what is done";[22] Pickeryng's actors imitate rather than do. We are made aware that Horestes was, and that he is being played; indeed, there is a sense in which the fact that he is being played in itself proves him worth playing. In short, any performance of Pickeryng's drama constitutes an act of remembrance.

It should now be clear why the tragedians of the city are so prominent in *Hamlet*. Clearly, the Prince is interested in them because of his obsession with "seeming" and "being," and because they can act while divorcing themselves from their actions—which is what Hamlet would have to do if he were to revenge his father. But they fascinate him above all because they make remembrance their profession. The Prince must struggle to keep his promise to the ghost, to preserve his memory for only a few months, but the first player can reach back effortlessly to the crash of "senseless Ilium" and the murder of Priam (II.ii.434–522). So vividly does he make the dead King of Troy live, that Hamlet has the players do the same for the other dead king—his father—in "The Murder of Gonzago." The most extended and deliberate act of remembrance within *Hamlet*, "The Mousetrap" moves on from Troy to dramatise the more immediate past of Vienna and, through that, Denmark, before melting into the present of the larger play of which it is a part, the murder in the orchard being effected and unpunished, the murderer being happily in possession of both crown and queen.

Throughout *Hamlet*, the Prince's obsession with actors and acting, his allusions to revenge tragedy and his dramatic imagery work to divorce the character which he is from the actor who represents him. The first striking effect of this divorce is, obviously, that it protects Hamlet's privacy. When Burbage, Olivier or Jonathan Pryce calls on those who are "audience to this act" we are drawn within the scope of the hero's attention as surely as the pale and trembling Danes, but we are also made aware that, just as the squeaking boy is not Cleopatra, so the actor is not the Hamlet which in another sense he is. The character seems to protest through the imagery that he is too bafflingly himself to be inhabited by another. Nothing could more clearly mark the difference between the ancient Greek and Elizabethan conceptions of dramatic identity than the absence of such imagery from Greek tragedy.[23]

The second important effect which stems from a perceived discrepancy between a character and the actor representing him has already been touched on in the analysis of *Horestes*—again with a defining contrast against ancient Greek practice. When we are addressed as "audience to this act" we are made aware that we are witnessing in the theatre both the death of a "great man" and a performance which celebrates that man's memory. The duplicity is similar to that created by Cassius, when, having prepared "imperious Caesar" to patch a wall, he asks: "How many ages hence/Shall this our lofty scene be acted over/In states unborn and accents yet unknown!" (III.i.111–13). And the dramatic imagery which Hieronimo exploits when he, like Hamlet, faces death, might also be compared: "gentles, thus I end my play:/Urge no more words, I have no more to say. *He runs to hang himself*" (IV.iv.151–52). But if the mechanism at work in *Horestes*, *Julius Caesar* and *The Spanish Tragedy* is similar to that used in *Hamlet*, its felt effect is infinitely more poignant in the later play. In *Horestes*, the case for remembrance is put by an abstraction, Fame; in *Julius Caesar*, it is sought for the sake of a dead, rather than by a dying, man; and Hieronimo's dramatic imagery—as we would expect from a protagonist who has constantly subordinated remembrance to the revenge which it incites—has a memorial implication which is scarcely more than latent. But in *Hamlet* the appeal for remembrance has the full weight of the play behind it. It comes from a dying hero who, having devoted himself to the generosity of memory, now longs to be remembered. The appeal is enacted. It is satisfied in its performance.

Notes

1. Quoting from Hugh Lloyd-Jones's translation of *The Oresteia* (2nd ed., 1979), ll. 18–19.
2. ll. 143–44.
3. ll. 491–92. Lloyd-Jones rightly accepts the emendation ἐκαίνισαν.
4. ll. 510–13.
5. Throughout this essay I assume that the Elizabethan popular drama was not

directly influenced by Greek tragedy. For an interesting attack on this (the consensus) view, see John Harvey's "A Note on Shakespeare and Sophocles" (*E in C* XXVII, 1977, pp. 254–70.

6. Kyd quotations are taken from Philip Edwards's edition of *The Spanish Tragedy* (1959).

7. The field is described as "purple" with gore at I.ii.62. Whether the scarf is bloodstained or not depends, of course, on the director.

8. Quoting from the Geneva Version of *Romans* xiii.4. "Civil magistrate" is the Geneva marginal gloss on "the minister of God."

9. "The safe way for crime is always through crimes." The original reads: "*per scelera semper sceleribus tutum est iter.*"

10. This sense registers the more strongly because it represents the kind of Senecanism which the King of Portingale indulges in elsewhere in the play—at I.iii.5–42 and III.xiv.31–34, for example.

11. 1010–13.

12. *À la recherche du temps perdu*, Vol. III, p. 869 (Pléiade ed., 1954). Andreas Mayor's translation (1970) reads: "the napkin which I had used to wipe my mouth had precisely the same degree of stiffness and starchedness as the towel with which I had found it so awkward to dry my face as I stood in front of the window on the first day of my arrival at Balbec, and this napkin now, in the library of the Prince de Geurmantes's house, unfolded for me—concealed within its smooth surfaces and its folds—the plumage of an ocean green and blue like the tail of a peacock." The quotation which follows, in which Marcel contemplates the great difficulties which he must overcome in executing the work of art which he feels within him, is from pp. 870–71 of the Gallimard text.

13. The importance of remembrance is emphasised here by a parallel with an earlier scene: another father, Polonius, bids adieu to another son, Laertes, saying, "my blessing with thee!/And these few precepts in thy memory/Look thou character" (I.iii.57–59). Laertes, in turn, bidding adieu to his sister, asks her to "remember" (84).

14. The word "memory" occurs more than twice as often in *Hamlet* than in any other play by Shakespeare, "remember" is more plentiful than in the other plays, and in "remembrance(s)" only *All's Well* outnumbers the tragedy.

15. *Loss: Sadness and Depression*, Vol. III of *Attachment and Loss* (1980), p. 26.

16. *The Complete Psychological Works of Sigmund Freud*, Vol. XIII (1953), p. 65. The German *die trauer*, like "mourning," covers both the affect and the garb of bereavement.

17. Op. cit., Vol. II, p. 7.

18. *The Anatomy of Melancholy*, ed. Holbrook Jackson (1972), Pt. 1, Sec. 1, Mem. 2, Subs. 7 (p. 159).

19. "I am not as I was, you will not be as you are." For a general account of this tradition see A. Tenenti's *Il senso della morte e l'amore della vita nel Rinascimento* (Turin, 1957).

20. Ed. H. Bergson (for E.E.T.S.), Bk. V, II. 1011–12 and 1015–16.

21. Ed. A. Brandl, in *Quellen des Weltlichen Drama* (Strassburg, 1898); ll. 441 and 492–94.

22. *On Aristotle and Greek Tragedy* (1962), p. 59.

23. Oliver Taplin confirms this omission on pp. 132–33 of *The Stagecraft of Aeschylus* (1977). The closest approach made to dramatic self-consciousness in the ancient tragedies can be found in Euripides's *Electra*, where the heroine refuses to accept the lock of hair and the footprints which had satisfied her Aeschylean precursor (11. 487–595). She is defined against the earlier Electra as more centred, less subject to the directing flow of the μῦθος; she is less of, and more in, her play. But because the sense of dramatic artifice here lies outside the circumference of the heroine's intelligence, there is no suggestion of a divorce between character and actor. Euripides's roles, as surely as those of Sophocles and Aeschylus, live in the externality of the mask.

"Maimed Rites":
Violated Ceremony in *Hamlet*

DAVID BEVINGTON

And so, without more circumstance at all,
I hold it fit that we shake hands and part.
                              —1.5.128–129

"Th' appurtenance of welcome is fashion and ceremony," says Hamlet to Rosencrantz and Guildenstern in a rare moment of seeming relaxation when he is looking forward to the arrival of the players at Elsinore. "Let me comply with you in this garb, lest my extent to the players, which, I tell you, must show fairly outwards, should more appear like entertainment than yours. You are welcome" (2.2.371–375). As he offers the two young men his hand, he bids them accept this gesture as his well-meant observation of the proper civilities of the court. He appears to acknowledge the validity of such ceremony, yet he characteristically refers to it as "complying," a word he later uses pejoratively of Osric,[1] and as "garb," that is, fashion or outward appearance. His apparent concern is that his old acquaintances—he calls them "excellent good friends" at first, but quickly finds reason to qualify that epithet—should not feel snubbed by the outward show of a greeting to their social inferiors, the players. He has received the two young men, as they later report to Claudius, "Most like a gentleman," but with "much forcing of his disposition" (3.1.11–12). Even in this moment of playful acceptance of social convention, Hamlet's way of describing it is wry, quizzical, bordering on the satiric. He goes on in the very next part of this scene to answer the entering Polonius and his prolix ceremoniousness with studied though artful rudeness, and then to aggravate this insult by a genuinely warm greeting to the players.

Hamlet's antipathy to ceremony is more striking elsewhere in the play. It helps focus our attention on a pattern of "maimed rites" that extends from the very first scene, with its inversions of precedence on the guard platform, to the final scene, in which a banqueting table becomes a feast of

*From *Action Is Eloquence* (1984). Copyright © 1984 by the President and Fellows of Harvard College. Reprinted by permission of Harvard University Press, and David Bevington.

death and a gentlemanly duel becomes a scuffle over a poisoned sword. The "o'erhasty marriage" of Gertrude and Claudius before the play begins is a maimed rite; so is the awkward public scene at court in which the marriage is announced in the presence of Gertrude's inconsolable son, the dramatic entertainment presented by the players to Claudius but broken off by his sudden rising, Claudius' abortive attempt at prayer, the "obscure funeral" of old Polonius, the substituting of a forged death warrant sent by Claudius to the King of England, and the burial of Ophelia without the singing of "the service of the dead." As Francis Fergusson puts it, the maimed rites of Ophelia are full of cross-references: to Polonius' funeral, to Gertrude's corrupt marriage, to the marriage of Ophelia and Hamlet that never takes place, and to Ophelia's mad mixture of funeral and marriage.[2] Even the last ceremonial entrance of Fortinbras with his army, and the military funeral in which four captains "Bear Hamlet, like a soldier, to the stage," represent a disruption of the nominal ceremony of reconciliation with which the play's climactic scene begins. These and other inversions of ceremony, some of them visible on stage and some of them presented only to our imagination, function as signs of disorder in the play. Stage images of public ceremony alternate with those of isolation, darkness, and terror, allowing the more private glimpses of intense emotion to comment unfavorably on the hollow reassurances of public life in Denmark. Image patterns of clothes, of poison, and of the theater, both verbal and actualized on stage, contribute to the graphic picture of dislocation and misplacing of ceremonial observance.

The Elizabethan public theater itself, as Fergusson points out, fulfills a similar purpose.[3] Its potent symbolism of the cosmos provides an admirable backdrop for Hamlet's speech on the nature of man; its inclusive depiction of the heavens above and hell beneath gives a spatial immediacy to Hamlet's notion that "this goodly frame, the earth" is also "a foul and pestilent congregation of vapors." In the Elizabethan theater the spectators see a painted heavens corresponding to Hamlet's stirring invocation of "this most excellent canopy, the air . . . this brave o'erhanging firmament, this majestical roof fretted with golden fire" (2.2.299–304), but the spectators have also witnessed the "wondrous strange" workings of the Ghost in the "cellerage" beneath the stage (1.5.152–165). The "idea of the theater" embodied in this play begins with a majestic conception of order and "the celebration of the mystery of human life"; the spectators can see, in the very architecture of the Elizabethan stage as interpreted by George Kernodle, an image of monarchical authority and the dependency upon the throne of all social well-being.[4] Yet the central theatrical icon of this play is based on a premise that is shattered from the start by Claudius' secret crime. The terrible failure of the throne in *Hamlet* to meet the all-encompassing demands placed upon it is one source of the philosophical and moral conflict in which Hamlet, and we, are so absorbed.

In the play's opening scene, two sentinels, meeting on the guard platform in the dead of night, at the changing of the watch, betray their nervousness by reversing the customary roles of challenger and challenged. "Who's there?" asks the soldier who is coming on watch, usurping the challenge to be spoken by the man already on duty, and is properly corrected: "Nay, answer *me*. Stand and unfold yourself" (emphasis added). As Lawrence Danson suggests, their exchange is "an inversion of ceremonial order," the first of many of the play.[5] The intense darkness is conveyed not through the theatrical convention of burning torches, as later in the full court scene when King Claudius sees "The Murder of Gonzago"; in this scene the darkness is conveyed by guards who cannot recognize one another or who must rely on their sense of hearing. "I think I hear them,"says Francisco of the approaching Horatio and Marcellus. "Stand, ho! Who is there?" (1.1.1–14). Disembodied sound is important to this and the later scenes played on the battlements, in the crowing of the cock causing the Ghost to start "like a guilty thing / Upon a fearful summons," in the offstage braying of Claudius' kettledrum and trumpet that is so at variance with the eerie stillness of the castle battlements, in the cry of the Ghost *"under the stage,"* "Swear by his sword."[6]

The silent language of gesture assumes a significant role in these scenes of darkness, of whispered conferences, of terrifying otherworldly appearances. "See, it stalks away . . . 'Tis gone, and will not answer." *"It spreads his arms." "Beckons."* "It beckons you to go away with it . . . Look with what courteous action / It waves you to a more removed ground."[7] We learn in fact a good deal about the appearance of the Ghost. It comes "In the same figure, like the King that's dead," as like the King "As though thou art to thyself. / Such was the very armor he had on / When he the ambitious Norway combated. / So frown'd he once when, in an angry parle, / He smote the sledded Polacks on the ice" (I.I.41–63). It evades the attempts of Marcellus and the rest to strike at it with their partisans, and "starts" guiltily at the crowing of the cock.

Horatio's report to Hamlet in scene 2 of what the soldiers have seen in the night is as fully descriptive as any theatrical producer could wish; it reads almost like a promptbook:

> A figure like your father,
> Armed at point exactly, cap-a-pe,
> Appears before them, and with solemn march
> Goes slow and stately by them. Thrice he walk'd
> By their oppress'd and fear-surprised eyes
> Within his truncheon's length, whilst they, distill'd
> Almost to jelly with the act of fear,
> Stand dumb and speak not to him.
>
> (1.2.199–206)

Not only are the accoutrements exactly described, but also the pace, the gesture, the relative positioning of the figures on stage, the distance between them. The report would make no theatrical sense if it did not correspond fairly closely with what we as spectators have seen. Horatio adds more details from his own observation on the third night of watch: the Ghost "wore his beaver up," revealing "A countenance more / In sorrow than in anger," "very pale," with his eyes fixed upon Horatio "Most constantly." His beard was "as I have seen it in his life, / A sable silver'd." On one occasion the Ghost "lifted up it head and did address / Itself to motion, like as it would speak," but instead shrank away "in haste" at the crowing of the cock and "vanish'd from our sight" (ll. 216–241).

We learn a good deal about the physical appearance and gesture of the men on the battlements as well. Bernardo says to Horatio, "You tremble and look pale." They strike at the Ghost with their partisans, attempt to restrain Hamlet from following it, and reluctantly move from place to place at the Ghost's behest to swear secrecy on Hamlet's sword. One or two of these details, like the pallor, depend more on Elizabethan commonplace symptoms of sorrow and fear than on what spectators would actually be able to see, but the rest of the description points to the actors' performance on stage.

The emphasis on visual means of communication in these early scenes is appropriate to a play that poses so many enigmatic questions.[8] How are we, and Hamlet, to interpret these signs? What do they bode? As soon as Hamlet is informed of what Horatio and his companions have seen, he perceives at once the problem of interpretation. "My father's spirit in arms! All is not well. / I doubt some foul play . . . Foul deeds will rise, / Though all the earth o'erwhelm them, to men's eyes" (ll. 254–257). It is through his cross-examining that we learn so much about the Ghost's appearance. To the Ghost, when it reappears, his first questions are those of interpretation. "What may this mean, / That thou, dead corse, again in complete steel / Revisits thus the glimpses of the moon, / Making night hideous? . . . Say, why is this? Wherefore? What should we do?" (1.4.51–57). Hamlet later mistrusts his ability to interpret this apparition accurately because of his melancholy and because "the devil hath power / T' assume a pleasing shape" (2.2.600–601), and he is in fact misled by the seeming earnestness of Claudius at prayer (3.3). Hamlet's iconoclasm grows out of his perception of the complexity of signs.

As Hamlet nonetheless intuits and as the Ghost soon confirms, the terrible secret justifying so much alarm and puzzlement is one that attacks all basis of human order and civilization. The act of which the Ghost must speak represents at least three appalling disruptions: the killing of a king, the murder of a brother, and the desertion of a husband by his wife.[9] The act is thus an assault on monarchy, on blood relationship, and on marriage. The early part of *Hamlet* is filled with graphic visual images of this threefold horror. When the Ghost has led Hamlet to the crucial point of revealing how and by whom the Ghost was slain, he states the essential fact in an image of perverted monarchy: "know, thou noble youth, / The serpent that did sting thy father's life /Now wears his crown" (1.5.39–41)

The ensuing account repeatedly uses a tripartite rhetorical pattern to emphasize the crime of one who is a regicide-usurper, *bruder-morder*, and incestuous adulterer: "Thus was I, sleeping, by a brother's hand / Of life, of crown, of queen, at once dispatch'd, / Cut off even in the blossoms of my sin, / Unhous'led, disappointed, unanel'd" (ll. 75–78). The assault on the rite of marriage and on its sacred vows galls the Ghost, especially the "falling-off" of his queen, "From me, whose love was of that dignity / That it went hand in hand even with the vow / I made to her in marriage" (ll. 49–51). Later, in the play within the play, the player King similarly recalls his marriage in sacramental terms: thirty years have passed, he notes, "Since love our hearts, and Hymen did our hands / Unite commutual in most sacred bands" (3.2.157–158).

Hamlet too, even before the revelation of the murder to him, has been preoccupied with images of violated ceremony. His imagination dwells on the sad conflation of funeral and marriage, whereby the ceremonial objects properly devoted to the expression of grief have been perverted to the expression of joy. Gertrude has shown her frailty and change of appetite within "A little month, or ere those shoes were old / With which she followed my poor father's body, / Like Niobe, all tears." In a similar gesture of "thrift," as Hamlet wryly calls it, "The funeral bak'd meats / Did coldly furnish forth the marriage tables" (1.2.147–181). The violation of rites sacred to funeral or marriage, and the violation of the bonds of brotherhood, are seen as integral to the violation of a duty a subject owes his monarch.

Some of these pictures of disrupted custom in Denmark are reported to us as historical and social background rather than through direct visual signs in the theater; but even such verbal images of disorder are relevant to a presentational analysis of *Hamlet* because they anticipate the many ceremonial actions through which the play is rendered. The murder of Hamlet's father and his funeral (also, later, the funeral of Polonius) are not shown directly on stage, but they live in Hamlet's memory as in ours to be theatrically reincarnated in "The Murder of Gonzago," the abortive funeral of Ophelia, and Hamlet's killing of Claudius. Similarly, we do not literally see shipwrights and other workers exert themselves out of season, preparing for military action against Norway with a "sweaty haste" that "Does not divide the Sunday from the week" and makes "the night joint-laborer with the day" (1.1.76–78). Nor can we behold what makes this preparation necessary, the attempt by young Fortinbras to recover "by strong hand / And terms compulsatory" (ll. 102–103) the land won by old Hamlet from old Fortinbras of Norway in fair and chivalrous fight. We do, however, behold the consequence of these inversions of order in the figure of a King who must now walk nightly among men as a ghost, subjecting himself to further affronts undeserved by such a regal figure. "It is offended," says Marcellus, as the

Ghost "stalks away" and refuses to answer Horatio's challenges (l. 50). When the soldiers strike at the Ghost with their partisans, the fruitlessness of their endeavor brings home to them that they are offending a figure of unparalleled dignity. "We do it wrong, being so majestical, / To offer it the show of violence," Marcellus concludes (ll. 143–144).

This image of a kingly figure struck at by his own former soldiers accentuates the gravity of his recent fall from monarch to corpse and sufferer of the unspeakable torments of Purgatory. The image of this fall will recur visually in "The Murder of Gonzago," when we behold in dumb show and then in full performance the killing of a king, witnessed on stage by the usurping king who will also, in the fullness of time, be slain in public view. Several Shakespearean tragedies—*Richard II*, *Richard III*, *Henry VI*, *Macbeth*—make use of the devastating symbol of a killed king, but nowhere other than in *Hamlet* is the symbol used with such visible and murderous violence, practiced (in the case of the old King Hamlet) upon a reigning legitimate monarch. Richard II and Henry VI are deposed before they are slain, and have not reigned well; Richard III and Macbeth are usurpers killed in battle; Duncan is murdered offstage. King John, if in fact he is poisoned by a monk, is another weak ruler with a defective claim, like Henry VI. Even *Hamlet* depicts the murder of the old King Hamlet indirectly, through report and through the play within the play. Truly, as Rosencrantz observes (though he applies it with unconscious irony to the usurper, not the true king), "The cess of majesty / Dies not alone, but like a gulf doth draw / What's near it with it . . . Never alone / Did the King sigh, but with a general groan" (3.3.15–23).

This central image of disruption, the killing of a king, is reinforced throughout the play of *Hamlet* by a repeated juxtaposition of King Claudius' fulsomely ceremonial royal presence and Prince Hamlet's lonely rejection of such hollow ritual. In scenes that roughly alternate with one another, we see on the one hand Claudius in full regalia, surrounded by his court, and on the other hand Hamlet, standing by himself in strikingly different costume from all the rest, or on the battlements in the cold night with a few trusted associates, or in soliloquy. The ritual scenes at court, as Fergusson points out, focus on the Danish body politic and its hidden malady; they are "ceremonious invocations of the well-being of society, and secular or religious devices for securing it."[10] Claudius' first entrance is to an official court function. The stage direction in the second Quarto measures the formality and extent of the processional appearance: "*Flourish. Enter Claudius, King of Denmark, Gertrude the Queen, Councilors, Polonius and his son Laertes, Hamlet, cum aliis*" (1.2).[11] "*Cum aliis*" includes the ambassadors Voltimand and Cornelius, whose dispatch to Norway is a first order of business. The stage is filled with richly costumed persons, and (although the stage directions do not so specify) the occasion would seem to demand a throne on stage, centrally located.[12] Certainly when they later watch "The Murder of Gonzago" on a state occasion, the King and Queen are seated. Gertrude is at Claudius' side throughout the play, enabling them to confer confidentially. Those advisers on whom the new king will rely most, such as Polonius, are evidently closest at hand. Stage business requires repeated signs of obeisance to the King: Cornelius and Voltimand undertake to "show our duty" to Claudius before they depart, and Laertes, similarly on hand to "show my duty in your coronation," now "bows" his thoughts and wishes of departure for France "to your gracious leave and pardon" (ll. 40–56). The flourish of trumpets announces the King's departure in procession as it has announced his arrival.

The positioning of Hamlet's name last in the opening stage direction of the second Quarto text suggests that he does not occupy a place in the procession appropriate to one who is proclaimed in this scene "the most immediate to our throne" (l. 109). The order of court business, proceeding from an official explanation of the King's marriage to the negotiations with Norway to the request for Laertes' departure and at last to Hamlet's situation, underscores once again his physical and psychic distance from the throne. Although he protests that his "inky cloak" and "customary suits of solemn black" cannot truly denote his inner grief, there can be no doubt that he is dressed in mourning black, while the rest of the court tries politicly to keep pace with Claudius' "auspicious and a dropping eye, / With mirth in funeral and with dirge in marriage, / In equal scale weighing delight and dole."[13] Nor can his mordant view of "windy suspiration of forc'd breath," of "the fruitful river in the eye," and of "the dejected havior of the visage" as woefully inadequate "forms, moods, shapes of grief" deny the fact that Hamlet's gestures are those of grief. His mother tells us that with "vailed lids" he continually seeks for his father "in the dust." The point of contention between Claudius and Hamlet logically becomes one of determining the proper extent of "mourning duties" for a dead father, of "filial obligation for some term" in what Claudius calls "obsequious sorrow"—that is, sorrow suited to obsequies or funerals, though the choice of term may also betray Claudius' complacency (ll. 11–92). How should sorrow manifest itself? And what are the signs of true monarchy? In the contest between these outward showings, presented to us as stage images, lies much of the dramatic conflict of the early scenes.

These same images, when Hamlet appears on the battlements, call upon our perception of what we see and what is to be imagined offstage. The juxtaposition of court and lonely battlements creates what Fergusson calls a "rhythm of performance" as we shift from scenes of hollow ceremony to "improvisational" scenes that "throw doubt upon the efficacy of the official magic."[14] Hamlet is with a few trusted followers, in the cold night air, awaiting the Ghost, but for the moment (scene 4) listening to Claudius' noisy revelry inside the castle. "*A flourish of trumpets, and two pieces go off*," specifies the stage direction, indicating that Claudius is now fulfilling his earlier command that trumpet and cannon are to greet each occasion of the King's drinking: "No jocund health that Denmark drinks today / But the great cannon to the clouds shall tell, / And the King's rouse the heaven shall bruit again, / Re-speaking earthly thunder" (1.2.125–128). The blasphemy of this inversion, whereby the heavens are to ape their human counterpart and master, is made still more offensive by its being a custom—"a custom," as Hamlet wryly qualifies it, "More honor'd in the breach than the observance" (1.4.15–16). Claudius' vast gift for evil can be seen in his ability to usurp custom, to make ceremony and observance serve his debased interests. He is the true corrupter of ceremony, by perverting its forms to his own use.[15] As a result, Hamlet, despite the reverence for proper ceremony that is suggested in his sorrow over the debasements of his father's funeral, is driven into the posture of a rebel.

Hamlet's "antic disposition" is more than a test of Claudius' guilt; it is also a protest aimed at the conventionality he sees perverted to the use of one who is a "cutpurse of the empire and the rule" (3.4.102).[16] The "wild and whirling words" with which Hamlet perplexes Horatio and the rest after the Ghost's departure are only one mark of his erratic behavior; he also makes an emphatic point of dispensing with ceremony. "And so, without more circumstance at all, / I hold it fit that we shake hands and part," he enjoins his comrades (1.5.128–129). After bidding them swear an oath of secrecy upon his sword, in a ceremony that is almost a comic travesty because of the Ghost's bizarre movements under the stage, after bidding them to hold "your fingers on your lips, I pray," and not to indulge in courtly games of leaking secret information through insinuating nods and folded arms, Hamlet insists on an exit that is fraternal rather than hierarchical. "Nay, come, let's go together," he insists, objecting to their habitual deference to him (ll. 188–191). Horatio has become indeed Hamlet's "good friend," one with whom he can honestly exchange that precious name of "friend" (1.2.163), one whom he can trust never to "flatter" or "crook the pregnant hinges of the knee / Where thrift may follow fawning," letting "the candied tongue lick absurd pomp" (3.2.59–61). Horatio's most precious gift for Hamlet is his ability to sort out what is real from what is specious in the elaborate ritual of courtly ceremony.

Most members of Claudius' court fail by this exacting standard, and their failure provokes in Hamlet further unconventional behavior as a protest against their conformity to a corrupted ethic. Stage image accentuates the contrast between a hollow ceremonial order and Hamlet's piercing through that apparent hierarchical structure; the metaphor of clothes, of inky cloaks and solemn suits of black, becomes literalized in Hamlet's aberrant dress. A notable instance of this, though described as happening offstage rather than before our eyes, is Hamlet's appearance to Ophelia in her closet in his "doublet all unbrac'd, / No hat upon his head, his stockings fouled, / Ungart'red, and down-gyved to his ankle, / Pale as his shirt, his knees knocking each other, / And with a look so piteous in purport / As if he had been loosed out of hell / To speak of horrors" (2.1.75–81). These costume effects and gestures, so minutely particularized, are in part a trap for Polonius, into which he obligingly falls: "Come, go with me, I will go seek the King. / This is the very ecstasy of love" (ll. 98–99). As such, these visual effects serve a major purpose of stage picture in the play, which is to test the nature of interpretation.[17] Polonius reads too simplistically, as Hamlet intends him to do, in the complex book of outward signs and their inner signification. Hamlet evokes in exaggerated fashion the "signs" of love melancholy, and Polonius is taken in.

The gestures and costume are more than love signs, however, for they reveal something to us of Hamlet's bitter disappointment at Ophelia's willingness to let her father interpret for her. It is surely no coincidence that Hamlet's "To be or not to be" soliloquy, with its profound questioning of "the law's delay," "The insolence of office," and other indicators of a corrupted ceremonial order, should be spoken while Ophelia is nearby, reading (or pretending to read) in a book of devotion, no doubt on her knees, and watched secretly by the King and Polonius. Her assumed piety is a stage literalization of what Polonius has just conceded, "that with devotion's visage / And pious action we do sugar o'er / The devil himself" (3.1.47–49). The stage business of kneeling at empty prayer is all the more arresting in the theater because it anticipates the scene, again witnessed by Hamlet, of Claudius' bowing his "stubborn knees" (3.3.70) to no effect. No matter how much we may pity Ophelia, and recognize the genuineness of her lament for the overthrow in Hamlet of "The courtier's, soldier's, scholar's, eye, tongue, sword," we find ourselves confronted with stage images in which her failure is, in Hamlet's eyes, all too apparent. Her suffering, appropriately, is to lose her sanity and to lament a father who, as Laertes protests, is interred with "No trophy, sword, nor hatchment o'er his bones, / No noble rite nor formal ostentation." Polonius' defective funeral anticipates Ophelia's own (4.5.214–216).[18] The elaborate procession of "*King, Queen, Laertes, and the Corse*," attended by priests, a lord, and others, conducting a young woman "of some estate" to an interment bereft of the sung requiem (5.1.217–221), is an overpowering token in this play of the end to which ceremonial observance has come.

Polonius and his son Laertes are no less foils for Hamlet's mordant observations on ceremonial forms.[19] Polonius is, after all, the author of that infamous advice to his son, "Costly thy habit as they purse can buy, / But not express'd in fancy; rich, not gaudy, / For the apparel oft proclaims the man" (1.3.70–72). This conventional approach to signs, usefully employed in Shakespeare's earlier plays, is inadequate to measure Hamlet's tragedy, and it leads to a contest between empty formality and inner truth in which Hamlet's sentiments often border on the satiric. Polonius' windy expostulation on "What majesty should be, what duty is" (2.2.87) characterizes the tediousness of his bowings and observances; the scenes in which he appears as chief adviser to the King are, with fitting contrast, either scenes of court ritual with flourishes, obeisances, and escorting of noble visitors, or scenes of concealment behind arrases where, in Hamlet's phrase, he may "play the fool . . . in 's own house" (3.1.134). Hamlet's unfeeling response to Polonius' death is no doubt deplorable, but we cannot forget the very different roles that these two men play, at court or in amateur drama; Polonius' prophetic role while at the university was that of Julius Caesar, being "so capital a calf" that he was killed in the Capitol.

Laertes is more admired by Hamlet and indeed becomes outwardly like him in his fury of protest at a father slain. Laertes is prepared "To cut his throat i' th' church" if he can encounter his father's slayer (4.7.126). No image could better convey the assault on rite and observance to which the tragic events of the play have led Laertes. He is similarly ready to mount a palace revolution in command of a "riotous head" or "rabble" who shout, "Choose we! Laertes shall be king!" and his bursting in upon Claudius is accompanied by that most telling stage sign of violent disorder: "The doors are broke" (4.5.104–114). It seems for the moment that Laertes is Claudius' nemesis, the revolutionary who will throw out the regicide and thereby demonstrate how murderous usurpation teaches others in turn to rebel. The irony, however, is that Laertes is still his father's son, unable to read beneath the plausible outward signs of Claudius' monarchical façade, and so condemned at last to serve the interests of this "king of shreds and patches." His first appearance in the play, as Lynda Boose observes, explicitly pairs and contrasts him with Hamlet, for he is dressed in ceremonial garb and presents a petition in the most courtly terms to be allowed to return to Paris, the city of fashion and gaming, whereas Hamlet clings stubbornly to unfashionable mourning clothes and is denied his petition to return to Wittenberg, a city of reform and intellectual ferment. Laertes is, like his father, concerned "with the exterior surfaces of objects, emotions, thoughts, and actions," and for that reason is obsessed with the lack of public ceremony at his father's funeral.[20] The assaults on correct courtly behavior to which he is goaded by his father's death—the poisoned sword, the unbated point, the poisoned cup as a last resort—are all directed ultimately not at achieving a true unconventionality but at a defense of the false monarchy Claudius has devised.

Hamlet's growing contempt for the obedient forms practiced by Rosencrantz and Guildenstern is fitly expressed in the mocking show of ceremony with which he greets their summons of him to the Queen's chambers, following the performance of "The Murder of Gonzago." "You are welcome," he jokes at their announcement that the Queen has sent for him "in most great affliction of spirit." Guildenstern's annoyed response to Hamlet's rudeness sums up the apparent case against irreverent treatment of social forms: "Nay, good my lord, this courtesy is not of the right breed" (3.2.310–314). Hamlet's mockery continues, directed always against their subservience to the outward forms of ceremony: "We shall obey, were she ten times our mother" (l. 331). Appropriately, Rosencrantz and Guildenstern are the persons appointed to wait upon Hamlet, to serve as his entourage, and, after his killing of Polonius, to guard him at the King's "pleasure" or convey him to England. Hamlet's impertinent response to this function is to play hide-and-seek: "Hide, fox, and all after" (4.2.31–32). Rosencrantz and Guildenstern are not practiced villains—"there is a kind of confession in your looks which your modesties have not craft enough to color," Hamlet tells them (2.2.280–282)—but they can never rise above the kind of superficial obedience to forms that Claudius knows how to exploit.

Hamlet's finest impatience with ceremonious behavior manifests itself in Act 5, after his return from England, in his encounter with the gravedigger and with Osric.[21] The gravedigger throws out various skulls, one of which might be that of a courtier, "which could say 'Good morrow, sweet lord! How dost thou, sweet lord?,' " though now, in a "fine revolution" of the ironies of history, he is being knocked about the mazard with a sexton's spade; or of a lawyer, with his "quillities, his cases, his tenures, and his tricks"; or of an important buyer of land, with his "recognizances, his fines, his double vouchers, his recoveries" (5.1.82–105). The almost good-natured satire of such behavior, the distance from it, the perception of its universality in human history embracing even Alexander the Great and Julius Caesar, all prepare us for Hamlet's conversation with Osric, who, like the anonymous land-owner, "hath much land, and fertile," but who cannot put his bonnet "to his right use" or refrain from posturing in his description of "six French rapiers and poniards, with their assigns, as girdle, hangers, and so on," including their "carriages" (5.2.86–151). Osric is the ultimate creature of Claudius' court, one who in Hamlet's phrase "did comply, sir, with his dug, before 'a suck'd it" (ll. 186–187), and his comic discomfiture is essential to establishing the mood of resignation and ironic detachment, side by side with the deeply passionate caring about his father's death and his mother's remarriage, that Hamlet brings to his final rendezvous with Claudius and Laertes.

Claudius is of course Hamlet's principal antagonist, the man against whom Hamlet's protesting of corrupted ceremony is ultimately directed. Thus it is appropriate that this mockery king, most of whose entrances and exits have been marked by flourishes and processions, who dispatches ambassadors and receives petitioners, who sits in regal splendor in the midst of courtiers and torchbearers to behold a play on the subject of his own crime, but who also hides behind arrases and appoints men to spy and poison, should preside over a final scene in which the hollow splendor of his court appears in all its fatal glory. This final scene is, as Fergusson observes, "the last time we see all the dramatis personae gathered to celebrate the social order upon which they all depend."²² "*A table*" is "*prepar'd*" for the duel of Laertes and Hamlet. "*Trumpets, drums, and Officers with cushions*" arrive, followed in regal procession by the "*King, Queen, and all the State,*" including Osric. Foils, daggers, and wine are borne in with a flourish. Once more, as he has done throughout the play, Claudius orders that "all the battlements" are to fire their ordnance when "The King shall drink to Hamlet's better breath." "Give me the cups," he proclaims, "And let the kettle to the trumpet speak, / The trumpet to the cannoneer without, / The cannons to the heavens, the heaven to earth, / 'Now the King drinks to Hamlet.' Come, begin." And the stage direction in Q2 specifies "*Trumpets the while*" (ll. 222–276).

This is Claudius' finest moment, the most impressive ceremony of his life as king, and the climactic moment of his secret plot on Hamlet's life. It is also the moment before he falls. The ritual act of throwing a pearl in Hamlet's cup, and the ceremonial drinking, conceal an attempt at poisoning Hamlet that instead becomes the means of Gertrude's death. The swordplay, ostensibly one more chivalrous manifestation of Claudius' royal magnificence, is instead the mechanism of his treachery. It fittingly precipitates the killing of a king, one who deserves to die, one whose violent death answers in visual terms the murder of old Hamlet and "The Murder of Gonzago" that have provided so dominant an image—to our imaginations and to our eyes—of inverted order. Through the killing of Claudius the stage action of regicide is at last legitimized; it enacts the vengeance demanded of Hamlet by his father, yet its unpremeditated suddenness on Hamlet's part makes it, in his eyes at least, the work of providential "rashness."

Hamlet's status as one likely "To have prov'd most royal" is confirmed by the play's final ceremonial in which he is borne to his grave accompanied by "The soldiers' music and the rite of war" (ll. 400–401). It is explicitly a rite of "passage," as Fortinbras insists (l. 400), a ceremony of death intended to offer some measure of comfort to those who must "draw [their] breath in pain" in this world and seek to understand the meaning of tragic events. For all the terrible sense of loss, the final ceremony does at least hint at a kind of reincorporation, one that we share in the liminal experience of theatergoing. The military orderliness of Hamlet's funeral procession may seem incongruous for one who was not a soldier, but it also completes something left unfinished in the abortive rites of passage for old Hamlet, Polonius, Ophelia, and others who have died—including Claudius, for whom no obsequies at all are proposed. Ceremony is at last not simply masquerade, as it was for Claudius, but a thing of substance that restores some hope of perceivable meaning in the ceremonial signs that hold together the social and moral order.²³ Hamlet's iconoclasm toward those signs, and his lament for a lost world in which those signs once had meaning, are answered to some degree (though not without irony as well) in the ritual solemnity of Hamlet's passage toward death.

Notes

1. Charney, *Style in "Hamlet."* (Princeton: Princeton University Press, 1969), p. 175.

2. Fergusson, *The Idea of a Theater* (Princeton: Princeton University Press, 1949), p. 138. See also Lynda E. Boose, "The Father and the Bride in Shakespeare, *PMLA* 97(1982): 325–347, esp. p. 330, for analysis of a "collision" of rituals in the mixture of funeral and marriage.

3. Fergusson, *The Idea of a Theater*, pp. 114–119.

4. Kernodle, *From Art to Theater* (Chicago: University of Chicago Press, 1944), pp. 5 ff. and passim; Fergusson, *The Idea of a Theater*, p. 116; and R. A. Foakes, *"Hamlet* and the Court of Elsinore," *Shakespeare Survey* 9(1956):35–43.

5. Danson, *Tragic Alphabet* (New Haven: Yale University Press, 1974), p. 24; see also Charles R. Forker, "Shakespeare's Theatrical Symbolism and Its Function in *Hamlet*," *Shakespeare Quarterly* 14(1963):215–229.

6. *Hamlet*, 1.1.148–149; 1.5.149–162. See Maurice Charney, *"Hamlet* without Words," in *Shakespeare's "More Than Words Can Witness*," ed. Homan (Lewisburg, Pa.: Bucknell University Press, 1980), pp. 23–42.

7. *Hamlet*, 1.1.50–52, 129; 1.4.57–61. See Charney, *Style in "Hamlet*," p. 169.

8. See Maynard Mack, "The World of *Hamlet*," *Yale Review* 41(1952):502–523; and Harry Levin, *The Question of Hamlet* (New York: Oxford University Press, 1959).

9. See Maynard Mack, Jr., *Killing the King: Three Studies in Shakespeare's Tragic Structure* (New Haven: Yale University Press, 1973).

10. Fergusson, *The Idea of a Theater*, p. 114. See also Foakes, *"Hamlet* and the Court of Elsinore," pp. 35–43; and Rose, *Shakespearean Design*, pp. 95–125.

11. The literal reading of the 1604–5 second Quarto is: *"Florish. Enter Claudius, King of Denmarke, Gertrad the Queene, Counsaile: as Polonius, and his Sonne Laertes, Hamlet, Cum Aliis."* The Folio text reads: *"Enter Claudius King of Denmarke, Gertrude the Queene, Hamlet, Polonius, Laertes, and his Sister Ophelia, Lords Attendant."*

12. Charney,*"Hamlet* without Words," p. 36; George F. Reynolds, *"Hamlet* at the Globe," *Shakespeare Survey* 9(1956):49–53.

13. See Coghill, *Shakespeare's Professional Skills* (Cambridge: Cambridge University Press, 1964), chap. 1, esp. p. 1.

14. Fergusson, *The Idea of a Theater*, p. 114.

15. Paul Hamill, "Death's Lively Image: The Emblematic Significance of the Closet Scene in *Hamlet*," *Texas Studies in Literature and Language* 16(1974–75):249–262, argues that Claudius' Elsinore is a castle of lechery, complete with riotous banqueting.

16. See Jacqueline E. M. Latham, "The Imagery in *Hamlet*: Acting," *Educational Theater Journal* 14(1962):197–202; and Kent W. Cartwright, "Ceremony in *Hamlet, Lear*, and *Macbeth*," *Dissertation Abstracts International* 39(1979):6773–A.

17. See Francis Berry, *The Shakespeare Inset: Word and Picture* (London: Routledge & Kegan Paul, 1965), pp. 116–143.

18. See Thiselton Dyer, *Folk-Lore of Shakespeare*, pp. 340–361; and Bridget Gellert Lyons, "The Iconography of Ophelia," *English Literary History* 44(1977):60–74.

19. Lynda E. Boose, "The Fashionable Poloniuses," *Hamlet Studies* 1(1979):66–77.

20. Ibid., pp. 69–73.

21. Bridget Gellert, "The Iconography of Melancholy in the Graveyard Scene in *Hamlet*," *Studies in Philology* 67(1970):57–66; and John P. Sisk, "Ceremony and Civilization in Shakespeare," *Sewanee Review* 86(1978):396–405.

22. Fergusson, *The Idea of a Theater*, p. 138.

23. See Wendy Coppedge Sanford, *Theater as Metaphor in "Hamlet"* (Cambridge, Mass.: Harvard University Press, 1967), pp. 23–24.

Hamlet: letters and spirits

MARGARET W. FERGUSON

"The letter killeth," said Saint Paul (2 Cor. 3:6). His words can serve as an epigraph—or epitaph—to my essay, which approaches some broad questions about the genre of Shakespearean tragedy by exploring the connections between certain techniques of wordplay in *Hamlet* and a process of dramatic literalization that is associated, in this play, with the impulse to kill. In the early part of the play, Hamlet frequently uses language to effect a divorce between words and their conventional meanings. His rhetorical tactics, which include punning and deliberately undoing the rhetorical figures of other speakers, expose the arbitrariness, as well as the fragility, of the bonds that tie words to agreed-upon significations. His language in dialogues with others, though not in his soliloquies, produces a curious effect of *materializing* the word, materializing it in a way that forces us to question the distinction between literal and figurative meanings, and that also leads us to look in new ways at the word as a spoken or written phenomenon. Hamlet's verbal tactics in the early part of the play—roughly through the closet scene in Act III—constitute a rehearsal for a more disturbing kind of materializing that occurs, with increasing frequency, in the later part of the drama. This second kind of materializing pertains to the realm of deeds as well as to that of words; in fact it highlights the thin but significant line that separates those realms, while at the same time it reminds us that all acts performed in a theater share with words the problematic status of representation. This second type of materializing might be called *performative*,[1] and since in *Hamlet*, in contrast to the comedies, it almost always results in a literal death, it might also be described as a process of "incorpsing"—to borrow a term that is used once in *Hamlet* and nowhere else in Shakespeare's corpus.

Hamlet begins his verbal activity of materializing words with the first line he speaks: "A little more than kin, and less than kind" (I.ii.65).[2] With this riddling sentence, spoken aside to the audience, Hamlet rejects the social and linguistic bond that Claudius asserted when he addressed Hamlet in terms of their kinship: "But now, my cousin Hamlet, and my son" (I.ii.64). Hamlet not only refuses to be defined or possessed by Claudius's

*Reprinted from *Shakespeare and the Question of Theory*, Patricia Parker and Geoffrey Hartman, eds., (1986), by permission of the publisher, Routledge, Chapman and Hall, Inc.

epithets, the second of which confuses the legal relation of stepson with the "natural" one of son; he also refuses to accept the principle of similarity that governs Claudius's syntax, which here, as elsewhere, employs the rhetorical figure of *isocolon*: balanced clauses joined by "and."[3] Claudius's isocolonic style is also characteristically oxymoronic: opposites are smoothly joined by syntax and sound, as for instance in these lines from his opening speech:

> Therefore our sometimes sister, now our queen,
> Th'imperial jointress to this warlike state,
> Have we, as 'twere with a defeated joy,
> With an auspicious and a dropping eye,
> With mirth in funeral and with dirge in marriage,
> In equal scale weighing delight and dole,
> Taken to wife.
>
> (I.ii.8–14)

Hamlet's remark "A little more than kin, and less than kind" unbalances the scale Claudius has created through his rhetoric—a scale in which opposites like "delight" and "dole" are blandly equated. Hamlet's sentence disjoins what Claudius has linked; it does so through its comparative "more" and "less," and also through the play on "kin" and "kind" which points, by the difference of a single letter, to a radical difference between what Claudius seems or claims to be, and what he is. The pun on the word "kind" itself, moreover, works, as Hamlet's puns so often do, to disrupt the smooth surface of another person's discourse. Hamlet's pun, suggesting that Claudius is neither natural nor kindly, is like a pebble thrown into the only pool of the king's rhetoric. As Lawrence Danson observes in *Tragic Alphabet*, Hamlet's puns challenge Claudius's "wordy attempts at compromise" by demanding "that words receive their full freight of meaning."[4] If the puns work to increase semantic richness, however—the Elizabethan rhetorician George Puttenham characterized the pun or *syllepsis* as "the figure of double supply"[5]—they do so by driving a wedge between words and their ordinary meanings. The pun, Sigurd Burckhardt argues, characteristically performs "an act of verbal violence. . . . It asserts that mere phonetic—i.e., material, corporeal—likeness establishes likeness of meaning. The pun gives the word as entity primacy over the word as sign."[6]

If Hamlet's punning wit makes an oblique attack on Claudius's rhetorical penchant for "yoking heterogeneous ideas by violence together"—to borrow the phrase Dr Johnson used in a similar attack on what he felt to be indecorous conceits—Hamlet is, of course, attacking much more than Claudius's rhetorical style. For Claudius has yoked not only words but bodies together, and it therefore seems likely that Hamlet's style reflects his (at this point) obscure and certainly overdetermined desire to separate his uncle from his mother. His dialogue with Polonius in II.ii offers further support for my hypothesis that Hamlet's disjunctive verbal techniques constitute not only a defense against being entrapped by others' tropes but also an aggressive, albeit displaced, attack on the marriage union of Gertrude and Claudius. By the time Hamlet speaks with Polonius, of course, he has not only had his worst suspicions about the king confirmed by the Ghost, but has also met with a rebuff from Ophelia, a rebuff dictated by Polonius's and Laertes' suspicions. It is no wonder, then, that his rhetoric is now directly deployed against the very idea of fleshly union. "Have you a daughter?" he asks Polonius (II.ii.182), and goes on to draw Ophelia into his morbid train of thought, which has been about the sun's power to breed maggots in the dead flesh of a dog. "Let her not walk i'th' sun," he says, echoing his earlier statement, in the opening scene with Claudius, "I am too much in the sun" (I.ii.67). The echo hints that Ophelia is already in some sense Hamlet's double here: both are endangered by the sun which is an emblem of kingly power, and both are also endangered—though in significantly different ways—by Hamlet's terrible burden of being a biological son to a dead king and a legal son to Claudius. As if dimly aware that his own way of thinking about Ophelia is tainting her with maggoty conceptions about sonship, Hamlet says to her father, "Conception is a blessing, but as your daughter may conceive—friend, look to't" (II.ii.184–6). It is at this point that Hamlet strikes yet another rhetorical blow against union in the realm of discourse: "What do you read, my lord?" asks Polonius. "Words, words, words," Hamlet replies. "What is the matter, my lord?" Polonius persists. "Between who?" is the perverse, ungrammatical, and fascinating reply, not an answer but, characteristically, another question. In this peculiar dialogue Hamlet disjoins words from their conventional meanings both rhetorically and thematically; in so doing, he breaks the social contract necessary to ordinary human discourse, the contract which mandates that there be, in Roman Jakobson's words, "a certain equivalence between the symbols used by the addressor and those known and interpreted by the addressee."[7]

In his first answer, "Words, words, words," Hamlet deliberately interprets Polonius's question literally; in his second reply, however, he does something more complicated than substituting a literal sense for a figurative one: he points, rather, to the problem that has always plagued classical theories of metaphor, which is that a word or phrase may not *have* a single, "literal" sense.[8] And it seems strangely appropriate that Hamlet should expose the problem of distinguishing between multiple—and perhaps equally figurative—meanings through the example of the word *matter*—a word that appears 26 times in the play, more than in any other by Shakespeare, in locutions ranging from Gertrude's acerbic remark to Polonius, "More matter with less art" (II.ii.95), to Hamlet's poignant comment to Horatio in the last act: "Thou wouldst not think how ill all's here about my heart; but it is no matter" (V.ii.208–9).

As is apparent from even a cursory examination of the play's manifold uses of this word, the relation between matter and spirit, matter and art, matter and anything that is "no matter," is altogether questionable for Hamlet; he is therefore quite accurate in presenting matter as an obstacle to unity of opinion: "Between who?" suggests only that any definition of matter will be a matter for dispute. Hamlet has indeed effectively disjoined this word from any single conventional meaning we or Polonius might want to give it; and it is no accident, I think, that Hamlet's rapier attack on the word "matter" foreshadows the closet scene in which he both *speaks* daggers to his mother and literally stabs Polonius, mistaking him, as he says to the corpse, "for thy better." In this scene, the concept of matter is linked to that of the mother by a pun that marries Shakespeare's mother tongue to the language known, in the Renaissance, as the *sermo patrius*: the language of the Church fathers and also of the ancient Romans.[9] "Now, mother, what's the matter?" asks Hamlet at the very outset of the closet scene (III.iv.7), and this query makes explicit an association of ideas already implied by a remark Hamlet made to Rosencrantz: "Therefore no more, but to the matter. My mother, you say—" (III.ii.315–16).

As we hear or see in the word "matter" the Latin term for mother, we may surmise that the common Renaissance association between female nature in general and the "lower" realm of matter is here being deployed in the service of Hamlet's complex oedipal struggle.[10] The mother is the matter that comes between the father and the son—and it is no accident that in this closet scene Hamlet's sexual hysteria rises to its highest pitch. Dwelling with obsessive, disgusted fascination on his mother's unseemly passion for her second husband, Hamlet appears to be struggling with his own feelings about her body even as he argues for his dead father's continuing rights to her bed. Hamlet's act of stabbing Polonius through the curtain, which occurs almost casually in the middle of the tirade against Gertrude's lust, seems only to increase his passionate desire to make her *see* her error in preferring Claudius to her first husband. For Hamlet, however, the problem of seeing a genuine *difference* between his original father and the man Gertrude has called his father assumes enormous significance at precisely this juncture in the drama; immediately before Hamlet refers to Claudius as a "king of shreds and patches," the Ghost appears, or rather reappears, with a dramatic entrance that allows the phrase "king of shreds and patches" to refer to the Ghost as well as to Claudius. As if to underscore the fact that Hamlet's dilemma here is a hermeneutic as well as an ethical one, Shakespeare has him address the Ghost with the pregnant question, "What would your gracious figure?" (III.IV. 105). If Claudius is a figure of the father, so is the Ghost; according to what standard of truth, then, is Hamlet to distinguish between them?

Shakespeare give this problem a further turn of the screw, as it were, by making the Ghost invisible and inaudible to Gertrude. Like the governess in Henry James's tale, who sees the ghostly figure of Miss Jessell when the "gross" housekeeper does not, Hamlet is forced to confront and deny the possibility that the Ghost may be a figment of his own imagination. He, and the audience, must at least fleetingly experience a conflict between the evidence provided by their eyes and ears and Gertrude's statement that she perceives "nothing." And even if this scene's stage directions confirm the Ghost's existence and support Hamlet's argument that what he has seen is not, as Gertrude insists, a "bodiless creation" of "ecstasy," we may well not feel entirely easy about giving credence to Hamlet here; after the Ghost exists, Hamlet declares to Gertrude that his "pulse" keeps time just as "temperately" as hers does (III.IV. 142). Then, having claimed to be no less (but also no more) sane than is the woman whose perceptions we have just been forced to discount, Hamlet proceeds to promise that "I the matter will re-word, which madness / Would gambol from." The relation between the "matter" of the Ghost and the matter Hamlet will "re-word" in the ensuing passionate dialogue with Gertrude remains deeply mysterious.

By stressing the epistemologically doubtful status of the Ghost, we can usefully supplement the classic psychoanalytic explanation for why Hamlet defers performing the deed of revenge. That explanation, outlined by Freud in a famous footnote to the *Interpretation of Dreams* and elaborated by Ernest Jones, suggests that Hamlet obscurely knows that in killing Claudius he would be satisfying his repressed oedipal desire to be *like* Claudius, who has become a king and husband by killing the elder Hamlet.[11] Jacques Lacan, in his brilliant, albeit elliptical, essay on "Desire and the interpretation of desire in *Hamlet*," speculates that Hamlet's invectives against Claudius in the closet scene are an example of *dénégation*, that is, the words of dispraise and contempt are indications of repressed admiration.[12] Building on both Freud and Lacan, we might read Hamlet's frantic efforts to draw a clear epistemological distinction between his father and Claudius as a defense against his perception of an excessive degree of *likeness* between himself and Claudius, or, more precisely, between his desires and Claudius's. In fact, the distinctions Hamlet draws between Claudius and Old Hamlet seem no less questionable, in their hyperbole, than the distinction he draws between himself and his mother when, alluding to the simple moral system of medieval religious drama, he calls her a vice and himself a virtue. A parallel dualistic oversimplification informs his sermon-like speech on the pictures of the two kings, "The counterfeit presentment of two brothers," as he calls them:

> See what a grace was seated on this brow,
> Hyperion's curls, the front of Jove himself,
> An eye like Mars to threaten and command,
> A station like the herald Mercury
> New-lighted on a heaven-kissing hill
>   (III.iv.55–9)

He doth protest too much, methinks, in this plethora of similitudes designed, as he says, to make his mother relinquish that passion which is blind to difference. Hamlet's own passion, we might say, is making him blind to similarity. His description of his father's incomparable virtue hardly accords with what the Ghost himself said to his son when he lamented having been "Cut off even in the blossoms of my sin" and "sent to my account / With all my imperfections on my head" (I.v.76–9). Nor does it accord with what Hamlet himself said in III.iii, where he described his father dying with "all his crimes broad blown, as flush as May" (81).

Hamlet's doubts about his father's character, about the Ghost's status as a figure, and about his own relation to both his father and Claudius, constitute one reason why he cannot resolve the matter of his mother or his revenge. Another and related reason is that he is too filled with disgust at female flesh to follow the path Freud describes for those who eventually emerge, however scarred, from the oedipal complex. That path leads to marriage with a woman who is not the mother. In Hamlet's case, the obvious candidate is Ophelia, whom Hamlet actually seems to prefer to his mother in the play within the play scene. "Come hither, my dear Hamlet, sit by me," says Gertrude, and Hamlet replies, "No, good mother, here's metal more attractive" (III.ii. 108). The metaphor is misogynistically reductive— and ominously allied to Hamlet's pervasive concern with debased currency; nonetheless, for a moment it seems that he may find in Ophelia a matter to replace his mother. "Lady, shall I lie in your lap?" he asks, and when she says no, taking him literally, he specifies his meaning, offering to lay in her lap only that part of him which houses the higher faculties: "I mean, my head upon your lap?" "Ay, my lord," she answers; but he twists her affirmation by indicating that his head is filled with thoughts of her—and his—lower parts: "Do you think I meant country matters?" he asks, punning on the slang term for the female genitals. "I think nothing, my lord," Ophelia replies; and Hamlet once again bawdily literalizes her words: "That's a fair thought to lie between maids' legs" (III.ii.110–17). While his speeches in this dialogue seem like an invitation to sexual union (in one sense he is enticing her to realize that the matter between *his* legs is not nothing but something), the final effect of this exchange, as of all the encounters between Ophelia and Hamlet we see in this play, is to separate her from him, to push her naive love away and reduce her to incomprehension of what he later calls his "mystery." Hamlet's relation to Ophelia seems aptly epitomized a little later in this scene, when he leaves off interpreting the tropical ambiguities of the *Mousetrap* play being presented before them to say to her, "I could interpret between you and your love if I could see the puppets dallying" (III.ii. 241–2). The role of the interpreter who stands *between* others and their loves is the role he has at once had thrust upon him by fate and which he chooses to continue to play. It is dangerous to suggest that he had any alternative, for the play notoriously foils critics who think themselves ethically or intellectually superior to this tragic hero.[13] Nonetheless, I would like to argue that the play does provide a critical perspective on Hamlet, a perspective that implies a questioning of the genre of tragedy itself more than a moral critique of the hero as an individual subject.

The critical perspective I hope to trace does not result in our feeling that Hamlet *should* have done something else at any point in the play; rather, it heightens our awareness that the drama itself is the product of certain choices which *might have been different*. Like many students of Shakespeare, I have often felt that certain of his plays strongly invite the audience to imagine how the play would go if it were written according to a different set of generic rules. Certain turns of plot are made to seem somehow *arbitrary*, and the effect of such moments is to shift our attention from the story-line to the invisible hand manipulating it; we are reminded that the dramatist's decisions about his material are *not* wholly preordained. A strange sense of potentiality arises at such moments; we enter a metadramatic realm where movements of plot and characterization no longer seem simply given or "necessary." The death of Mercutio in *Romeo and Juliet* is an example of the kind of moment I have in mind; it seems so accidental, so unmotivated, that we may well wonder how the play would have turned out had he been allowed to live. The play *could* have been a comedy—as Shakespeare later explicitly indicated by including a parody of it in Act V of *A Midsummer Night's Dream*. Shakespeare's tendency to blur generic boundaries throughout his career has often been remarked; but critics have not, to my knowledge, related this phenomenon to the peculiar way in which Shakespearean tragedy, in contrast to Greek or classical French examples of the genre, seems so often to imply a questioning of the necessity of casting a given story *as* tragedy.

The critical perspective on Hamlet—or on *Hamlet* as a "piece of work"—begins to emerge, I think, with the first death in the play, the stabbing of Polonius in the pivotal closet scene of III.iv. Here we see a darker, literalized version of Hamlet's verbal technique of separating others' words from their conventional meanings. That technique was dissociative but also semantically fecund; now, however, a spirit is definitively separated from its body, which becomes mere matter. "It was a brute part of him to kill so capital a calf," Hamlet had punningly remarked apropos of Polonius's fate when he played Julius Caesar in a university theatrical (III.ii.104); now, by killing Polonius, Hamlet makes the earlier insult seem prophetic; he "realizes" it, transforming the old man into a sacrificial calf on another stage. This performative mode of materializing a figure, with its grim effects of tragic irony, is what I want to call "incorpsing."

Although the play raises all sorts of questions about the boundary between speaking and doing, in the closet scene there is no doubt that Hamlet passes from speaking daggers to using them. But he has stabbed Polonius only through a curtain—yet another figure for that position of "in betweenness" Hamlet himself is structurally bound to occupy. That curtain may also be seen, I think, as a material emblem not only for Hamlet's ignorance of Polonius's identity, but also for his inability to pursue a certain ethical line of interpreting the meaning of his deed. Hamlet does not inquire very deeply either here or later, when he kills Rosencrantz and Guildenstern, into the meaning of his action. This seems odd, since he has shown himself so remarkably capable of interrogating the meaning of his *inaction*. There is a thinness, even an uncharacteristic patness, to his response to his killing of Polonius: "For this same lord / I do repent," he says, adding, "but heaven hath pleas'd it so, / To punish me with this and this with me, / That I must be their scourge and minister" (III.iv.174–7). It seems to me that the play questions this kind of self-justification, supplementing if not altogether invalidating Hamlet's view of himself as a divinely appointed "scourge." The questioning occurs most generally through the play's scrutiny of kingship; kings, like divinely appointed "scourges," may easily abuse their power by seeing themselves as heavenly instruments, beyond the authority of human laws. Shakespeare, I would argue, invites us to see that one meaning of Hamlet's "incorpsing" activity is that through it he becomes more and more like a king—or, perhaps, like a playwright. Indeed, with the killing of Polonius—the "rat" Hamlet mistakenly takes for the king he had already symbolically caught in the *Mousetrap* play—Hamlet takes a crucial step towards occupying the place of the king as the play defines it: not in terms of an individual, but in terms of a *role* associated both with the power to kill and with the tendency to justify killing with lines of argument unavailable to lesser men. Horatio darkly suggests this in V.ii. Hamlet has just described how he disposed of Rosencrantz and Guildenstern. "They are not near my conscience," he says:

> 'Tis dangerous when the baser nature comes
> Between the pass and fell incensed points
> Of mighty opposites.
>
> (V.ii.60–2)

"Why, what a king is this!" Horatio ambiguously exclaims or queries. Does he refer to Hamlet or to Claudius? It doesn't much matter, Shakespeare seems to say: a king is one who thinks himself capable of literally disposing of whatever comes between him and his desires.

It is no accident that Hamlet kills Rosencrantz and Guildenstern by means of a forged letter. For Claudius's letter ordering the king of England to kill Hamlet, Hamlet substitutes a letter ordering the king to kill Rosencrantz and Guildenstern. He seals that letter with his father's ring, the signet or sign of royal power; Claudius of course possesses a copy of this ring, and it is worth noting that there is no difference between the *effect* of Claudius's copy and that of the original seal. Both have the power to order instant death. Communication among kings in this play would, indeed, appear to be a grim illustration of Saint Paul's dictum that the letter killeth. The play suggests, however, that it is not only the letter, but the desire to *interpret* literally, to find one single sense, that leads to murder. The Ghost that appeared "In the same figure like the King that's dead" commands Hamlet to take action by means of several equivocal and mutually contradictory phrases, including "bear it not," "Taint not thy mind," and "Remember me" (I.v.81, 85, 91); even when he reappears to whet Hamlet's almost blunted purpose, all the Ghost commands is "Do not forget" (III.iv.110). So long as Hamlet remains perplexed by the multiple potential meanings of these commands, he remains in a realm where destruction of meanings goes hand in hand with the creation of new ones: the verbal and hermeneutic realm of his puns. Unyoking words from their conventional meanings is not the same thing as unyoking bodies from spirits. In coming to resemble Claudius, Hamlet is driven to forget this distinction, and Shakespeare, I think, asks us to see the cost of this forgetting. He does so by giving the audience a letter (of sorts) that invites a radically different interpretation from those which Claudius and Hamlet take from the messages they receive from mysterious places.

Shakespeare's "letter to the audience," as I want to characterize it, appears in a passage immediately following Claudius's receipt of Hamlet's letter announcing his return—naked and alone—to the shores of Denmark (IV.vii.42–5): let me try to show why the juxtaposition of passages is significant. Claudius says that he cannot understand Hamlet's letter ("What should this mean?" he asks Laertes (IV.vii.47)); but he recognizes Hamlet's "character" in the handwriting and proceeds quickly enough to give it a kingly interpretation. For he immediately tells Laertes of his "device" to work Hamlet's death in a way that will appear an accident. His response to the letter—which comes, after all, from someone he believed he had sent to the country from which no traveler returns—is eerily similar to Hamlet's response to the Ghost's message from the land of the dead. Like Hamlet, Claudius wonders about the ambiguity of the message: "is [the letter] some abuse?" he asks Laertes (IV.vii.48), echoing Hamlet's earlier question to himself about whether "The spirit that I have seen" is or is not a devil that "perhaps . . . / Abuses me to damn me" (II.ii.596, 599). Also like Hamlet, although much more quickly, Claudius chooses a single interpretation of the message, finding in it an incentive to kill. It hardly seems to matter whether the message comes from a spirit or a letter: the interpreter's *decision* about its meaning creates the deadliness. But in the passage that follows, Shakespeare offers an oblique criticism of the kind of interpretive decision that the kings or would-be kings make in this play. He does so by using Claudius as the unwitting spokesman for a greater king, the one who will really win the duel in the final scene. This is the king whom Richard II describes in Act III of his play:

> within the hollow crown
> That rounds the mortal temples of a king,
> Keeps Death his court, and there the antic sits
> Scoffing his state and grinning at his pomp,
> Allowing him a breath, a little scene,
> To monarchize, be fear'd, and kill with looks;
> Infusing him with self and vain conceit,
> As if this flesh which walls about our life
> Were brass impregnable.
> (*Richard II*, III.ii.160–8)

With wonderful irony, Shakespeare has Claudius metaphorically describe this king of kings while *thinking* he is pursuing his own aims—devising his own plot—by manipulating Laertes' competitive spirit to transform his rage against Claudius for Polonius's death into anger against Hamlet. "Two months since," Claudius says,

> Here was a gentleman of Normandy—
> I have seen myself, and serv'd against, the French,
> And they can well on horseback, but this gallant
> Had witchcraft in't. He grew unto his seat,
> And to such wondrous doing brought his horse
> As had he been incorps'd and demi-natur'd
> With the brave beast. So far he topp'd my thought
> That I in forgery of shapes and tricks
> Come short of what he did.
> (IV.vii. 81–9)

"A Norman was't?" Laertes asks, and then, in one of the subtlest nonrecognition scenes in all of Shakespeare, Laertes tells us the Norman's name: "Upon my life, Lamord" (91).[14] The spirit behind these letters from the text of the Second Quarto is invisible to Laertes and Claudius; it was also invisible to the compilers of the First Folio, who spelled the Frenchman's name "Lamound," and to eighteenth-century editors like Pope and Malone; the former gave the name as "Lamond," the latter, citing the phrase which describes the character as "the brooch and gem of all the nation," suggested "Lamode," fashion.[15] But I contend that Shakespeare meant us to hear or see the word "death" in and through the letters of this name; "Upon my life, Death," is the translation we are invited to make[16]—and for those who are uncertain of their French but willing to suspect that puns which depend on mere changes of letters have metaphorical significance, Shakespeare provides an English pun in the word "Norman," which is all too close for comfort to the phrase used by the gravedigger in the next scene: "What man dost thou dig it for?" Hamlet asks. "For no man, sir," is the equivocal reply (V.i.126–7).

The play offers other intratexual clues to the identity of "Lamord." Laertes' phrase "Upon my life, Lamord," echoes a phrase Horatio used in his discussion of the Ghost in I.i: "Let us impart what we have seen tonight / Unto young Hamlet; for *upon my life* / *This spirit*, dumb to us, will speak to him" (I.i.174–6; my italics).

Horatio here unwittingly exposes the same eerie truth that Laertes does in Act IV: the "spirit" of Death, whether in the figure of the Ghost or in the figure of Lamord, sits upon the lives of all the characters in the play. And the scene which introduces Lamord seems deliberately designed not only to make Death's past and future presence manifest, but to link it, ominously and obscurely, to the playwright's own activities of "forging shapes," of persuading, and of creating elegiac song: immediately after Claudius successfully persuades Laertes to envenom his sword so that if he "galls" Hamlet in the duel "It may be death" (146–7), the queen enters with news of Ophelia's fate of being pulled, by her garments, from her "melodious lay / To muddy death" (181–2).

In the description of the mysterious Norman, Shakespeare paradoxically insists on the presence of Death by animating the dead metaphor in the common phrase "upon my life"; he also creates a new adjective, "incorpsed," which editors (and the *OED*, citing this line as the first use of the term) gloss as "made into one body," but which may also evoke the image of a dead body if we hear the Norman's name as "Death." The lines make us "see" Death, as it were, in a strangely materialized and emblematic figure: that of the rider sitting on—and controlling—the horse that traditionally represents human passion and ambition: "A horse, a horse, my kingdom for a horse," Richard III famously cries, when he is about to lose the powerful vitality that animal symbolizes.[17] The figure of Lamord sitting on his horse as if he were "incorps'd and demi-natur'd / With the brave beast" is richly evocative, reminding us, as Harry Levin suggests, both of the apocalyptic image of Death as a rider on a "pale horse" (Revelation 6:8), and of Hamlet's broodings on the inherently double or centaur-like nature of man, the angel and beast, the "beauty of the world" and the "quintessence of dust" combined into one "piece of work" (II.ii.307ff).[18]

The description of Lamord, which I would like to see as Shakespeare's figurative letter to the reader, is somber and mysterious, a *memento mori* admonition. But it contrasts in a curious way with the other messages and admonitions in this play; for there is all the difference in the world between a message that asks us, with the paradoxical temporality of literature and dream, to *remember* our own future death, and messages that ambiguously incite characters to kill and thereby to forget, as it were, the potential future of another. It seems to me significant, therefore, that Shakespeare uses the trope of personification—the animation of inanimate things—to describe Lamord. A premonitory and admonitory figure he certainly is—but how interestingly different from the literalized *memento mori* that appears in the next scene, in Yorick's skull. I do not think Hamlet grasps the meaning of Yorick's skull very completely because he so quickly forgets its implications for the fate of kings. Although seeing the skull leads him to brood on the idea that great men such as Alexander and Caesar finally become, like commoners, no more than dust to stop a bunghole, in the very next scene (V.ii.58–62) we find Hamlet still thinking of *himself* as a "mighty opposite" in a kingly war that makes humble men like Rosencrantz and Guildenstern irrelevant to conscience. Paradoxically, the death drive in Hamlet seems too strong to allow him to understand either a graphic *memento mori* such as Yorick's skull or the more unusual, figurative one offered to the audience (but not to Hamlet) in the Lamord passage. For truly to understand a *memento mori*, one must have at least some love of life—on earth or beyond. And Hamlet lacks this love; he was speaking truly when he told Polonius that there was nothing he would prefer to lose more than Polonius's company "except my life, except my life, except my life" (II.ii.216–17).[19] It is therefore appropriate that, in the description of Lamord that Hamlet can neither read nor hear, Shakespeare asks us to remember not only death, but also love and life—particularly the life of Hamlet as Ophelia remembers it from a time before the play began. Lamord, Laertes admiringly says, is "the brooch indeed / And gem of all the nation" (IV.vii. 92–3); the phrasing and rhythm recall Ophelia's description of Hamlet as "Th'expectancy and rose of the fair state. The glass of fashion and the mould of form" (III.i.154–5).

The implied parallel between Lamord and Hamlet—not the gloomy and disheveled prince we see throughout most of the play, a man obsessed with a sense of sexual impotence, but rather a prince made present to us only through the mediation of Ophelia's memorializing description—this parallel suggests that there is yet another way of interpreting Lamord's name and symbolic significance. If one listens closely to his name, one may hear in it a pun not only on Death but also on Love—there is, after all, only the slightest difference in pronunciation between the French "la mort" and "l'amour"; and the Latin *amor* is contained within the Norman's name. French Renaissance poets often punned on "l'amour" and "la mort" in ways that suggest the two forces are no less "demi-natured" than Lamord and his horse.[20]

In a play as concerned as this one is with problems of translation, it seems quite plausible that Shakespeare would pun bilingually here no less richly than he does in the bawdy "French lesson" scene of *Henry V*. It also seems plausible that he would be particularly interested in puns that strike the reader's eye even more than the listener's ear; *Hamlet* is after all a play that broods on the relation between elite and "general" audiences, and also on the relation between written texts and dramatic performances of them.[21] The play on Lamord's name suggested by the Second Quarto in any case invites those of us who read *Hamlet* now, knowing all the problems presented by the existence of its different textual versions, to imagine the playwright asking of himself a question similar to the one Horatio voices in Act V, apropos of Osric's inability to understand Hamlet's parody of the inflated courtly style Osric himself uses: "Is't not possible to understand in another tongue?" (V.ii.125). Horatio's question, like so many questions in this play, is left unanswered. But even if most of Shakespeare's later readers and editors have *not* understand the other tongue, or tongues, spoken by the text in the Lamord passage, that passage is nonetheless significant as a kind of window that allows us briefly to look out from the dark and claustrophobic world of *Hamlet* to another verbal universe, one whose metaphysical economy is less depressed than the one we see in *Hamlet*. The description of Lamord, often cut in production and apparently so irrelevant to the play's plot that it is sometimes described as a "personal allusion" on Shakespeare's part,[22] seems to me a significant digression from the world of tragedy itself. The language of this passage is strangely foreign to *Hamlet* because here letter and spirit are joined in a message that insists on the union of life and death but does not present that union as a horror. For Hamlet, questioner of tropes and incorpser of bodies, all unions are tainted with poison, like the literal "union" (the pearl) in the cup Claudius prepares for Hamlet in the final scene. After Gertrude has mistakenly drunk from that cup and Claudius has been wounded with the envenomed sword, Hamlet ironically offers the poisoned vessel to Claudius, asking bitterly, "Is thy union here? / Follow my mother" (V.ii.331–2).

There is a different perspective on unions in the personification of Lamord. Shakespeare explores that perspective more fully in some of his later plays, notably the romances; one might indeed see the passage on Lamord as a kind of prophecy of Shakespeare's later career, when he experimented with a genre characterized by "wondrous" escapes from potentially tragic plots. In the romances, and in a play like *Antony and Cleopatra* which blurs the boundary between tragedy and romance, we find a vision of the relation between death and life that sharply contrasts with the tragic vision represented in *Hamlet*. Characters like Antony, Florizel (*The Winter's Tale*) and Ferdinand (*The Tempest*) inhabit verbal universes in which the verb "to die" often has a double meaning; and the playwright himself exploits the theatrical analogue to this pun by reminding us, as he does conspicuously in *Antony*, that actors, like lovers, may die many times and come again to life.[23] Antony's marvelous dialogue with Eros envisions death as a dissolving of boundaries that is more erotic than terrible, and that may well be compared to the image of Lamord "incorps'd and demi-natur'd" with his horse. "Thou hast seen these signs, / They are black vesper's pageants," Antony tells Eros after describing to him the various forms clouds take; he goes on to conjure an image that anticipates Prospero's famous "cloud-capp'd towers" speech in *The Tempest* (IV.i. 148ff.). Antony says: "That which is now a horse, even with a thought / The rack dislimns, and makes it indistinct / As water is in water" (IV.xiv.9–11).

Such a way of conceiving death allows for the possibility of new shapes rising from the dissolution of old ones; death is acknowledged but also, one might say, embraced, in a romance vision similar to the one incarnated in a dialogue in Act IV of *The Winter's Tale*. Speaking of the spring flowers she lacks (for the pastoral world of Shakespearean romance is never an Eden of timeless spring), Perdita says that if she had such flowers she would use them on her lover, "To strew him o'er and o'er." "What, like a corpse?" he asks, and she replies: "No, like a bank, for love to lie and play on: / Not like a corpse; or if—not to be buried, / But quick, and in mine arms" (IV.iv.130–2). Here again is language like that in the Lamord passage, which speaks of something "incorps'd" and lively at once, the quick and the dead "demi-natur'd." In such visions there is a kind of sublime punning, an equivocation that holds life and death in solution or delicate balance. "We must speak by the card or equivocation will undo us," Hamlet says in the graveyard scene (V.i.133–4). Shakespeare, I think, infuses this statement with an irony Hamlet cannot see; for Hamlet is undone, and undoes others, not because he equivocates, but because he inhabits a world where equivocation tends, as if by a fatal entropy, to become "absolute for death." The play, however, renders its own generic drive toward death just equivocal enough to make us question the rules of tragedy.

Notes

I am grateful to Mac Pigman for his helpful comments on an earlier version of this essay. I am also grateful to the many friends and strangers who listened to this paper and criticized it constructively when it was presented in various forms at Wellesley, Smith, Vassar, Bennington, Williams and Mount Holyoke colleges, and at Brown and The Johns Hopkins universities.

1. I borrow the term "performative" from J. L. Austin, *How To Do Things With Words* (1962), 2nd edn (Cambridge, Mass., 1975), 5 and *passim*. Austin, however, notoriously seeks to exclude from his discussion the type of performative utterance that interests me here, namely that which occurs on a stage or in a literary text. Such performatives, he writes, "will be *in a peculiar way* hollow or void" (22, Austin's italics).

2. All quotations from *Hamlet* and other Shakespeare plays are from the New Arden editions, general editors Harold F. Brooks, Harold Jenkins and Brian Morris (London and New York). The Arden *Hamlet*, ed. Harold Jenkins, was published in 1982.

3. See Stephen Booth's excellent discussion of the syntactic and rhetorical devices Claudius uses to achieve "equation by balance"; "On the value of *Hamlet*," in *Reinterpretations of Elizabethan Drama*, ed. Norman Rabkin (New York, 1969), esp. 148–9. [Reprinted in this volume.]

4. Lawrence Danson, *Tragic Alphabet: Shakespeare's Drama of Language* (New Haven and London, 1974), 27.

5. See George Puttenham's *The Arte of English Poesie*, ed. Gladys Willcock and Alice Walker (Cambridge, 1936), 136. "Syllepsis" is the classical trope that corresponds most closely to the modern notion of the pun—a term that did not appear in English until the

eighteenth century, according to the *OED*. Oswald Ducrot and Tzvetan Todorov define syllepsis as "the use of a single word that has more than one meaning and participates in more than one syntactic construction"; they cite as an example Falstaff's remark, from *The Merry Wives of Windsor*, "At a word, hang no more about me; I am no gibbet for you" (*Encyclopedic Dictionary of the Sciences of Language*, tr. Catherine Porter (Baltimore, 1979), 2–8). I am indebted for this citation and for my general understanding of punning tropes to Jane Hedley's unpublished essay on "Syllepsis and the problem of the Shakespeare sonnet order."

      6.   Sigurd Burckhardt, *Shakespearean Meanings* (Princeton, 1968), 24–5. Burckhardt's comment is cited in part by Danson, op. cit., 27, n. 2.

      7.   Roman Jakobson and Morris Halle, *Fundamentals of Language* (The Hague, 1956), 62; cited by Danson, op. cit., 27, n. 3.

      8.   See, e.g., Paul de Man's discussion of Locke's condemnation of *catachresis*, the trope that most notoriously dramatizes the difficulty of grounding a theory of figurative language in a concept of referential correspondence between words and "reality"; "The epistemology of metaphor," in *On Metaphor*, ed. Sheldon Sacks (Chicago and London, 1979), 11–28. Locke's condemnation of catachresis, in *The Essay Concerning Human Understanding*, eventually "takes all language for its target," de Man argues, "for at no point in the course of the demonstration can the empirical entity be sheltered from tropological deformation" (19–20).

      9.   On Latin as a *sermo patrius*, see my *Trials of Desire: Renaissance Defenses of Poetry* (New Haven and London, 1983), 24, and Leo Spitzer, "Muttersprache und Muttererziehung," in *Essays in Historical Semantics* (New York, 1948), 15–65.

      10.   See Ian Maclean, *The Renaissance Notion of Woman* (Cambridge, 1980), for a survey of Renaissance authors who adopted the Aristotelian scheme of dualities "in which one element is superior and the other inferior. The male principle in nature is associated with active, formative, and perfected characteristics, while the female is passive, material, and deprived" (8). See also Linda Woodbridge, *Woman and the English Renaissance: Literature and the Nature of Womankind, 1540–1620* (Urbana and Chicago, 1984), esp. ch. 3. It seems likely that an association between baseness, "matter," and his mother is at work even earlier in the play, when Hamlet vows that the Ghost's "commandment all alone shall live / Within the book and volume of my brain, / Unmix'd with baser matter. Yes, by heaven! / O most pernicious woman!" (I.v.102–5). Cf. Avi Erlich's comments about this passage in *Hamlet's Absent Father* (Princeton, 1977), 218.

      11.   Freud's famous discussion of Hamlet as a "hysteric" whose guilt about his own repressed oedipal wishes prevents him from taking vengeance "on the man who did away with his father and took that father's place with his mother" was originally published as a footnote to ch. 5 of *The Interpretation of Dreams* (1900); from 1914 onward the passage was included in the text. See *The Standard Edition of the Complete Psychological Works of Sigmund Freud*, ed. James Strachey *et al.*, 4 (London, 1953), 264–6. See also Ernest Jones, *Hamlet and Oedipus* (Garden City, 1949). But see also, for a critique of the "Freud–Jones" interpretation and a discussion of other psychoanalytic readings of *Hamlet*, Theodore Lidz, *Hamlet's Enemy: Madness and Myth in "Hamlet"* (New York, 1975), esp. 9–13, 184–6.

      12.   Jacques Lacan, "Desire and the interpretation of desire in *Hamlet*," tr. James Hulbert, French text ed. Jacques-Alain Miller from transcripts of Lacan's seminar, in *Literature and Psychoanalysis, The Question of Reading: Otherwise*, ed. Shoshana Felman (*Yale French Studies*, 55–6 (1977), 11–52). The mention of *dénégation* occurs on p. 50; my explanation of the term draws on the translator's note 6. I should observe, however, that Lacan's analysis departs from Freud's, or rather claims to "shed light on what Freud [had to] . . . leave out" (48), by interpreting the play with reference to the Lacanian theory of the "phallus." The fundamental reason why Hamlet cannot raise his arm against Claudius, Lacan argues, is that "he knows that he must strike something other than what's there" (51). That "something other" is the

phallus, the symbolic object which, for Lacan, signifies "the law of the father," and which cannot be mastered by the individual subject because it is an *effect* of repression and of one's insertion into a cultural system of meaning. "[O]ne cannot strike the phallus," Lacan asserts, "because the phallus, even the real phallus, is a *ghost*" (50).

13. Many critics have succumbed to the temptation to reproach Hamlet for incompetence (Bradley) or for possessing "a moral sensibility inferior to our own," as Helen Gardner characterizes T. S. Eliot's rebuke to Hamlet for "dying fairly well pleased with himself" despite the fact that he has made "a pretty considerable mess of things" ("The stoicism of Shakespeare and Seneca," cited in Gardner's useful survey of the problems critics have encountered in trying to find ethical or logical "consistency" in the drama; see her chapter on "The historical approach: *Hamlet*," in *The Business of Criticism* (Oxford, 1959), 35–51).

14. The Norman's name is spelled "Lamord" in the Second Quarto and in many modern editions of the play, e.g. the Arden, the Signet, the Riverside; the entire passage is absent from the First ("Bad") Quarto.

15. See the variants and notes for IV.vii.93 in the New Variorum *Hamlet*, ed. H. H. Furness, 5th edn (Philadelphia, 1877), I, 363. The Variorum itself prints the name as "Lamond."

16. Although most modern editors who use the Second Quarto's spelling of the name do so without explaining their choice, Harold Jenkins in the New Arden edition does comment on his decision, suggesting that "the name of the 'wondrous' messenger (91) is a presage of fatality" and is most plausibly interpreted as a play on "La Mort" (see his note to IV.vii.91, p. 369, and his longer note about the passage on 543–4). To the best of my knowledge, Harry Levin is the only other modern commentator who has devoted much attention to the passage; in *The Question of Hamlet* (New York, 1959), Levin discusses the "easily possible slip of typography or pronunciation" that would make "La Mort" into the Second Quarto's "Lamord" (95).

17. The common Renaissance allegorization of the horse as a symbol for those passions which need to be controlled by reason (figured in the rider or driver) frequently harks back to Plato's image of the soul as a charioteer with two winged horses (*Phaedrus*, 246–8). Shakespeare uses the horse as a figure for uncontrolled anger in *2 Henry IV*, l.i.9–11, and again in *Henry VIII*, l.i.133.

18. See Levin, op. cit., 95; see also Harold Jenkins's editorial comment (op. cit., 544) that the description of Lamord recalls the image of Claudius as a satyr (I.ii.140) and "kindred animal images, even while the horseman, in contrast with the satyr, is invested with a splendour of which no touch is ever given to Claudius."

19. Cf. Lacan's remarks on Hamlet's rejection of Ophelia once she becomes, in his eyes, "the childbearer to every sin"; she is then "the phallus, exteriorized and rejected by the subject as a symbol signifying life" (Lacan, op. cit., 23).

20. My favorite example, for which I am indebted to Joseph Shork, of the University of Massachusetts at Boston, is the following:

> Amour en latin faict amor;
> Or donc provient d'amour la mort,
> Et par avant, soulcy qui mord,
> Deuils, plours, pieges, forfaitz, remords.

Stendhal uses this *blason* as an epigraph to chapter 15 of *Le Rouge et le Noir*. I have been unable to locate a Renaissance source for this epigraph and it may of course have been composed by Stendhal himself; nonetheless, "se non è vero, è ben trovato." Its play on "mordre" as "to bite" makes it a particularly apt gloss on the Lamord passage, since one editor of *Hamlet*, Edward Dowden, connects the Second Quarto's Lamord with the French *mords*, a horse's bit. For simpler examples of wordplay on love and death in sixteenth-century

French poetry, see *Poètes du XVIe siècle*, ed. Albert-Marie Schmidt (Paris, 1953), 725 (Jodelle's *Les Amours*, Sonnet 35), and 827, 823, 820 (poems from Philippe Desportes's *Les Amours d'Hippolyte*).

21. For whatever reasons—one possibly having to do with the complex publication and production history of *Hamlet* in Shakespeare's own lifetime—the play emphasizes the difference between written scripts and actors' versions of them in a way unique in Shakespeare's canon; see, e.g., Hamlet's remark to the Player in II.ii.430–1 apropos the speech that "was never acted" (" 'twas caviare to the general") and his later directive, again addressed to the Player, that "your clowns speak no more than is set down for them" (III.ii.38–9). The play is also unusually full of references to books, tablets, letters, and forgeries of written texts; some critics have suspected that Hamlet's letter to Ophelia (II.ii.109ff.) is a forgery by Polonius. For a discussion of the theme of writing in the play, see Daniel Sibony, "*Hamlet*: a writing effect" (*Yale French Studies*, 55–6(1977), 53–93). On other passages in the text that contain bi- and trilingual puns, see Lidz, op. cit., 23–5.

22. As Harold Jenkins notes (Arden *Hamlet*, 369), a number of editors have suggested a "personal allusion" in the passage to the cavalier in Castiglione's *The Courtier* named Pietro Monte (rendered by Hoby in his Tudor translation as Peter Mount; cf. the Folio's "Lamound"). I do not dispute the idea of an esoteric allusion; I am simply arguing what can never be definitively proved, that an allusion to Death is more plausible.

23. See, for examples of erotic puns on "die," *Antony and Cleopatra*, I.ii.138–42 and IV.xv.38–9; *The Tempest*, III.i.79–84.

Hamlet—the "Mona Lisa" of Literature

Jacqueline Rose

It does not seem to have been pointed out that T. S. Eliot's famous concept of the "objective correlative," which has been so influential in the assessment of literature and its values, was originally put forward in 1919 in the form of a reproach against the character of a woman.[1] The woman in question is Gertrude in Shakespeare's *Hamlet*, and the reproach Eliot makes is that she is not good enough aesthetically, that is, *bad* enough psychologically, which means that in relationship to the affect which she generates by her behaviour in the chief character of the drama—Hamlet himself—Gertrude is not deemed a sufficient *cause*.

The question of femininity clearly underpins this central, if not indeed *the* central, concept of Eliot's aesthetic theory, and this is confirmed by the fact that Eliot again uses an image of femininity—and by no means one of the most straightforward in its own representation or in the responses it has produced—to give us the measure of the consequent failure of the play. *Hamlet* the play, Eliot writes, is "the Mona Lisa of literature,"[2] offering up in its essentially enigmatic and indecipherable nature something of that maimed or imperfect quality of appeal which characterises Leonardo's famous painting. The aesthetic inadequacy of the play is caused by the figure of a woman, and the image of a woman most aptly embodies the consequences of that failure. Femininity thus becomes the stake, not only of the internal, but also of the critical drama generated by the play.

Equally important, however, is the fact that femininity has been at the heart of the psychoanalytic approach to *Hamlet*, from Ernest Jones onwards—a fact which has again been overlooked by those who have arrested their attention at the famous Oedipal saga for which his reading of the play is best known. "Hamlet was a woman"[3] is just one of the statements about *Hamlet* which Jones quotes as indicating the place of the "feminine" in a drama which has paradoxically been celebrated as the birth of the modern, post-Renaissance, conception of man. In this essay, I will try to focus what I see as the centrality of this question of femininity to an aesthetic theory which has crucially influenced a whole tradition of how we conceptualise literary writing, and to the psychoanalytic theory which was being elaborated

---

*From *Sexuality in the Field of Vision* (1986). © 1986, Verso. Reprinted by permission of Verso.

at exactly the same time, at the point where they converge on the same object—Shakespeare's *Hamlet*—described by Freud as an emblem of "the secular advance of repression in the emotional life of mankind."[4]

I

To start with T. S. Eliot's critique of *Hamlet*. T. S. Eliot in fact sees his reading of the play as a move away from psychological approaches to *Hamlet* which concentrate too much on the characters to the exclusion of the play itself: "*Hamlet* the play is the primary problem, and Hamlet the character only secondary."[5] Eliot therefore makes it clear that what he has to say exceeds the fact of the dramatis personae and strikes at the heart of aesthetic form itself. The problem with *Hamlet* is that there is something in the play which is formally or aesthetically unmanageable: "like the *Sonnets*" (another work by Shakespeare in which a question of sexual ambivalence has always been recognised) "*Hamlet* is full of some stuff that the writer could not drag to light, contemplate, or manipulate into art."[6] Eliot then describes the conditions, as he sees it, of that in which *Hamlet* fails—the successful manipulation of matter into artistic form. It is here that he produces the concept of the "objective correlative" for the first time: "The only way of expressing emotion in the form of art is by finding an 'objective correlative'; in other words, a set of objects, a situation, a chain of events which shall be the formula of that *particular* emotion; such that when the external facts . . . are given, the emotion is immediately evoked. . . . The artistic 'inevitability' lies in this complete adequacy of the external to the emotion."[7]

Emotion, or affect, is therefore only admissable in art if it is given an external object to which it can be seen, clearly and automatically, to correspond. There must be nothing in that emotion which spills over or exceeds the objective, visible (one could say conscious) facts, no residue or trace of the primitive "stuff" which may have been the original stimulus for the work of art. This is where *Hamlet* fails: Hamlet the man is dominated by an emotion which is inexpressible, because it is in *excess* of the facts as they appear. And that excess is occasioned by Gertrude who precipitates Hamlet into despondency by her "o'er hasty" marriage to his dead father's brother and successor, who turns out also to have been the agent of the former king's death. For Eliot, Gertrude is not an adequate equivalent for the disgust which she evokes in Hamlet, which "envelopes and exceeds her"[8] and which, because she cannot adequately contain it, runs right across the fabric of the play. Gertrude is therefore disgusting, but not quite disgusting *enough*. Eliot is, however, clear that he is not asking for a stronger woman character on the stage, since he recognises that it is in the nature of the problem dealt with in this play—a son's feelings towards a guilty mother—that they should be in excess of their objective cause. On this count, Gertrude's inadequacy turns around and becomes wholly appropriate: "it is just *because* her character is so negative and insignificant that she arouses in Hamlet the feeling which she is incapable of representing."[9]

What is at stake behind this failing of the woman, what she fails to represent, therefore, is precisely unrepresentable—a set of unconscious emotions which, *by definition*, can have no objective outlet and which are therefore incapable of submitting to the formal constraints of art. What we get in *Hamlet* instead is "buffoonery"—in Hamlet himself the "buffoonery of an emotion which can find no outlet in action," for the dramatist the "buffoonery of an emotion which he cannot express in art."[10] Such "intense," "ecstatic" (Gertrude uses the word "ecstasy" to describe Hamlet's madness in the bedchamber scene of the play) and "terrible" feeling is for Eliot "doubtless a subject of study for the pathologist" and why Shakespeare attempted to express the "inexpressibly horrible" we cannot ever know, since we should have finally "to know something which is by hypothesis unknowable and to understand things which Shakespeare did not understand himself."[11]

Today we can only be struck by the extraordinary resonance of the terms which figure so negatively in Eliot's critique—buffoonery, ecstasy, the excessive and unknowable—all terms in which we have learnt to recognise (since Freud at least) something necessarily present in any act of writing (*Hamlet* included) which only suppresses them—orders them precisely into form—at a cost. Eliot's criticism of *Hamlet* can therefore be turned around. What he sees as the play's weakness becomes its source of fascination or even strength.

In this context, the fact that it is a woman who is seen as cause of the excess and deficiency in the play and again a woman who symbolises its aesthetic failure starts to look like a repetition. Firstly, of the play itself—Hamlet and his dead father united in the reproach they make of Gertrude for her sexual failing ("O Hamlet what a falling off was there"), and *horror* as the exact response to the crime which precedes the play and precipitates its drama ("O horrible! O horrible! most horrible!").[12] Secondly, a repetition of a more fundamental drama of psychic experience itself as described by Freud, the drama of sexual difference in which the woman is seen as the cause of just such a failure in representation, as something deficient, lacking or threatening to the system and identities which are the precondition not only of integrated artistic form but also of so-called normal adult psychic and sexual life. Located by Freud at the point where the woman is first seen to be different,[13] this moment can then have its effects in that familiar mystification or fetishisation of femininity which makes of the woman something both perfect and dangerous or obscene (obscene if *not* perfect). And perhaps no image has evoked this process more clearly than that of the "Mona Lisa" itself, which at almost exactly this historical moment (the time of Freud and Eliot alike) started to be taken as the emblem of an inscrutable femininity, cause and destination of the whole of human mystery and its desires: "The lady smiled in regal calm: her instincts of conquest, of ferocity, all the heredity of the species, the will to seduce and to ensnare, the charm of deceit, the kindness that conceals a cruel purpose—all this appeared and disappeared by turns behind the laughing veil and buried itself in the poem of her smile. Good and wicked, cruel and compassionate, graceful and feline she laughed."[14]

By choosing an image of a woman to embody the inexpressible and inscrutable context which he identified in Shakespeare's play, Eliot ties the enigma of femininity to the problem of interpretation itself: "No one has solved the riddle of her smile, no one has read the meaning of her thoughts, "a presence . . . expressive of what in the way of a thousand years men had come to desire."[15] Freud himself picks up the tone in one of his more problematic observations about femininity when he allows that critics have recognised in the picture "the most perfect representation of the contrasts which dominate the erotic life of women; the contrast between reserve and seduction, and between the most devoted tenderness and a sensuality that is ruthlessly demanding—consuming men as if they were alien beings."[16]

What other representation, we might ask, has so clearly produced a set of emotions without "objective correlative," that is, in excess of the facts as they appear? T. S. Eliot's reading of *Hamlet* would therefore seem to suggest that what is in fact felt as inscrutable, unmanageable or even horrible (ecstatic in both senses of the term) for an aesthetic theory which will only allow into its definition what can be controlled or managed by art is nothing other than femininity itself.

At the end of Eliot's essay, he refers to Montaigne's "Apologie of Raymond Sebond" as a possible source for the malaise of the play. Its discourse on the contradictory, unstable and ephemeral nature of man has often been seen as the origin of Hamlet's suicide soliloquy; it also contains an extraordinary passage anticipating Freud where Montaigne asks whether we do not live in dreaming, dream when we think and work, and whether our waking merely be a form of sleep.[17] In relation to the woman, however, another smaller essay by Montaigne—"Of Three Good Women"—is equally striking for the exact reversal which these three women, models of female virtue, represent vis-à-vis Gertrude herself in Shakespeare's play, each one choosing self-imposed death at the point where her husband is to die.[18] The image is close to the protestations of the Player Queen in the Mousetrap scene of *Hamlet* who vows her undying love to her husband; whereupon Gertrude, recognising perhaps in the Player Queen's claims a rebuke or foil to her own sexual laxness, comments "The lady doth protest too much" (a familiar cliché now for the sexual 'inconstancy' of females).[19] So what happens, indeed, to the sexuality of the woman, when the husband dies, who is there to hold its potentially dangerous excess within the bounds of a fully social constraint? This could be seen as one of the questions asked by *Hamlet* the play and generative of its terrible effect.

Before going on to discuss psychoanalytic interpretations of *Hamlet*, it is worth stressing the extent to which Eliot's theory is shot through with sexuality in this way and its implications for recent literary debate. Taking their cue from psychoanalysis, writers like Roland Barthes and Julia Kristeva have seen the very stability of the sign as index and precondition for that myth of linguistic cohesion and sexual identity which we must live by but under whose regimen we suffer.[20] Literature then becomes one of the chief arenas in which this struggle is played out. Literary writing which proclaims its integrity, and literary theory which demands that integrity (objectivity/correlation) of writing, merely repeat that moment of repression when language and sexuality were first ordered into place, putting down the unconscious processes which threaten the resolution of the Oedipal drama and of narrative form alike. In this context, Eliot's critical writing, with its stress on the ethical task of writer and critic, becomes nothing less than the most accomplished (and influential) case for the interdependency and centrality of language and sexuality to the proper ordering of literary form. Much recent literary theory can be seen as an attempt to undo the ferocious effects of this particularly harsh type of literary super-ego—one whose political repressiveness in the case of Eliot became more and more explicit in his later allegiance to Empire, Church and State.

Eliot himself was aware of the areas of psychic danger against which he constantly brushed. He was clear that he was touching on "perilous" issues which risk "violating the frontier of consciousness," and when he talks of writing as something "pleasurable," "exhausting," "agitating," as a sudden "breakdown of strong habitual barriers," the sexuality of the writing process which he seeks to order spills over into the text.[21] And Eliot's conception of that order, what he sees as proper literary form, is finally an Oedipal drama in itself. In his other famous essay "Tradition and the Individual Talent," which was written in the same year as the *"Hamlet"* essay, Eliot states that the way the artist can avoid his own disordered subjectivity and transmute it into form is by giving himself up to something outside himself and surrendering to the tradition that precedes and surrounds him. Only by capitulating to the world of dead poets can the artist escape his oppressive individuality and enter into historical time: "Set [the artist] for contrast and comparison among the dead" for "the most individual parts of his work are those in which the dead poets, his ancestors, assert their immortality most vigourously."[22] Thus, just as in the psychoanalytic account, the son pays his debt to the dead father, symbol of the law, in order fully to enter his history, so in Eliot's reading the artist pays his debt to the dead poets and can only become a poet by that fact. Eliot's conception of literary tradition and form could therefore be described as a plea for appropriate mourning and for the respecting of literary rites—that mourning whose shameful inadequacy, as Jacques Lacan points out in his essay on *Hamlet*,[23] is the trigger and then constant refrain of the play: the old Hamlet cut off in the "blossom" of his sin: Polonius interred "hugger mugger"; Ophelia buried wrongly—because of her suicide—in consecrated ground.

In Eliot's reading of *Hamlet*, therefore, the sexuality of the woman seems to become the scape goat and cause of the dearth or breakdown of Oedipal resolution which the play ceaselessly enacts, not only at the level of its theme, but also in the disjunctions and difficulties of its aesthetic form. Much has been made of course of the aesthetic problem of *Hamlet* by critics other than Eliot, who have pondered on its lack of integration or single-purposiveness, its apparent inability to resolve itself or come to term (it is the longest of Shakespeare's plays), much as they have pondered on all these factors in the character of Hamlet himself.

Hamlet poses a problem for Eliot, therefore, at the level of both matter and form. Femininity is the image of that problem; it seems in fact to be the only image through which the problem can be conceptualised or thought. The principal danger, femininity thus becomes the focus for a partly theorised recognition of the psychic and literary disintegration which can erupt at any moment into literary form.

One more example, and perhaps the most graphic, can serve to illustrate how far femininity is implicated in this aesthetic theory—the lines which Eliot uses from Tourneur's *The Revenger's Tragedy* to describe the artist surrendering to his inspiration before ordering it into form:

> And now methinks I could e'en chide myself
> For doating on her beauty, though her death
> Shall be revenged after no common action.
> Does the silkworm expend her yellow labours
> For thee? For thee does she undo herself?
> Are lordships sold to maintain ladyships
> For the poor benefit of a bewildering minute?
> Why doth yon fellow falsify highways,
> And put his life between the judge's lips,
> To refine such a thing—keeps horse and men
> To beat their valours for her?[24]

For a play that has also been discussed as excessive and perhaps even more than *Hamlet*, this moment gives the strongest measure of that excess. The speech is made by Vindice, the Revenger, to the skull of his former mistress who was poisoned by the Duke for resisting his advances. His revenge takes the form of wrapping this skull in the full bodied attire of the woman and dowsing its mouth with poison so that the Duke will first be seduced and then poisoned in its embrace. In this crazed image, the woman appears at once as purity and lust, victim and destroyer, but the split representation shows how the feminine can serve as a receptacle for a more fundamental horror of sexuality and death. Femininity becomes the place in which man reads his destiny, just as the woman becomes a symptom for the man.[25]

Likewise in *Hamlet*, these two themes—of death and sexuality—run their course through the play, both as something which can be assimilated to social constraint and as a threat to constraint and to the social altogether. For *Hamlet* can be seen as a play which turns on mourning and marriage—the former the means whereby death is given its symbolic form and enters back into social life, the latter the means whereby sexuality is brought into the orbit of the law. When *Hamlet* opens, however, what we are given is *too much* of each (perhaps this is the excess)—too much mourning (Hamlet wears black, stands apart, and mourns beyond the natural term) and too much marriage (Gertrude passes from one husband to another too fast). As if these two regulators of the furthest edges of social and civil life, if they become overstated, if there is too much of them, tip over into their opposite and start to look like what they are designed to hold off. Eliot's essay on *Hamlet*, and his writing on literature in general, gives us a sense of how these matters, which he recognises in the play, underpin the space of aesthetic representation itself and how femininity figures crucially in that conceptualisation.

II

If Eliot's aesthetic theories move across into the arena of sexuality, Ernest Jones's psychoanalytic interpretation of *Hamlet* turns out also to be part of an aesthetic concern. His intention is to use psychoanalysis to establish the integrity of the literary text, that is, to uncover factors, hidden motives and desires, which will give back to rational understanding what would otherwise pass the limits of literary understanding and appreciation itself: "The perfect work of art is one where the traits and reactions of the character prove to be harmonious, consistent and intelligible when examined in the different layers of the mind."[26] Jones's reading, therefore, belongs to that psychoanalytic project which restores to rationality or brings to light, placing what was formerly unconscious or unmanageable under the ego's mastery or control. It is a project which has been read directly out of Freud's much contested statement *"Wo Es war, soll Ich werden,"* translated by Strachey "Where id was, there ego shall be."[27] Lacan, for whom the notion of such conscious mastery is only ever a fantasy (the fantasy of the ego itself) translates or reverses the statement: "There where it was, so I must come to be."[28]

For Jones, as for Eliot, therefore, there must be no aesthetic excess, nothing which goes beyond the reaches of what can ultimately be deciphered and known. In this context, psychoanalysis acts as a key which can solve the enigma of the text, take away its surplus by offering us as readers that fully rational understanding which Shakespeare's play—Jones recognises like Eliot—places at risk. The chapter of Jones's book which gives the Oedipal reading of *Hamlet*, the one which tends to be included in the anthologies of Shakespeare criticism, is accordingly entitled "The psychoanalytic solution."[29] Taking his reference from Freud's comments in *The Interpretation of Dreams*, Jones sees Hamlet as a little Oedipus who cannot bring himself to kill Claudius because he stands in the place of his own desire, having murdered Hamlet's father and married his mother.[30] The difference between Oedipus and Hamlet is that Oedipus unknowingly acts out this fantasy, whereas for Hamlet it is repressed into the unconscious revealing itself in the form of that inhibition or inability to act which has baffled so many critics of the play. It is this repression of the Oedipal drama beneath the surface of the text which leads Freud to say of *Hamlet*, comparing it with Sophocles's drama, that it demonstrates the "secular advance of repression in the emotional life of mankind.[31]

But Jones's book and the psychoanalytic engagement with *Hamlet* do not stop there and it is finally more interesting than this Oedipal reading which, along with Jones's speculations on Hamlet's childhood and Shakespeare's own life, has most often been used to discredit them. For while it is the case that Jones's account seems to fulfil the dream of any explanatory hypothesis by providing an account of factors which would otherwise remain unaccountable, a closer look shows how this same reading infringes the interpretative and sexual boundaries which, like Eliot, it seems to be putting into place.

The relationship of psychoanalysis to *Hamlet* has in fact always been a strange and repetitive one in which Hamlet the character is constantly given the status of a truth, and becomes a pivot for psychoanalysis and its project, just as for Eliot *Hamlet* is the focal point through which he arrives at a more general problem of aesthetic form. For Freud, for instance, Hamlet is not just Oedipus, but also melancholic and hysteric, and both these readings, problematic as they are as diagnoses of literary characters, become interesting because of the way they bring us up against the limits of interpretation and sexual identity alike. The interpretative distinction between rationality and excess, between normality and abnormality, for example, starts to crumble when the melancholic is defined as a madman who also speaks the truth. Freud uses *Hamlet* with this meaning in "Mourning and Melancholia" written in 1915: "We only wonder why a man has to be ill before he can be accessible to a truth of this kind. For there can be no doubt that if anyone holds an opinion of himself such as this (an opinion which Hamlet holds of himself and of everyone else) he is ill, whether or not he is speaking the truth or whether he is being more or less unfair to himself.[32]

Taken in this direction, *Hamlet* illustrates not so much a failure of identity as the precarious distinction on which this notion of identity rests. In "Psychopathic Characters on the Stage," Freud includes *Hamlet* in that group of plays which rely for their effect on the neurotic in the spectator, inducing in her or him the neurosis watched on stage, crossing over the boundaries between onstage and offstage and breaking down the habitual barriers of the mind.[33] A particular *type* of drama, this form is nonetheless effective only through its capacity to implicate us *all:* "A person who does not lose his reason under certain conditions can have no reason to lose." [34] Jones makes a similar point and underscores its fullest social import when he attributes the power of *Hamlet* to the very edge of sanity on which it moves, the way that it confuses the division which "until our generation (and even now in the juristic sphere) separated the sane and the responsible from the irresponsible insane." [35] T. S. Eliot also gave a version of this, but from the other side, when he described poetry in "Tradition and the Individual Talent" as an escape from emotion and personality, and then added "but, of course, only those who have personality and emotion can know what it means to want to escape from these things." [36] So instead of safely diagnosing Hamlet, his Oedipal drama, his disturbance, and subjecting them to its mastery and control, the psychoanalytic interpretation turns back onto spectator and critic, implicating the observer in those forms of irrationality and excess which Jones and Eliot in their different ways seek to order into place.

Calling Hamlet a hysteric, which both Freud and Jones also do,[37] has the same effect in terms of the question of sexual difference, since it immediately raises the question of femininity and upsets the too tidy Oedipal reading of the play. Freud had originally seen the boy's Oedipal drama as a straightforward desire for the mother and rivalry with the father, just as he first considered the little girl's Oedipal trajectory to be its simple reverse. The discovery of the girl's pre-Oedipal attachment to the mother led him to modify this too easy picture in which unconscious sexual desires in infancy are simply the precursors in miniature of the boy's and the girl's later appropriate sexual and social place.[38] We could say that psychoanalysis can become of interest to feminism at the point where the little girl's desire for the father can no longer be safely assumed. But equally important is the effect that this upset of the original schema has on how we consider the psychic life of the boy. In a section called "Matricide" normally omitted from the anthologies, Jones talks of Hamlet's desire to kill, not the father, but the mother.[39] He takes this from Hamlet's soliloquy before he goes to his mother's bedchamber in Act III, scene ii of the play:

> Let not ever
> The soul of Nero enter this firm bosom;
> Let me be cruel, not unnatural.
> I will speak daggers to her, but use none.[40]

and also from Gertrude's own lines "What wilt thou do? Thou wilt not murder me? Help! Ho!"[41] (the murder of Polonius is the immediate consequence of this). "Thus desire spills over into its opposite and the woman becomes guilty for the affect which she provokes.

This is still an Oedipal reading of the play since the violence towards the mother is the effect of the desire for her (a simple passage between the two forms of excess). But the problem of desire starts to trouble the category of identification, involving Jones in a discussion of the femininity in man (not just desire *for* the woman but identification *with* her), a femininity which has been recognised by more than one critic of the play.[42] Thus on either side of the psychoanalytic "solution," we find something which makes of it no solution at all. And Hamlet, "as patient as the female dove,"[43] becomes Renaissance man only to the extent that he reveals a femininity which undermines that fiction. Femininity turns out to be lying behind the Oedipal drama, indicating its impasse or impossibility of resolution, even though Freud did himself talk of its dissolution, as if it suddenly went out of existence altogether. But this observation contradicts the basic analytic premise of the persistence of unconscious desire.

The point being not whether Hamlet suffers from an excess *of* femininity, but the way that femininity itself functions *as* excess—the excess of this particular interpretative scheme (hence presumably its exclusion from the summaries and extracts from Jones), and as the vanishing-point of the difficulties of the play. And in this, Ernest Jones outbids T. S. Eliot vis-à-vis the woman: "The central mystery [of Hamlet] has well been called the Sphinx of modern literature."[44] The femininity of Hamlet is perhaps finally less important than this image of the feminine which Jones blithely projects onto the troubled and troubling aesthetic boundaries of the play.

III

If the bad or dangerous woman is aesthetic trouble, then it should come as no surprise that the opposite of this disturbance—an achieved aesthetic or even creativity itself—then finds its most appropriate image a gain in femininity, but this time its reverse: the good enough mother herself. As if completing the circuit, André Green turns to D.W. Winnicott's concept of the maternal function as the basis for his recent book on *Hamlet*.[45] Femininity now appears as the very principle of the aesthetic process. Shakespeare's Hamlet forecloses the femininity in himself, but by projecting onto the stage the degraded and violent image of a femininity repudiated by his character, Shakespeare manages to preserve in himself that other femininity which is the source of his creative art: "Writing *Hamlet* had been an act of exorcism which enabled its author to give his hero's femininity—cause of his anxieties, self-reproaches and accusations—an acceptable form through the process of aesthetic creation. . . . By creating *Hamlet*, by giving it representation,

Shakespeare, unlike his hero, managed to lift the dissociation between his masculine and feminine elements and to reconcile himself with the femininity in himself."[46]

The reading comes from Winnicott's paper "Creativity and its Origins," which ends with a discussion of Shakespeare's play.[47] It is a fully psychological reading of the author, but its interest once again lies in the way that femininity moves and slips across the different levels of the text and the analytic process—the enigma and source of the analysis as of the play. More clearly and explicitly for Winnicott than for the other writers discussed so far, it is aesthetic space itself that is conceptualised in terms of sexual difference and the place of femininity within that. Creativity *per se* (the creativity in all of us—so this is not just the creativity of the artist) arises for Winnicott out of a femininity which is that primordial space of being which is created by the mother alone. It is a state of being which is not yet a relationship to the object because there is as yet no self, and it is, as Green defines it, *"au-dela de la représentation,"* the other side of representation, before the coming of the sign (this comes very close to French feminists such as Luce Irigaray on femininity and language).[48] But it is worth noting how the woman appears at the point either where language and aesthetic form start to crumble or else where they have not yet come to be. "Masculinity does, femininity is" is Winnicott's definition. It took a sceptical analyst in the audience when Winnicott first presented the paper to point to its fully literary and mythical origin; it transpires that Winnicott had been reading Robert Graves' "Man does, Woman is," but the observation from the floor was not included when Winnicott's famous paper was subsequently published in his book.[49]

Winnicott's definition, like Green's, and like that of Eliot before them, once again starts to look like a repetition (one might ask what other form of analysis can there be?) which reproduces or repeats the fundamental drama of *Hamlet*, cleaving the image of femininity in two, splitting it between a degradation and an idealisation which, far from keeping each other under control (as Green suggests), set each other off, being the reverse sides of one and the same mystification. And like Eliot, Green also gets caught in the other face of the idealisation, the inevitable accusation of Gertrude: "Is the marriage of Gertrude consequence or cause of the murder of Hamlet's father? I incline towards the cause (*Je pencherai pour la cause*)."[50] And at the end of his book he takes off on a truly wild speculation which makes Gertrude the stake in the battle between the old Fortinbras and the old Hamlet before the start of the play.

But the fact that *Hamlet* constantly unleashes an anxiety which returns to the question of femininity tells us above all something about the relationship of aesthetic form and sexual difference, about the fantasies they share— fantasies of coherence and identity in which the woman appears repeatedly as both wager and threat. "Fantasy in its very perversity" is the object of psychoanalytic interpretation,[51] but this does not mean that psychoanalysis might not also repeat within its own discourse the fantasies, or even perversions, which it uncovers in other forms of speech.

In Lacan's own essay on *Hamlet*, he puts himself resolutely on the side of the symbolic, reading the play in terms of its dearth of proper mourning and the impossibility for Hamlet of responding to the too literal summons of the dead father who would otherwise represent for the hero the point of entry into his appropriate symbolic place (the proximity between this essay and Eliot's "Tradition and the Individual Talent" is truly striking). Lacan therefore places the problem of the play in the symbolic, on the side of the father we might say; Green in the "before" of representation where the mother simply *is*. The difference between them is also another repetition, for it is the difference between the law of the father and the body of the mother, between symbol and affect (one of Green's best known books in France was an account of the concept of "affect" in Freud and a critique of Lacan's central premise that psychic life is regulated by the exigencies of representation and the linguistic sign).[52] But it is a difference with more far-reaching implications, which reconnect with the question of the fantasy of the woman and her guilt with which this essay began. For the concentration on the mother, on her adequacies and inadequacies, was the development in psychoanalytic theory itself which Lacan wanted to redress, precisely because, like *Hamlet*, it makes the mother cause of all good and evil, and her failings responsible for a malaise in all human subjects, that is in men *and* in women, which stems from their position in the symbolic order of culture itself. The problem of the regulation of subjectivity, of the Oedipal drama and the ordering of language and literary form—the necessity of that regulation and its constant difficulty or failing—is not, to put it at its most simple, the woman's fault.

Finally, therefore, a question remains, one which can be put to André Green when he says that Shakespeare saved his sanity by projecting this crazed repudiation of the feminine onto the stage, using his art to give it "an acceptable form."[53] To whom is this acceptable? Or rather what does it mean to us that one of the most elevated and generally esteemed works of our Western literary tradition should enact such a negative representation of femininity, or even such a violent repudiation of the femininity in man? I say "esteemed" because it is of course the case that Eliot's critique has inflated rather than reduced *Hamlet*'s status. In "Tradition and the Individual Talent," Eliot says the poet must "know" the mind of Europe;[54] *Hamlet* has more than once been taken as the model for that mind. Western tradition, the mind of Europe, Hamlet himself—each one the symbol of a cultural order in which the woman is given too much and too little of a place. But it is perhaps not finally inappropriate that those who celebrate or seek to uphold that order, with no regard to the image of the woman it encodes, constantly find themselves up against a problem which they call femininity—

a reminder of the precarious nature of the certainties on which that order rests.

Notes

1. T. S. Eliot, *"Hamlet"* (1919), in *Selected Prose of T. S. Eliot*, ed. Frank Kermode, London 1975. This essay was first presented as a talk at the Pembroke Center for Teaching and Research on Women, Brown University, 1984; printed in *Critical Quarterly*, Autumn 1986; a different version appeared as "Sexuality in the reading of Shakespeare: *Hamlet* and *Measure for Measure*" in *Alternative Shakespeares*, ed. John Drakakis, London and New York 1985.
2. *"Hamlet,"* p. 47.
3. Ernest Jones, *Hamlet and Oedipus* (1949), New York 1954, p. 88.
4. Freud, *The Interpretation of Dreams*, p. 264; p. 366.
5. *"Hamlet,"* p. 45.
6. Ibid., p. 48.
7. Ibid.
8. Ibid.
9. Ibid., pp. 48–49.
10. Ibid., p. 49.
11. Ibid.
12. William Shakespeare, *Hamlet*, 1,v, 47 and 1,v,80. All references to the Arden Shakespeare unless otherwise specified.
13. Freud "The Dissolution of the Oedipus Complex;" "Some Psychical Consequences of the Anatomical Distinction Between the Sexes."
14. Angelo Conti, cit. Freud, "Leonardo da Vinci and a Memory of his Childhood" (1910), SE 11, p. 109; PF 14, p. 201.
15. Muther and Walter Pater, cit. in ibid., pp. 108, 110; pp. 200, 202.
16. Ibid., p. 108; p. 200.
17. John Florio, tr., *The Essays of Michael, Lord of Montaigne* (1603), London and New York 1885, pp. 219–310.
18. Ibid., pp. 378–382.
19. *Hamlet*, III, ii, 225.
20. See, in particular, Roland Barthes, "La mythologie aujourd'hui," *Esprit* 1971 (tr. Stephen Heath, "Change the Object itself," *Image, Music, Text*, London 1977) and *S/Z*, Paris 1970 (tr. Richard Miller, *S/Z*, London and New York 1974); Julia Kristeva, *La révolution du langage poétique*. Paris 1974 (excerpts from Part I of this book have been translated in *The Kristeva Reader*, ed. Toril Moi, Oxford 1986).
21. T. S. Eliot, "The Use of Poetry and the Use of Criticism" (1933), in *Selected Prose*, pp. 92, 89.
22. T. S. Eliot, "Tradition and the Individual Talent" (1919), in ibid., p. 38.
23. Lacan, "Desire and the interpretation of desire in *Hamlet*" in Felman ed., *Literature and Psychoanalysis*.
24. Tourneur, cit. in "Tradition and the Individual Talent," p. 42.
25. Lacan, "Seminar of 21 January, 1975," p. 168.
26. *"Hamlet,"* p. 49.
27. Freud, "The Dissection of the Psychical Personality," *New Introductory Lectures* (1932), SE 22, p. 80; PF 2, p. 112.
28. Lacan, "The Agency of the Letter in the Unconscious," p. 171 (translation modified).

29. See, for example, Laurence Lerner ed., *Shakespeare's Tragedies. An Anthology of Modern Criticism*. Harmondsworth 1963.

30. *The Interpretation of Dreams*, pp. 264–266; pp. 364–368.

31. Ibid., p. 264; p. 366.

32. Freud, "Mourning and Melancholia" (1915), SE 14, pp. 246–247; PF 11, p. 255.

33. Freud, "Psychopathic Characters on the Stage" (1905 or 1906), SE 7.

34. Lessing, cit. in ibid., p. 30n.

35. Jones, p. 70.

36. "*Hamlet*," p. 43.

37. Freud, *The Origins of Psychoanalysis*, letters to Wilhelm Fliess, Drafts and Notes, 1887–1902, ed. Marie Bonaparte, Anna Freud and Ernst Kris, London 1954, p. 224; Jones, p. 59.

38. Freud, "Female Sexuality."

39. Jones, chapter 5, pp. 105–114.

40. *Hamlet*, III, ii, 384–387.

41. Ibid., III, iv, 20–21.

42. Jones, pp. 88, 106. The concept of femininity in relation to Hamlet's character appears again in Marilyn French, *Shakespeare's Division of Experience*, London 1982, p. 149 and in David Leverenz, "The Woman in *Hamlet*: an interpersonal view," in *Representing Shakespeare, New Psychoanalytic Essays*, eds. Murray M. Schwarz and Coppélia Kahn, Baltimore and London 1980.

43. *Hamlet*, V,i,281. The image of the female dove was objected to by Knight as a typographical error in the Variorum edition of the play, ed. H. H. Furness, 15th ed., Philadelphia 1877, Part 1, p. 410n.

44. Jones, pp. 25–26.

45. In *Hamlet et HAMLET*, Paris 1982, André Green continues the work he began in *Un oeil en trop*, Paris 1969, (tr. Alan Sheridan, *Tragic Effect: Oedipus Complex and Tragedy*, Cambridge 1979) on the psychoanalytic concept of representation in relation to dramatic form, and argues that, while the explicit themes of *Hamlet* (incest, parricide, madness) have the clearest links with the concerns of psychoanalysis, the play's central preoccupation with theatrical space and performance also falls within the psychoanalytic domain through the concept of psychic representation and fantasy. Green examines the way that theatricality, or show, and femininity are constantly assimilated throughout the play (I,ii, 76ff, II, ii, 581ff, III,i, 50ff). In the remarks which follow, I concentrate on the concept of femininity which he sets against this negative assimilation in his final section on Shakespeare's creative art (pp. 25–62).

46. *Hamlet et HAMLET*, p. 256.

47. D. W. Winnicott, "Split-off male and female elements found clinically in men and women" (1966), *Psychoanalytic Forum*, ed. J. Linden, New York 1972.

48. See especially Luce Irigaray, *Speculum of the Other Woman*, and Michèle Montrelay, "Inquiry into Femininity."

49. Winnicott first presented this paper to the British Psycho-Analytic Society in 1966 under the title "Split-off male and female elements found clinically in men and women: theoretical inferences" (see note 47 above). It was then included in *Playing and Reality*, London 1971. The discussion of sexual difference in the paper as a whole is far more complex and interesting than the final descent (ascent) into mythology which is addressed here, although it is this concept of femininity, with its associated emphasis on mothering, which has recently been imported directly into psychoanalytic readings of Shakespeare (see especially Leverenz and the whole anthology in which the article appears).

50. *Hamlet et HAMLET*, p. 61.

51. Lacan, "Desire and the interpretation of desire in *Hamlet*," p. 14.

52. Green, *Le discours vivant, le concept psychanalytique de l'affect*, Paris 1973.
53. *Hamlet et HAMLET*, p. 256.
54. "Tradition and the Individual Talent," p. 39.

Hamlet and the Security
of the South African State

MARTIN ORKIN

I

The true nature of the state power portrayed in *Hamlet* declares itself in Act IV when Claudius, knowing that Hamlet is aware of his secret murder of the previous ruler of Denmark, announces that he has decided to send the young prince to England. Then, left alone on stage, he confirms that he intends to eliminate his opponent:

> And England, if my love thou hold'st at aught—
> As my great power thereof may give thee sense,
> Since yet thy cicatrice looks raw and red
> After the Danish sword, and thy free awe
> Pays homage to us—thou mayst not coldly set
> Our sovereign process, which imports at full,
> By letters congruing to that effect,
> The present death of Hamlet. Do it, England;
> For like the hectic in my blood he rages,
> And thou must cure me.
>
> (IV.iii.70)[1]

Claudius's intention to have Hamlet murdered—although he does not succeed in the play—and the duplicity with which he proceeds confirm him as a practitioner of violence, recalcitrant and ruthless when it comes to the preservation of his own power. The text also identifies the interrelatedness of such a ruler and his society directly when Rosencrantz, unaware of the ironies of what he is saying, observes elsewhere in the play to the King himself:

> The cess of majesty
> Dies not alone, but like a gulf doth draw
> What's near it with it. Or it is a massy wheel

*From *Shakespeare Against Apartheid* (1987), 23–54. Reprinted by permission of Martin Orkin and Ad. Donker (Pty) Ltd.

> Fix'd on the summit of the highest mount,
> To whose huge spokes ten thousand lesser things
> Are mortis'd and adjoin'd, which when it falls,
> Each small annexment, petty consequence,
> Attends the boist'rous ruin. Never alone
> Did the King sigh, but with a general groan.
>
> (III.iii.23)

This recognition of the interrelatedness of ruler and ruled reflected a well-known Elizabeth notion. A similar identification which registers the magnitude of impact of the dominant class not only in its retaliation against those who threaten aspects of, or oppose, the existing social order but also in its domination of those who submit to it emerges from an account in present day South Africa of a recent tragic event, representative of many other similar cases. The 1981 Race Relations Survey contains the following report relating to the death of Steve Biko:

A committee appointed by the Medical Association of South Africa (MASA) to investigate the medical ethical issues arising from the conduct of two doctors involved in the treatment of Black Consciousness leader Mr Steve Biko shortly before his death, published its report in August. Mr Biko died in detention on September 14, [*sic*] 1978, after being detained on August 18, and widespread criticism of Drs Ivor Lang and Benjamin Tucker followed the inquest into his death. The committee, consisting of Mr I.A. Maisels, QC and Dr J.N. de Villiers, found that:
 —it was undesirable that the security police headquarters in Pretoria should have the power to decide whether or not a detainee should be removed to a non-prison hospital;
 —medical practitioners should directly ask detainees themselves what their health problems were;
 —the medical profession should not allow a doctor to absolve himself of responsibility if his medical advice was rejected by security police headquarters;
 —in the event of being overruled by the security police, the doctor should report this to the Minister of Police and try to obtain the support of his local medical association.
Because it did not have any subpoena powers, the committee did not attempt to establish whether the doctors involved were guilty of disgraceful or unprofessional conduct. However, the committee did find that a medical certificate issued by Dr Lang, presently the Port Elizabeth District Surgeon, concerning Mr Biko's condition shortly before his death was "unsatisfactory and incomplete, if not a deliberate suppression of the facts."
In the certificates he drew up, Dr Lang said he could not establish the existence of any abnormality affecting Mr Biko's health, even though Mr Biko was behaving strangely and would not speak. The committee also found that Colonel P.J. Goosen, the security policeman in charge of Mr Biko's detention, regarded himself and the security police as being above the law. Dr Lang and

Dr Tucker were forbidden by the Deputy Director of Health Services, Dr
D.J. Gillilland, from participating in the committee's proceedings. The committee was refused permission to inspect the Walmer Police Station cells
where Mr Biko was held.[2]

This report does not simply involve the mysterious death of a political
detainee whilst in the custody of state power. It mentions a number of
individuals directly involved in or subsequently drawn into the incidents
described. Moreover it raises disturbing questions of responsibility involving
support for, acquiescence in or opposition to the actions of the dominant
order. And it underlines the extent to which individuals within the state
are in one way or another implicated in political events of terrible magnitude.

The presentation of a ruler such as Claudius in *Hamlet* should not
surprise us. Relationships between the dominant and subordinate orders and
between different interest groups within the dominant order in the Elizabethan state were problematic. Apart from anything else, although Elizabeth
towards the end of her reign remained the accepted monarch, this was not
a simple matter. For one thing the ruling class continued to encounter,
coerce and persecute dissent or opposition; to do this it was never averse to
the use of methods of government we now term totalitarian: censorship,
spies, unlimited power of arrest, detention, torture and execution. B.L.
Joseph describes the treatment of Puritans, for instance, in the last two
decades of the sixteenth century:

> Between the end of 1587 and . . . 1589 Puritan opposition to the Crown
> showed itself in the Marprelate pamphlets, but eventually the anonymous
> authors had to stop to avoid discovery. One of the chief writers, John Penry,
> escaped to Scotland, but was lured back and executed in 1593. . . . The
> government treated extreme Puritans as if they were Anabaptists, dedicated
> in the imaginations of the ruling circles and of the populace to the subversion
> of church, state and public morals. In 1589 a group of Presbyterian leaders,
> including Cartwright, were summoned by the commission, refused to take
> the oath and were sent to prison until 1592, when they were released because
> no open infringement of the law could be proved against them. But the more
> extreme Puritans suffered much more. John Udall, suspected of being a
> Martinist, was sentenced to death but died in prison before execution in 1590.
> One, Hackett, accused of plotting against the Queen's life, was executed in
> 1592. In 1593, Barrow and Greenwood, the separatists, were executed for
> seditious speeches.[3]

Such governmental methods were obviously not applied only in the case of
Puritan opponents. And if Elizabeth herself was never perceived to be a
tyrant by the majority of her subjects, religious issues throughout Europe
made the problem of a tyrannous ruler highly topical. The English uncertainty about a future without Elizabeth only intensified the topicality of this

subject. Yet interestingly it was a modern East European critic, amongst others, who was to encourage attention to the importance of the political concerns in *Hamlet*. Praising a production of the play which he saw in Poland, Jan Kott wrote in 1965:

> The *Hamlet* produced in Cracow a few weeks after the XXth Congress of the Soviet Communist Party lasted exactly three hours. It was light and clear, tense and sharp, modern and consistent. . . . It was a political drama *par excellence*. "Something is rotten in the state of Denmark"—was the first chord of *Hamlet's* new meaning. And then the dead sound of the words "Denmark's a prison," three times repeated. Finally the magnificent churchyard scene, with the gravediggers' dialogue rid of metaphysics, brutal and unequivocal. Gravediggers know for whom they dig graves. "The gallows is built stronger than the church" they say.[4]

Within the Elizabethan dominant classes too, there was considerable conflict of interest. For many reasons, Elizabeth's position as monarch was far from absolute. She could maintain her position only through a combination of

> political adroitness, patronage and force—and all these, the latter especially, could be exercised only by and through the aristocracy itself. Elizabeth could oppose the Earl of Leicester if supported by Burghley, or vice versa, but she could not for long oppose them both. After the death of Leicester in 1589 the power struggle was not so symmetrical. The rise of the youthful, charismatic and militarily impressive Earl of Essex introduced a new element: he rivalled the Queen herself, as Burghley and Leicester never did. The more service, especially military, Essex performed, the more he established a rival power base, and Elizabeth did not care for it. . . . The Irish expedition was make or break for both; Essex would be away from court and vulnerable to schemes against him, but were he to return with spectacular success he would be unstoppable. In the event he was not successful, and thus found himself pushed into a corner where he could see no alternative but direct revolt.[5]

David Bevington makes a strong case against topical identification in the plays of historical personages and events.[6] But there is no need to suggest that Hamlet is Essex to recognise the significance, in 1601, of a play presenting conflict within the ruling class. Furthermore Essex's hopes for the succession centred round James of Scotland, but great uncertainty surrounded the prospect of such a ruler ascending the English throne. If Elizabeth herself was never perceived to be a tyrant by the majority of her subjects the religious question made tyrannous action in a ruler the issue for all dissenters in every country in Europe, including, as we have just seen, those dissenting in matters of religion in England. The fact that James was untested and also, in his religious sympathies, suspected, might in 1601 have encouraged the exploration on stage of issues involving opposition to a tyrannous ruler.

Such antagonisms, divisions and uncertainties within the dominant order, as well as religious and other forms of dissent, to say nothing of the economic and social flux of the period, were for obvious reasons resisted in the propositions of Elizabethan state ideology. These worked to legitimate the existing social order and to present it as unified, naturally hierarchical and ultimately sanctioned by God. Rosencrantz's flattery of Claudius in Act III, scene iii, lines 15–23 not only recognises the interrelatedness of ruler and ruled but also presupposes the principle of hierarchy. Claudius himself relies on this proposition when he is confronted by a potentially rebellious Laertes:

> Do not fear our person.
> There's such divinity doth hedge a king
> That treason can but peep to what it would,
> Acts little of his will.
>
> (IV.v.125)

Claudius knows that he can count on the ignorance of the court and its support of the official view of monarchy; indeed, the first word that is uttered when he is finally killed is "treason" (V. ii. 328). But the contradictions in such a claim set against the man who utters it are evident. That such an attitude to monarchy was deliberately promoted by the ruling class might never have seemed a more inviting inference, held in check, perhaps, by the rider that the speaker is a usurper and a tyrant. This strategy of legitimation, as we in the twentieth century may readily recognise, often goes hand in hand with the misrepresentation of opposition or dissent as treachery. The claim of "treason" appears to be purely a function of the partisan views of the accusers. In the famous treason trials of the late fifties in South Africa, many individuals were brought to a lengthy and disruptive trial, only to be acquitted at the end of it all. Soon after this, detention without trial was introduced, enabling the minister, at his own discretion, to decide who was a danger to the state. Nor did this present any problem of conscience for the man who introduced these laws. When asked, "Are you saying that if the government of the day identifies a man as a threat to the State then it is its duty to lock that man up, even without the benefit of a trial?" he was happy to reply, "If I see a man or a woman as a threat to the State and if there are valid reasons for not bringing that person to trial, then I must take them out of circulation one way or another. That is my responsibility as Minister of Justice."[7]

II

The moral issues precipitating Hamlet's dilemma about revenge have been described by many critics.[8] The Ghost asks of the prince adherence to the code of family honour; thrusting against this, Christianity forbids murderous action, warning that God alone is the only judge. Before the end of the play-scene, moreover, Hamlet's problems are exacerbated by the uncertain origins of the ghost.[9] To this we need to add the fact that legitimation (with the help of the doctrines of hierarchy and the Divine Right of Kings), of the ruling class's position within the social order also occurred in a context of lively debate about the right of resistance to rulers. Roland Mushat Frye, who is some respects follows a traditional approach to *Hamlet*, has demonstrated at length that in Shakespeare's day a variety of attitudes on the subject were current.[10]

The official Tudor view forbade resistance to the ruling monarch, however questionable his rights to the throne, a perspective, which Frye claims, many Englishmen shared. Thus *The Book of Homilies*, appointed to be read in churches, commands obedience and condemns wilful rebellion.[11] But Frye argues that even among those who held the official Anglican doctrine of nonresistance to the crown, cases of conscience involving obedience and disobedience were not always easy to resolve.[12] He cites as one example of this, Bishop Hooper's support of Princess Mary, despite the fact that, with the support of Archbishop Cranmer, the virtually unanimous support of the judges of the realm and the unanimous acceptance of the royal council, Lady Jane Grey had already been proclaimed the new monarch, on the death of King Edward VI. Shortly before his execution as a heretic in 1555, Hooper, defending himself, recalled his support of Mary despite the fact that the council had already "freely gone along" with Lady Jane Gray:

> As for my truth and loyalty to the Queen's highness, the time of her most dangerous estate can testify with me, that when there was both commandments and commissions out against her, whereby she was, to the sight of the world, the more in danger, and less like to come to the crown; yet, when she was at the worst. I rode myself from place to place . . . to win and stay the people for her party; and whereas another was proclaimed [Jane Grey], I preferred her [Mary] notwithstanding the proclamations.[13]

And during Edward VI's reign Hooper had preached a sermon which reasoned that the process of coronation itself did not make the king, but only the right of succession.[14]

Another view of resistance attempted to define it in the context of retribution or retaliation. Tyndale argued that Christ's absolute commandment against vengeance applied to the private citizen only, not to the ruler or magistrate, who is not disabled from administering justice, thus developing a long established distinction between private person and official ruler: "Christ here intended not to disannul the temporal regiment, and to forbid rulers to punish evil doers . . . [the ruler] not only mayest, but also must, and art bound under pain of damnation to execute [his] office.[15]

Frye recalls in this context the notorious murder of James I's father, Lord Darnley, who, after he was married to Mary Queen of Scots, was referred to as "King Henry." His murdered body was found in an orchard, and his most likely assassin, the Earl of Bothwell, married the widowed queen and moved toward the crown. James's paternal grandparents laid the challenge of revenge squarely upon their infant grandson in a memorial painting the details of which actively enjoined on him the task of exacting retribution.[16]

Finally, Frye points out that European Catholics and Protestants in certain instances argued that resistance was a necessity:

> The Protestant monarchomachs . . . [attempted] to establish inclusive justifi-cations for overthrowing a tyrant. Even though he might not be a usurper, a ruler who "violates the bonds and shatters the restraints by which human society has been maintained," as Althusius put it, would in this view leave magnates and princes of the blood no other recourse than to take up arms. In striking down a tyrant, according to Buchanan, they would be engaged in "the most just of wars." Not only did princes and magistrates have the right to destroy a tyrant, but they had the duty to do so, according to teachings shared by Calvinists and Jesuits. As the Huguenot du Plessis-Mornay put it, they are not only permitted "to use force against a tyrant . . . but obliged as part of the duty of their office, and they have no excuse if they should fail to act." In a somewhat more general context, Calvin wrote of inactive magis-trates that if they "put up their sword and hold their hands pure from blood while in the meantime desperate men do reign with murders and slaughters, then they shall make themselves guilty of most great wickedness.[17]

Ideological legitimation stressing hierarchy and order occurred, in the context then, of a range of views regarding resistance to a usurper or tyrant who was also the crowned monarch. Moreover attempts on the ruler's life happened in the sixteenth and seventeenth centuries both in England and in Europe; two of these, against Henry III of France in 1589 and against Henry IV of France in 1610, were successful.

If the issues in Hamlet's situation are, in these ways, highly suggestive, the fact that the prince spends the first four acts debating them places him in considerable political danger. From the official point of view to avenge his father means also to rid his class of its established ruler. Were his movement into a position of contestation with this ruler made public he would be classifiable as the equivalent of what some twentieth century govern-ments mean by an "enemy" of the state. His first concern therefore is to ensure absolute secrecy—he realises he will have to "go underground." After the departure of the Ghost he urges his friends to swear that they will never reveal what has transpired—in seventeenth-century Christian terms his insistence upon an oath has obvious importance. Furthermore, envisaging

what measures of self-protection will in future have to be adopted, he tries
to prevent discovery by a watchful and suspicious ruler:

> But come,
> Here, as before, never, so help you mercy,
> How strange or odd some'er I bear myself—
> As I perchance hereafter shall think meet
> To put an antic disposition on—
> That you, at such time seeing me, never shall,
> With arms encumber'd thus, or this head-shake,
> Or by pronouncing of some doubtful phrase,
> As "Well, we know," or "We could and if we would."
> Or "If we list to speak," or "There be and if they might."
> Or such ambiguous giving out, to note
> That you know aught of me—this do swear,
> So grace and mercy at your most need help you.
>
> (I.v.188)

Shakespeare took the device of madness from his sources, but used it in
more than one way. Hamlet's subsequent "antic disposition" may in part
be an emblem of torment, or a means of communicating his satire about
the tendency to compromise with and accept the prevailing behaviour of the
dominant order. It is as well a mask, adapted as a political tactic to hide
as best he can the truth of his antagonism towards the established ruler.
Furthermore, in a social order where behaviour is never free of the surveillance
of agents of the ruling class Hamlet understands that every move of his
associates will be scrutinised for their political implications. The young
prince of Denmark is well aware of the political difficulties arising from the
demand which the ghost of his father has made.

III

Hamlet's understanding of the political implications of what the Ghost has
asked him to do, and his awareness of the alertly watchful and potentially
treacherous nature of members of the court make him tread warily, but he
must do so also because Claudius is a formidable opponent.

If the King has the doctrine of the Divine Right of Kings and absolute
power as a means of self-protection the text also presents Claudius, as many
critics observe, as a ruler with a great deal of political acumen.[18] His opening
speech to the court, despite its ironies, displays great skill in reconciling
the old dispensation with the new and in using the possibility of foreign
threat as a rallying point; in the course of the play, he resolves the crisis
with Norway without war and without compromising the rights of Denmark.

Claudius's political adroitness is also revealed in his ability to exploit the unsuspecting loyalty of his subjects. In the name of legitimate rule he involves them in duplicity; in fact he uses those prepared to work for him to hunt out and if possible destroy any threat to the retention at all costs of his own power.

In the dealings which the King has with Polonius and with Rosencrantz and Guildenstern, the text demonstrates Claudius's skill in exploiting the loyalty of his subjects whilst at the same time illustrating the nature of those prepared to compromise their own actions in the names of their rulers. There is one moment when Polonius, compromising Ophelia too in the business of spying upon Hamlet, recognises the betrayal of honesty and straight dealing which his readiness to spy for the King involves.

> Read on this book,
> That show of such an exercise may colour
> Your loneliness.—We are oft to blame in this,
> 'Tis too much prov'd, that with devotion's visage
> The devil himself
>
> (III.i.49)

Polonius is never aware of the real motive for Claudius's concern about Hamlet, nor does he understand the nature of Claudius's kingship. In him *Hamlet* presents to us the man who operates within the dominant order unquestioningly. Our first real glimpse of the councillor occurs in Act I scene iii when we see him giving advice to both his children. The precepts he offers to Laertes were well known, often memorised by children who attended grammar schools.[19] Shakespeare's first audiences would recognise in Polonius's predilection for such commonplace expressions of worldly wisdom a mind that runs along conventional tracks, sticking only to what is practically useful in terms of worldly self-advancement. His advice to Laertes, as with his advice to Ophelia, focuses on social survival and success within the dominant order. Thus when he speaks to Ophelia about Hamlet he sees her relationship with the prince exclusively in expedient social terms. He may of course be entitled to point out to his daughter the "political realities" that might make any real relationship with Hamlet difficult, but he does not for a moment credit either Ophelia or Hamlet with any capacity for mutual love and respect.

He describes Hamlet's behaviour as that of a worldly exploiter, setting "springes to catch woodcocks" (I.iii.1 15), and he sees love in the language of financial broking or later, in the context of his son's activities in Paris, in the language of promiscuity.[20] This failure of Polonius's mind and imagination to go beyond the mundane, more cynical worldly view of experience is evident too when Hamlet discusses theatre. Polonius's consciousness appreciates neither the value of theatre nor the richness of Hamlet's response to it. It is precisely because he tends to the well worn path, eschewing or pouring scorn on the exceptional in human experience that Polonius becomes so useful a tool to a ruler like Claudius. His readiness to accept, compromise, follow the empirical and expedient path becomes a readiness to accept that the end justifies the means, as he himself admits, that to catch the "carp of truth" the "bait of falsehood" (II.i.63) is necessary: "thus do we of wisdom and of reach,/With windlasses and with assays of bias,/By indirections find directions out" (II.i.66). Not himself a man of conscious malice he is not a man of principle either, and in this he is exactly like Rosencrantz and Guildenstern. Young as they are they hold a similar pragmatic and expedient political attitude. They are ready to return to Denmark at the summons of the ruling power, and to spy upon the prince with whom they were school-fellows. If it is Rosencrantz who gives expression to the notion of the interre-latedness of ruler and ruled it is Guildenstern who asseverates: "Most holy and religious fear it is/To keep those many many bodies safe/That live and feed upon your Majesty" (III.iii.10). Their observations about the centrality of rulers in their society may be true enough, but in having the two young men speak in this way to a ruler who is, as the audience knows, totally self-interested, the play underlines the speciousness of such arguments when they are used to justify all kinds of behaviour. This implies a ready acceptance of whatever it is that the state demands of the individual; a multitude of sins may be committed in the name of the security of the state and the preservation of order. Moreover, the security of the rule of a man like Claudius, and the task of defending it, is invested, by Guildenstern's lan-guage—"holy and religious"—with the aura of religious sanctity. As we know such a habit is only too noticeable in the verbal practice of certain twentieth-century governments. An extreme example of this, but neverthe-less pertinent, may be found in the comment which Dr Verwoerd made in a broadcast to his people after recovering from the first assassination attempt upon his life: "I trust that I will be permitted to testify to my conviction that the protection of Divine Providence was accorded one with a purpose, a purpose which concerns South Africa too. May it be given me to fulfil that task faithfully."[21] His view was endorsed by his supporters, as evidenced by the progovernment newspaper *Die Burger* which wrote: "In this miraculous escape, all believers will see the hand of God himself."[22]

The play shows that the failure of men such as Polonius, Rosencrantz, and Guildenstern to think about their world and their actions, their ready conformity to the wishes of the powerful, and their willingness to compromise their own integrity implicate them by default in a process of domination from which they are not themselves safe. All three, in the course of pursuing their ruler's wishes, are destroyed.

Because of their innocence of the really destructive force to which they minister, these servants of the King are especially interesting to audiences in South Africa. In this context too, we may recall the case of Adolph

Eichmann. It may be true that his experience provides the best example of the consequences of action on behalf of a self-interested order ready to take any measures to deal with that which is different from it. Although Eichmann claimed diminished responsibility for his actions, he carried out the policies of his superior, and has been seen to be culpable for that. But it may be argued that, despite his legal argument at his trial, Eichmann was fairly well informed about the nature of his work and, more obviously, was an active and willing participant in the role assigned him. The position of Polonius, Rosencrantz, and Guildenstern is more interesting to some of us precisely because of their genuine innocence of the King's hidden evil. We may remember the innocence that some of us have claimed in southern Africa, not necessarily because we believe that we disagree with what is happening or because we do not know about what is happening, but because we claim we have no power over what is happening. True as this may be, the unquestioning acceptance which results is not very different from the unquestioning acceptance with which Polonius, Rosencrantz, and Guildenstern obey their king. It is true that the three have very little alternative. They can hardly disobey an absolute monarch when he asks them to serve him, just as in southern Africa it has been very difficult for some genuine dissenters to find a means of confronting the dominant order. But in *Hamlet* such qualifications in no way free the dramatic characters from the process of dishonesty and destruction that eventually includes them. Moreover we know that silence and compliance have their rewards, and the recipients, as Hamlet on one occasion has it, are to be compared to a "sponge" that "soaks up the King's countenance, his rewards, his authorities." (IV. ii. 15). Christopher Hope has written pointedly about the lives of similar beneficiaries in southern Africa:

> In the foyer a sugar baron's rifles rust,
> they've not been pulled through in years.
> In the bar, bottle tops shower the wooden slats
> which save the floor, hiding slopped beers
> and totwash sluiced away. Two cricket bats
> in the umbrella stand unpeel the smell of linseed.
> In the lavatory someone is hawking phlegm.
> A planter declares the Zulu a broken nation.
> Rumour has it there are some so rich
> they allow the air-conditioning to breathe for them
> and employ servants merely for observation.[23]

The Hungarian writer George Konrad, it is worth noting, has observed that "the true symbol of the totalitarian state is not the executioner but the exemplary bureaucrat who proves to be more loyal to the state than to his friend."[24]

IV

Roland Mushat Frye points out that various characteristics attached to Claudius suggest certain sixteenth- and seventeenth-century versions of the traits of the tyrannous ruler. Whitney's *A Choice of Emblems*, for instance, presents a visualisation of the tyrant and the sponge, pointing to the tyrant's exploitation of dependent flatterers.[25] Claudius's use of "Switzers" (IV. v. 97), he argues, recalls the fact that, as Erasmus noted, mercenaries were considered the necessary choice for any tyrant: "the tyrant guarantees safety for himself by means of foreign attendants and hired brigands. The king deems himself safe through his kindness to his subjects and their love for him in return."[26] Furthermore, Claudius's fear of Hamlet's popularity amongst the people may bespeak the tyrant's fear of being supplanted. His entire mode of ruling seems summarised, argues Frye, by "one of the most influential political theorists of the later sixteenth century," George Buchanan: "tyrants, cherishing the false appearance of a kingdom, when by fair means or foul they have once obtained it, cannot hold it without crime, nor can they give it up without destroying it."[27] In addition to this, *Hamlet* pays particular attention to the use of surveillance and spying as a means of control. Moreover, Shakespeare shows that a government such as that of Claudius, with its capacity to manipulate men such as Polonius, Rosencrantz, and Guildenstern, depends not only upon spying but in the end also upon violence to retain that control.

Acts II and III are partly structured around the activity of spying. The procurement of spies is demonstrated in Act II scenes i and ii, the business of spying in Act II scene ii and Act III scene ii, and the report back by informants to their "instigator" in Act II scene ii and Act III scene i.[28] Hamlet comments directly on the corrupting effect that such methods of government bespeak when he replies to Guildenstern's admission that he cannot play the recorder:

> Why, look you now, how unworthy a thing you make of me. You would play upon me, you would seem to know my stops, you would pluck out the heart of my mystery, you would sound me from my lowest note to the top of my compass; and there is much music, excellent voice, in this little organ, yet cannot you make it speak. 'Sblood, do you think I am easier to be played on than a pipe? Call me what instrument you will, though you fret me, you cannot play upon me.
>
> (III.ii.363)

The denial of human dignity and trust which the practice of spying entails, and the consequent reduction of the human subject to an object solely of exploitation, is something of which Hamlet is well aware—even as he asserts the precious integrity, "much music, excellent voice," of the inner life of the individual which ought not to be so recklessly or ruthlessly ignored.

Hamlet concentrates especially in Act IV upon the inherent violence in Denmark's ruler, which surfaces when his self-interest is threatened. At the same time the text demonstrates the increasing disruption that Claudius's method of government produces in the social order. Claudius's self-interest is apparent in Act IV scene i when he deliberately reinforces Gertrude's alarm over the death of Polonius, hoping perhaps to prepare her for the planned murder of her son (IV.i.12–15). Even as he speaks, it is clear that Claudius's mind runs continually to the political implication for himself of what has happened (IV.i.16–19, 38–45). When he reappears in the third scene, the text presents him as actively persuading the court of the "justice" of his action in removing the prince, heir to the throne (IV.iii.1–11). Then, when on his own, he reveals his real, murderous intentions.

The play also shows that for Claudius the consequences of his actions prove uncontrollable. Polonius, the first overt casualty of this spy-ridden order, is followed soon after by another casualty, his daughter. When Claudius encounters her madness directly on stage, he broods about the implications such developments have for his position. From what he says, it is clear that the effect of his rule and its consequences now impinge upon the consciousnesses of his subjects. The people, he muses, are "muddied,/Thick and unwholesome in their thoughts and whispers/For good Polonius' death" (IV.v.83). They are concerned too about the "hugger-mugger" (IV.v.84) behaviour of their rulers. The process of destabilisation continues when Laertes, returning from abroad and convinced Claudius is responsible for his father's death, makes his way to the King, while, in the words of the messenger:

> The rabble call him lord,
> And, as the world were now but to begin,
> Antiquity forgot, custom not known—
> The ratifiers and props of every word—
> They cry, "Choose we! Laertes shall be king."
> Caps, hands and tongues applaud it to the clouds,
> "Laertes shall be king, Laertes king."
> (IV.v.108)

The text confirms Claudius's great persuasive skills as politician and the immensely destructive effect of that skill and its self-interested centre upon those around him most explicitly in the encounter between the King and Laertes. Claudius deflects the reckless animus of the young Laertes, redirecting it against Hamlet. He encourages Laertes to an act of revenge which, as critics have noted, commits him to "damnable" action.[29] The play provides here a rich image of the poisonous ruler corrupting his subject, for Laertes, in agreeing to Claudius's plans, becomes himself an agent of the ruler's thrust to maintain his dominant position.

V

This depiction of the process of spying and violence in the play suggests, however, more than simply the tyranny of Claudius. The King refers to the "muddied" and "unwholesome" thoughts of the populace. The messenger emphasises that members of the subordinate order are voicing support for Laertes as antagonist to the King. Both speakers assume the ready agreement of the court as a whole to the undesirability of any involvement of the subordinate classes in events. These brief references offer a glimpse of the ruling class's attitude to those it dominates; but its own claims to legitimacy and natural rights of government, its claim moreover to class (and national) unity of purpose is brought into question in the events of *Hamlet*, not merely by those aspects of surveillance that the play foregrounds, but precisely by the fact that the text is directly concerned with antagonisms within the dominant order. Thus although it is true that almost no other attention is given to the subordinate classes in the play, the text conveys a distinct uneasiness about the real nature of the ruling class. This unease is clearly present in the central situation where two "mighty opposites" (V. ii. 62) confront one another. Claudius, king within the dominant order, is threatened or opposed by the second most powerful individual within that order— the prince who has right of inheritance to the throne. Later, for a short while, Claudius is challenged too by Laertes. Moreover, the fact that the young Hamlet is confronted by the ghost of his father who confirms that he was victim of his own brother's ambitions implies that such antagonisms within the ruling class are not particularly new. We may recall the brief observation made at the beginning of this chapter about the actuality of antagonisms within the Elizabethan dominant order. In this context Lawrence Stone emphasises that everything depended upon Elizabeth's particular skills: "At court and throughout the central administration, Elizabeth spent her reign walking the tightrope, balancing one noble faction off against another, and the Essex Revolt was the only occasion in forty years when the royal acrobat slipped. 'The principall note of her raigne,' remarked Naunton, 'will be that she ruled much by faction and parties, which she her selfe both made, upheld, and weakned as her owne great judgement advised.' "[30] Claudius's decisions at the beginning of the play might reflect just such a need to strengthen and weaken faction, as *his* judgement devises. Thus Laertes is favoured and promoted over the Hamlet whom he suspects and who must, accordingly, be restrained under the watchful eye of the Danish court. Rosencrantz and Guildenstern understand their brief from the King as one which requires discovery of the exact nature of Hamlet's ambitions. And certain of the points which Frye argues about Hamlet's recognition, just before he kills the King, that Denmark is an elective monarchy, suggest a sensitivity of the text to its own subversive implications about antagonism within the dominant order. These in turn are held in check to prevent the play and presumably the players from falling foul of the censor and the authorities.

Frye argues that "in England the hereditary principle was so strong that most Englishmen would have assumed Claudius to be a usurper until they were told in the last scene that the Danish monarchy was elective."[31] Hamlet says, at that point:

> Does it not, think thee, stand me now upon—
> He that hath kill'd my king and whor'd my mother,
> Popp'd in between th'election and my hopes,
> Thrown out his angle for my proper life
> And with such coz'nage—is't not perfect conscience
> To quit him with this arm? And is't not to be damn'd
> To let this canker of our nature come
> In further evil?
>
> (V.ii.70)

In this context, Frye recalls Bishop Thomas Bilson's work, *The True Difference between Christian Subjection and Unchristian Rebellion*, commissioned by Queen Elizabeth and issued three times between 1585 and 1595. It suggests that although a hereditary monarch who becomes a tyrant may be opposed, he may not be deposed, whereas elective monarchs who are tyrannous may be removed.[32] Frye suggests that, although Shakespeare's company had been exonerated over their performance of *Richard II* just before the Essex uprising, nevertheless:

> to present the killer of a king as a sympathetic character could entail misunder-standing. . . . Shakespeare introduced the fact that Denmark was an elective monarchy just before . . . and . . . shortly after the king's death. [Thus] Shakespeare . . . presented Hamlet in a more favourable way while protecting himself and his company from the danger of dramatising a scene in which a sympathetic and attractive hero kills a crowned king. Should the authorities object, the Lord Chamberlain's men could point to the official Elizabethan doctrine as presented by Bishop Bilson.[33]

This resonance of unease in the text about possible disruption within the dominant order is most evident in the presentation of Hamlet himself. The prince is portrayed as a young man adhering to traditional values of human justice and right action. In one sense this depiction of Hamlet, located in a world he considers unjust at its core, has obvious point for many twentieth-century audiences—Hamlet's "integrity" is reflected in his manifest concern with the problem of action in the play. The profundity of this concern to understand himself and his world, to act with honour against the trend of ruthless violence in the social order, emerges from everything he says, and especially from his soliloquies: the fluctuating emotions, contradictions, and the violent as well as the rational thoughts to which he is given, bear witness to the intensity of his endeavour.[34] This "integrity" in Hamlet is established especially in language that draws on Christian discourse, evident in the moral undercurrents in his satirical awareness, in his ability to speak not only for the general but for the particular and personal in human experience, and in his capacity for and concern with human feeling—all of which contrast powerfully with the ruler of Denmark and those who work for him. At the same time the play seems to bring into question the effectiveness of these traditional values within the realities of the social order, itself undergoing increasing change—dramatically hinted at by the sudden transference of power from the old to the new monarch at the beginning of the play. Thus Hamlet, who believes in those doctrines and especially their underlying Christian thrust which the ruler himself uses to legitimate his position of domination within the social order, is brought by these very same doctrines into a position of antagonism towards, and confrontation with, his monarch.

VI

Although it expresses unease, the play does not hint at an effective means of eradicating those problems it identifies. Indeed, *Hamlet* offers, in the death of Claudius, only an apparent resolution to those elements in the play which register disturbing aspects in the operation of state power, and those elements which identify the existence of tensions and antagonisms within the dominant order. For one thing, despite all that Hamlet's own language about action suggests in terms of traditional Christian discourse—and despite the final death of Claudius—those less deliberately exploitative than the King, and especially Hamlet himself, are dead too. Moreover the Fortinbras who replaces him, is, in certain senses at least, as committed to force as his predecessor. And a sense of the indifference of agents of state power is generated in one of Hamlet's soliloquies by the lines which recognise the Norwegian prince's callously exploitative attitude to the subordinate orders. In battle he is happy to countenance:

> The imminent death of twenty thousand men
> That, for a fantasy and trick of fame,
> Go to their graves like beds, fight for a plot
> Whereon the numbers cannot try the cause,
> Which is not tomb enough and continent
> To hide the slain.
>
> (IV.iv.66)

Hamlet appears to respond to these various problems only by stressing enigma and mystery. These are the conditions within which the tragic loss of those who believe in traditional notions of goodness and justice occurs. The indeterminacy and mystery of these deaths, particularly, contribute to the play's assertion of tragedy. We should further note that in scrutinising human action in this way, *Hamlet* places it, intermittently, in the context of Christian discourse and in the context of the uncontrollable factor of accident in a fallen world.

Hamlet's accidental slaying of Polonius is only one of a string of uncontrollable incidents or indications in the text that appear to assert the significance of accident as a factor affecting the realisation of human intentions in action. Claudius's plan to murder Hamlet is partly undone by the accident of Hamlet's discovery of the letter on board the ship carrying him to England, as well as the chance attack by pirates. The emphasis upon death in the first scene of Act V not only acknowledges its finality but, in the detailed texture of the language, underlines the limits of human endeavour—"Imperious Caesar, dead and turn'd to clay,/Might stop a hole to keep the wind away" (V.i.207). And in the final scene, the text presents at last that action about which the whole play has been concerned. It offers, in the duel itself, a powerful dramatic enactment of accident and of the proposition that man cannot in action anticipate or control the outcome of his intentions. Claudius, in the presence of a compliant Gertrude, a Laertes who has become his tool, and a court largely supportive of his rule and unaware of its evil, attempts to implement the murder of Hamlet, but the unpredictability of experience appears to dominate. Hamlet dies but Gertrude, Laertes, and the King himself meet their deaths as well. Or, to put this more appropriately, although the poisonous ruler is finally killed, many others die in the process. Hamlet may in the penultimate scenes of the play recognise a "divinity that shapes our ends" (V.ii.10) but this must be set against the "quarry" that "cries on havoc" (V.ii.369) concluding it. The sweet prince whose heroic consciousness, more than any other in the play, has sought goodness and justice dies even as he frees the kingdom of its unjust ruler. The sense of loss at this—"Now cracks a noble heart" (V.ii.364)—at the text's end, includes the acknowledgement of mystery of a kind too profound, apparently, to be reducible to any one system or explanation—as Hamlet, dying, has it, "the rest is silence" (V.ii.363).

VII

Traditional Anglo-American approaches to the Shakespeare text were never so narrow as the South African version of them. Thus location of that language in *Hamlet* relating to accident and mystery, ultimately perceived in terms of traditional Christian discourse, is rare in South African criticism. This narrowness is in part a consequence of the determination to react to tragedy primarily in terms of character; it is also, "Shakespeare Depoliticised," the result of the South African habit of treating the Shakespeare text as a particular kind of "moral gymnasium." This approach endeavours continually to turn the Shakespeare text to use in order to detect and inculcate certain appropriate attitudes, the possession of which constitutes the right kind of "self-improvement." Thus, another South African critic writing on *Hamlet* observes in the course of his discussion: "we read literature, presumably, at least in part, to grow: by entering into a vision of life that is not our own we extend our awareness and our capacity, and a commitment to a particular approach should not be such as to preclude the possibility of literature changing us.[35] His version of what such self-improvement and growth might entail, however, is not as liberating as his avoidance of "recourse to the logic of the whole [as] the authoritative determinant of interpretation" (p. 87) might promise. Indeed his procedure suggests little more than a skilful reenactment (and by implication advocation) of a version of New Criticism. He poses as alternative interpretations of Act V scene i lines 239–256 either "the prince's striving for and ultimately finding an adequate role in terms of which to perform a called-for action" or what he calls "the sickness at the heart of life" (p. 87) and eventually concludes:

> If one had hitherto been preoccupied with the sense of Hamlet's searching for an appropriate role or mode of action, one would have to ensure . . . that that hypothesis was broad enough to include the tragic necessity of surrendering other more devoutly-to-be-wished roles . . . which would not have left a man with a sense of "how ill all's here about my heart." If, to take another example, one had been preoccupied with the sense of Hamlet's coming to terms with the sickness at heart of life, one would have to ensure that the hypothesis was broad enough to include the dignity of finding stature and purpose in the very heart of loss (pp. 89–90).

Although the discussion appears to reject a unitary response to the play, the alternative possibilities it postulates prove to be different versions of the same emphasis—both foreground aspects of human nature and action as these may be deduced from the character Hamlet alone.

But the concern with accident in the language and situation of *Hamlet* develops in a way that moves beyond such narrowness of focus. Rather than leading to perceptions enabling a certain kind of attitude to or conclusions about human nature and action that will allow us to "grow," the text, in its scrutiny of action, encounters complexity, difficulty, and problem. And even within traditional frameworks of response, set against such narrowness in the South African traditional approach, we may discern a different version of the tragedy. In his book *The Unnatural Scene,* Michael Long identifies some notions of Schopenhauer, although he applies these in ways different from that aspect I consider here.[36] Long connects the concerns of Shakespeare's tragedies with Schopenhauer's observation that tragedy as well as comedy results from "the consciousness's inability to control or even understand the world which it so limitedly captures in its concepts . . . here . . . is an idea of tragedy which sees it as central to the dynamics of mental and psychological life . . . comprehensible to a mind . . . fully apprised of a high energy world of on-going destructive power before which, at any moment, the mind may be rendered powerless" (p. 16). Such a force, continues Long, for Schopenhauer, "made a destructive mockery of the human world which offered to understand or control it" (pp. 16–17). The "tragic response" is proposed as one means of dealing with this view of experience. Long quotes from Schopenhauer on the impact of this tragic realisation: "we feel ourselves urged to turn our will away from life, to give up willing and loving life . . . we become convinced more clearly than ever that life is a bad dream from which we have to awake . . . the dawning of the knowledge that the world and life can afford no true satisfaction, and are therefore not worth our attachment to them. It is this that the tragic spirit consists [sic]; accordingly it leads to resignation" (p. 17). Schopenhauer's concern with the world as a refraction of the perceiving mind and his concept of the world as *die Wille* are not ideas which Shakespeare in any way shared.[37] However, the sense of the "consciousness's inability to control or even understand the world which it so limitedly captures in its concepts" does, as Long seems to suggest, relate to a similar recognition (naturally, amongst several others) in Shakespeare's play. The text's sense of the mysterious aspects of human experience, moreover, is expressed not merely through the acknowledgement of the fact of accident. The concern with human, individual endeavour, which we have no difficulty in identifying, is often balanced in the language of the text against more overt recognition of the limited effectiveness of human action when set in a larger, apparently uncontrollable universe. Again the diverse nature of these attempts to describe or define action and its outcome in the play intensifies the sense of problem and mystery, which the text appears to assert as inevitably attendant upon any attempt to fathom the secret of human action.

Several of the lines given to the Player King, for example, argue the limitation of human action directly. The Player King tells the Queen:

> I do believe you think what now you speak;
> But what we do determine, oft we break.
> Purpose is but the slave to memory,
> Of violent birth but poor validity,
> Which now, the fruit unripe, sticks on the tree,
> But fall unshaken when they mellow be.

> Most necessary 'tis that we forget
> To pay ourselves what to ourselves is debt.
> What to ourselves in passion we propose,
> The passion ending, doth the purpose lose.
>
> . . . .
>
> Our wills and fates do so contrary run
> That our devices still are overthrown:
> Our thoughts are ours, their ends none of our own.
>
> (III.ii.208)

Furthermore, Hamlet's consideration of action from a variety of perspectives contributes to this effect of mystery. His attempts may, admittedly, be read as his scrutiny of the possible ways of resisting or adopting an oppositional stance against the dominant power.[38] At the same time, in the multiplicity of attempts he makes, the difficulty of defining precisely the nature of human action is foregrounded. When, for instance, he requests the Second Player to speak about the revenge of Phyrrus, it is clear the prince is considering action in the aspect of unrestrained violence, the end result of the revenge impulse (II.ii.442–514). Then again, in conversation with Horatio, Hamlet contemplates commitment to the opposite kind of action, suggested by the capacity of his friend who, "in suff'ring all . . . suffers nothing" (III.ii.66). Hamlet says admiringly of this:

> Give me that man
> That is not passion's slave, and I will wear him
> In my heart's core, ay, in my heart of heart,
> As I do thee.
>
> (III.ii.74)

At times, Hamlet appears motivated by the seventeenth-century sense of original sin, when, with bitterness, he refers to man's incapacity to act in love with any reliability—"for virtue cannot so innoculate our old stock but we shall relish of it" (III.i.118). But, by contrast again, in his discussion with Horatio about Danish drinking customs he laments the extent to which man's capacity for noble action can be underrated because of his imperfections. Man's natural limitations, suggests Hamlet, may be used to cloud the "pith and marrow" (I.iv.22) of what he does achieve.

In the detail of the language of other speakers too the imperfection of action in this world is delineated. The appearance of the Ghost in Act I scene i, starting like a "guilty thing" (I.i.153) prompts Marcellus to glimpse, by contrast with the world of the play, for a moment, a world at Christmas, closest to one without blemish when

> no spirit dare stir abroad,
> The nights are wholesome, then no planets strike,

> No fairy takes, nor witch hath power to charm,
> So hallow'd and so gracious is that time.
>
> (I.i.169)

Laertes speaks to his sister of the world's imperfections in general terms, significantly with natural imagery, when he observes:

> Virtue itself scapes not calumnious strokes.
> The canker galls the infants of the spring
> Too oft before their buttons be disclos'd,
> And in the morn and liquid dew of youth
> Contagious blastments are most imminent.
>
> (I.iii.42)

and his father, in seeking to know the imperfections of his son's behaviour in Paris, instructs Reynaldo to:

> breathe his faults so quaintly
> That they may seem the taints of liberty,
> The flash and outbreak of a fiery mind,
> A savageness in unreclaimed blood,
> Of general assault.
>
> (II.i.35)

The richness of the differing perspectives on human action and the varied attempts to account for it in *Hamlet*, then, also posit a mystery surrounding human endeavour as men struggle to comprehend and make sense of action in this world. Indeed, the darkness of the first scene together with the appearance of the Ghost, may be taken as two key images which direct the audience at once to the fact of the unknown and the mysterious in experience. It juxtaposes this recognition against an instinctive human need for knowledge and order, suggested in the eagerness of the dramatic characters to identify each other, their references to the order and rhythm of nature, the urgency with which they question the Ghost, the relief, touched with religious reverence, with which they greet the dawn.

VIII

This resort to mystery as a means of accounting for tragic loss within an established but conflict-ridden social order seems present too in certain modern South African narratives. Sipho Sepamla's novel *The Root Is One*,[39] for instance, tells the story of two young friends who at the commencement of the book are both concerned to struggle against a world which they consider to be unjust and oppressive. But in the course of events their intentions go awry. They become involved in a strike and attempt to form a resistance movement against the authority's plan to institute removals from their location and to demolish the dwellings which remain. By the end of the story there have been riots in protest at the removals, there has been bloodshed, and the bulldozers have moved in. One of the young men has been arrested and the other kills himself for having informed upon his friend to the ruling powers. Sepamla at the conclusion of the novel describes the reaction of the people of the location to these events:

> The crowd waited: this crowd of women and children and a sprinkling of men. To kill the time, they began to chatter, to ask questions, to discover the truth they lived but were unable to articulate. They were turning themselves inside out; they were rubbing their sore spots in an effort to reduce to nothingness this huge hurt which followed their lives like the shadows tailing daylight. The dead were praised, the living were damned. In all they said, they hoped to reveal before their own eyes the meaning of their lives. But the mystery of it remained, only its particles were revealed in such events as the removals and the suicide of men.
>
> Night was creeping in, confirming a dying—of men as well, and of the place. A sadness pervaded all moments. The sight of ruins had become common by nightfall—these ruins which some said were the extension of human decay.
>
> Some things were said in whispers, others loudly. And in the process of it all someone summed up the tragedy of the moment: Spiwo was in jail awaiting serious charges; Juda was dead after saying he had let down his friend. Then it was asked: how was survival? Each of these young men had sought survival. Each had been harassed by the moment and, in a desperate bid for survival, had dug his own grave. How ought people to behave in order to attain certain survival? The question remained unanswered, for the "black maria" was heard screaming from afar. Now the tension, which had held the people gathered in knots near the house of Baloyi, heightened. There had been moments when it had risen with the expectation of some development and dropped with the sighs of disappointment.
>
> "Listen," some man said in one group, "I am not God to sit in judgement over the deeds of others. I've grown grey watching and seeing many people do wrong, and yet I've always come forward to bury these same people. It is our duty as human beings to do just that in the end. For, when an enemy has died, what harm can he do in the coffin? Tell me that, what harm, m'm?"
>
> "He speaks the truth" added another.
>
> Encouraged, the first speaker said: "You see, I'm concerned with the pain which the living must endure, which must be carried in the hearts of the living for days on end. The pain of suffering is like mist: it settles on every home" (pp. 129–30).

In Sepamla's description, a similar concern for the personal as well as the more general sense of experience, as may be found in *Hamlet*, is evident.

The crowd waits, aware in its own personal way of the need to "ask questions, to discover the truth they lived but were unable to articulate," experiencing as always the "sore spots" and "huge hurt" of the life it is forced to live. Hamlet we should remember, with a murdered father and a political opponent who has "Popp'd in between th'election and my hopes" (V. ii. 65), speaks with precision about:

> Th'oppressor's wrong, the proud man's contumely,
> The pangs of dispriz'd love, the law's delay,
> The insolence of office, and the spurns
> That patient merit of th'unworthy takes,
>
> (III.i.74)[40]

Sepamla's text, too, speaks of this—as the "pain the living must endure" that "settles on every home." It identifies an impenetrable mystery in experience—"only its particles were revealed in such events as the removals and the suicide of men." And in the context, both of the problematic nature of human action and determined self-interest, Sepamla's text, like Shakespeare's, salutes the heroism of those prepared to "take arms against a sea of troubles" (III.i.59) and to search for just and good action.

IX

Different levels of signification, then, more numerous than many traditional South African critics have been ready to admit, operate in *Hamlet*. The language that directs us towards values evident in Christian discourse occurs in a context that suggests the absence of these values, and also, disturbingly, their possible impotence. Hamlet's convictions, as we have seen, bring him into confrontation with the principal ruler of that order of which he is himself part, an order that appears in practice to operate in terms only of the retention and assertion of dominance, and moreover one that seems in practice to be riven by internal rivalry and conflict. Nevertheless, although the principal agent of that order is removed by the play's conclusion, no essential change appears to have occurred. The play's unease about the dominant order endures, despite its apparent attempt to contain this unease by the death of Claudius and by reference to accident and mystery in a fallen world.

We might note in this context that the emergence of the present South African social formation was not the instant product of the Afrikaner Nationalist accession to power in 1948. The increase in control by mining and agricultural capital in the early years of this century generated a process that would go on to include the Land Act of 1913, a whole web of detailed legislation such as that contained in the Apprenticeship Act and the Industrial Conciliation Act, the Native Administration Act of 1927 and the 1936 Herzog Bills. All these contributed to a system of relationships that was, again, intensified further after 1948. Similarly, despite the claims made about the potential of individual rulers to change the South African social formation at the time of their accession to powerful positions within the state apparatus, no essential change has in fact occurred—only the continuation of a particular process. This applies, indeed, to important aspects of the roles played by General Herzog and Jan Christiaan Smuts when they held positions of power as much as it does, more recently, to Prime Minister John Vorster and President P.W. Botha.[41]

We may note briefly too that *Hamlet* becomes particularly interesting to us precisely because of the uncertainty it suggests about that world which has produced it. If we detect the hint of a recognition in *Hamlet* that the dominant classes perpetuate their own position despite changes in individual rulers, and we are aware of the unease about this with which the play ends, this is because such unease points to the conflicting and contradictory forces in the late Elizabethan world as it experienced movement from a feudal society to the beginnings of a capitalist society. And when we seek direct evidence of these forces we encounter descriptions of a social order, which, inevitably, includes, as well as other factors we have already registered, different class-political divisions. One version of these may be cited here:

> The Catholic position was associated with attempts to support a traditional conception of social hierarchy with the monarch representing the epitome of the social power of the aristocracy, in a system based on qualification by blood, stable wealth in land, and rule by personal domination; while the Protestant position was associated with a "levelling" tendency in which the sovereign was coming to represent a rational conception of necessary social order, in a system based on qualification by moral legitimacy, expanding wealth in money, and rule by popular recognition or even consent. King James's watchword, "No bishops no king" succinctly captured the fear of radical Protestantism, and the intensifying ideological-political bind in which the English monarchy found itself as a result of Henry VIII's actions in tying the fate of the institution to the developing Reformation—actions which, ironically, were meant to, and in the short run did, strengthen the power of the monarchy itself against the aristocracy and the Church.[42]

Such observations may point the way forward for us as we attempt, increasingly, to study the Shakespeare text as a signifying practice that is, most importantly, located in the material struggles taking place within the social order from which it comes.[43]

I would argue therefore that the young men and women in Soweto and elsewhere in South Africa, who know they are living in a system which is less than just, despite its official claims, will recognise many aspects of the situation depicted in *Hamlet*. They will respond to the unease we may detect in the text about the working of state power within the social order, an unease which the resort in the language to accident, mystery, and an imperfect world does not dissipate. Furthermore, if they themselves care about justice they will understand Hamlet's anger at a society that compromises with injustice and they will share his agony at the problem of finding the proper action that will at last realise that justice. They will also know, distressingly, that the "pain of living" is often the pain of a Horatio, who at the end of the play understands, as does Sipho Sepamla, that it is more and more frequently the dead who must be praised. They, most of all, have cared and because they have challenged injustice they have died. Not all such men and women may be interested in Shakespeare, but the experience of *Hamlet* is in their blood.

Notes

1.   All references to *Hamlet* in this chapter are taken from *Hamlet* ed. Harold Jenkins (London: Methuen, 1982). References are to act, scene, and line. Where more than one line is quoted, the number for the "last" quoted line is given.

2.   Muriel Horrell ed., *Survey of Race Relations in South Africa 1981*, (Johannesburg: South African Institute of Race Relations, 1982) pp. 85–6.

3.   B.L. Joseph, *Shakespeare's Eden* (London: Blandford Press, 1971), p. 197. The short essay by J. Hurstfield, "The Historical and Social Background" in *A New Companion to Shakespeare Studies*, ed. K. Muir and S. Schoenbaum (Cambridge: Cambridge University Press, 1971), still provides a useful summary of some main features of the period.

4.   Jan Kott, *Shakespeare Our Contemporary* (London: Methuen, 1975), p. 48.

5.   Dollimore and Sinfield, "History and Ideology: the instance of *Henry V*," p. 219

6.   Bevington, *Tudor Drama and Politics*, p. 25.

7.   Quoted in John D'Oliveira, *Vorster the Man* (Johannesburg: Ernest Stanton Publisher, 1977), pp. 157–8.

8.   A brief and clear statement of the problem posed by the revenge ethic is to be found in Winifred Nowottny's article on "Shakespeare's Tragedies" in *Shakespeare's World*, ed. J. Hurstfield and J. Sutherland (London: Edward Arnold, 1964), pp. 48–78.

9.   Hamlet himself comments on this, for instance in II.ii.594–99.

10.   Roland Mushat Frye, *The Renaissance Hamlet: Issues and Responses in 1600* (Princeton: Princeton University Press, 1984). I am totally indebted in the discussion which follows to Frye, especially, for the immediate discussion, to chapters 2 and 3, pp. 11–75.

11.   Frye, *The Renaissance Hamlet*, p. 12.

12.   Frye, *The Renaissance Hamlet*, p. 50.

13.   Cited in Frye, *The Renaissance Hamlet*, p. 48.

14.   Frye, *The Renaissance Hamlet*, pp. 49–50. Frye quotes from this sermon:

As the king's majesty may not attribute his right unto the crown, but unto God and unto his father, who hath not only given him grace to be born into the world, but also to govern as a king in the world; whose right and title the crown confirmeth, and sheweth the same unto all the world. Whereas this right by God and natural succession precedeth, not the coronation, the ceremony availeth nothing. A traitor may receive the crown, and yet [be a] true king nothing the rather. So an hypocrite and [an] infidel may receive the external sign of baptism and yet no christian man nothing the rather.

15. Cited in Frye, *The Renaissance Hamlet*, p. 30. Aquinas wrote: "He who takes vengeance on the wicked in keeping with his rank and position does not usurp what belongs to God, but makes use of the power granted him by God" (p. 31).

16. Frye, *The Renaissance Hamlet*, pp. 31–7.

17. Frye, *The Renaissance Hamlet*, p. 264.

18. Nigel Alexander, *Poison, Play and Duel* (London: Routledge and Kegan Paul, 1971), pp. 51–2, writes: "in his opening speech Claudius displays a firm and impressive grasp of . . . rhetoric. In a series of striking phrases, he combines ideas of opposite meaning in an attempt to persuade his audience that, having weighed the arguments, he is pursuing a reasonable course of action. The rhetoric thus conceals the fact that his forceful and aggressive behaviour is based only upon one of the opposed views which he mentions."

19. There are numerous articles dealing with Polonius's use of proverbs. For opposing views see K. Lever, "Proverbs and *Sententiae* in the plays of Shakespeare," *The Shakespeare Association Bulletin* 13, 1938, pp. 173–83, 224–39 and Doris V. Falk, "Proverbs and the Polonius Destiny," *Shakespeare Quarterly* 18, 1967, pp. 23–36. See also, Joan Bennet, "Characterization in Polonius's advice to Laertes," *Shakespeare Quarterly* 4, 1953, pp. 3–9. The best comments on the subject are made by Leonard F. Dean, "Shakespeare's treatment of conventional ideas," *The Sewanee Review* 52, 1944, pp. 414–23.

20. Molly Mahood, *Shakespeare's Wordplay* (London: Methuen, 1968), has valuable observations about the language in this scene, pp. 119–28.

21. Broadcast to the South African people on 20 May 1960; quoted in Henry Kenney, *Architect of Apartheid* (Johannesburg: Jonathan Ball, 1980), p. 195.

22. Kennedy, *Architect of Apartheid*, p. 195.

23. Christopher Hope, *In the Country of the Black Pig* (Johannesburg: Ravan, 1981). From the poem "The Country Club," p. 3.

24. George Konrad, "The Long Work of Liberty," *The New York Review of Books*, 26 January 1978, p. 28.

25. Frye, *The Renaissance Hamlet*, p. 39.

26. Cited in Frye, *The Renaissance Hamlet*, p. 38.

27. Cited in Frye, *The Renaissance Hamlet*, p. 38.

28. Ophelia, who does not realise the implications of her behaviour, dutifully reports to her father about Hamlet, in effect, because of the use Polonius makes of what he is told, informing on the prince to the ruler.

29. Nigel Alexander, *Poison, Play and Duel*, writes: "Laertes . . . is prepared to violate sanctuary. . . . The contrast between this desire to prove oneself in 'deed' and Hamlet, who has spent the play, prayer, and closet scenes anatomizing his role as his father's son in words is deliberate and striking. . . . [The King's] appeal to conscience persuades Laertes to take part in an act which, if he had time to think and reflect, he would find against his conscience" (p. 191).

30. Lawrence Stone, *The Crisis of the Aristocracy 1558–1641* (Oxford: Oxford University Press, 1965) pp. 256–7.

31. Frye, *The Renaissance Hamlet*, p. 263.

32. Frye, *The Renaissance Hamlet*, p. 265.

33. Frye, *The Renaissance Hamlet*, p. 266, 265.

34. The point is often made about Hamlet that he refuses to choose the way of compromise, the way of the rash force of a Fortinbras, or the way of the thoughtless passion of a Laertes who ends by serving the designs of a wicked ruler.

35. B. D. Cheadle, "Hamlet at the Graveside: A Leap into Hermeneutics," *English Studies in Africa*, 22:2, 1979, pp. 83–90, p. 87.

36. Michael Long, *The Unnatural Scene* (London: Methuen, 1976).

37. In referring to these terms I rely upon the use made of them by Long in his book.

38. Frye, *The Renaissance Hamlet*, pp. 188–93, for example, argues that Hamlet's question "whether 'tis nobler in the mind to suffer/The slings and arrows of outrageous fortune/Or to take arms against a sea of troubles/And by opposing end them" (III.i.57–60) "could not have been raised in 1600 as though in some hermetically sealed philosophical isolation, because it was fundamental and divisive throughout Western Europe in the latter third of the sixteenth century . . . prominent Jesuits recommended violent action when necessary to achieve virtuous ends, and prominent Calvinists in France, Holland and Scotland, not only advocated but actually did take arms against a 'sea of troubles,' and by opposing did in some sense end them, overturning regimes and replacing monarchs by their own combination of activism and faith." He draws interesting parallels to Donne's "Satyre III" lines 77–84 and to Queen Elizabeth I "as she sat in gloomy isolation and wavered back and forth over what to do about Mary Stuart. . . . It might be necessary and one's moral duty to strike down a crowned sovereign, but it was not morally easy, even when one already wore a crown oneself."

39. Sipho Sepamla, *The Root is One* (London: Rex Collings, 1979).

40. See Harold Jenkins, ed., *Hamlet*, note on I. ii. 1, pp. 433–4.

41. See for instance H. J. Simons and R. E. Simons, *Class and Colour in South Africa 1850–1950* (Harmondsworth: Penguin, 1969).

42. Note to James H. Kavanagh, "Shakespeare in Ideology" in Drakakis, *Alternative Shakespeares*, pp. 144–65, p. 233.

43. For further clarification see Catherine Belsey, *Critical Practice* (London: Methuen, 1980) and Catherine Belsey, *The Subject of Tragedy* (London: Methuen, 1985).

"His semblable is his mirror": *Hamlet* and the Imitation of Revenge

David Scott Kastan

Through the streets of Jerusalem at the present day crawls one who is mad and carries a wooden cross on his shoulders. He is a symbol of the lives that are marred by imitation.

—Oscar Wilde

What replication should be made by the son of a king?

—*Hamlet*, IV.ii.11–12

I

Hamlet is not alone in attending to the compelling voice of a ghost; Shakespeare himself apparently remembered the "ghost which cried so miserally [*sic*] at the Theator, like an oister wife, *Hamlet, revenge.*"[1] *Hamlet's* source, almost certainly, is the play that Lodge recalls, the *Hamlet* for which Henslowe records a performance at Newington Butts in June of 1594, and Hamlet, too, shares a name with a prior Hamlet. Both the play and the prince seek their individuality in their complex relationship with the past, relations obscurely inscribed in the name each takes from its forebear.

Hamlet worries about the "wounded name" he will "leave behind" (V.ii.346–47), but it is a name previously left to him, already "wounded," except perhaps in Hamlet's idealizing imagination. "This is I, / Hamlet the Dane" (V.i.257–58), he claims in his most determined assertion of self, but in naming himself he must echo his earlier act of naming as he stood before the ghost: "I'll call thee Hamlet, / King, father, royal Dane" (I.iv.44–45). He cannot name himself without simultaneously naming his father, and the shared name asserts his inescapable filiation. He is his father's son and namesake, and thus is he "bound to hear" and finally bound "to revenge" (I.v.7, 8), bound to his father and his father's cause.

For Hamlet, however, to accept the filial obligation sounded in his

* From *Shakespeare Studies*, 19 (1988): 111–124. Reprinted by permission of Associated University Presses.

name is to disregard and dismiss all other relations he has established. His filiation becomes a diminution. He would be *only* the son, sworn to remember and revenge his father.

> Yea, from the table of my memory
> I'll wipe away all trivial fond records,
> All saws of books, all forms, all pressures past
> That youth and observation copied there,
> And they commandment all alone shall live
> Within the book and volume of my brain,
> Unmix'd with baser matter.
>
> (I.v.99–104)

The complex intertextuality of the "book" of Hamlet's brain is denied as he subordinates himself to the authority of his father. What has been diligently "copied there" would be quickly erased. He hopes "with wings as swift / As meditation or the thoughts of love" to "sweep to his revenge" (I.v.30–32), though "meditation" and "love" would both suggest a less bloody course. Hamlet, however, commits himself to a "commandment" that other commandments, now readily forgotten, would supplant, to a text that more humane texts would censure if not suppress. He commits himself to his father, to being a son, to represent, that is, old Hamlet in both senses of the word—as the child who re-presents the father and as the agent who represents the father's interests—and his representation is confirmed as, for the first time, the ghost addresses him by name immediately following Hamlet's eager acceptance of his charge. "I find thee apt," the ghost says: "And duller shouldst thou be than the fat weed/ That roots on Lethe wharf/ Wouldst thou not stir in this. Now, Hamlet, hear" (I.v.32–35). The ghost does not speak their shared name until he is confident of their shared purpose. He demands the radical identification of son with father that their undifferentiated name suggests.

To be Hamlet, to deserve the name, at least as far as the ghost is concerned, is to be a revenger. The ghost would turn Shakespeare's play into the old play Lodge remembered, echoing the earlier ghost's command, "Hamlet, revenge"; yet what differentiates *Hamlet* from the Ur-*Hamlet*, as well as what differentiates Hamlet from old Hamlet, is that Shakespeare's prince can never fully credit the impulse to revenge.[2]

He is never quite as "apt" a revenger as either he or the ghost would like, puzzling both of them, as well as generations of critics, with his inability to act. Revenge, however, makes action problematic, for, though it would insist upon the singularity of the villainy it would punish, inevitably it duplicates the crime, dissolving all difference that could effectively motivate action in its inescapable imitative nature.[3] John Bereblock understood exactly this watching *Progne*, which was played before the Queen in 1566:

"It is wonderful how she longed to seek vengeance for the blood of her sister. She goes about therefore to avenge wrongs with wrongs and injuries with injuries; nor is it at all reverent to add crimes to crimes already committed."[4] Revenge is, as Hamlet reluctantly discovers, a desperate mode of imitation, avenging wrongs with wrongs. The revenger is prevented from originating an action. He is allowed only to react to—and to reenact—the original crime; Hamlet's delay may be understood as his resistance to accept his imitative relation either to the ghostly simulacrum of his father who urges him to revenge, or to the smiling villain of an uncle who would be its object.

Only when he can persuade himself that revenge is a mode of restoration rather than reprisal can Hamlet move toward its execution, but always he is reminded of the inescapable relatedness of victim/villain/avenger. Examples, both gross and fine, exhort him to the uncomfortable knowledge of the repetitions and resemblances that revenge effects. Like the defensive literary theorists of the English Renaissance, Hamlet values literature for its mimetic and didactic functions, its abilities to generate moral exempla that will "show virtue her feature, scorn her own image" (III.ii.22–23), and guided by his idealist mimetic principles, he recalls "the rugged Pyrrhus" (II.ii.450), a son who readily avenges his father's death, as an example that might animate his own revenge. Pyrrhus, however, serves only to confirm the disturbing resemblances Hamlet needs to deny.[5] As the example of Pyrrhus forecasts the future, it represents, of course, Hamlet himself pausing momentarily before he revenges his father's death; as the example recalls the past it represents Claudius killing the true king. Pyrrhus, then, becomes a figure both of the avenging son and of the father's murderer, subverting any moral distinction in the single example which shows at once "virtue her feature" and "scorn her own image."

Hamlet turns to a classical model hoping to clarify his obligation and confirm his resolve, but instead he discovers in the disturbing alignments of the example of Pyrrhus further inhibition of his ability to act upon his "motive and cue for passion" (II.ii.561). In his faulty recollection of the first line of the remembered speech, he unconsciously reveals his knowledge that Pyrrhus, as object of imitation, cannot stimulate and direct his energy: " 'The rugged Pyrrhus, like th'Hyrcanian beast,' /—'Tis not so. It begins with Pyrrhus—/ 'The rugged Pyrrhus, he whose sable arms . . . ' " (II.ii.450–52). Hamlet's misremembered line, of course, "begins with Pyrrhus" exactly as the corrected line does; the error comes in the second half. Hamlet anxiously misreads his text. In projecting Pyrrhus as "th'Hyrcanian beast," Hamlet betrays his unwanted awareness that revenge is an inhuman and pointless activity. The tigers of Hyrcania were proverbial for their ferocity, and they are apt images not only for the fury of revenge but also for its self-destructive nature. Barnabe Riche's Friar Sebastian laments how "beastly" soldiers are, preferring the far more sensible behavior of actual beasts: "the bruite beast by naturall instinct doe daily eschew the inconvenience that folowe them:

and have an eye to that whiche may profite them. Contrariewise, these Souldiers like to *Hircan Tigers*, revenge themselves on their owne bowelles, some *Parricides*, some *Fratricides*, all *Homicides*."[6]

Pyrrhus is, then, "like th'Hyrcanian beast," even if Vergil does not himself provide the simile. Pyrrhus is a parricide no less than Paris. He kills Priam as Priam's son killed Pyrrhus' father, and the symmetry and reciprocity mock the moral authority the revenger would claim. In a world where a son can only revenge (rather than prevent) his father's murder, and revenge him only by becoming the murderer of another father whose son will in turn seek his revenge, it is clear that revengers do "revenge themselves on their own bowelles," accomplishing nothing but a concatenation of hatred and death.

Hamlet, however, has not invented the figure he mistakenly if appropriately applies to Pyrrhus. His language recalls Vergil's, or rather Dido's, identification of Aeneas with the Hyrcanian beast as he prepares to leave Carthage.

> No goddess was your mother, false Aeneas,
> and Dardanus no author of your race;
> the bristling Caucasus was father to you
> on his harsh crags; Hyrcanian tigresses
> gave you their teats.
>> (IV.497–501; *trans. Mandelbaum*)

These are not thoughtless insults spat out in fury, but are carefully calculated to deny the *pietas* Aeneas claims, and which she—and even he—feels as bitter loss.

Aeneas is identified with the Hyrcanian beast when he rouses himself to fulfill the destiny the gods have chosen for him, not, as one might expect, when he rouses himself to vengeance after witnessing Priam's slaughter. There, confronted with the "hated" Helen, he reveals his own passion for revenge: "it will be a joy to fill my soul with vengeful fire, / to satisfy the ashes of my people" (II.791–92). But his mother, Venus, quickly extinguishes the flames of his vengeance, resigning him to the will of the gods who would have fallen Troy not revenged but refounded at Rome.[7]

> My son, what bitterness has kindled thy
> fanatic anger? Why this madness? What
> of all your care for me. . . .
> . . . . .
>> you must not fear
> the orders of your mother; do not doubt,
> but carry out what she commands
>> (ll. 802–04, 820–22)

Hamlet in seeing Pyrrhus "like th'Hyrcanian beast" thus at once registers the beastliness of revenge and represses an alternative course suggested by the example of Aeneas. To revenge, he fears, is to be a beast; but his need to revenge, determined (even overdetermined) by the identification with his father, denies him full consideration of any alternative, so that not to revenge is also to be a beast: "What is a man/ If his chief good and market of his time/ Be but to sleep and feed? A beast, no more" (IV.iv.33–35). To be or not to be a beast? Perhaps that is the question, but not for Hamlet, whose imitative poetics have denied him the choice.

Hamlet's consideration of "Aeneas' tale of Dido" (II.ii.446) leads him neither to accept nor to reject the ghost's charge. The example of Pyrrhus neither confirms Hamlet's commitments to revenge nor dissuades him from it. Indeed, Pyrrhus is soon passed over for Hecuba's grief. "Say on, come to Hecuba" (II.ii.501), Hamlet urges, eager for a correlative of his own self-pity. He resists any identification with Pyrrhus, even in Pyrrhus' frozen moment facing Priam when he "stood, / And like a neutral to his will and matter, / Did nothing" (II.ii.480–82); but, quickly, faced with the player's skillful imitation of Hecuba's passionate suffering, Hamlet stands self-convicted of failure.

> What would he do
> Had he the motive and cue for passion
> That I have? He would drown the stage with tears
> And cleave the general ear with horrid speech,
> Make mad the guilty and appal the free,
> Confound the ignorant, and amaze indeed
> The very faculties of eyes and ears. Yet I
> A dull and muddy-mettled rascal, peak
> Like John-a-dreams, unpregnant of my cause,
> And can say nothing—
>
> (II.ii.560–69)

Oddly, Hamlet wishes to imitate the player rather than Pyrrhus. He envies the player's dramatic technique, his ability to

> force his soul so to his own conceit
> That from her working all his visage wann'd,
> Tears in his eyes, distraction in his aspect,
> A broken voice, and his whole function suiting
> With forms to his conceit.
>
> (II.ii.553–57)

Hamlet is angry that he, unlike the player, is incapable of acting expressively, rather than angry that, unlike Pyrrhus, he is incapable of acting effectively; the problem he admits is not that he can *do* nothing but that he can *say* "nothing."

It is hardly a charge anyone else would dare bring against Hamlet, who speaks over 1,400 lines, or three hundred more than even the most defiantly vocal of Shakespeare's other characters.[8] But Hamlet here believes he has at the very least said nothing memorable, nothing, that is, that an actor, in the Senecan revenge play in which the ghost would cast Hamlet, can wrap his tongue around. Admittedly he gives it a try: "I should have fatted all the region kites/With this slave's offal. Bloody, bawdy villain!/Remorseless, treacherous, lecherous, kindless villain!" (II.ii.579–81). Here he struts and bellows with the impassioned theatricality of the stage revenger, but he cannot sustain his belief in the conventional role:

> Why, what an ass am I! This is most brave,
> That I, the son of a dear father murder'd,
> Prompted to my revenge by heaven and hell,
> Must like a whore, unpack my heart with words.
>
> (II.ii.583–86)

No longer is he concerned that he "can say nothing." In fewer than twenty lines he has reversed himself completely, deciding now that to say anything is to say too much, is to allow speech to substitute for the revenge he has been charged to enact. No longer would he be a player "in a fiction" (II.ii.552), prompted by some stage manager; now he would be an actor in truth "prompted to [his] revenge by heaven and hell."

Even this resolve, however, fails finally to motivate his action, for again Hamlet's moral imagination generates a disabling symmetry. Hamlet is "the son of a dear father murder'd," and prompted by heaven alone, he would be God's avenging minister. "Avenge not yourselves," St. Paul, of course, had warned the Romans, "for it is written, vengeance is mine: I will repaye" (Romans 12:19, Geneva Bible); but in the next chapter Paul writes that the prince "is the minister of God to take vengeance on him that doeth evil" (Romans 13:4). As an agent of God's vengeance Hamlet, then, could act, and his revenge would have the authority and finality of God's judgment; but prompted by "heaven *and* hell," revenge cannot sustain the moral differentiation that would make it justice. The copulative does not effect an addition but enforces a subtraction. Coupling heaven and hell does not double the authorizing pressure; it cancels the essential difference between moral alternatives necessary to permit his revenge.

Thus it is that Hamlet returns to his fictions. "The play's the thing" (II.ii.605) with which he will search for the singularity his revenge requires. "The Murder of Gonzago" is a simple mimetic plot. It is "the image of a murder done in Vienna" (III.ii.236) which Hamlet, through the addition of "a speech of some dozen or sixteen lines" (II.ii.541), transforms into the image of a murder done in Denmark. Hamlet's play is designed to imitate Claudius' crime in order to "catch the conscience of the king" (II.ii.607), but Hamlet's imitative practice, conflating his moral desire and his psychological need, denies the play the clarity he presumes. He wants to see Claudius and himself as "mighty opposites" (V.ii.62), but the play reveals their disturbing similarity. If Lucianus serves as an image of Claudius, murderer of the king, he serves more openly as an image of Hamlet, "nephew to the king" (III.ii.242). In holding the mirror up to degenerate nature Hamlet unwittingly establishes the symmetry that revenge must deny.

Claudius, of course, does rise, "frighted with false fire" (III.ii.264), but Hamlet and the audience of his play cannot know, unlike the audience of Shakespeare's, if Claudius rises maddened by the moving image of his crime or appalled by the audacity of his nephew. In unnecessarily identifying Lucianus as "nephew to the king," Hamlet allows his play to imitate both Claudius' guilty secret and his own: his desperate desire to kill the king. The play becomes at least in part, then, a murderous threat which establishes how thoroughly the revenger becomes "soil'd i'th working" (II.i.40), obscuring the differences Hamlet desires between the villain and the agent who would avenge the prior crime.

If, throughout, Hamlet is prevented from enacting his revenge by the discomforting ratios that his literary imitations generate, he is equally prevented from repudiating his revenge by his inability to emancipate himself from his father, to be other than an imitation of what has generated him. Caught in this double bind,[9] between an inescapable psychological obligation to revenge and unavoidable moral abhorrence of it, between a certainty that he must revenge and a certainty that he cannot, when he finally kills Claudius, appropriately he does so to avenge not his father's murder but his own. "The King—the King's to blame," Laertes confesses; and Hamlet turns on Claudius in fury: "The point envenom'd too! Then, venom, to thy work" (V.ii.324). Laertes dies, relating his and his father's death, but Hamlet dies with no word of the father he has sworn to "remember." The act he finally commits is more reflex than revenge.

In his reflexive killing of Claudius, Hamlet acts for himself not for his father, but it is still a reaction rather than an original and originating act. Mortally wounded, he retaliates against his murderer, but even in his death he cannot escape the imitative relation to his father that is figured in their shared name. Like old Hamlet, Hamlet too dies poisoned by Claudius' treacherous hand; and, also like old Hamlet, he dies urgently demanding to be remembered.[10] "Absent thee from felicity awhile," he begs Horatio, "And in this harsh world draw thy breath in pain / To tell my story" (V.ii.349–51). What is different, however, is that old Hamlet demands to be remembered in (violent) action: "Revenge [my] foul and most unnatural murder" (I.v.26); Hamlet demands to be remembered in (violent) language: "Tell my story." Remembering old Hamlet leads to death; remembering Hamlet leads to drama.

Imitation is effective for Hamlet neither as a mode of action nor as a mode of knowing. "*Imitari* is nothing," Holofernes asserts in *Love's Labor's*

Lost: "so doth the hound his master, the ape his keeper, the tired horse his rider" (IV.ii.125–26). The familiar metaphors of imitative theory reveal that *Imitari* is, as Hamlet discovers, to be a beast, to be less than fully human. However, for "the soul of great article," Hamlet understands that "his semblable is his mirror and who else would trace him, his umbrage, nothing more." (V.ii.118–20). Hamlet's parody here of Osric's affected praise of Laertes is an aggressive appropriation of Osric's imitative courtly discourse, and is itself an attack on the value of imitation. More significantly, however, Hamlet reveals his knowledge that "the soul of great article" will not be forged imitatively. It will be an original; and "who else would trace him," that is, imitate him, can be no more than his "umbrage," merely his shadow.

Hamlet, once "the glass of fashion and the mould of form, / Th'observed of all observers" (III.i.156–57), the object of other's anxious imitation, becomes in his commitment to revenge an imitator rather than the imitated. He becomes the "umbrage," or rather the umbrage of an umbrage, "a shadow's shadow" (II.ii.263), in Rosencrantz' phrase, reduced to tracing patterns rather than providing them. *Hamlet*, on the other hand, is not content to trace its models. Shakespeare is not "bound" as his hero is to the imitation of revenge. Shakespeare's *Hamlet* refuses servilely to imitate the revenge play—not least in its hero's refusal to take revenge—and in that refusal it creates the imaginative space for tragedy.[11]

II

In his commendatory poem to the 1640 edition of Shakespeare's *Poems*, Leonard Digges enthusiastically if improbably asserts:

> Thou shalt find he doth not borrow
> One phrase from Greekes, nor Latines imitate,
> Nor once from vulgar Languages Translate,
> Nor Plagiari-like from others gleane,
> Nor begges he from each witty friend a Scene,
> To peece his Acts with, all that he doth write,
> Is pure his owne.
>
> (ll. 12–18)

Obviously nothing that Shakespeare writes is *"pure* his owne." The sedimentation of language and of writing itself would deny the radical originality that Digges claims for Shakespeare, and, of course, scholarly activity, beginning with Langbaine's *Account of the English Dramatick Poets* (1691), has doggedly tracked Shakespeare's reading as it is inscribed in his writing. Even with the Ur-*Hamlet* unavailable for comparison, *Hamlet* reveals itself as a text in its etymological sense, as a *web* of indebtedness to prior texts.

Perhaps predictably in an age that defined itself in the language of recovery and rebirth, Renaissance literary theory gave prominence to imitation in its understanding of literary creativity.[12] Castiglione advises: "take diligent heede to following [Thomas Hoby's translation of *imitazioni*], without the wiche I judge no man can write well";[13] and the thought is often echoed in England. Thomas Wilson, for example, writes: "All men of any understanding seeke to follow someone unto whom they desire to be lyke, or if it may be, to passe him."[14] Poets are to seek, embrace, and, in Wilson's remarkably unanxious phrase, "if it may be," surpass the literary model "they desire to be lyke." The past is a repository of literary authority and cultural value to which imitation grants success. Certainly, as Jonson writes, the poet is "not, to imitate servilely, as *Horace* saith, and catch at vices, for vertue: but, to draw forth out of the best, and choisest flowers, with the Bee, and turne all into Honey."[15]

If the prominence of imitation in Renaissance literary theory is unsurprising, so too is the resistance to it that surfaces. However much the authority of the model is sought and welcomed, inevitably it generates significant anxieties. Jonson uncomfortably acknowledges his fear that imitation will always leave the writer subordinate to the model: "never no Imitator ever, grew up to his *Author*" (8, 590); but Jonson recognizes an even more disturbing danger: not that imitation might fail but that it might succeed, for successful imitation threatens the independence and integrity of the writing self. "*I have* considered," writes Jonson, "our whole life is like a *Play*, wherein every man forgetfull of himselfe, is in travaile with expression of another. Nay, we so insist in imitating others, as we cannot (when it is necessary) returne to our selves: like Children, that imitate the vices of *Stammerers* so long, till at last they become such; and make the habit to another nature, as it is never forgotten" (8, 597). The imitator runs the risk of being overwhelmed by his model, trapped in and by the excellence he admires. Though Jonson usually emphasizes the transformative aspect of poetic imitation, occasionally the threat is unmistakably voiced. The poet, he says, is "to make choise of one excellent man above the rest, and so to follow him, till he grow a very *Hee:* or so like him, as the Copie may be mistaken for the Principall" (8, 638).

Imitation writes the tensions of Renaissance England small. The ambivalence that Jonson betrays is the ambivalence of a culture that socially and politically attempts to contain, if not resolve, the conflicts between the duty of submission and the desire for autonomy.[16] Just as the aggressively self-assertive political voice could not always successfully be silenced, so too the aggressively self-assertive literary voice is heard. In spite of its central position in the Humanist educational and literary program, imitation by some is felt as limitation; thus, Thomas Nashe "will proudly boast, that the vaine which

I have (be it a *median* vaine or a madde man) is of my owne begetting, and cals no man father in England but my selfe."[17]

Somewhat like Milton's Satan, Nashe asserts his autogenesis, accepting, or at least acknowledging, no literary patrimony. Nashe's self-assertion is only in part defensively motivated by Harvey's accusation of his borrowings; at least as important as the personal quarrel is a literary environment in which the precepts and practice of imitation have become not an invitation to creativity but an evasion of it:

> It is a common practise now a daies amongst a sort of shifting companions, that runne through every arte and thrive by none, to leave the trade of *Noverint*, whereto they were borne, and busie themselves with the indevors of Art, that could scarcelie latinize their neck-verse if they should have neede; yet English Seneca read by candle light yeeldes manie good sentences, as *Bloud is a begger*, and so foorth; and, if you intreate him faire in a frostie morning, hee will affoord you whole *Hamlets*, I should say handfuls of tragical speaches.[18]

The Ur-*Hamlet* serves Nashe here as a convenient sign for both the theatrical excess of the conventional revenge play and the "servile imitation" that produces it; nonetheless, Shakespeare, in naming his play *Hamlet*, pointedly calls attention to its relation to the imitations of "English *Seneca*" that Nashe derides. Even in an age where plots, characters, and even "handfuls of tragical speaches" were readily borrowed, it seems strange that with the infinite number of available names for a play and an eponymous hero Shakespeare would choose one already claimed, and one so familiar that Nashe can use it for an easy joke about defective literary practice.

If Shakespeare's purpose were to exploit the popularity of the revenge play, any name other than "Hamlet" would better serve his needs. One does not climb aboard a bandwagon by announcing a new contribution as a mere replica of what has already been done. Marlowe's *Tamburlaine* spawned numerous imitators of the conqueror drama, but not one thought to exploit the popularity of that form by calling a new play *Tamburlaine*. (The anonymous *Tamer Cham* comes close, but the example, in fact, confirms my point, as does Marlowe's own sequel, *Tamburlaine, Part II.*) For Shakespeare, then, to call his play *Hamlet* is not to follow in the tracks of his precursor but to obliterate those footsteps. It is not a gesture of respect toward a worthy model but a revisionary proclamation ostentatiously announcing its own originality.

Shakespeare, who is called by his first editors a "happie imitator of Nature," is revealed to be a no less happy imitator of his literary precursors, free of the ambivalence that marks the theory and practice of his contemporaries.[19] Harold Bloom exempts him entirely from any anxiety of influence; what we see in his relations with prior texts, Bloom writes, is "the absolute absorption of the precursor."[20] Certainly *Hamlet* reveals exactly this full and confident appropriation (and even more literally than Bloom intends, as the text of the Ur-*Hamlet* no longer exists). Shakespeare borrows, parodies, quotes, echoes—imitates, in its various senses—but always to make something that meaningfully can be said to be "pure his owne." In shaping a play that interrogates rather than merely enacts the rhythms of revenge, Shakespeare creates something that is more than a revenge play—a play finally that is neither an imitation nor one that is imitatable, something whose semblable, as Hamlet might say, is its mirror.

Hamlet originates in a revision of the revenge tradition, but a revision, unlike Hamlet's own, that demonstrates, indeed advertises, the difficulty but also the possibility of escaping the reduction of belatedness. *Hamlet* does not repeat the Ur-*Hamlet* but reimagines and revises it, performing a humane, if not humanist, act of imitation. *Hamlet* does not become "a very *Hee*" in spite of taking the name of its precursor. Like his hero, Shakespeare responds to the words of a ghost demanding to be remembered, but Shakespeare's revisionary act of remembrance recognizes and transcends (what is for Hamlet, anyway, literally) the deadening effects of imitation.[21]

Notes

1. Thomas Lodge, *Wits Miserie* (1596), in *The Complete Works of Thomas Lodge* (n.p.: Hunterian Club, 1883), 4, 56.

2. James L. Calderwood has a suggestive account of these relations in his *To Be and Not to Be* (New York: Columbia Univ. Press, 1983), esp. pp. 27–28.

3. See Rene Girard, "To Entrap the Wisest: A Reading of *The Merchant of Venice*," in *Literature and Society: Selected Papers from the English Institute*, ed. Edward W. Said (Baltimore: Johns Hopkins Univ. Press, 1980), esp. pp. 104–07; and his recent extension of the argument in "Hamlet's Dull Revenge," *Stanford Literary Review* 1 (1984), 159–200.

4. Quoted in Fredson Bowers, *Elizabethan Revenge Tragedy* 1587–1642 (1940; rpt. Princeton, N.J.: Princeton Univ. Press, 1971), p. 81.

5. Clifford Leech speculatively discusses these relations in his "The Hesitation of Pyrrhus," in *The Mortality of Art*, ed. D. W. Jefferson (London: Routledge and Kegan Paul, 1969), pp. 41–49.

6. *The Second Tome of the Travailes and Adventures of Don Simonides* (London, 1584), Sig. C. See also *3 Henry VI*, I.iv. 154–55.

7. Gregory des Jardins, "The Hyrcanian Beast," *Notes and Queries*, 228 (1983), 124–25, also notes the transposition of the simile from Aeneas to Pyrrhus, though he focuses his attention on Hamlet's responsibility for "the care of the city."

8. According to the analysis on p. 31 of *William Shakespeare: The Complete Works*, ed. Alfred Harbage (Baltimore: Penguin Books, 1969), Hamlet speaks 1,422 lines. Richard III has the next longest role: 1,124 lines. Iago speaks 1,097; Henry V, 1,025, and no other character more than 820.

9. Anna K. Nardo, in "Hamlet, 'A Man to Double Business Bound,' " *Shakespeare Quarterly*, 34 (1983), 181–200, suggestively explores the application of recent psychological theories of the double bind to the play.

10. See James P. Hammersmith, "*Hamlet* and the Myth of Memory," *ELH* 45 (1978),

597–605, though Hammersmith equates the efforts of Hamlet and the ghost each to be kept alive through memory.

11. See Howard Felperin's chapter, "O'erdoing Termagant: *Hamlet*" in *Shakespearean Representation* (Princeton, N.J.: Princeton Univ. Press, 1977), pp. 44–67.

12. For a masterful account of imitative theories and practice in the Renaissance, see Thomas Greene's *The Light in Troy: Imitation and Discovery in Renaissance Poetry* (New Haven, Conn.: Yale Univ. Press, 1982). See also the important studies of Renaissance imitation by Margaret W. Ferguson, *Trials of Desire* (New Haven, Conn.: Yale Univ. Press, 1983), esp. pp. 18–53; G. W. Pigman, III, "Versions of Imitation in the Renaissance," *Renaissance Quarterly*, 33 (1980), 1–32; and Marion Trousdale, "Recurrence and Renaissance: Rhetorical Imitation in Ascham and Sturm," *English Literary Renaissance*, 6 (1976), 156–79.

13. *The Book of the Courtier*, trans. Thomas Hoby (1561), ed. J. H. Whitfeld (London: Dent, 1974), pp. 52–53.

14. *The Three Orations of Demosthenes* (London: 1570), Sig. *4.

15. "Discoveries," in *Ben Jonson*, ed. C. H. Herford, Percy and Evelyn Simpson (Oxford: Clarendon, 1947), 8, 638–39. Additional citations from this volume will be cited parenthetically in the text.

16. See Richard C. McCoy's discussion of these cultural tensions in his *Sir Philip Sidney: Rebellion in Arcadia* (New Brunswick, N.J.: Rutgers Univ. Press, 1979), esp. pp. 1–68.

17. "Strange News of the Intercepting of Certaine Letters" (1592), in *Works of Thomas Nashe*, ed. Ronald B. McKerrow (London: Sidgwick and Jackson, 1910), 1, 319.

18. Thomas Nashe, preface to Greene's *Menaphon* (1582), in *Elizabethan Critical Essays*, ed. G. Gregory Smith (1904; rpt. Oxford Univ. Press, 1967), 1, 311–12.

19. The distinction between *imitatio* and *mimesis* that some modern critics would make to differentiate imitations of literary models from imitations of nature was not regularly observed in the Renaissance. Indeed Scaliger, in Stephen Orgel's paraphrase, observes that "we can best imitate nature by imitating Virgil." Orgel's essay "The Renaissance Artist as Plagiarist," *ELH* 48 (1981), 476–95, is another of the extremely important contributions to our understanding of Renaissance theories and practices of imitation.

20. *The Anxiety of Influence* (Oxford: Oxford Univ. Press, 1975), p. 11.

21. I would like to record my thanks to the friends and colleagues whose comments helped in the preparation of this paper, especially Richard Corum, Margaret Ferguson, Peter Travis, Nancy Vickers, and Marguerite Waller; and thank Donna Hamilton and the seminar of The Shakespeare Association for whom an early version of this essay was prepared.

The Textual Mystery of *Hamlet*

PAUL WERSTINE

The '80s have seen a large number of Shakespeareans—myself among them—rise up to advocate the possibility that Shakespeare revised his plays. Some of us would like to imagine that we are the first to entertain the idea seriously; it has been said, for example, that "editors and critics have long resisted the obvious conclusion, that Shakespeare occasionally—perhaps, if we could only see it, habitually—revised his work."[1] Yet the notion of revision had its heyday in the nineteenth century just as it is having another one now; what's more, discussion of the question has hardly languished in the last three decades. Fredson Bowers, whose name has become almost synonymous with Shakespeare bibliography and textual criticism since the '50s, has repeatedly addressed the possibility that Shakespeare revised the version of *Hamlet* that was printed in the second quarto of 1604/1605 and that his revisions may appear among the variants evident in the Folio version published in 1623.

Far from resisting revision as an explanation of variation between quarto and Folio *Hamlet*, Bowers declared the question entirely open as early as his Sandars Lectures in Bibliography of 1958. Citing a number of single-word quarto/Folio variants, he said:

> I hold it to be an occupation eminently worth while, warranting any number of hours, to determine whether Shakespeare wrote one, or the other, or both. The decision, if clear-cut, might be crucial in the accumulation of evidence whether on the whole the Folio variants from the quarto *Hamlet* are corruptions, corrections, or revisions. . . . Depending upon what can be proved, some hundreds of readings will be affected if an editor decides that Shakespeare revised the text after its second quarto form; for in that case there could be an argument for choosing the Folio variants in all but the most obvious cases of sophistication. Or he might decide that in only a few cases, where the second-quarto compositors have corrupted the text, should the Folio readings take precedence over the generally authoritative second quarto.[2]

In the 1962 article "Established Texts and Definitive Editions," Bowers extended the possibility of revision to a range of plays: "Such plays as *Troilus*

---

* From *Shakespeare Quarterly*, 39 (Spring (1988), 1–26. Reprinted by permission of *Shakespeare Quarterly*.

and Cressida, Hamlet, and *Othello* exist in two authoritative textual versions, Quarto and Folio. For *Troilus* there is some reason to believe that the two versions represent original and authorial revision, perhaps in reverse order; but the situation for *Othello* and *Hamlet* is complicated by what seems to be evidence of theatrical alterations, some of doubtful authority, perhaps mingled with some authorial revision."[3] Again and again he raised the complex problem of identifying authorial revision among the variants between early printed versions without claiming to resolve it one way or the other.

Recent assertions that the issue has been resolved in favor of Shakespeare's occasional or habitual revision of his plays seem seems to me rather exaggerated.[4] Probably Shakespeare did revise, whether in the course of original composition or at some later date, but we would be fortunate indeed if the variations between extant printed texts of his plays represented only authorial changes of mind. There are a great many other ways in which variation can be produced in printed texts—scribal transcription, unauthorized playhouse cuts or additions, printing-house errors, to name only three. Can we realistically expect to identify the source of every variant of the hundreds between the quarto and Folio texts of such plays as *Hamlet* or *Othello?* When it is so difficult to prove or disprove authorship of an entire play or even a whole canon, there is little chance of conclusively demonstrating that Shakespeare's must have been the hand that originally wrote the eighty or so lines in the Folio text of *Hamlet* that have no counterparts in the second-quarto version. Nor are we likely ever to know whose hand(s) cut the more than two hundred lines from the second-quarto text that do not appear in the Folio; in the very nature of the case, there is simply no evidence for determining the authorship of cuts.

Rather than continue the quest for the indeterminable origins of variants between the second-quarto and Folio versions of *Hamlet,* why not examine what we have—namely, the early printed texts themselves—with a view to assessing the extent to which the two may be compatible or incompatible with each other? Why not ask what consequences flow from yoking the texts together, as has been the practice of almost every editor since Rowe, who stands at the foundation of the editorial tradition? This essay pursues these questions, and although it cannot claim to have run them to ground, tentatively suggests that much of the enduring mystery that is *Hamlet*/Hamlet has been produced through the editorial construction of *Hamlet* as the combination of the second-quarto (Q2) and Folio (F) versions.[5]

I

To begin near the end of *Hamlet,* we might consider the minor mystery created by the inclusion in almost all editions since the eighteenth century of both of the alternative motives provided in Q2 and F for the apology that Hamlet offers to Laertes before the fencing match in the last scene: "Give me your pardon, sir. I have [F: I'ue] done you wrong" (V.ii.224 ff. [Q2 & F]).[6] Hamlet is referring to the wrong he did by challenging Laertes's grief at Ophelia's burial, provoking Laertes to violence: "I prithee, take thy fingers from my throat" (V.i.260 [Q2 & F]). As he exits from V.i, Hamlet represents himself as the aggrieved party:

> Hear you, sir:
> What is the reason that you use me thus?
> I lov'd you ever. But it is no matter.
> Let Hercules himself do what he may,
> The cat will mew, and dog will have his day.
> (V.i.288–92 [Q2 & F])

Yet when he next meets Laertes at the fencing match, it is with the words, "Give me your pardon, sir."

What intervenes between the stormy encounter of V.i and the fencing match in V.ii to move Hamlet to beg Laertes's pardon? Here Q2 and F differ. In Q2 the answer to this question arrives in the form of a nameless lord who inquires, on behalf of Claudius, whether Hamlet will fence with Laertes. I quote this lord's brief interview with Hamlet in its entirety to show how, in large part, it merely repeats the exchange with Osric that occurred a few lines earlier:

> *Enter a Lord.*
>
> LORD: My lord, his Majesty commended him to you by young Osric, who brings back to him that you attend him in the hall. He sends to know if your pleasure hold to play with Laertes, or that you will take longer time.
>
> HAMLET: I am constant to my purposes; they follow the King's pleasure. If his fitness speaks, mine is ready; now or whensoever, provided I be so able as now.
>
> LORD: The King and Queen and all are coming down.
>
> HAMLET: In happy time.
>
> LORD: The Queen desires you to use some gentle entertainment to Laertes before you fall to play.
>
> HAMLET: She well instructs me.   [*Exit Lord.*]
> (V.ii.194–206 [Q2])

Since it scarcely seems necessary to introduce this lord for the purpose of confirming Hamlet's intention to play with Laertes—Hamlet has done nothing to raise doubts about his intention in the ten lines since Osric's exit—and since he need not be brought on to announce the entrance of Claudius,

Gertrude, "and all," which will be evident enough when they appear seven-teen lines later, the primary function of the lord would seem to be to advise Hamlet of his mother's wish for a reconciliation between Hamlet and Laertes. George Hibbard calls this lord "superfluous," but the lord is a most necessary character in Q2; without his message from the queen, Q2 would leave us quite unprepared for Hamlet's apology to Laertes at the fencing match.

In F there is no trace of the nameless lord and so no mention of Gertrude's intercession with Hamlet. Instead in F, but not in Q2, Hamlet expresses regret for his treatment of Laertes before Osric ever enters:

> But I am very sorry, good Horatio,
> That to Laertes I forgot myself,
> For by the image of my cause I see
> The portraiture of his. I'll court [F: count] his favors.
> But, sure, the bravery of his grief did put me
> Into a tow'ring passion.
>
> (V.ii.75–80 [F])

According to F, then, Hamlet's later apology to Laertes springs from empathy with him.

What happens when the Q2 interview with the nameless lord is com-bined with Folio Hamlet's empathetic speech in the modern text of *Hamlet*? Quite simply, the modern text doubles up Hamlet's motives for the apology to Laertes before the fencing match and leaves readers and theatre-goers unsure as to how much Hamlet's apology arises from his sympathy with Laertes, how much from a desire to satisfy Gertrude. The problem is aggra-vated in the combined Q2/F text by the note on which the F-only speech ends, namely Hamlet's recollection of the "tow'ring passion" into which Laertes's allegedly ostentatious grief had thrown Hamlet—a self-justificatory theme that might qualify Hamlet's resolve to court Laertes's favor. To readers of the modern combined Q2/F text, it could well seem that Hamlet began to empathize, remembered his rage, and finally needed a push from Gertrude to apologize. Readers of the F text can know that Hamlet's empathy alone was sufficient to prompt his kindness to Laertes, for Gertrude does not intervene in F. Readers of Q2 may assess Hamlet's motives in a different way, but with equal clarity: in Q2 Hamlet's apology is inspired only by Gertrude's instruction to him, not by any spontaneous regret for his treatment of Laertes in V.i.[7]

This minor mystery scarcely calls for a revolution in conventional editing of *Hamlet*. But other mysteries also cloud the modern combined Q2/F text of V.ii. In modern editions, Hamlet's expression of empathy with Laertes is immediately, and I think contradictorily, followed by an extended ex-change with Osric (found only in Q2) in which Hamlet reduces Laertes to an object of ridicule in the course of parodying Osric's overmannered speech:

OSRIC: Nay, good my lord; for my ease, in good faith. Sir. here is newly
            come to court Laertes—believe me, an absolute gentleman [Q2:
            gentleman], full of most excellent differences, of very soft society and
            great showing. Indeed, to speak feeling [Q2 corr.: fellingly; *uncorr.*:
            sellingly] of him, he is the card or calendar of gentry, for you shall
            find in him the continent of what part a gentleman would see.

HAMLET: Sir, his definement suffers no perdition in you, though, I know, to
            divide him inventorially would dozy [Q2 *corr.*: dazzie] th'arithmetic
            of memory, and yet but yaw [Q2 *corr.*: raw] neither in respect of his
            quick sail. But, in the verity of extolment, I take him to be a soul of
            great article, and his infusion of such dearth and rareness, as, to
            make true diction of him, his semblable is his mirror, and who else
            would trace him, his umbrage, nothing more.

OSRIC: Your lordship speaks most infallibly of him.

HAMLET: The concernancy, sir? Why do we wrap the gentleman in our more
            rawer breath?

OSRIC: Sir?

HORATIO: Is't not possible to understand in another tongue? You will do't [Q2
            uncorr.: too't], sir, really.

HAMLET: What imports the nomination of this gentleman?

OSRIC: Of Laertes?

HORATIO: [*To Hamlet*] His purse is empty already; all's golden words are spent.

HAMLET: Of him, sir.

OSRIC: I know you are not ignorant—

HAMLET: I would you did, sir; yet, in faith, if you did, it would not much
            approve me. Well, sir?

OSRIC: You are not ignorant of what excellence Laertes is—

HAMLET: I dare not confess that, lest I should compare with him in excellence;
            but to know a man well were to know himself.

OSRIC: I mean, sir, for his [Q2: this] weapon; but in the imputation laid on
            him by them, in his meed he's unfellow'd.

HAMLET: What's his weapon?

(V.ii.105–43 [Q2])

As parodies of Osric's pretentious mode of address, Hamlet's speeches call
far more attention to their style than to their reference to Laertes, but Hamlet
cannot mock Osric in speaking of Laertes without swiping Laertes at the
same time. Hamlet attacks Laertes in a number of different ways: sometimes
Hamlet achieves a bathetic effect through inflated praise of Laertes ("to divide
him inventorially would dozy th'arithmetic of memory"); sometimes Hamlet
makes compliments collapse upon themselves in tautology ("his semblable
is his mirror") or he affects exaggerated deference to Laertes ("Why do we

wrap the gentleman in our more rawer breath"). The callousness with which Hamlet makes Laertes's reputation the vehicle of extended mimickry of Osric hardly seems consistent with the sympathy that Hamlet has just shown towards Laertes in conversation with Horatio. Instead, the tone of Hamlet's references to Laertes is in line with the hostility with which Hamlet parted from Laertes at Ophelia's grave. In the modern combined Q2/F text, then, we are required to follow a Hamlet whose anger toward Laertes in V.i has become empathy in the exchange with Horatio that opens V.ii, only to find that Hamlet's newly discovered regard for Laertes is not equal to the temptation to ridicule him in the exchange with Osric.

Read independently of each other, both Q2 and F plot a straighter (though not necessarily a better) course for Hamlet from V.i through V.ii. The long exchange between Hamlet and Osric that I have just quoted appears only in Q2; in that text, as I have already noted, Hamlet's V.ii conversation with Horatio contains no expression of sympathy for Laertes. So when Osric enters in Q2, Hamlet, as far as we can know, remains as angry with Laertes as he was at the end of V.i and finds Laertes's fame a fit object for mockery. In Q2, then, Hamlet's tone toward Laertes changes only once—after Osric has exited and the nameless lord has given Hamlet Gertrude's instruction to "use some gentle entertainment to Laertes." Then Hamlet acknowledges, "She well instructs me," and treats Laertes courteously as soon as the latter enters.

In F, Hamlet's tone toward Laertes also changes only once—during the conversation with Horatio before Osric enters—and it does not change again in Hamlet's dialogue with the "water-fly." In F, the long Q2 passage I have quoted appears only in this much abbreviated form:

> OSRIC: Nay, in good faith, for mine ease
> in good faith: Sir, you are not
> ignorant of what excellence *Laertes*
> is at his weapon.
> HAMLET: What's his weapon?
> (Folio, TLN 3610–13)

Through the elimination of Hamlet's ridicule of Laertes, F presents a Hamlet who does not waver in his attitude to Laertes, once Hamlet has decided to court Laertes's favor. The modern text of V.ii, which contains all that both Q2 and F have to offer, provides a Hamlet who sways mysteriously in his attitude toward Laertes, but Q2 and F each present a Hamlet whose feelings toward Laertes change only once and then are constant.

Once one has sorted out the variant motivations of Hamlet in V.ii, one is still left, if one is a reader of the combined Q2/F text, with the mystery of why Laertes should win Hamlet's respect and empathy in the F version of this scene, but not in the Q2 version. This mystery results from the fact that the combined Q2/F text collapses a number of other differences in the presentation of Laertes throughout the rest of the play. If Laertes's part were invariant in the two texts in all but V.ii, we might well be comfortable with what is only, taken by itself, a minor emotional fluctuation in Hamlet. But V.ii is not the exclusive site of sizeable variants between Q2 and F in the representation of Laertes, both in his own words and in those of other characters. From his first appearance in I.ii, F offers a Laertes who seems stronger and a bit more reflective and therefore more worthy, in his own right, of the respect that he eventually wins from Hamlet in V.ii than the Laertes that Q2 depicts.

In both these early printed versions, Laertes appears in I.ii to beg of Claudius "leave and favor to return to France" (1. 51). In both texts, Claudius's consent is conditional upon the will of Polonius, whose son Claudius promises in advance to favor for the father's sake. F, however, accords Laertes the opportunity to plead successfully in his own right. In contrast, Q2 has Claudius accede to Laertes's request only after Polonius elaborately emphasizes Laertes's dependence upon paternal authority. In quoting this passage, I enclose the Q2 variant in pointed brackets:

KING: What wouldst thou have, Laertes?

LAERTES: My dread lord [F: Dread my Lord],
Your leave and favor to return to France,
From whence though willingly I came to Denmark
To show my duty in your coronation,
Yet now I must confess, that duty done,
My thoughts and wishes bend again toward France
And bow them to your gracious leave and pardon.

KING: Have you your father's leave? What says Polonius?

POLONIUS: H'ath, [F: He hath] my lord, <wrung from me my slow leave
By laborsome petition, and at last
Upon his will I seal'd my hard consent.>
I do beseech you, give him leave to go.

KING: Take thy fair hour, Laertes.

(I.ii.50–62)

Polonius's speech in Q2 emphasizes Laertes's status as a supplicant, an acknowledged dependent; that status is less obtrusive in the F version of the scene.[8]

Laertes appears onstage only three more times between I.ii and his encounter with Hamlet in V.i. Two of these three occasions follow his return from France; in both there are sizeable variants in his role between Q2 and F. The first of these arises in the lines given to him upon his first sight of the now mad Ophelia (this time I enclose the F-only passage in pointed brackets):

> Dear maid, kind sister, sweet Ophelia!
> O heavens, is't possible a young maid's wits
> Should be as mortal as an old [Q2: a poore] man's life?
> <Nature is fine in love, and, where 'tis fine,
> It sends some precious instance of itself
> After the thing it loves.>
>
> (IV.v.160–65)

The last three lines—the ones found in F alone—represent Laertes's discourse moving from a particular dramatic situation to a generalizing reflection upon "human nature." First, in both Q2 and F, Laertes draws an analogy between Polonius's mortality and the loss of Ophelia's wits; then, in F alone, he induces from this single instance the generalization that, in the words of Harold Jenkins's note, "Human nature, when in love, is exquisitely sensitive, and being so, it sends a precious part of itself as a token to follow the object of its love. Thus, the fineness of Ophelia's love is demonstrated when, after the loved one has gone, her mind goes too."[9] Nowhere else in either F or Q2 does Laertes indulge in such generalizing in the company of anyone but Ophelia alone (I.iii). Yet here in F he is given the opportunity to generalize in the company of his seniors, and thus to enhance his public stature. As a generalization of a particular sentiment, Laertes's F-only speech resembles the pattern of so many of Hamlet's, which insistently build huge generalizations upon individual observations. Among the most evident examples are the "vicious mole of nature" speech (I.iv.17–38 [Q2]), prompted by Claudius's drunken revel, or the conclusion that "There's a divinity that shapes our ends" drawn from Hamlet's good fortune in detecting Claudius's plot to have him killed in England (V.ii.4–11 [F & Q2]). The F Laertes's generalization about love thus brings his part in the latter half of the play into closer relation to Hamlet's and perhaps provides, for the audience, a further basis for the analogy that Hamlet will later draw between Laertes and himself.

Laertes next appears, alone with Claudius, in the scene in which they plot the treacherous fencing match, a scene substantially abbreviated in F in comparison to Q2. Two major passages are affected (the lines appearing in Q2 alone are in pointed brackets):

LAERTES: It warms the very sickness in my heart
     That I shall [Q2: *omit* shall] live and tell him {Hamlet} to his teeth,
     "Thus didst [F: diddest] thou."

KING: If it be so, Laertes—
     As how should it be so? How otherwise?—
     Will you be rul'd by me?

LAERTES: <Ay, my lord,>
       So you will [F: If so you'l] not o'errule me to a peace.

KING: To thine own peace. If he be now returned,
       As checking [Q2: the King] at his voyage, and that he means
       No more to undertake it, I will work him
       To an exploit, now ripe in my device,
       Under the which he shall not choose but fall;
       And for his death no wind of blame shall breathe,
       But even his mother shall uncharge the practice
       And call it accident.

<LAERTES: My lord, I will be rul'd,
       The rather if you could devise it so
       That I might be the organ.

KING: It falls right.
       You have been talk'd of since your travel much,
       And that in Hamlet's hearing, for a quality
       Wherein, they say, you shine. Your sum of parts
       Did not together pluck such envy from him
       As did that one, and that, in my regard,
       Of the unworthiest siege.

LAERTES: What part is that, my lord?

KING: A very riband in the cap of youth.
       Yet needful too, for youth no less becomes
       The light and careless livery that it wears
       Than settled age his sables and his weeds,
       Importing health and graveness.> Two [F: Some
       two] months since [F: hence]
       Here was a gentleman of Normandy.

                            (IV.vii.54–82)

Claudius then goes on to praise the gentleman, whom Laertes identifies as Lamord and also praises.

KING: He made confession of you,
       And gave you such a masterly report
       For art and exercise in your defense,
       And for your rapier most especial [F: especiallye],
       That he cried out, 'twould be a sight indeed,
       If one could match you. <The scrimers of their nation,
       He swore, had neither motion, guard, nor eye,
       If you oppos'd them.> Sir, this report of his
       Did Hamlet so envenom with his envy
       That he could nothing do but wish and beg
       Your sudden coming o'er, to play with you [F: him].
       Now out of this—

LAERTES: What [F: Why] out of this, my lord?

KING: Laertes, was your father dear to you?
Or are you like the painting of a sorrow,
A face without a heart?

LAERTES: Why ask you this?

KING: Not that I think you did not love your father,
But that I know love is begun by time,
And that I see, in passages of proof,
Time qualifies the spark and fire of it.
<There lives within the very flame of love
A kind of wick or snuff that will abate it,
And nothing is at a like goodness still,
For goodness, growing to a plurisy,
Dies in his own too much. That we would do,
We should do when we would; for this "would" changes
And hath abatements and delays as many
As there are tongues, are hands, are accidents,
And then this "should" is like a spendthrift's [Q2: spend thirfts] sigh,
That hurts by easing. But, to the quick o' th' ulcer:>
Hamlet comes back. What would you undertake
To show yourself your father's son in deed [F: indeed; Q2: indeede your fathers sonne]
More than in words?

LAERTES: To cut his throat i' th' church.

KING: No place, indeed, should murder sanctuarize;
Revenge should have no bounds
Thereafter the two devise the mechanics of their plot.)

(IV.vii.95–128)

In the first Q2-only passage (11. 67–81), Laertes is subjected to much double-edged flattery that demeans him more than it elevates him. While appearing to praise Laertes's mastery of fencing, Claudius is careful never to indicate his own acceptance of what is said of it ("you have been talk'd of," and "they say"), nor is Claudius willing to grant that, however attractive Laertes's mastery may be to others, including Hamlet, it is in any way truly noble or substantial: of all of Laertes's achievements (the rest of which are never cited), Claudius represents Laertes's fencing as the "one . . . in my regard, / Of the unworthiest siege," merely a "riband in the cap of youth." Because it is "in the cap of youth," it may seem prominent, but it is a mere decoration, a "riband," part of "the light and careless livery" of youth, which Claudius contrasts with signs of the "graveness" of "settled age." Claudius's Q2 flattery of Laertes appears especially hollow and demeaning in contrast with the king's unqualified praise of Lamord's horsemanship (ll. 81–90). Then, in the last Q2-only passage (ll. 114–23), Claudius lengthens considerably his taunting suggestions that Laertes's devotion to his dead father is transient, in a speech that at the same time postpones Claudius's disclosure of the details of his plot against Hamlet, which Laertes wants to hear.[10] Meanwhile Laertes, in Q2, is reduced to offering himself up unconditionally as the king's tool ("My lord, I will be rul'd") and begging to be used ("The rather if you could devise it so / That I might be the organ"); but his capitulation fails to elicit from Claudius the particulars of the king's scheme and, instead, forces Laertes almost silently to endure Claudius's lightly veiled mockery, now that the king has him on the hook.

In the F version, Laertes can hardly be said to escape either domination or needling by Claudius, but in F Laertes stops short of utter capitulation to the king, never withdrawing the condition he places on cooperation with Claudius ("so you'l not o'errule me to a peace" [TLN 3070]) and never begging to be used. Simply because so much of what Claudius says in Q2 is omitted from F, Laertes is not forced to wait so long for Claudius to divulge the scheme and is not mocked half so much. Without overemphasizing the differences between the two texts produced by the shortening of this exchange in F, I believe it can be said that Laertes escapes in the F version of this scene with a measure of dignity and independence that is denied him in Q2. Whichever version of the scene we read, Claudius bests Laertes, but readers of F may find the regard that Hamlet privately expresses for Laertes in the last scene of F more appropriate to the Laertes that F presents to us (if not directly to Hamlet) than to Q2's Laertes. But in Q2 Hamlet does not privately express any regard for Laertes in V.ii. Only in the modern combined Q2/F text is Laertes represented as delivering himself up to humiliation by Claudius as the king's tool in IV.vii and then as somehow winning respect from Hamlet in V.ii. The variations between Q2 and F in IV.vii affect Claudius's role as much as they affect Laertes's, and I will return to Claudius in a consideration of the way in which F and Q2 vary in their presentation of his relation to Hamlet.

II

When revisionist textual critics began to advance the argument that Shakespeare revised *King Lear*, altering the text printed in quarto to become the Folio version, others wondered, with some justification, why Shakespeare would undertake revision merely to adjust the roles of so many secondary characters (Albany and Edgar, Kent, Goneril, the Fool) and do so little, in the course of alleged revision, with the part of Lear himself. While it is not my contention that Shakespeare must have been responsible for any or all of the variations between Q2 and F Hamlet, the same objection would not apply. No role varies so much between these two texts as does Hamlet's.

Philip Edwards has already discussed some of the major variants in the conventional terms of textual criticism—that is, in terms of the putative origins of the variants. His account of them involves adapting a longstanding hypothesis about a handful of minor variants between Q2 and F and applying it to whole passages present in one text but absent from the other. I cannot share Edwards's views regarding either the minor or the major variants that he assesses, yet because his analysis, by the time he completes it, represents a strongly innovative approach to the textual problem of *Hamlet*, it deserves respect and detailed consideration. (Readers who have no interest in the minutiae of textual criticism may wish to bypass the rest of section II of this article.)

I begin where Edwards does—with the minor variants. According to Edwards (and many others), Q2 *Hamlet*, like the second quarto of *Romeo and Juliet* and the first quarto of *Love's Labour's Lost*, was set into type from Shakespeare's own working papers, in which the playwright failed to mark deleted passages in a way that might later command the attention of the compositors who set all three quartos into type. Consequently, according to the tradition that Edwards follows, Q2 *Hamlet*, like the other two quartos, contains both Shakespeare's "first shots" and "second thoughts." Yet in the case of *Hamlet* alone we fortunately possess an F-text that preserves only the authoritative "second thoughts," and we can use F to correct Q2 in these cases, even though, according to the tradition that Edwards follows, a great many other variants in F are judged to be quite unauthoritative.[11]

I hope that the last few sentences fairly represent the hypothesis that Edwards states, but when he begins to employ it to generate examples from Q2 and F, the hypothesis applies to only four variants, not all of which it can entirely account for; and when Edwards tries to use it to generate a fifth example, he falls into contradiction. In the first of these, Shakespeare, it is said, revised a couplet as he wrote it, but he failed properly to delete his first use of "I be":

> Q2: Both heere and hence pursue me lasting strife,
>   If once I be a widdow, euer I be a wife.
>
> F: Both heere, and hence, pursue me lasting strife,
>   If I once a Widdow, euer I be Wife.
>   (III.ii.220–21)

(This explanation completely ignores Q2's extrametrical "a wife" for F's "Wife.") In another case, according to the tradition Edwards follows, Shakespeare got into a muddle with the couplets in the Player King's speech, which he did not adequately clarify in his papers, so that again Q2 prints the playwright's various attempts to resolve it: "For women feare too much, euen as they loue,/And womens feare and loue hold quantitie,/Eyther none, in neither ought, or in extremitie." Again, according to Edwards, F prints only Shakespeare's "second thought," in which the first of the Q2 lines, which is only half a couplet in Q2, is deleted and the third smoothed out: "For womens Feare and Loue, holds quantitie,/In neither ought, or in extremity" (III.ii.165–66). (This time there arises the improbability of Shakespeare's managing to write so many other couplets before and after this passage, but getting into two difficulties here in the space of three lines.) In another case, Shakespeare is supposed to have originally inscribed "threescore" and then changed his mind to "three thousand," neglecting adequately to erase "-score": Q2 reads "threescore thousand crownes" and F "three thousand Crownes" (II.ii.73). Later in II.ii, Q2 reads "some dosen lines, or sixteene lines" but F "some dosen or sixteene lines," and so Shakespeare, it is asserted, originally hit upon "dosen lines" and then later decided on "dosen or sixteene lines" but did not completely cross out his earlier "lines" (1. 541). Even if Edwards's hypothesis is sometimes less than adequate for some of these examples, so far his arguments are logically consistent—in each he asserts that by overlooking Shakespeare's (allegedly inadequate) deletion marks, the Q2 compositors printed both of Shakespeare's alternatives.

Yet in the fifth example that Edwards offers, a Q2 compositor is said to have fallen into error precisely because he did register one of Shakespeare's deletion marks (in quoting this passage I again place the lines present only in Q2, not in F, in pointed brackets):

> And [F: To] let them know both what we mean to do
> And what's untimely done,
> <Whose whisper o'er the world's diameter
> As level as the cannon to his blank,
> Transports his pois'ned shot, may miss our name
> And hit the woundless air.> O, come away!
> My soul is full of discord and dismay.
>
> (IV.i.39–45)

This time the Q2 compositor is represented as correctly deleting the last half of the second line, but incorrectly printing the next three and a half lines, and the F text is represented as correctly omitting all four lines beginning with the half-line omitted from Q2. So, by addressing this case, Edwards and the tradition that he follows are having it both ways, explaining some variants as the consequence of Shakespeare's failure to mark deletions adequately, but this variant as the result of Shakespeare's clear indication of a deletion in the manuscript from which Q2 was printed.[12]

Furthermore, when Edwards draws an analogy between the alleged "first shots" and "second thoughts" in Q2 *Hamlet* and those in *Love's Labour's Lost* and *Romeo and Juliet*, he asserts a continuity in Shakespeare's habits of composition across the three texts—a continuity I believe to be specious. In *LLL* and *Rom.* we find nearly identical versions of four or more lines of verse printed in close succession to each other, one presumably the "first shot," the other the "second thought"; for example, in the second quarto of *Rom.*, the following lines are first given to Romeo near the end of II.ii and then again to the Friar at the beginning of II.iii (I include the few variants between the two versions in square brackets):

> The grey eyde morne smiles on the frowning night,
> Checkring [Checking] the Easterne Clouds with streaks of light,
> And darknesse fleckted [fleckeld darknesse] like a drunkard reeles,
> From forth daies pathway [path], made by [and] *Tytans* [burning] wheeles.
>
> (sig. D4ᵛ)

In *Hamlet* there are no comparable duplicate passages—at most a word or two gets repeated (see the discussion of "lines" or "I be" above), not four or more complete lines. No proper analogy is evident between the minor variants between Q2 and F *Hamlet* quoted above and the major duplications in *Rom.* and *LLL*. Only by assuming that the manuscript from which Q2 *Hamlet* was printed contained duplications similar to those evident in the *Rom.* and *LLL* quartos is it possible to explain variants between Q2 and F *Hamlet* as arising from duplication, yet the most evident difference between Q2 *Hamlet* and the other quartos is that Q2 *Hamlet* contains no comparable duplications. Indeed it is surprising that the five coincidences between errors in Q2 *Hamlet* and omissions of Q2 readings and lines from F have ever been thought to need such elaborate explanation as is provided by the tradition that Edwards follows. Editors have detected hundreds of errors in Q2, and hundreds of Q2 readings and lines are omitted from F. That in a small handful of cases a Q2 error should coincide with an F omission is hardly cause for elaborate theorizing about the origin of these few variants. Only a desire to recover the lost moment of Shakespeare's original composition of *Hamlet* can account for the arbitrary projection of a few selected variants upon Shakespeare's habits of composition.

III

Nevertheless, according to Edwards, Q2 contains not only Shakespeare's first and second tries at isolated readings, but also long speeches that Shakespeare experimented with but then rejected. Edwards finds evidence of Shakespeare's dissatisfaction with these speeches in their omission from F. But Edwards would have it that Shakespeare remained pleased with other passages that are nonetheless omitted from F; these, on Edwards's theory, failed to please a hypothetical bookkeeper who, Edwards believes, made further cuts to the F text after Shakespeare had finished with it. Edwards denies that either F or Q2 preserves Shakespeare's final intentions for *Hamlet*, and he denies that combination of these two early texts can provide what Shakespeare finally wanted. Instead, Edwards demands that an editor determine what in both texts finally pleased Shakespeare. To discover Shakespeare's pleasure at this late date may, I'm afraid, tax not only an editor's scholarship but also his or her powers of divination.

Edwards concentrates primarily on the omission from F of two major Q2 passages and the inclusion in F of an extra line in Hamlet's conversation with Horatio in V.ii. The first omission affects the conclusion of Hamlet's interview with his mother in her closet. While in both texts, Hamlet parts from Gertrude by alluding to his imminent journey to England, only in Q2 does Hamlet voice his aggressive suspicions of Rosencrantz and Guildenstern, who are to accompany him to England, and his plan to use against them whatever device they are to use, wittingly or unwittingly, against him. Again, in quoting the texts, I place the lines unique to Q2 in pointed brackets:

HAMLET: I must to England; you know that?

QUEEN: Alack, I had forgot. 'Tis so concluded on.

HAMLET: <There's letters seal'd, and my two schoolfellows,
Whom I will trust as I will adders fang'd,
They bear the mandate; they must sweep on my way,
And marshal me to knavery. Let it work.
For 'tis the sport to have the enginer
Hoist with his own petar, and 't [Q2: an't] shall go hard
But I will delve one yard below their mines,
And blow them at the moon. O, 'tis most sweet,
When in one line two crafts directly meet.>
This man shall set me packing.
I'll lug the guts into the neighbor room.

(III.iv.207–19)

Edwards argues that Shakespeare himself deleted this passage for several reasons: among them, "Hamlet has been given no means of learning that [Rosencrantz and Guildenstern] are to go with him" and "the audience has still to be told . . . that Claudius is using the voyage to England to liquidate Hamlet" (p. 15), since Claudius does not reveal this intention until three scenes later (IV.iii.62–72). Yet the very same objections apply to Hamlet's and the queen's references to his impending journey to England, which are not omitted from F and so, according to Edwards's theory, were not cut by Shakespeare. Although Claudius first broaches the idea of sending Hamlet to England at III.i.172 ff., the king agrees, at Polonius's request, to postpone a decision until after Gertrude interviews Hamlet (III.iv). Upset by "The Mousetrap" play, Claudius announces his decision to Rosencrantz and Guildenstern alone at the beginning of III.iii, when Gertrude is represented as awaiting Hamlet in her closet and Hamlet as coming to her. Since F preserves Hamlet's reference to the journey to England—something he can no more know, according to Edwards's criteria, than he can that Rosencrantz and Guildenstern are to accompany him or that the king is planning his death— F is as vulnerable to Edwards's objection as is Q2.

But Edwards has other reservations about the Q2 "engineer" speech— reservations that he assumes Shakespeare shared. Edwards assumes that the speech expresses Hamlet's "new conviction . . . that Rosencrantz and Guildenstern are accomplices in a plot to destroy him" (p. 15)—and Edwards means *knowing accomplices* because he later contrasts the word *accomplices* with "unwitting agents in the king's plot" (p. 16). Motivated by this alleged "conviction," Hamlet, according to Edwards, formulates, in the "engineer" speech, a definite plan against his schoolfellows; in order to carry it out, Hamlet neglects "his main task of revenge" against Claudius, "in spite of the recent re-appearance of the Ghost urging" him to it, and, instead, "accepts the journey to England" (p. 15). But, Edwards goes on, the "definiteness of Hamlet's plans" in the "engineer" speech contradicts Hamlet's later account—common to both Q2 and F—of his escape from Rosencrantz and Guildenstern. In V.ii.4–25, Hamlet describes his "idea of entering the cabin of Rosencrantz and Guildenstern [as] a sudden inspiration, a wild rashness, in which he saw the hand of Providence"— an "unplanned move" (p. 15).

Because of this alleged contradiction in Q2, Edwards concludes that the "engineer" speech is another "first shot" ultimately rejected by Shakespeare, who in a "second thought" added a line to Hamlet's exchange with Horatio in V.ii to compensate for the cut. When Hamlet describes how he rewrote the "grand commission" to call for Rosencrantz and Guildenstern's deaths, Horatio comments, in both the early printed texts, "So Guildenstern and Rosencrantz go to 't," but, in F alone, the first line of Hamlet's reply is the self-justification, "Why, man, they did make love to this employment" (V.ii.56–57). Shakespeare added this line, Edwards says, to etch Hamlet's "wish to exculpate himself in the new moral context for the deaths of Rosencrantz and Guildenstern" (p. 16), for, in what Edwards regards as Shakespeare's revised version, Hamlet has not destroyed the two out of the conviction, allegedly expressed in the Q2 "engineer" speech, that they are Claudius's accomplices; rather, Hamlet sends to their deaths these men he knows to be "no more than repulsive sneaks, royal toadies, who are unwitting agents in the king's plot, [and] their grim punishment is a more sensitive affair" (p. 16).

Finally, according to Edwards, the "Hoist on his own petar" speech also produces other contradictions within Q2, this time with Hamlet's soliloquy, "How all occasions do inform against me," which is unique to Q2 and which, Edwards believes, is another "first shot" that Shakespeare ultimately rejected. The soliloquy, on Edwards's account, "looks like an alternative to the 'engineer' speech. . . . As Hamlet faces being sent to England, we are given first a demonstration of defiance and determination; then we are to see him in a state of nerveless drifting, bafflement, indecision and inactivity," expressed, for Edwards, in what he regards as the "core" of "How all occasions do inform against me":

> Now, whether it be
> Bestial oblivion, or some craven scruple
> Of thinking too precisely on th' event—
> A thought which, quarter'd, hath but one part wisdom
> And ever three parts coward—I do not know
> Why yet I live to say "This thing's to do,"
> Sith I have cause and will and strength and means
> To do't.
>
> (IV.iv.39–46)

Edwards then goes on to denigrate this soliloquy at length: it is "a second attempt, a contradictory attempt, and a weaker attempt [than the "engineer" speech] to provide a psychological bridge for this very difficult stage of the plot. . . . Hamlet has become so immense in his mystery, so unfathomable, that the speech is scarcely adequate for the speaker" (p. 17). Since, according to Edwards, Hamlet deliberately postpones his revenge against Claudius by choosing to accept Claudius's plan to send him to England, Hamlet's reference here to having "cause and will and strength and means" to undertake revenge makes no sense; the speech, Edwards says, "does not know all that has gone before it" (p. 17).

Like most recent attempts to argue for Shakespeare's revision of a play, Edwards's is marked by a reduction of passages in each of the polysemous versions to a single "meaning" that can readily be contrasted to the "meaning" of the other to indicate an alleged revision between the two. Also typical of revisionism is Edwards's denigration of the allegedly earlier version, so that revision can be plausibly represented as producing a substantial improvement in the play. Because I find neither of these revisionist moves persuasive, all that I can accept from Edwards's case is that Hamlet's self-justificatory line "Why, man, they did make love to this employment" does, in fact, seem appropriate to the F version, in which Hamlet, having decided on impulse to send Rosencrantz and Guildenstern to their deaths, is forced to reflect upon this sudden decision, apparently for the first time. I can find nothing in Q2 to support Edwards's view that the "engineer" speech (found in Q2 alone) reveals Hamlet's "conviction" that Rosencrantz and Guildenstern are knowing accomplices in Claudius's plan to have Hamlet assassinated. Hamlet can mistrust Rosencrantz and Guildenstern "as adders fang'd" merely because he knows that Claudius is making use of them; they can bear a mandate, sweep his way, and marshall him to knavery without knowing the contents of the mandate or the destination toward which they guide him; Hamlet may resolve to "hoist" or undermine them simply because they have agreed to act on Claudius's behalf, whether or not they are privy to the king's plot. Equally difficult to accept is Edwards's insistence upon the "definiteness of Hamlet's plans" in the "engineer" speech and therefore upon the so-called contradictions in Q2 between that speech and Hamlet's conversation with Horatio in V.ii, in which Hamlet represents his discovery of the assassination plot against him and his reversal of it as spontaneous acts, not a deep plot. Indeed the language of the "engineer" speech is so highly figurative that anyone experiencing Q2 *Hamlet* diachronically would probably find it impossible to put such a precise construction on the speech as to imagine later that it contradicts Hamlet's words to Horatio.[13]

There is much in Q2 to contradict Edwards's assertions that Hamlet *chooses* to accompany Rosencrantz and Guildenstern to England and thereby deliberately *postpones* revenge against Claudius. Claudius's plot to send Hamlet to England does not depend upon any choice by Hamlet, nor is Hamlet represented as making any choice. After all, Hamlet's travel, like Laertes's, has been controlled by the king since the beginning of the play. In I.ii when Claudius declares that Hamlet's "intent / In going back to school in Wittenberg / . . . is most retrograde to our desire" (ll. 112–14 [F & Q2]), Hamlet must stay in Denmark. No matter how Hamlet and Gertrude learn of Claudius's intention to dispatch Hamlet to England, Hamlet and the queen recognize that Hamlet has no choice: "I must to England," Hamlet says, and Gertrude replies, "'Tis so concluded on" (III.iv.207–8 [F & Q2]). Hamlet recognizes that Claudius will find in the slaughter of Polonius a pretext for Hamlet's immediate departure—"This man shall set me packing" (III.iv.218 [F & Q2])—as indeed Claudius does in an announcement to Hamlet, now under guard, that brooks no denial: "Hamlet, this deed . . . / . . . must send thee hence./ . . . Therefore prepare thyself. . . . / . . . everything is [F: at] bent / For England" (IV.iii.41–47). Hamlet's only expressions of enthusiasm for the journey—"Good"; "Come, for England!" (ll. 50, 57 [Q2 & F])—are voiced to Claudius and so can hardly be represented as expressive rather than rhetorically deceptive. Finally, when Edwards alleges a contradiction between the defiance of the "engineer" speech and the "nerveless drifting" in what he calls the "core" of "How all occasions . . ." he simply ignores most of the soliloquy, whose conclusion, for example, is wholly defiant: "O, from this time forth, / My thoughts be bloody, or be nothing worth!" (IV.iv.65–66). The following analysis of variations in Hamlet's role between Q2 and F does not depend on any theory of the origins of these texts and thus differs widely from Edwards's.

IV

Readers of the modern combined Q2/F text may, like Edwards, find Hamlet's Q2 "engineer" speech problematic, since, in the combined text, Hamlet has never before this speech been represented as so suspicious of Claudius's motives or of Rosencrantz and Guildenstern. A reader of Q2, on the other hand, might perhaps be less surprised by the "engineer" speech and might well perceive in Hamlet's facility for anticipating Claudius's devices the continuation of a pattern already established in Q2. The first episode in this pattern may occur as early as II.ii of Q2, in which Claudius and Gertrude set Hamlet's schoolfellows upon him to glean the cause of his antic disposition. Q2 gives its readers no indication of how Hamlet can possibly have developed the suspicion that Rosencrantz and Guildenstern have been summoned to court by the king and queen (just as Q2 will later fail to provide any account of why Hamlet suspects Claudius of "knavery" in sending the prince to England). Yet Q2 nevertheless represents Hamlet as identifying his schoolfellows as Claudius's informers before they have an opportunity to expose themselves. This first encounter between Hamlet and his former schoolfellows begins as follows in Q2 (printed in Bevington as II.ii.222–36, 271–93):

GUYL: My honor'd Lord.

ROS: My most deere Lord.

HAM: My extent good friends, how doost thou *Guyldersterne?* A *Rosencraus*, good lads how doe you both?

ROS: As the indifferent children of the earth.

GUYL: Happy, in that we are not euer happy on Fortunes lap. We are not the very button.

HAM: Nor the soles of her shooe.

ROS: Neither my Lord.

HAM: Then you liue about her wast, or in the middle of her fauors.

GUYL: Faith her priuates we.

HAM: In the secret parts of Fortune, oh most true, she is a strumpet, What newes?

ROS: None my Lord, but the worlds growne honest.

AM: Then is Doomes day neere, but your newes is not true; But in the beaten way of friendship, what make you at *Elsonoure?*

ROS: To visit you my Lord, no other occasion.

HAM: Begger that I am, I am euer poore in thankes, but I thanke you, and sure deare friends, my thankes are too deare a halfpeny: were you not sent for? is it your owne inclining? is it a free visitation? come, come, deale iustly with me, come, come, nay speake.

GUY: What should we say my Lord?

HAM: Anything but to'th purpose: you were sent for, and there is a kind of confession in your lookes, which your modesties haue not craft enough to cullour. I know the good King and Queene haue sent for you.

ROS: To what end my Lord?

HAM: That you must teach me: but let me coniure you, by the rights of our fellowship, by the consonancie of our youth, by the obligation of our euer preserued loue; and by what more deare a better proposer can charge you withall, bee euen and direct with me whether you were sent for or no.

ROS: What say you.

HAM: Nay then I haue an eye of you? If you loue me hold not of.

GUYL: My Lord we were sent for.

(Q2, sigs. F1^v–F2^r)

Hamlet is not represented here as knowing in advance that Rosencrantz and Guildenstern have been sent for. Instead he is portrayed as being alert to the possibility of Claudius's setting spies upon him, and so, as soon as the former schoolfellows have greeted each other and bantered about the strumpet Fortune, Hamlet asks if his "friends" have been sent for. When he gets no answer, he claims to "know the good King and Queene haue sent for you," but he does not yet *know*. If he *knew*, he would not continue to pester them to admit they have been summoned, and he would not wait until Rosencrantz speaks "aside" to Guildenstern ("what say you")—an obvious admission of collusion with Claudius—to confide to the audience in his own aside, "Nay then I haue an eye of you." Yet by confidently exploiting his initially groundless suspicions that Rosencrantz and Guildenstern are spies and by accusing them, Hamlet not only foils Claudius's plot to discover Hamlet's mind but also achieves a strategic advantage over the king by confirming his own suspicions of the king's intention of spying on him. Perhaps having already "hoist[ed]" the king "on his own petar" here in II.ii of Q2, long before delivering the "engineer" speech in the closet scene, Hamlet may, in the later scene, confidently predict a repetition of his success if he again pursues his suspicions—this time, the suspicion that Claudius is dispatching him to England in order to harm him. Until the Q2 Claudius devises the fencing match, he is represented as quite overmatched by a Hamlet who is led by his almost preternatural wariness to suspect even the seemingly innocuous.

In F's II.ii, in contrast, Rosencrantz and Guildenstern betray themselves to Hamlet. First they deny his representation of Denmark as a "prison," and then they clumsily accuse him of ambition, a charge that could logically come only from supporters of the reigning king. F interpolates the passage (signaled here by pointed brackets) between the jokes about strumpet Fortune and Hamlet's revelation of his suspicion that Rosencrantz and Guildenstern are the king's informers:

> HAMLET: In the secret parts of Fortune? O, most true; she is a strumpet. What [F: What's the] news?
>
> ROSENCRANTZ: None, my lord, but [F: but that] the world's grown honest.
>
> HAMLET: Then is doomsday near. But your news is not true. <Let me question more in particular. What have you, my good friends, deserv'd at the hands of Fortune that she sends you to prison hither?
>
> GUILDENSTERN: Prison, my lord?
>
> HAMLET: Denmark's a prison.
>
> ROSENCRANTZ: Then is the world one.
>
> HAMLET: A goodly one, in which there are many confines, wards, and dungeons, Denmark being one o' th' worst.
>
> ROSENCRANTZ: We think not so, my lord.
>
> HAMLET: Why then 'tis none to you, for there is nothing either good or bad but thinking makes it so. To me it is a prison.
>
> ROSENCRANTZ: Why then, your ambition makes it one. 'Tis too narrow for your mind.
>
> HAMLET: O God, I could be bounded in a nutshell and count myself a king of infinite space, were it not that I have bad dreams.
>
> GUILDENSTERN: Which dreams indeed are ambition, for the very substance of the ambitious is merely the shadow of a dream.
>
> HAMLET: A dream itself is but a shadow.
>
> ROSENCRANTZ: Truly, and I hold ambition of so airy and light a quality that it is but a shadow's shadow.
>
> HAMLET: Then are our beggars bodies, and our monarchs and outstretch'd heroes the beggars' shadows. Shall we to th' court? For, by my fay, I cannot reason.
>
> ROSENCRANTZ,
> GUILDENSTERN: We'll wait upon you.
>
> HAMLET: No such matter. I will not sort you with the rest of my servants, for, to speak to you like an honest man, I am most dreadfully attended.> But, in the beaten way of friendship, what make you at Elsinore?
>
> (II.ii.235–71)

Because Rosencrantz and Guildenstern give away the king's game themselves, F's Hamlet need not be and does not seem to be as suspicious of Claudius's plotting against him as Q2's Hamlet. It would then be less characteristic of F's Hamlet, in the closet scene, immediately to suspect the possible treachery of Claudius's plan to send him to England. Because F contains neither the "engineer" speech nor "How all occasions . . . ," F presents a silent Hamlet departing from Denmark. In F, then, Claudius's plot may seem to have quelled Hamlet, and the king may appear very much in control; his soliloquy divulging the planned assassination is uncontested in conditioning expectations of the outcome of Hamlet's voyage.[14]

The differences between Q2 and F in their representation of the contest between Hamlet and Claudius become most marked in the scenes concerning the voyage. In Q2, the advantage that Claudius believes he has attained over Hamlet in forcing the voyage on him seems, in light of Hamlet's speeches, merely illusory. While Hamlet cannot resist going, he nevertheless presents himself as capable of opposing Claudius, if not directly, at least in the persons of the king's agents, and by besting them, he can return to attack Claudius himself. Hamlet's general intention to do so, his conviction of his success, and his justification for whatever future acts he must undertake against either Claudius or his agents are among the topics of Q2's "engineer" speech and "How all occasions do inform against me," which are not necessarily inconsistent with each other in spite of Edwards's allegation.

Paradoxically, then, in Q2, Claudius's dispatch of Hamlet for England, rather than establishing an advantage for the king, instead hardens Hamlet's resolve relentlessly to oppose him and his agents—the resolve that in Q2 carries Hamlet through the interrupted voyage to England and back to Denmark to kill the king. In Q2 the expression of this resolve in the "How all occasions . . ." soliloquy makes this speech seem the pivot upon which that version turns. There is much more to this soliloquy than Edwards allows in arbitrarily privileging a few lines of it as its alleged "core." The soliloquy may indeed begin on a note of impatient self-castigation (IV.iv.32–46 [Q2]). Yet the speech goes on to reveal a Hamlet who discovers a basis for action in the concept of honor, which he finds superlatively exemplified in Fortinbras:

> . . . Examples gross as earth exhort me:
> Witness this army of such mass and charge
> Led by a delicate and tender prince,
> Whose spirit with divine ambition puff'd
> Makes mouths at the invisible event,
> Exposing what is mortal and unsure
> To all that fortune, death, and danger dare,
> Even for an egg-shell. Rightly to be great
> Is not to stir without great argument,
> But greatly to find quarrel in a straw
> When honor's at the stake. How stand I then,
> That have a father kill'd, a mother stain'd,
> Excitements of my reason and my blood,
> And let all sleep, while, to my shame, I see
> The imminent death of twenty thousand men,

> That, for a fantasy and trick of fame,
> Go to their graves like beds, fight for a plot
> Whereon the numbers cannot try the cause,
> Which is not tomb enough and continent
> To hide the slain? O, from this time forth,
> My thoughts be bloody, or be nothing worth!
>   (IV.iv.46–66 [Q2])

Briefly itemizing his grievances against Claudius and contrasting these powerful "excitements" against the "egg-shell" motives of Fortinbras, who, "for
a fantasy," will send thousands to their death, Hamlet represents himself as
compelled by honor to prosecute his revenge. "How all occasions . . ."
marks the last time in Q2 that Hamlet is given an opportunity to determine
the necessity of Claudius's death and the deaths of his agents, and it presents
the secular concept of honor as the ground of this determination.

   F, on the other hand, reserves Hamlet's ultimate justification of his
revenge until his V.ii conversation with Horatio, which, as has already been
noticed, is much expanded in F. This expansion initially takes the form of
the continuation and completion of a speech by Hamlet that is interrupted
by the entrance of Osric in Q2 (the F-only lines are in pointed brackets):

> Does it not, think thee, stand me now upon—
> He that hath kill'd my king and whor'd my mother.
> Popp'd in between th'election and my hopes,
> Thrown out his angle for my proper life,
> And with such coz'nage—is't not perfect conscience
>   [Q2: *Enter a Courtier.* {Osric}]
> <To quit him with this arm? And is't not to be damn'd
> To let this canker of our nature come
> In further evil?

> HORATIO: It must be shortly known to him from England
>   What is the issue of the business there.

> HAMLET: It will be short. The interim is [F: interim's] mine.
>   And a man's life's no more than to say "One."">
>   (V.ii.63–74)

In F, Hamlet finally justifies his revenge in terms of its necessity to his
salvation ("And is't not to be damn'd . . . ?"), rather than, as in Q2, in
terms of the obligations of the purely secular concept of honor. However
unintelligible to a modern audience the concept of a sacred act of violence
may be, Edwards, who much prefers F's alternative to Q's, has argued, citing
Tyndale, that the concept was available to a Renaissance audience. Although
Edwards stops short of elevating Hamlet's revenge to the realm of the sacred,

he suggests that, in F at least, *Hamlet* is a profoundly religious play in which the prince is tormented by the problematic status of revenge as possibly sacred, possibly damnable.[15] In V.ii of F, Hamlet resolves this debate by concluding that his salvation depends upon revenge.

This conclusion of Hamlet's may be related to his representation of the voyage from which he has just returned. In F, Hamlet departed for England in silence, seemingly vulnerable to Claudius's plot, a plot that Hamlet, so far as we can tell, failed entirely to anticipate. The F Hamlet then represents himself as completely surprised by the events that have so quickly returned him to Denmark: he writes to advise Claudius of his "sudden and more strange return" (IV.vii.46–47 [F]). This reading, unique to F, may throw considerably more emphasis on Hamlet's reference in V.ii (common to Q2 and F) to "a divinity that shapes our ends, / Rough-hew them how we will" (ll. 10–11), whose agency Hamlet represents as having preserved him. If, in F, Hamlet credits his survival to a special providence, he may go on, later in F's V.ii, to conclude that he has been preserved in order to execute sacred vengeance upon Claudius, into whose kingdom he has been so strangely returned. Now he thinks that he has recovered the advantage over Claudius that he seemed to have lost when the king sent him off—"The interim is mine."

In Q2, on the other hand, Hamlet writes to Claudius only of his "sudden return," which need not seem "strange" because Hamlet left Denmark suspicious of Claudius's "knavery" and determined to undermine it in however "bloody" a manner was necessary. Thus, while Hamlet may refer in Q2 to the "divinity that shapes our ends" as providing him with the specific occasion on which to discover and reverse Claudius's plot, the emphasis in Q2 may not fall nearly so heavily upon providence as an agent in Hamlet's deliverance. Nor would it seem appropriate for the Q2 Hamlet to declare "The interim is mine," because he is not represented as ever conceding that he has lost the advantage over Claudius, even when the king sent him to England. To enjoy at least an imagined ascendancy over Claudius is not a new experience for Q2's Hamlet and would scarcely call for remark.

What I have so far argued to be a contrast in the representation of Hamlet between Q2 and F can, of course, be construed with equal justification as a contrast in the relation between Hamlet and Claudius to each other in the two printed versions. Claudius seems a stronger adversary to Hamlet in F because the king appears to gain the upper hand much earlier in sending off an apparently unsuspecting Hamlet to what seems certain death in England. It may therefore seem appropriate that, at one other point, F portrays Claudius as a more competent plotter in other ways as well. While in the Q2 version of IV.vii Claudius is interrupted quite unexpectedly as he is referring obliquely to the English assassination plot, in F Claudius appears much more cautious in anticipating interruption, breaking off his conversation with Laertes upon the approach of the messenger. Again in quoting the variant passage, I place the F-only lines in pointed brackets:

KING: . . . You must not think
That we are made of stuff so flat and dull
That we can let our beard be shook with danger
And think it pastime. You shortly shall hear more.
I lov'd your father, and we love ourself;
And that, I hope, will teach you to imagine—
Enter a Messenger with Letters [F: omit *with Letters*]
<How now? What news?

MESSENGER: Letters, my lord, from Hamlet:>
These [F: This] to your Majesty, this to the Queen.
(IV.vii.30–37)[16]

The alternative representations of Hamlet in Q2 and F may also affect other roles, most notably those of Fortinbras and Laertes. Jenkins writes that Shakespeare presents Claudius in I.ii as dealing with Fortinbras and Laertes before turning to Hamlet because later "their situations are designed to reflect his" (p. 133). But Fortinbras looms large only in Q2 with "How all occasions . . . ," and the reflection of Hamlet's situation in Laertes's becomes explicit only in F. The double reflection of Hamlet in Fortinbras and in Laertes is thus restricted to the modern combined Q2/F text. There Hamlet, about to undertake his enforced expedition to England, first contrasts himself with Fortinbras, finding that honor, which Hamlet regards as no more than a "fantasy" propelling Fortinbras's military expedition, absolutely requires Hamlet's revenge against Claudius and, perhaps, against his tools Rosencrantz and Guildenstern as well. Then the combined text presents Hamlet, upon his return to Denmark, unaccountably ignoring, but never explicitly renouncing, the claims of honor when he recasts revenge as a sacred obligation enjoined by providence. Then Hamlet stands in contrast to Laertes, who has represented himself to Claudius as caring so little for the sacred that he consigns "Conscience and grace, to the profoundest pit" (IV.v.131 [Q2 & F]), promises, if necessary, to "cut [Hamlet's] throat i' th' church" (IV.vii.125 [Q2 & F]), and, in the fencing scene, overrides the prompting of his conscience in order to kill Hamlet: "And yet it is [F: 'tis] almost against [F: 'gainst] my conscience" (V.ii.299 [Q2 & F]).

So far the combined Q2/F text provides, in this double reflection of Hamlet's situation in both Fortinbras's and Laertes's, a neat, if problematic antithesis. It is neat because one reflection (Hamlet/Fortinbras) belongs entirely to the secular realm of honor, the other (Hamlet/Laertes) to the religious in its emphasis on salvation. It is problematic because the contexts for the contrasts seem incommensurate with each other, and so may the sides of

Hamlet that they reveal. Yet even the neatness has disappeared by the end of V.ii in the combined Q2/F text, for there Laertes is represented as being as punctilious on questions of honor as Hamlet has earlier found Fortinbras to be. Laertes accepts Hamlet's apology at the beginning of the fencing match only upon conditions: "But in my terms of honor / I stand aloof, and will no reconcilement / Till by some elder masters of known honor / I have a voice and precedent of peace / To keep my name ungor'd [F: vngorg'd]" (V.ii.244–48 [Q2 & F]). Finally, then, in the combined Q2/F text, Hamlet contrasts in exactly the same way with Fortinbras and with Laertes, who are both represented, unlike Hamlet, as extremely jealous of their honor upon the least provocation, but Hamlet also contrasts in a second way with Laertes alone, since Hamlet seeks revenge as a matter of conscience, while Laertes takes revenge in spite of conscience.

Q2 and F again each offer a straighter course. In Q2, Hamlet explicitly contrasts himself only with Fortinbras, not with Laertes ("How all occasions . . ."), and only in terms of honor; Hamlet dismisses the Norwegian's conception of honor as fantastic but accepts honor as an unavoidable imperative for himself; an audience may later contrast Hamlet with Laertes in the same terms, when Laertes's refusal even to pretend to accept an apology without consulting "elder masters of known honor" may seem as nice as the issue that has sent Fortinbras to war. In sum, the basis for contrasts and comparisons among the three characters provided in Q2 is honor. In F, however, Hamlet compares himself only with Laertes, who stands out in F (which lacks "How all occasions . . .") as the only remaining exponent of the secular value of honor because the F Hamlet regards his own revenge as sacred. In the F antithesis, then, Hamlet lays claim to religious values, which Laertes rejects; Laertes lays claim to honor, a matter on which Hamlet is silent.

V

According to the conventions of revisionist textual criticism, I should now rise in an *o altitudo* to invoke Shakespeare as necessarily the source of the divergent patterns in Q2 and F unearthed here: "all that is needed is Shakespeare, capable of preternatural brilliance, well within his observed capacity to strike us dumb with amazement."[17] Probably this convention stands in need of reform. While, like other revisionists, I have been intent upon asserting continuities within each of the early printed texts and discontinuities between them, there are no grounds for privileging the alleged integrity of each of Q2 and F to the host of aesthetic forms that critics have produced from their reading of the combined Q2/F text. Indeed, the divergent aesthetic patterns that I have abstracted from Q2 and F are radically unstable and threaten, at every turn, to collapse into the combination with each other that is so familiar from the editorial tradition. For example, as I have already allowed, it seems impossible to disentangle Hamlet's F speech representing revenge as necessary to salvation ("And is't not to be damn'd . . . ?") from his reference to "a divinity that shapes our ends," and, it could be added, from his earlier conception of himself as "scourge and minister" of heaven (III.iv.182), even though both the latter speeches are in both Q2 and F. Instances quickly multiply: the acutely suspicious Hamlet, whom I have tried to confine to the Q2 version, leaps up in the nunnery scene in *both* versions to ask suspiciously of Ophelia, "Where's your father?" (III.i.131).

The only imaginable grounds for privileging Q2 and F with unassailable integrity would be evidence that each is independently linked to Shakespeare. While the historicity of the variants discussed in this paper is evident from the printed documents themselves, just as the historicity of the playwright Shakespeare is well documented, there is no document to link the variants to the playwright. As purely aesthetic patterns the variations discussed in this paper can have no claim to historicity; they do not exist beyond this paper. To claim that such patterns must originate with Shakespeare is to abolish the distinction between history and aesthetics.[18] In addition, the patterns of variation displayed here are hardly coterminous with the variants between the historical documents designated Q2 and F. Many of the Q2/F variants are so trivial that they defy discussion; but there are also a number of sizeable variations between the two texts that resist inclusion in any of the continuities proposed here. Among them are Horatio's speech on the death of Caesar (I.i.108–25 [Q2]), Hamlet's on the "vicious mole of nature" (I.iv.17–38 [Q2]), and the "little eyases" passage (II.ii.337–62 [F]). If an aesthetic design determined the formation of each of the early printed texts and if that design transcended history—necessary assumptions for those who would infer Shakespearean authorship from the aesthetic forms they, as readers, constitute in variants between early printed texts—it would be possible now to account for all the Q2/F variants in terms of it. But no such design is self-evident; without it, the possibility of imagining that in reading F and Q2 we are in the presence of Shakespeare's true art, in both its original and revised forms, disappears.

Lacking evidence of revision between early printed versions of the plays, revisionist critics have resorted to arguments from analogy to assign these versions to Shakespeare. In an attempt to establish a trans-historical conception of the author as tireless reviser, E.A.J. Honigmann has presented the manuscript revisions of poets as far removed from Shakespeare as Keats and Burns to show that the minor verbal changes they habitually introduced in recopying their own work often resemble the variants between early printed texts of Shakespeare's plays.[19] Since the capacity of scribes and typesetters to introduce changes indistinguishable from those of poets themselves was already well attested, Honigmann's research left the problem of the origin of such variants in early printed plays unresolved.[20] Then John Kerrigan examined documented authorial revisions of English Renaissance plays and compared the variants in them to those produced in the course of theatrical adaptations of plays by non-authorial hands. He concluded that authorial revisions issued not only in major additions, deletions, and substitutions (such as those treated in this paper) but also in a plethora of minor verbal alterations throughout the play (of the sort documented in many of the passages common to Q2 and F quoted in this paper). In contrast, nonauthorial adaptation produced only major variants, leaving the verbal texture of the rest of a play untouched.[21] Still the problem of identifying the origin of printed texts containing both major variants and many minor verbal differences remains in dispute: obviously such a printed play could preserve authorial revision, but it just as likely could represent a nonauthorial theatrical adaptation (hence the major variants) that had been copied one or more times by scribes (hence the numerous minor variants, to which the typesetters would have added).

Others have preferred to redefine the function of the author with reference to the fragmentary evidence of Shakespeare's biography. As dramatic poet, player, and sharer in a dramatic company, Shakespeare, it is asserted, would have embraced every stage in the production of one of his plays. He might write it without reference to the theatrical purpose to which it finally would be put: hence, the argument goes, the many ambiguities and even confusions in the designations of characters in some early printed plays. But then Shakespeare would be on hand during rehearsals to provide the necessary clarification and to cooperate with his fellow actors in trimming and shaping his play for the stage: hence, this argument continues, the many deletions from F *Hamlet* in comparison with Q2. Finally, according to George Hibbard, Shakespeare would even transcribe the revised version. Thus, on this theory, the author absorbs within himself the roles of theatrical adapter (or bookkeeper) and scribe to whom traditional textual critics, like Edwards, would consign much of the variation between printed texts. Yet no matter how much the concept of Shakespeare the author is distended, it fails to include the publication of the Folio versions of his plays in 1623, seven years after the historical Shakespeare's death. Such an attempt to force the Folio text to yield up the history of its transmission merely reveals the persistence of the same desire to recover lost origins that produced the more conventional accounts of the genesis and transmission of Q2 and F *Hamlet* that constitute Edwards's point of departure. To project all the Q2/F variants upon Shakespeare is to substitute one fiction of origin for another.

Close examination of an actual dramatic manuscript from Shakespeare's own period, such as *Thomas of Woodstock*, indicates the presence of no fewer than nine hands. How many of these, if any, are authorial can probably never be determined.[22] Had the play been printed from this manuscript, its printing would probably have erased nearly all the evidence of collaborative inscription. Such a historical document supports Foucault's characterization of the search for origins as ultimately futile and misleading, "an attempt to

capture the exact essence of things, their purest possibilities and their carefully protected identities, because this search assumes the existence of immo-
bile forms that precede the external world of accident and succession. This
search is directed to 'that which was already there,' the image of a primordial
truth fully adequate to its nature, and it necessitates the removal of every
mask to ultimately disclose an original identity. However, if the genealogist
refuses to extend his faith in metaphysics, if he listens to history, he finds
that there is 'something altogether different' behind things: not a timeless
and essential secret, but the secret that they have no essence or that their
essence was fabricated in a piecemeal fashion from alien forms."[23]

On this formulation, assertions of Shakespeare's agency alone in the
production of first the Q2 and then the F text of *Hamlet* translate these
printed versions out of the realm of history, where things are fabricated in
piecemeal fashion from alien forms through accident and succession, into
the world of metaphysics, where timeless and tireless genius produces and
then reproduces the essence of *Hamlet*. The older editorial tradition of combining Q2 and F *Hamlet* usefully acknowledges the possibility of accident
in the production of printed versions, but in attempting to recover Shakespeare's full *Hamlet* from the combination of the disparate early texts, this
tradition may simply compound the accidents of history in fashioning a
Hamlet piecemeal from what I have tried to show to be the alien forms of
Q2 and F. The critical enigmas of *Hamlet* and Hamlet that have been
projected as Shakespeare's solitary creation may, at least to some extent,
then, be the product of the latter-day accident of an editorial tradition.

Notes

1. Gary Taylor, "General Introduction," in *William Shakespeare: The Textual Companion* (Oxford: Clarendon Press, 1987), p. 14.

2. *Textual and Literary Criticism* (Cambridge: Cambridge Univ. Press, 1959), reprinted, in part, as "Textual Criticism and the Literary Critic," in Fredson Bowers, *Essays
in Bibliography, Text, and Editing* (Charlottesville: Univ. Press of Virginia, 1975), p. 304.

3. *Bibliography, Text, and Editing*, p. 373; cf. pp. 524 ff.

4. Most discussion thus far has focused on *King Lear:* Michael J. Warren, "Quarto
and Folio *King Lear* and the Interpretation of Albany and Edgar," in *Shakespeare, Patterns of
Excelling Nature*, eds. David Bevington and Jay L. Halio (Newark: Univ. of Delaware Press,
1978), pp. 95–107; Steven Urkowitz, *Shakespeare's Revision of* King Lear (Princeton: Princeton
Univ. Press, 1980); Gary Taylor. "The War in *King Lear*," *Shakespeare Survey*, 33 (1980),
27–34; and the essays by my fellow contributors to *The Division of the Kingdoms: Shakespeare's
Two Versions of* King Lear, eds. Gary Taylor and Michael Warren (Oxford: Clarendon Press,
1983). While now, as in 1983, I cannot share the belief of a number of these writers that
the two early printed versions of *Lear* must be distinct authorial versions, I could not have
approached *Hamlet* as I do without the benefit of their work and that of P.W.M. Blayney,
Nicholas Okes and the First Quarto (Cambridge: Cambridge Univ. Press, 1982), Vol. I of *The
Texts of* King Lear *and their Origins*.

5. Combining Q2 and F is hardly an unreasonable strategy and is founded on the

belief that all (or, for some editors, almost all) of both Q2 and F were written by Shakespeare but that variation between the printed versions may have been produced by other agents in the transmission of the play into print. And so editors since Rowe (1709) have preferred to provide their readers with what they regard as all of Shakespeare's *Hamlet* rather than only with what may have been chosen by someone else as printer's copy for Q2 (1604–5) or for F (1623).

Exceptions to usual modern practice are Stanley Wells and Gary Taylor, *William Shakespeare, The Complete Works* (Oxford: Clarendon Press, 1986) and G. R. Hibbard, *Hamlet*, The Oxford Shakespeare (Oxford: Clarendon Press, 1987). These editors base their editions upon F, which they believe represents Shakespeare's revision, and relegate most, but not all, Q2-only passages to the end of the text. Yet these editors often print passages and readings from Q2 in their texts when Q2 agrees with the first quarto (1603), which these editors believe is, like F, a witness to what was performed on stage. The first quarto differs so widely from Q2 and F in length (less than 2200 lines), order of scenes, naming of characters, and so on, that their decision to regard such materially different texts as witnesses to the same event (performance of *Hamlet*) seems to demonstrate the power, in the formation of modern editions, that theory about the origins of texts enjoys over material evidence. Steven Urkowitz once contended that the first quarto, Q2, and F all represented distinct authorial versions of the play: " 'Well-sayd olde Mole': Burying Three *Hamlets* in Modern Editions," *Shakespeare Study Today: The Horace Howard Furness Memorial Lectures* [1982], ed. Georgianna Ziegler (New York: AMS Press, 1986), pp. 37–70.

6. I quote *Hamlet* only occasionally from Q2/F themselves, more often from *The Complete Works of Shakespeare*, ed. David Bevington, 3rd ed. (Glenview: Scott, Foresman and Co., 1980). I include F and Q2 substantive and semi-substantive variants in square brackets within quotations; when there are substantive press variants in Q2 or F, I mark the first state *uncorr.* and the second *corr.*

7. Gary Taylor and I each learned in conversation in the summer of 1986 that we had independently discovered this "duplication" between Q2 and F. Taylor discusses the duplication in *The Textual Companion*, but his Introduction and Notes in the *Companion* were not yet in print when this article was written.

8. Wells and Taylor and Hibbard print the Q2-only lines of Polonius in their texts because the first quarto has this "equivalent" to these lines: "He hath, my lord, wrung from me a forced graunt" (sig. B3ᵛ). But they later print IV.iv in its truncated F form, even though the first quarto (in which the scene is even shorter) has a phrase found only in the longer Q2 version of IV.iv: "*Fortenbrasse* nephew to old *Norway*" (sig. G4ᵛ). See W. W. Greg, *The Shakespeare First Folio* (Oxford: Clarendon Press, 1955), p. 317, n. 38.

9. Harold Jenkins, ed., *Hamlet*, The New Arden Shakespeare (London: Methuen, 1982), p. 358. Those editors who are intent upon explaining the differences between F and Q2 in terms of the origins of the two texts and who want to represent the F text as a cutdown and linguistically simplified theatrical version fail to explain how such a difficult passage that does nothing to advance the plot should have found its way into F and into F alone. Hibbard bases his theory on the absence from F of some but not all the generalizing reflections on human nature found in the Q2 roles of Hamlet and Claudius (pp. 106–10).

10. Cf. Jenkins, pp. 543–44; Hibbard, p. 108; Philip Edwards, ed., *Hamlet*, The New Cambridge Shakespeare (Cambridge: Cambridge Univ. Press, 1985), pp. 207–9.

11. This long tradition includes, among others, J. Dover Wilson, *The Manuscript of Shakespeare's "Hamlet,"* 2 vols. (Cambridge: Cambridge Univ. Press, 1934); W. W. Greg, *The Shakespeare First Folio* (Oxford: Clarendon Press, 1955), pp. 314, 332; as well as Jenkins, pp. 41–42, and Hibbard, p. 96. On the usually insuperable difficulties that impede identification of the character of the manuscript underlying a printed text, especially by the traditional methods of noting actors' names and the variable naming of characters in stage directions and speech prefixes, see Fredson Bowers. "Authority, Copy, and Transmission in Shakespeare's

Texts," in *Shakespeare Study Today*, pp. 24–25 and my " 'Foul Papers' and 'Promptbooks': Printer's Copy for Shakespeare's *Comedy of Errors*," *Studies in Bibliography* 41 (1988):232–46.

12.   Edwards believes there are three other readings in Q2 that result from the compositor's failure to note deletions: III.ii.335, IV.iii.74–76, IV.vii.8. If the preliminary identification of the stints of two different compositors in Q2 can be accepted, then Edwards would have it that both compositors missed deletions marked by Shakespeare but that the compositor who most often overlooked Shakespeare's deletion marks was the same one who noticed them on a single occasion (IV.i.39–45)—an improbable hypothesis. See John Russell Brown, "The Compositors of *Hamlet* Q2 and *The Merchant of Venice*," *Studies in Bibliography*, VII (1955), 17–40.

13.   As Jenkins writes, "Hamlet's confidence in the outcome will prepare the audience for it, but affords no justification for supposing that he has any precise plan for bringing it about" (pp. 331–32).

14.   Editors have speculated that the "prison" passage, unique to F, was censored in Q2 for fear of offending Anne of Denmark by calling her native land a prison; then the passage was restored in F because Anne had died by 1623. If this passage would have offended the queen, how much would she have liked the whole play's portrayal of the Danish royal family preying on each other until they had destroyed their line and delivered up the throne to a foreigner?

15.   Philip Edwards, "Tragic Balance in *Hamlet*," *Shakespeare Survey*, 36 (1983), 43–52.

16.   Harold Jenkins, in "Playhouse Interpolations in the Folio Text of *Hamlet*," *SB*, XIII (1960), 31–47, sought to associate this variant with a number of other F-only readings, many of them simple repetitions to which this variant is not obviously related, and dismiss the lot as "actors' interpolations." He never did explain satisfactorily why "actors' gag" should ever have been inscribed in a manuscript—another incomplete fiction of origin.

17.   Urkowitz, *Revision*, p. 149.

18.   Cf. Marion Trousdale, "A Trip through the Divided Kingdoms." *Shakespeare Quarterly*, 37 (1986), 218–23. Attempts to support the hypothesis of revision by fixing different dates of composition upon Q2 and F merely defer the problem of dating the Q2 and F versions into unresolvable problems of dating the composition of the documents that allude to *Hamlet* or that mark the events to which either Q2 or F is alleged to allude. For an optimistic view, see E.A.J. Honigmann, "The Date of *Hamlet*." *ShS*, 9 (1956), 24–34.

19.   *The Stability of Shakespeare's Text* (London: Edward Arnold, 1965).

20.   Charlton Hinman, "Shakespearean Textual Studies: Seven More Years," in *Shakespeare 1971, Proceedings of the World Shakespeare Congress*, ed. Clifford Leech and J.M.R. Margeson (Toronto: Univ. of Toronto Press, 1972), p. 40.

21.   John Kerrigan, "Revision, Adaptation, and the Fool in *King Lear*," in *The Division of the Kingdoms*, pp. 195–245.

22.   Wilhelmina P. Frijlinck, ed., *The First Part of the Reign of King Richard the Second or Thomas of Woodstock*, Malone Society Reprints (Oxford: The Malone Society, 1929) and William B. Long, " 'A bed for woodstock': A Warning for the Unwary," *Medieval and Renaissance Drama in England*, II (1985), 91–118.

23.   Michel Foucault. *Language, Counter-Memory, Practice*, ed. Donald F. Bouchard. trans. Bouchard and Sherry Simon (Ithaca: Cornell Univ. Press. 1977), p. 142.

Hamlet: Growing

BARBARA EVERETT

BBC Radio has started a pleasant practice of filling the Christmas season with murder plays, mostly dramatized detective stories from the classic English phase of the 1920s and 1930s. This joining of the festive with the lethal provokes thought. There may well be some long line in English culture that links the Christmas visit to *The Mouse Trap* with a point at least as far back as that splendid moment in medieval literature when the Green Knight, his head cut off, stoops to pick up the rolling object, and rides out of Arthur's Christmas Court with the head lifted high and turned in the hand to smile genially here and there at the gathered knights and ladies as he goes. "A sad tale's best for winter." If there is such a tradition of smiling violence, then clearly there must be a place in it for the original "Mouse Trap" itself, Shakespeare's tragedy of Court life. Indeed, as the work of the most formally inventive of all literary geniuses, *Hamlet* could even be called— particularly since its presumed Kydian predecessor is lost—the first ever detective story or civilized thriller. The drama critic James Agate, who once savagely described Donald Wolfit's Hamlet as a private detective watching the jewels at the Claudius–Gertrude wedding feast, may have said more than he knew.

Yet to praise *Hamlet* as the first detective story makes sense mainly in terms of a conceit, feasible partly because ridiculous. Literary artists have worked in the genre: Poe, Wilkie Collins, Simenon, Chandler, and Michael Innes among others. But the true English "classics" of the 1920s and '30s, the books we evoke in recalling a body in a locked library in a country house, hardly go in for artistry. V. S. Pritchett once wrote down the whole genre as Philistine, and many are notably badly written, their characters a stereotype and their language a cliché. These particular classics of the 1930s are fictions that evade not only the public horrors they seem faintly to shadow, but more private intensities of self-contemplation: they work in short as ritual games and puzzles, effective by their exclusions—their interesting mix of violence and nullity the opium, perhaps, of the English rectory and manor-house during the troubled inter-war period.

With an extraordinary unanimity, good representative Introductions to *Hamlet* and critical essays on it speak of it as the most enigmatic play in the canon, "the most problematic play ever written by Shakespeare or any other playwright":[1] a theme that has been with us since the late eighteenth century or thereabouts, when the tragedy for the first time began to become "a mystery," a "question," most of all a "problem." Some critics assume that for all its interest *Hamlet* simply fails to hold together; others more tentatively voice the difficulty of knowing "what the play is really about."[2] There can be a kind of relief in recognizing that the problematic may itself be subdued into entertainment—that "Whodunit?" is in itself a pleasurable system, with the Prince as detective, victim, and villain rolled into one. Acted out in a confined world of rituals and conventions—court politics, revenge, a clock that records time always passing—the tragedy of *Hamlet* gives the deep if quizzical solace of all games and puzzles. Its hero an undergraduate, the dominance in the play of a great freewheeling exercised intelligence ("I will walke heere in the Hall . . . 'tis the breathing time of day with me") makes the work what it is, the world's most sheerly entertaining tragedy, the cleverest, perhaps even the funniest: Dr Johnson meant this when he gave it "the praise of variety," adding "The pretended madness of Hamlet causes much mirth."

Yet even Johnson had something like "problems" with the play: he was too honest not to mention that "Of the feigned madness of Hamlet there appears no adequate cause"—for the very distinction of *Hamlet* is the degree to which it makes us reach out and in for "causes." The tragedy is, even when compared with those earlier dramas of Shakespeare which have done so much to nourish it, the English Histories in particular, self-evidently great. But this is not *just* because it is entertaining: or rather, it has managed to stay so for four hundred years because the human mind, which is entertainable in a large variety of ways, is always discovering "a hunger in itself to be more serious." The Christmassy detective stories of the Twenties and Thirties we are nostalgically reviving now precisely for their unseriousness, the efficiency with which they don't matter. Shakespeare's tragedy matters. It means something.

Hamlet is sometimes described as the first great tragedy in Europe for two thousand years. The achievement perhaps owes something to Shakespeare's unique mastery of ends hard not to state as opposites: the power to entertain and the power to mean. The bridging of the two in the writer's work gives some sense of his giant reticent power of mind. To quote William Empson, on another subject, "The contradictions cover such a range"—yet they are always reciprocal, in communication with each other. The meaning of *Hamlet* must be intrinsic with what in it holds audiences and readers. And, even if *King Lear* has come, at this point in a violent and in some sense paranoiac culture, to be ranked highest as "the greatest," *Hamlet* is still manifestly enjoyed, indeed loved by readers and audiences, even by critics. It has always been so, ever since the extraordinary furore caused by its early performances, probably in the last year of the sixteenth century. The tragedy seems to have been one of the world's great successes, producing—we can tell from the profusion of admiring, amused and envious contemporary references, quotations and parodies—a kind of matching madness in its audiences. It may be that this was the response of human beings to a literary work that went deeper, not just entertainingly wider but truthfully, deeper, than any aesthetic work of their experience: deep in a way that was slightly out of their control.

There is an old joke about *Hamlet* being full of quotations. So it is; but perhaps so it always was, even for its first audiences. If we can associate this great drama with detective stories and thrillers trivial at their best, as a "sad tale . . . best for winter," the reason is that "Christmassy" quality I have tried in passing to hint at: something in the drama profoundly reminiscential, nostalgic, obscurely looking back, so that the murderous Court and castle are none the less eerily cosy, as if we had always lived there. This familiarity may be explained on one level by the fact that the tragedy is so deep-rooted in our literature, our culture, even our schooling; and its first audiences perhaps savoured in much the same way the work's relation with a now nonexistent predecessor. But this harking-back quality is intrinsic, not merely incidental. The play's opening scene builds a great past for the work to inhabit; even the Ghost has been before, last night and the night before that. Recurrence has its climax at the end of the scene, which features an actual mention of Christmas, "that Season . . . / Wherein our Saviour's Birth is celebrated." The play would be different without this curiously stirring legend that "The Bird of Dawning singeth all night long"—it would lack some endorsement, some sense of otherwhere. Commentators don't seem to ask why Shakespeare failed to use the more conventional association of cockcrowing with Easter. But the New Arden editor is surely right to hint that the writer invented rather than found this myth of Christmas. And if Shakespeare did so, then his reason was that Christmas was needed in his play.

One of the great Christmas texts is Isaiah's "Unto us a child is born, unto us a son is given." Horatio answers Marcellus's Christmas speech with "Let us impart what we have seene to night/ Unto yong *Hamlet*.[3] Coming as this does so soon after the visitation by the late King's Ghost, this designates Hamlet as the Son, the Prince, Hamlet Junior. But the phrase "Young Hamlet" has a more absolute meaning. In an interesting early allusion, the writer of an elegy for Richard Burbage after his death in 1619 names the actor's great roles as "young Hamlet, ould Hieronymoe,/ Kind Leer, the Greved Moore"[4]—where Hamlet is young as Lear is kind and the Moor grieved. The phrase, which may have been regular in use, gives a valuable suggestion as to something vital in the tragedy that we have now largely lost.

Artists may work through a highly sophisticated complexity—such as Shakespeare certainly mastered in his career—to achieve a startlingly original simplicity. That simplicity comes into being with the existence of "Young" Hamlet. The Court that holds him is a brilliant creation reflecting back to us high-level existence of the period in all its details, both mundane and powerfully formal: the "World" as Shakespeare perceived it at this height of his career. And it is this Court which makes the tragedy so real, so permanently interesting, so unshakeably ambiguous. But we see it through a given very individual observer, an innocence, however corruptible, locked inside its experience: Young Hamlet.

Our tragic sense is mainly inherited from two sets of ancestors: the universalizing Victorians and the symbolizing Modernists. Both in their antithetical ways may equally neglect simple facts about Elizabethan life and art. The only great tragedy we have derives from a materialistic culture whose philosophy is obsessed by Crime and Punishment. Its highbrow reading is characterized by Seneca's closet-drama, whose dingy gang-warfare of revenge bequeathes to *Hamlet* itself its local claustrophobia. The two brilliantly gifted predecessors to whom Shakespeare perhaps owed most, Marlowe and Kyd, were both in their very different ways absorbed by this same mechanism of sheer human will, Marlowe through the great thugs who became his heroes and Kyd through his insight into the Machiavellian Court.

What is original to Shakespeare is his revelatory sense of the natural, of what is both fresh and classic in human feeling and human experience. In a now rather underrated comedy, *The Merry Wives of Windsor*, the burgher Master Ford thinks of experience as a jewel he has purchased "at an infinite rate."[5] But purchasing experience is what all Shakespeare's characters are in the end engrossed by. And what manifests the writer's original genius from the beginning is his unique sense of what makes experience fully human, shareable yet monolithic in its elements. In his very first two tragedies, Titus Andronicus is a father, and Romeo and Juliet are children. The long, rich series of what may be formally Shakespeare's own invention, the English History Plays, work in *Henry IV*, Parts I and II, to a climax that could be subtitled *Fathers and Sons*.

Implicit in these Histories from the first is a tragic potential: the weak Henry VI must observe the effect of his weakness, a son who has killed his father, and a father who has killed his son. Only in *Hamlet* does that potential fulfil and complete itself, as the play gives to history dimensions at once mythical and internal. Its soliloquizing hero is the Prince, the Son, the "young 'un": his remembering consciousness is a surrogate for, almost at moments a part of the past of, the play's readers and audiences, reflecting as they watch a drama itself holding "a mirror up to nature." Young Hamlet, as it were all Europe's "Elder Son," the white hope of history, grows up to find that he has grown dead: his is the body in the library not merely of Elsinore but of Western culture at large.

Victorian literary critics sometimes asked questions whose literalism makes them equally wrong-headed and useful. The practice is summarized in the mocking footnote we attach to Bradley, "How Many Children Had Lady Macbeth?" A similar topic once much debated though now rarely reverted to is: "How old, exactly, is Hamlet?" The dimensions of the problem are these. The Prince is introduced to us as an undergraduate. But in the last phase of the tragedy, when Hamlet is returning home after long absence on the high seas, he meets in the graveyard a Clown who tells him how old he must be, by dating his own long career as gravedigger: "I came too't that day that our last King *Hamlet* o'ercame *Fortinbras*. . . . It was the very day, that young *Hamlet* was borne, hee that was mad, and sent into England. . . . I have bin sixteene [sexton] here, man and Boy thirty yeares" (v.i. 159–77).

The undergraduate is therefore thirty years old. Scholars and commentators once used to try to resolve these figures by dissolving them. But this is a mistake. The "thirty" is confirmed by Hamlet's own contribution to the chain of figures, his evocation of his own childish self on Yorick's shoulders—and Yorick has, we are told, been dead just twenty-three years. Equal solidity is the rule early in the play. Shakespeare has worked at Hamlet's establishment as an undergraduate, and the confusions of Horatio's role may in part depend on it. Moreover, those haunting repetitions in the Prince's speech which occur only in the Folio ("Indeed, indeed sirs"; "Wormwood, wormwood") and which the New Arden attributes to actors' interference may rather be, in my opinion, Shakespeare's additions to help characterize the undergraduate by making him do what the type still touchingly does: imitate the pedantic mannerisms of an admired tutor.

Why should Shakespeare so desire to make real Hamlet's attachment to Wittenberg? The place had of course its own connotations—it was Faustus's university, as well as one much attended then by Danes of good birth. But Wittenberg is surely no more than likely; what is necessary is making Hamlet an undergraduate. And it is necessary because it is the simplest, solidest but most economical way of showing the Prince as young. Further, although Hamlet's age in years is not the important issue, as an undergraduate he would by no means be thirty years old. The play takes us directly and deeply at many points into a social history whose loss can cut off from us a sense of the work's simplicities. A university education at this almost incomparably well-educated period was too important, yet also too common a factor for a dramatist to play games with, particularly given that most of Shakespeare's literary contemporaries and a good number of his audience had been to Oxford or Cambridge or the Inns of Court, or some combination of these. If Hamlet went to the university, he was between about sixteen and about twenty-three, the seven years that allowed for first the BA then, for those who stayed on, the MA.[6] Aristocrats and Roman Catholics went to the university earlier, sometimes much earlier; only eccentrics like Gabriel Harvey stayed for ever.

These are the norms, and Hamlet's intellectual youth, high in nuisance value, indicates that he adhered to these norms. Even the black of his mourning garments must have helped suggestively to support the point of his youth (attention is drawn to it): for university "subfusc" was so much more intensive at this time, and so unavoidable by the young, that black indicated the scholar as much as the bereaved.[7] The peculiarly social, even legal role of academic black, the part it played in holding certain youthful orders in thrall, serves as a useful key to a larger question. There are issues here not at all easy to disentangle, and both *Hamlet* and Elizabethan society in general positively refuse to keep them apart. I have hinted that to ask precisely how old Hamlet was has to be classed as a nonquestion. Many Elizabethans would have agreed in regarding it as a nonquestion, partly because—as Keith Thomas has pointed out in an admirable lecture on "Age and Authority in Early Modern England"—many didn't themselves know how old they were. What they did know, or resentfully wished not to know, was their place—and youth had, or resentfully wished not to have, a place in sixteenth-century society. This issue even has for historians its special focus in terms of undergraduates: "In the history of the universities in England the late 16th century stands out as the age when a young man's 'university days' first came to be regarded as a period for the 'sowing of wild oats'. . . . A gentleman of Renaissance England fitted himself for his future role of governour . . . *after* he left university."[8] The university is the characteristic anteroom or waiting-place for the life of mature years: the life of power.

"Age" in Renaissance Europe is politically and socially adjusted. Behind that adjustment is a very thorough negation of modern systems of timing and ageing. There are in short figures and numbers in Shakespeare's tragedies, and they matter, but they are not our figures and numbers. Recent studies from both social and literary historians have documented that vague sense which any reader can get from Elizabethan literature that its characters simply don't know how old they are. The most complete and compendious of these scholarly works, John Burrow's *The Ages of Man*, reaches back through medieval to classical times to show how very differently existence was measured before our own pervasive if shallow mathematical and technological revolution. He reminds us that the Gospels record no fact in Jesus's life between his boyhood encounter with the Doctors at twelve, and the beginning of his ministry at thirty or thereabouts. This pair of dates blended with the classical, principally Aristotelian, patterning of human life into what were sometimes seven but more often three stages: the loose and variable but influential categories of "youth," "maturity," and "age." The dates of these stages can shift considerably; their concepts cannot. This is the "positive" Burrow argues. His book contains a "negative" which seems to me of equal importance: "Most ancient and mediaeval authorities speak of the course of human life not as a process of continuous development but as a series of transits from one distinct stage to another. . . . They generally saw the transitions between these estates as datable events rather than gradual processes. Mediaeval narrative displays a corresponding lack of interest in the process of change from one age to another."[9]

An example Burrow gives is the reminder that "the events of Chaucer's Knight's Tale occupy more than a decade," but that "Palamon and Emily remain 'young' throughout." *Hamlet*, too, shows signs of spanning something like a decade—though we should be unwise to time the play on these terms. But Hamlet does *not* "remain 'young' throughout," unlike any medieval or indeed contemporary character. Shakespeare is imagining that procedure of development and continuity, at once internal and psychological yet locked up in public events, which seems simply nonexistent in most earlier thinking. But to appreciate this we have to "set back" our clocks, and—as when crossing some geographical dateline—allow for a very different time-system.

The vital question of development or "growing" I shall return to. For the moment I want only to establish that the notion of time most relevant here is a definition not merely in terms of human life and human procedures, but specifically political. Age is status, age is power. Or rather, maturity is status and power: for in this period, so Keith Thomas argues, age recedes to join youth among the disadvantaged: "In early modern England the prevailing ideal was gerontocratic: the young were to serve and the old were to rule. . . . By analogy it justified the whole social order; for the lower classes at home, like the savages abroad, were often seen as 'childish' creatures, living in a state of arrested development, needing the mature rule of their superiors."[10] But, Thomas points out, the sixteenth and seventeenth centuries—except when social crises like war enforced otherwise—defined "maturity" so narrowly within the forty-and fifty-year-olds, as to create in practice an enormous class (over 90 per cent) of the "young" and the "very old" who were disadvantaged and dependent.

It may not be irrelevant to remember the main characters of the first three of Shakespeare's great tragedies: Hamlet, whose youth disadvantages him; Lear, whose extreme age debilitates him; and Othello, whose Moorish distinctiveness allows the vicious to alienate him as a "stranger" within his own society, so undermining his power and apparent maturity. Macbeth like Eliot's Gerontion seems to have relationship with all three human estates, youth, maturity, and age, and to forfeit the rewards of all three by the damage he does to his own humanity. Of the first three, Hamlet, Othello, and Lear, the young man, the "alien" mature man, and the old man, we must surely feel that these choices of character are not accidental. Shakespeare is spanning the full range of adult experience. Yet to their disadvantage or capacity for suffering the writer adds a complicating factor: each of these heroes is royal, or has some relation to royalty. The fact that Hamlet is the Prince, in a play that carefully obscures Denmark's politics of primogeniture, gives a clue to what Shakespeare has done with the role. Hamlet is all the double strength *and* weakness of youth and sonship; and this always ambiguous state of youth, held in the memory of every grown member of Shakespeare's audience ("you your selfe Sir, should be as old as I am, if like a Crab you could go backward"—"going backward" is at once remembering, retrogressing, and making obeisance to royalty) in its turn generates a large and wholly original tragedy of consciousness.

I am suggesting that the unusual degree of political vulnerability attending the out-of-power "young" in Shakespeare's England helped him towards the creative ambiguities locked up in his first great tragic hero. Three hundred years after Shakespeare, a writer possibly influenced by *Hamlet* in this, Henry James, made a fascinating near-tragedy out of the subject of the "Awkward Age," the period in the lives of young late-Victorian women when they were neither in the schoolroom nor entirely out in the world, safely married—a period of cruel subservience and limitation yet also of heroic freedom to see and to think. Because of the political conditioning of "youth" in the English Renaissance, Shakespeare's Prince himself exists at an "Age" or time which the dramatist has invented, a time also savagely confined yet endowed with peculiar freedoms. To grasp this time which is the heroic medium is perhaps to resolve into simplicity some of the elements in the drama which have become its most inordinately examined problems. I have already mentioned Dr Johnson's protest that though he found it entertaining he saw no dramatic "cause" for Hamlet's "madness." But he had perhaps forgotten what he once said (or Boswell at least makes him say) of his own undergraduate youth at Oxford: "Ah, Sir, I was mad and violent. It was bitterness which they mistook for frolic."[11] Hamlet too, and many real young people after him, might have added that like Johnson he "thought to fight his way by his literature and his wit," and that he "disregarded all power and all authority." Hamlet's dangerous subversive humour—which is neither madness nor sanity, but a denial of the authority of the society that holds him—permanently defines a freedom and impotence of the young. The same kind of simplifying process may be used for some illumination on literature's best-known line and indeed the whole soliloquy that follows it, "To be or not to be": long debated as to whether its subject is suicide, or revenge, or any other topic positively. There is a certain relevance in a line from a Philip Larkin poem, *"Vers de Société"*: "Only the young can be alone freely." Only the young can so detachedly if tormentedly survey the prospect of adult existence as to believe that they have the option "To be or not to be"; the adult, with "promises to keep," more often has to shrug and trudge on.

Some part of this extreme originality of insight clearly came to Shakespeare from the Elizabethan political situation—from the dramatist's ability to render private and internal what began in public life. The Jacobean Hamlet, who drove audiences mad with pleasure, amusement and alarm, was a Malcontent, a political subversive—as indeed was the play's Hamlet, being from the first too much the "son," overfathered by too much (and too unkind) "kin"; and so were all those who felt that their society made of them no more than a "captive good attending Captain III." The new political studies of Shakespeare in general take the stance of assuming that the chief of the King's Men must have been conservative. But the writer of the Sonnets can envisage that "Captains" might or must be "III"; and poetry itself was in Elizabethan society specifically no more than a toy for the young. The mature man, the man of power, had his attention engaged elsewhere. Thus, "Authors" (E. H. Miller tells us, in his valuable study of *The Professional Writer in Elizabethan England*) "viewed themselves as prodigal son." Fundamentally, Miller points out, "Elizabethan writers accepted the premises as well as the fears and aspirations of Tudor culture. 'Profite,' or utility, was an obsession with English humanists,"[12] who therefore speak through Claudius's rebuke to Hamlet for the frank wastefulness, the sheer childishness of his grief for his dead father. Indeed, formally most Tudor writers themselves spoke with him, apologizing for what they tended to throw away (like Puttenham) as "but the studie of my yonger yeares in which vanitie raigned."[13] The rest of the world concurred. "Though they be reasonable wittie and well don yet" (a letter of John Chamberlain's groans over elegiac lines by Donne when Dean of St Paul's) "I could wish a man of his yeares and place to give over versifieng."[14]

The point here is in the "yeares" and "place." Even a social and cultural theory most repressive to the young could grudgingly accept the kind of stress laid in Cicero's *Pro Caelio* on the necessary element of "ludus" to be allowed to the very young: "Everybody agrees in allowing youth a little fun. . . . Let some fun be granted to youth." With this near-identification of "youth" with "a little fun," or in a word *"play"*—with which most Elizabethan educationalists and politicians would have been in nominal accord—we come directly and fully back into Shakespeare's play. I have been hoping to suggest the very large and significant network of conditions—some contemporary, some much more permanent and lasting—"Young Hamlet" brings with him into his Court and his play. It is hard to imagine any of the later heroes as what the Prince is, an amateur but devout poet and playwright and even producer; and Shakespeare plainly gets a good deal of quiet ambiguous pleasure from dramatizing the lordly certainty with which his brilliant young aristocrat tells the tired polite professionals how to act. This amusing detail helps to illustrate the point at which I began, the peculiar entertainingness to be found in the tragedy. From his first wild, dangerous but liberating evasions of Claudius, the ironies that are also (politically) his first "madness" of youth ("More then kin, and lesse then kinde"; "I am too much i'th'Sun"), Hamlet brings into the confining world of power exercised that spaciousness of intellectual play which gives the work its largeness. It is significant, in the context, that Claudius first addresses him with a "But"—"But now my Cosin *Hamlet*, and my Sonne?"—a remark which accompanies the turn from the easily handled Laertes with a certain casual offensiveness, and Hamlet repays the insult with muffled interest. But Hamlet's own father, loved as he is, reacts to his son with something like the irritation of his hated brother-King; the quick true skittering sympathy proper to Hamlet's age and type, "Alas poore Ghost," the Ghost himself crushingly repels: "Pitty me not, but lend thy serious hearing / To what I shall unfold." Both Father-Kings identify the "serious" with the purposive. From his first skirmish of wit to the final Court-duel that kills him, Hamlet defines the "serious" so as to contain a violent play, his dance around the two revenge-held Kings opening out in the drama those dimensions and depths which we associate in the comedies with women and Fools, in the preceding Histories with such characters as the Bastard Faulconbridge and the great "player," Falstaff. But the game gives the Kings and the play itself both time and occasion to destroy him—or Hamlet time to destroy himself.

Hamlet's involvement with "play" in the first half of the action has its climax, naturally enough, in the arrival of the Players—the more usual Elizabethan word for what we now describe as "actors." The Players are often discussed as one of the tragedy's major problems, the randomness of their presence characterizing all in the drama that is wayward and enigmatic. There is of course something in this; Hamlet's whole world is, by accident and by principle, wayward and enigmatic. Yet there is at the same time a very marked decorum in the Players, an appropriateness in their appearance. Two important circumstances seem never to be noted. The Players are carefully introduced by Rosencrantz and Guildenstern, who make them indeed appear to "hold the mirror up to nature": for their case both resembles and reverses Hamlet's. Where his youth is trapped by Authority in a humiliating close Court, they have been driven out of the city by triumphant children, who—Hamlet at once perceives the relevance—"Exclaim against their own succession," verbally war against the stage of life they must themselves in time come to. The point is underlined immediately as the adult Players arrive, for Hamlet greets them affectionately as the only-just-not-children-themselves that they are: this young face so newly bearded, that boy-girl player suddenly grown tall.

The Players represent what both Kings would no doubt see (Polonius's enthusiasm is depressing in its patronage) as evasion, unseriousness, irrelevance—and in one sense the Kings are right. But Hamlet's comparable "marginality" also leaves him free to look at things. And what he sees in the Players is not merely a capacity to act "revenge" entertainingly; he also sees what they are or embody, beyond what they act: a struggle or conflict in human existence that is deeper and more permanent than the revenge-system which it resembles. The helpless division of the generations can lead to mutual destruction. Yet in the understanding of every observant human individual, the generations are really one and the same, mere "stages" held in one by memory and sympathy—as Young Hamlet, watching the Player weep for long-dead Hecuba, becomes an audience, crossing a great gulf to join us in the present.

The play scene (III.iii) has become one of the tragedy's great problems, in that it seems to tell us nothing of what Claudius sees in the play-within-the-play, and therefore tells us nothing to the point. But what the play scene does tell us is that "points" are of more than one kind, as Age and Youth are two different generations. Hamlet's delight in his play, which to him spells the truth, emerges in his succeeding near-intoxication. As readers and audiences we are in no position to belittle his enchantment; the tragedy begins and ends with first Barnardo and last Horatio rendering all its past into the terms of hypnotic story, and while the play lasts it invents those terms by which reader and audience alike become "young" again, cut off from Time, exchanging active power for a freedom more detached and contemplative.

But the murderous King is hardly a natural playgoer. If he were capable of accepting this kind of truth he would be less successful at his own. He lives by a different clock: "That we would do, we should do when we would." Truth as he sees it is not what happened to his brother in some theoretical past but what happens to himself in the real present. "The Mouse Trap" shows that a King may be killed by his nephew—a term that to Elizabethans could mean a bastard or a grandson or a successor: possibility enough to indicate that the King's stepson was getting far too much of a nuisance: "Our estate may not endure / Hazard so dangerous as doth hourely grow / Out of his bourds"[15] (III.iii.5–7)—a theme precisely echoed by Polonius's "Tell him his prankes have been too broad to beare with." "Bourds" and "prankes" nicely focus the Court insistence on the menace of Hamlet's youth.

It may even be Hamlet's youth which prevents him from killing the King at prayer, for reasons he gives with a savagery partly dependent on frustration. A theoretician, a perfectionist, not yet habituated to brutality, he has accepted Revenge as a system antithetical to most of himself which must be carried out with all the more Old Testament exactitude of eye-for-eye and tooth-for-tooth. To stab on other terms would be dishonouring, a mere act of murder—and Young Hamlet is as much an aristocrat as his royal father. His rage at the indecencies and injustices of mere life carries him straight to the fury of the scene in his mother's bedroom and to the accidental killing of Polonius. From this point of randomness at the centre of the play, clumsy life's mirror-image of the murder recalled by the fiction of "The Mouse Trap," Hamlet is done for. Claudius corrupts the young and courtly conventional Laertes and they unite against him. The Avenger has become the object of Revenge.

* * *

Readers and audiences of *Hamlet* seem to have experienced remarkably little difficulty with the play until a point late in the eighteenth century. Then, though as ever much loved, the drama began to be found a "mystery," an "enigma," and at last a "problem." To understand the importance of "Young Hamlet" may be a way of grasping this interesting critical shift. For literature itself records for us what happened to the reader's image of the tragedy in this period. During the last two decades of the eighteenth century, while in England Wordsworth was living through the materials of his future poem, on the "Growth of a Poet's Mind," in Germany Goethe was putting together a long, loose yet oddly powerful and even spell-binding romance, which recounted the adventures of a young bourgeois who leaves home to join a troupe of wandering actors, hoping to advance what he believes to be his calling as a writer, an artist: but in the end the hero changes his mind, and goes back to real life with a more practical determination to serve humanity. Renowned through Europe for a century or more, Goethe's story *Wilhelm Meister* is hardly now a current classic, though still saluted by literary historians as the first of the enormously influential literary mode which it invented: the *Bildungsroman*, or story of the life-education of a young person, whose growing-up is specifically defined as a turning-away from a self-centred "artistic" existence and a committed entry into society at large.

The "action" of *Wilhelm Meister* is really an intense and sustained brooding on the work which obsesses the young writer Wilhelm—Shakespeare's *Hamlet*, a production of which forms the culmination of the story. The English tragedy becomes something close to a play-within-the-play, an obscure yet suggestive paradigm of the new, organically free, always-emergent life of Goethe's own novel—yet it has this fertilizing power despite or perhaps because of the fact that Wilhelm cannot understand the tragedy, which seems to him a work "full of plan" that holds at its centre a hero "without a plan" (the phrases are his own). This paradox assumes considerable significance, if we recall that this is the exact moment when the tragedy begins to become a "mystery." Moreover, Goethe is hardly exceptional. After a century of English novels of which the most distinguished are plainly in the line of the *Bildungsroman*, the use made of *Hamlet* by the arch-Romantic writer Goethe is strikingly paralleled in the work of the arch-Modernist Joyce. James Joyce, who knew and (with reservations) admired *Wilhelm Meister* and even owned a copy, includes in *Ulysses*, his great tragicomic story of a "Father" and "Son" reconciled, a long Goethean library-discussion of the meaning of *Hamlet* and its possible provenance in Shakespeare's own life.

The enormous, rich and various inheritance of later English literature from Shakespeare's first great tragedy is not my subject here. One brief point may be made about some of the very best nineteenth-century writing in that area. Though the post-Romantic novel is of course strongly rooted in the *Bildungsroman*, the "story of life-education," the English imagination at its best turns aside from the German form and intuitively harks back to the Shakespearian ancestor, more at home with the dark or tragic than with the optimistic, socially orientated and progressive Romantic fiction. We ought perhaps to explain the unusual formality and aesthetic coherence of *Great Expectations*, for instance, in terms of the book's being a kind of reverie on the work which actually appears in its thirty-first chapter as Mr Wopsle's *Hamlet*: a reverie which brought into the novel the Christmas graveyard, the dead children, the ritualistic games of "Beggar-my-Neighbour" in the "Court" of Satis House, the cruel Petrarchan heroine, the lawyers of Little England, and above all the terrible returner from the dead who is "your second father. You're my son":—everything in the book, in fact, which seems to say to the reader, with an unnerving dark cosiness of memory, what the last chapters say to Pip: "Do not thou go home, let him not go home, let us not go home." And one might add to Dickens the very different but almost equally rich case of Henry James, whose story of a father-destroyed and haunted youth of military family, *Owen Wingrave*, reads like a late-Victorian paraphrase of *Hamlet*. I have already suggested that James owed something to Shakespeare when he began his late studies in isolated heroic consciousness with novels and stories whose protagonists were not merely young, but sometimes children. None ends happily.[16]

My point in introducing *Wilhelm Meister* was to propose the dependence of that major form of the European novel, the *Bildungsroman*, on Shakespeare's tragedy. *Hamlet*, the first great story in Europe of a young man growing up, in a sense originates the *Bildungsroman* itself. But if *Hamlet* invents or inspires the form, it also denies it. Romantic culture, taking its stand on the revolutionary hope of youth's great growing-stages, found itself forestalled by Shakespeare in more ways than one. And if the play begins at this period to become a "mystery," an "enigma," a "problem," the reason surely is what the latter half of the tragedy is actually saying. For Young Hamlet grows up and grows dead in the same instant. "The Court's a learning place" says Helena in *All's Well*, thinking of what may become of her love in the Court at Paris. Elsinore has been for Hamlet a "learning place" too: more so, perhaps, than Wittenberg. But "growing up," "becoming mature," so easily taken for granted by us now as virtues, are in Elsinore's tragic Court as doubtful, as hard to sustain as Hamlet's brief ownership of his father's crown; and if achieved at all, these conditions bring death with them. It is in a grave, Ophelia's grave, that the Prince at last and for the first time identifies himself with his father, taking on his father's royal title: "This is I, Hamlet the Dane."

At the beginning of the fifth Act Hamlet returns to Elsinore after an absence that makes itself felt as marked. When he comes back to it again, his mysterious encounter with the pirates serves to embody time passing, and to make believable those subtle changes often visible in human beings only when they return after absence. Learning for Hamlet is a kind of departure, a going away from his origins; and he comes back different. The play even hints by the word "naked," of course metaphorical, used in Hamlet's letter, and by his talk of his sea-gown, that he has left behind for ever his undergraduate, grieving, and courtly black clothes: the image that he makes is different, closer to that of Everyman. It is symptomatic, too, that we hear no more of the Ghost. His adventures on the high seas have been subject both to chance and to moral confusion—he has been saved only by pirates, "thieves of mercy," and he has substituted for himself in the net of his fate two men once friends of his own. These bewilderments and defeats are a hard burden like the dead bodies of Rosencrantz and Guildenstern, joining the dead Polonius in the shadows of Hamlet's now extensively stained past. The Prince comes home, in short, through a graveyard, where he is just in time for Ophelia's obsequies.

The Court of Elsinore is what was once known as a "man's world," one given up to the pursuit of power in a conventional system of rivalries. There is little place for women in such a world, and the women of this tragedy are markedly shadowy and faint. Gertrude can only signify her (doubtful) fidelity by moving from the side of her (politically) strong husband to that of her (politically) weak son; Ophelia is shattered by the conflict of her father, her brother, and her lover. Significantly, madness comes to this pathetic and evidently virginal young girl as the belief that she has been brutally seduced, almost raped. Her passivity is essential. And this is a point very interestingly underlined by the verbal by-play of the Clowns over the morality of her death—a passage unjustly neglected by commentators. The Gravediggers' common sense, aspiring to legal expertise, tells them that Ophelia must have committed and been guilty of a willed action—she must have drowned herself. And yet, "if the water come to him & drowne him; hee drownes not himselfe. Argall, hee that is not guilty of his owne death, shortens not his owne life." She may even have "drowned her selfe in her owne defence."

In its context, and within the formal peculiarities of the whole play— shapely, logical, yet deeply undermining what we sometimes allow ourselves to hope about human freedom—this nonsense makes a curious and haunting sense. Ophelia is a shadow of Hamlet, a moon by his sun: "cressant," as Laertes calls the Prince, her spirited yet defeated attempts to "grow" in the presence of her officious father and aggressive brother only betray her, and condemn her Court existence to an end among "Coronet weeds," the "envious sliver," "the weedy Trophies," "the weeping Brooke," "as one incapable of her owne distress." But her very unfreedom transmutes real guilt in her death. Really, she "drowned her selfe in her owne defence"—even, "the water came to her & drowned her." The preceding scenes of the fourth Act have distinctively entwined the morally dark with the natural—Claudius's corruption of her brother with the flowers the mad girl gives, the songs she sings, the Court's disturbed tenderness to her. That natural darkness, together with the silences of Hamlet's own failure, lie in the shadows of the Graveyard Scene as it begins, and even enter the Clown's songs about youthful love as "solace," and about "Age with his stealing steps." And they convert the violence of young Ophelia's madness and death to something quieter, more profoundly natural, like the inevitable passing of time.

These things flow together as Hamlet comes back from the sea to hold the skull of the fool Yorick, a man who has in memory performed momentarily something like the role of Juliet's Nurse—the age of seven is surely used here, like Juliet's weaning and then her arrival at fourteen, as one of the great Elizabethan age-divides: it was the age for starting school or, in harsher social circumstances, for starting work.[17] Hamlet is suddenly in the presence of his lost childhood. This is one of the moments at which Shakespeare, writing within an Elizabethan culture that neither cared greatly for children nor took much interest in them (attitudes shared to some extent by the writer's own work), reveals startlingly how he has transformed a story of Crime and Punishment to a tragedy of experience, in which—to use Yeats's trenchant phrase—"The crime of being born / Blackens all our lot."

When Hamlet thinks of Ophelia later in this scene, he moves into the past tense—"I loved Ophelia"—with the kind of clarity and simplicity he was far from finding as her lover; his at last loving glimpse of her pastness is like that strange, silent encounter recorded earlier through Ophelia's own memory. The two young people really only meet in their imaginations, even their fantasies (the Hamlet we see is superb, but he is not Ophelia's "expectancie and Rose of the fair State, / The glasse of fashion and the mould of Forme": the delicious young girl's images are faded, stereotypical). Similarly, the earlier undergraduate was simply more at ease with members of his own sex, both adoring and frightened of women, seeing only his mother through them. In the past tense he is certain. But Hamlet can use the past tense because he now has a past tense—he has, as used to be said of women, "a past." Once human beings have a past felt as dark, as irrecoverable, and as their own, their life is beginning to be over. They are in any case no longer young.

For Hamlet, "growing up" is also growing dead. He has reached thirty (the Gravedigger tells us), that ancient agreement as to the year of human maturity: but he will not live much longer. This arrival simultaneously both at full manhood and at death gives the play its mythical quality: it drafts out one of the great human rites of passage. But the play's progress is uniquely realistic as well as mythical. Hamlet's growing is given some of that haunted naturalness with which the water reaches Ophelia; merely waiting, watching, feeling, existing and always talking. Hamlet becomes something more than the busily conforming Laertes and the marching Fortinbras, who are no more than modes of behaviour. Supported as he is by the highly original and existential rhythms of the play, divergent, lingering, contradictory, and accidental, Hamlet's growing becomes a statement of being in itself, of human experience.

One of the characters in a novel by Ivy Compton-Burnett, *Elders and Betters*, says of the painful growing-up of the book's children, "The process of getting used to the world seems to be too much for us." The novel is one of those innumerable English fictions about which we can feel in passing that they perhaps might not have been written if Shakespeare's tragedy had not existed. At all events, that dry and trivial phrase "getting used to the world" could be used to gloss the deep and subtle power with which the very end of *Hamlet* is handled. A completely new character arrives, called in the Folio "young Osric"—a menacing young fop, and a King's Man in person—whose triviality is the keynote of all this last movement. Hamlet himself finds a new tone, adult and grim, light and disturbed, wearily impatient now to have things over and done with: "I shall winne at the oddes: but thou wouldest not thinke how ill's all heere about my heart: but it is no matter." His formal Court apology to his adversary, Laertes, brilliantly sustains the same tired and impenetrably public surface, his manner like the duel that follows honourable, empty, and—because empty—lethal. Young Hamlet's time is all but over. Its real end is soon marked by words from Horatio: "Goodnight sweet Prince,/ And flights of Angels sing thee to thy rest."

Horatio's "Goodnight" needs a word of comment it never seems to get. It might almost seem too sweet, too sentimental for the play. If it doesn't, this may be because of a shadowy irony the lines carry in themselves. Horatio, we feel, might almost be talking to a child—but perhaps he is talking to a child. Holding as they do that private sound of a nurse's good-night many times over delivered to well-born well-behaved Tudor children, the lines perhaps contain all the ironies of the play's own good-night to Hamlet's compromised youth, his freedom and his life.

And this possibility is conceivably strengthened by a curious fact in Shakespeare's own life. Biographers sometimes speculate on the relevance to the tragedy of the death, some four or five years before the play was first performed, of Shakespeare's only son, the eleven-year-old Hamnet. What doesn't however seem to be noticed is that in the very year of the boy's death Shakespeare's father—or the writer on his behalf—successfully applied for a coat of arms, thus ambitiously attaining the status of Gentleman. These two events perhaps became one in Shakespeare's mind, the seed from which his tragedy of a son began growing.

Notes

1. Harry Levin, *Shakespeare Quarterly*, 7 (1956), 105. Both this and "what the play is really about" (see n. 2 below) are quoted in the Introduction to the New Arden *Hamlet* (1982; ed. Harold Jenkins).

2. A. J. A. Waldock, *Hamlet: A Study in Critical Method* (1931), 7.

3. Shakespeare quotations are from *The Norton Facsimile: The First Folio of Shakespeare* (1968), prepared by Charlton Hinman.

4. *The Shakespeare Allusion Book* (1909), 272.

5. *The Merry Wives of Windsor*, II. ii. 216–17.

6. Lawrence Stone, "The Educational Revolution in England, 1560–1640," *Past and Present*, 28 (1964), 57.

7. See, e.g., John Earle, *Micro-cosmographie* (1628), No. 24, "A Meere young Gentleman of the University": "Of all things he endures not to be mistaken for a Scholler, and hates a black suit though it be of Sattin."

8. Kenneth Charlton, *Education in Renaissance England* (1965), 150.

9. John Burrow, *The Ages of Man* (Oxford, 1986), 177–8.

10. Keith Thomas, "Age and Authority in Early Modern England," *Proceedings of the British Academy*, LXII (1976), 207–10.

11. *Boswell's Life of Johnson*, ed. G. B. Hill and L. F. Powell (1934), i. 73–4. Dr Keith Walker has kindly mentioned to me Marshall Waingrow's opinion (*The Correspondence and Other Papers of James Boswell* (1969), 57 n. 10) that Boswell misread the "rude" of his notes as "mad". I suspect, however, that Boswell may here as elsewhere in the *Life* have improved on his first thoughts. "Mad" could be used during the whole period 1500–1800 to mean "foolish, unwise, extravagant in gaiety."

12. E. H. Miller, *The Professional Writer in Elizabethan England* (1959), 17–18.

13. George Puttenham, *The Arte of English Poesie*, ed. G. D. Wilcock and A. Walker (1936), 308.

14. *The Letters of John Chamberlain*, ed. N. E. McClure (Philadelphia, 1939), ii. 613.

15. I here emend F's "Lunacies" (itself an apparent compositorial emendation of Q2's brow's) to "bourds."

16. I explore this point further in "Henry James's Children," in *The Child and the Book* (Oxford, 1989), ed. Gillian Avery and Julia Briggs.

17. See, e.g., Philippe Aries, *Centuries of Childhood*, tr. R. Baldick (1962), 66.

"No offence i' th' world":
Hamlet and Unlawful Marriage

LISA JARDINE

HAMLET:	Madam, how like you this play?
QUEEN:	The lady doth protest too much, methinks.
HAMLET:	O, but she'll keep her word.
KING:	Have you heard the argument? Is there no offence in't?
HAMLET:	No, *no*, they do but jest—poison in jest. No offence i' th' world.[1]

This piece is part of the groundwork for a larger project on the relationship between cultural history and textual studies.[2] It is therefore both exploratory and incomplete—characteristics which will, I hope, make the work available for use by others besides myself who are trying to make explicit some of the assumptions behind recent historically based text-critical practice. The aim is to set up a dialogue with others writing similarly reflectively—an aim which was the starting-point for the Essex Symposium for which an earlier draft of this chapter was written.[3]

As a start, the remarks which follow are prompted by my reading of a helpful article by David Simpson, entitled "Literary criticism and the return to 'history.' "[4] It is that *"return to,"* and then "history" in quotation marks, in his title, which immediately takes my attention. And indeed, Simpson sets out to show that "the status of historical inquiry has become so eroded that its reactive renaissance, in whatever form, threatens to remain merely gestural and generic. 'History' promises thus to function as legitimating any reference to a context beyond literature exclusively conceived, whether it be one of discourse, biography, political or material circumstances.[5] In other words, he believes that many so-called historicist critics are using the catchword "history" to mask a quite conventional (and conservative) commitment to a set of unscrutinised, idealised premises about a past already modelled to the ideological requirements of the present.[6] The implication

*Reprinted from *Uses of History: Marxism, Postmodernism and the Renaissance*, eds. Francis Barker, Peter Hulme, and Margaret Iversen (1991): 123–139. Used by permission of Manchester University Press, and Lisa Jardine.

258

of that idea of "return," then, is that there is something retrograde, and above all something *positivistic*, about the undertaking—that is, that in invoking history we are privileging something called "facts" or "real-life events," whereas in truth we are all now supposed to know that there are only texts, that our access to facts and to history is only and inevitably textual.[7]

I start my own argument by making it clear that I do not regard the present endeavour as either a turn or a *return*. I do not think that we should let the marketing tag, "new" (targeted at eager academic consumers, after the latest product), suggest fashionable change, any more than we should allow "historicist" to suggest retroactive, backward-looking positivism (once historicism always historicism). What we should be looking at, I suggest, is the converging practices of social historians, intellectual and cultural historians, text critics and social anthropologists, as they move together towards a more sensitive integration of past and present cultural products. It is to this generally progressive trend or development that I consider my own work belongs.[8]

Both historians and text critics have learnt a lot from recent literary theory. We do, indeed, now begin from that position of understanding that our access to the past is through those "textual remains" in which the traces of the past are to be found—traces which it will require our ingenuity to make sense of. Nevertheless, it is by no means the case that this inevitably leaves us in a position of radical indeterminacy. In fact, I begin to believe that it only appears to lead us in such a direction if we are committed (wittingly or unwittingly) to the view that what textual remains yield, in the way of an account of the past, is evidence of *individual subjectivity*. In this case, indeterminacy is apparently doubly inevitable. For what we recognise as individual subjectivity is the fragmented, partial, uncertain, vacillating trace of first-person self-expression. And if we take on board Stephen Greenblatt's suggestive idea of *self-fashioning*—an aspiration on the part of the individual, embedded in past time, towards a coherence of self, which is inevitably endlessly deferred, and historically incomplete—it can be argued that what the cultural historian can retrieve and reconstruct of the past will of necessity be correspondingly incomplete and indeterminate. Here, Greenblatt's primary model is an anthropological one, his methodology that of the social anthropologist (and with it some of his assumptions about the strangeness of other selves).[9]

But those of us who are committed to social and political change may consider that we have another agenda altogether, the focus of which is *group* consciousness (and intersubjectivity).[10] In my recent work, I have emphasised that the specified ground for my own textual and cultural interpretations is a strongly felt need to provide a historical account which *restores agency to groups hitherto marginalised or left out of what counts as historical explanation*—nonélite men and all women. And since that means the focus of my critical attention is social relations within a community, the shaping of events in telling the tale is part of the given of the kind of excavation of the past I am engaged in.[11] In other words, I find that I am able to accommodate competing accounts of a set of textually transmitted events (competing versions of what makes collections of incidents in past time culturally meaningful), without discarding as illusory the lost incidents in past time which gave rise to them. That is a methodological matter to be negotiated, the very fabric out of which perceived social relations are constructed, not a breakdown or paradox within the community as such. Texts may be *generated* by individual, gendered selves, but we may nevertheless choose to give our attention to the way in which in any period, membership of a community is determined by a shared ability to give meaning to the shifting unpredictability of everyday life. This is the group consciousness on which social practice depends, and which provides the boundary conditions for individual self-affirmation and action.

"Restoring agency" is, for me, a matter of countering the apparent passivity of nonélite groups within the historical account. But this needs a little further glossing. The counterposition to passivity (by implication, powerlessness), is *active participation*, but not (without falsifying the account) *power*. In my recent exploration of the defamation of Desdemona in *Othello*, I was not able to give back to Desdemona *power* to accompany her activity— but I was able to reposition our attention in relation to the events which take place on the stage,so that representation no longer overwhelmed the interpersonal dynamics of an early modern community to which the text gives expression.[12] In so far as I was successful, this retrieval of agency for Desdemona was achieved by my treating the individual subject in the drama as a "cultural artefact":[13] the play gives us a tale of Desdemona's actions in the (then) recognisably shared terms of the early modern community. We can retrieve that recognition, I argued, by juxtaposing the tales told in contemporary court depositions (where the recognition of the *infringing* of shared codes of behaviour is the essence of the story) with the dramatic text— both being "performances" before "audiences" in that same community. Our access to something like "who Desdemona is" is given by learning to "read" in the social relations dramatised, those situations which were meaningful— which established or expressed Desdemona's relationship to her community in ways acknowledged as socially significant. Those "events" (as I choose to call such socially meaningful sets of relationships) are the expressed form of Desdemona's "lived experience," and I mean that, since in my view it will not make a significant difference whether the "person" who is presented via this shaped version of experience is real or fictional.[14]

What distinguishes this kind of retrospective critical activity from that of the social historian, I think, is that we want to position ourselves so as to *give meaning* to early modern agency, not simply to record it, to show that it was there. As Geertz says:

We are seeking, in the widened sense of the term in which it encompasses much more than talk, to converse with [our 'native' informants], a matter a great deal more difficult, and not only with strangers, than is commonly recognized. "If speaking *for* someone else seems to be a mysterious process," Stanley Cavell has remarked, "that may be because speaking *to* someone does not seem mysterious enough."[15]

Or as Greenblatt puts it—consciously alluding to the Geertz, as he specifies his own methodological starting-point:

I began with the desire to speak with the dead.
   This desire is a familiar, if unvoiced, motive in literary studies, a motive organized, professionalized, buried beneath thick layers of bureaucratic decorum: literature professors are salaried, middle-class shamans. If I never believed that the dead could hear me, and if I knew that the dead could not speak, I was nonetheless certain that I could re-create a conversation with them.[16]

What distinguishes the kind of analysis I am after, in the new "interdiscipline" I see my work as moving towards, from much literary criticism, and from much recent text criticism, is that it seeks to engage with the *external manifestations* of selfhood. It does not treat the "lived experience" of the individual, as something with which the modern critical self can engage, and which it can make meaningful in its own terms. Nor does it posit an unchanging human nature immune to local circumstances, which it is the critic's task to retrieve.[17]

   This brings me to a crucial distinction which in the consideration I shall be giving to *Hamlet* I shall particularly need to sustain, between the version of the term "subject" which my own approach addresses, and the one which I introduced earlier—individual internalised selfhood (of which the related term "subjectivity" is symptomatic).

   The form that the pursuit of the "lived experience" or untramelled universal se'fhood in textual criticism currently takes is grounded in psychoanalytical theory. It is the pursuit of a gendered first-person, authentic utterance—a discourse which inscribes the individual's unique experience of reality. The *subject*, in this sort of textual study, *is* that first-person discourse—which is the only access we have to individual selfhood.[18] And this discourse, which inscribes the individual's experience and determines her selfhood, is a discourse of desire and sexuality. And since this symbolic construction of the subject depends on a sign system which the receiver of the discourse shares with the discourser, subjectivity, in so far as it is grasped and understood is transhistorical.

   In Greenblatt's pioneering work, this pursuit of the psychoanalytical subject via psychoanalytic theory coexists with the methodology of social anthropology.[19] The individual critic acknowledges the distance which separates him from the discoursing subject in past time; he (*sic*) attempts to "speak with the dead." It follows that the *terms* of the dialogue he establishes are those which he can "hear" as the textual trace of selfhood, within his own discursive formation: desire and sexuality. By reaching back into texts which preserve desirous discourse in the early modern period, the new historicist critic retrieves those sign systems which he (from his own position in time and culture) can recognise; it is those shared discursive strategies which are, for him, all we can know of selfhood in past time.

The drawback in such an approach for the feminist critic is that sexuality is explicitly assumed to code "power" in ways which lead to the *subjection* of women (no longer *qua* women, but ostensibly as *standing for something else*)—even (ironically, and anachronistically) the subjection of Elizabeth I to her desirous male subjects.[20] But the main point to note is that, on this account of subjectivity, the "actual" is coextensive with what two discourses *share*—a matter of intertextual identity. This is, in my view, a fundamental difficulty for such a theory, and its methodology of power relations and subjectivity construction, when we are trying to deal with an inaccessible historical past, and particularly when we are trying to recover female agency from the cultural traces of the past.[21]

Which brings me finally to the problem of "feeling," and our access to it, in *Hamlet*. Hamlet's feelings towards his mother Gertrude were already described in recognisable terms of incestuous desire in the classic 1919 article on the play by T. S. Eliot:[22] "The essential emotion of the play is the feeling of a son towards a guilty mother . . . Hamlet (the man) is dominated by an emotion which is inexpressible, because it is in *excess* of the facts as they appear. . . . Hamlet is up against the difficulty that his disgust is occasioned by his mother, but that his mother is not an adequate equivalent for it; his disgust envelopes and exceeds her."[23]

This is an appropriate starting point, both because this idea of excess has been a feature of all *Hamlet* criticism since Eliot, and because it already makes clear that an account of Hamlet's "excessive" feelings in terms of *desire* (inexpressible emotion), immediately makes concrete and specific his *mother* as focus of attention for her *guilt*—she is pronounced guilty not as a judgement on her actions, but as a condition of her presence in the play in relation to Hamlet (thus textual rather than historical in my sense). If Hamlet's feeling is excessive it is because his sense of his mother's guilt exceeds what could possibly fit the facts of the plot: the guilt of a mother who has stimulated sexual desire in her son. Here "desire" is taken in the psychoanalytic and deconstructive sense, and is not an event but (according to Lacanian theory (and then Derrida)) a permanent condition of language, with regard to which Hamlet adopts a particular (problematic) orientation, one which produces mothers as guilty of arousing excessive desire in their sons.[24]

If desire is taken to be "a permanent condition of language," then the analysis of the subject, and the interpretation of the text (in our case, the text of *Hamlet*) tend increasingly towards one another. In a recent article entitled "Sexuality in the reading of Shakespeare," Jacqueline Rose writes:

> The psychoanalytic concept of resistance . . . assumes that meaning is never simply present in the subject, but is something which disguises itself, is overwhelming or escapes. Freud came to recognize that its very intractability was not a simple fault to be corrected or a history to be filled. It did not conceal a simple truth which psychoanalysis should aim to restore. Instead this deviation or vicissitude of meaning was the "truth" of a subject caught in the division between conscious and unconscious which will always function at one level as a split. Paradoxically, interpretation can only advance when resistance is seen not as obstacle but as process. This simultaneously deprives interpretation of its own control and mastery over its object since, as an act of language, it will necessarily be implicated in the same dynamic.
>
> In both *Hamlet* and *Measure for Measure*, the play itself presents this deviant and overpowering quality of meaning which appears in turn as something which escapes or overwhelms the spectator.[25]

And if we add the increasing interest of some critics in social anthropology, and in kinship systems as reflected in social forms, including language, the collapse of (specifically) "incest" from a specified, forbidden sexual union into a universal tendency towards nonconforming, problematic forms of desirous social relationships (manifested above all *in language*) is complete. In his recent book, *The end of kinship*: "*Measure for measure*," incest and the idea of universal siblinghood, Marc Shell writes:

> I have tried to bring to light a literary tradition associating physical and spiritual kinship and to suggest the manifestation of this tradition in the politics of the modern world. . . . [This] project involves reconsidering the polarity or the opposition between ascent into kinship and descent from kinship (or between incest and chastity) just as though "the way of descent and the way of ascent were one and the same."
>
> Some literary works display an inescapable vacillation between such descents and ascents, a vacillation from which society as we know it begins in an archaeological sense. Such vacillation takes place in *Hamlet*, where the hero thinks both about descent into incest or parricide, which he both desires and fears . . . and also about ascent into universal kinship. . . . The movements to and from absolute chastity and unchastity (incest), taken together, lend credence to a discomforting thesis: that there is no ultimately tenable distinction between chastity and incest, so that our ordinary understanding of marriage—as a middle way or as an adequate solution to the difficulties posed by society's exogamous need for an intersection of intertribal unity and intertribal diversity—is mistaken.[26]

I am not pretending, here, to cover this issue adequately. But I use this abbreviated discussion as a way of distinguishing "subjectivity" approaches from my own approach, focused as it is on *agency* and *event*, in terms I outlined at the beginning of this chapter. In my terms, what is striking in the play *Hamlet* is that Hamlet does not sleep with Gertrude; there is no incestuous "event" in the play, between mother and son, to match the excessive emotion on his side, and the excessive guilt on hers.[27] *Claudius* sleeps with (marries) Gertrude, and it is in fact on her sexual relations with *him* that Hamlet's excessive emotion concerning Gertrude is focused. And the point about Claudius's marriage to Gertrude historically (as event) is (a) that it is "unlawful" and (b) that it deprives Hamlet of his lawful succession. So I first turn my attention to what constituted unlawful marriage in the early modern period, and then show how the social relations of the play are altered if we put back the Gertrude/Claudius marriage in history—reinstate it as event—and look at the *offence* that it causes to Hamlet.

"Unlawful marriage," in early modern England, was a matter for the Ecclesiastical Courts. It is a key feature of the church canons (the legislation in canon law) that someone is *offended* by incest/unlawful marriage. As the 1603 canons put it:

> If any offend their Brethren, either by Adultery, Whoredome, Incest, or Drunkennesse, or by Swearing, Ribaldry, Usury, or any other uncleannesse and wickednesse of life, the Church-wardens . . . shall faithfully present all, and every of the said offenders, to the intent that they may be punished by the severity of the Lawes, according to their deserts, and such notorious offenders shall not be admitted to the holy Communion till they be reformed.[28]

And the crucial passage on incest itself in these canons runs:

> No person shall marry within the degrees prohibited by the lawe of god, and expressed in a table set forth by authority in the year of our lord 1563; and all marriages so made and contracted shall be adjudged incestuous and unlawful, and consequently shall be dissolved as void from the beginning, and the parties so married shall by course of law be separated. And the aforesaid table shall be in every church publickly set up, at the charge of the parish.[29]

Two depositions from the Durham Ecclesiastical Court Records, concerning an "unlawful marriage" (around 1560) show clearly how this idea of "offence caused" has a bearing on individual cases brought to the notice of the church courts:

> EDWARD WARD of Langton near Gainford husbandman, aged 40 years.
>   He saith that ther is dyvers writing hanginge upon the pillers of ther church of Gainford, but what they ar, or to what effect, he cannott deposse; saing that he and other parishioners doith gyve ther dewties to be taught such matters as he is examined upon, and is nott instruct of any such.

He saith, that he was married with the said Agnes in Gainford church by the curat Sr Nicholas, about 14 daies next after Christenmas last past, but not contrary to the lawes of God, as he and she thought. And for the resydew of the article he thinks nowe to be trewe, but not then. Examined whither that he, this deponent dyd knowe at and before the tyme of their mariadg, that she the said Agnes was, and had bein, his uncle Christofore Ward's wyfe, ye or no, he saith that he knew that to be trew, for she had, and haith yet, fyve children of his the said Christofer's. Examoned upon the danger of their soules, and evyll example, he saith that both he and mayny honest men in that parish thinks that it were a good deid that thei two meght still lyve to gyther as they doo, and be no further trobled. + AGNES WARD, ALIAS SAMPTON, aged 40 years.

—all the Lordship and paroch of Gainford knew howe nighe hir first husband and last husband was of kyn, and yet never found fault with their mariadg, neither when thei were asked in the church 3 sondry sonday nor sence—they haith bein likned [linked?] to gither more and 2 yere, and yett never man nor woman found fault—but rather thinks good ther of, bicause she was his own uncle wyf. +^30

The purposive narrative of these depositions is not difficult to unravel: Edward Ward's marriage to his uncle Christopher Ward's widow, Agnes, is incest under ecclesiastical law, but "mayny honest men in that Parish thinks that it were a good deid that thei two meight still lyve to gyther as they doo, and be no further trobled," and, as Agnes testified, everyone in the parish knew "howe nighe hir first husband and last husband was of kyn," and "yett never man nor woman found fault." Not only did no one find fault; they "rather thinks good ther of, bicause she was his own uncle wyf."

Church law holds the marriage unlawful; Christian charity suggests that no one is harmed by the marriage, and widow and children are appropriately cared for. The "dyvers writing hanginge upon the pillers of ther church" that Edward Ward refers to are the "table [to] to be in every church publickly set up, at the charge of the parish," specified in the 1603 canons quoted above: the tables of consanguinity and affinity which specified who might legally marry whom (as Edward Ward clearly deposes, he himself is illiterate, and unable to read the tables). And we may, I think, extend the idea of "offence caused" one stage further. *Someone* had to draw the marriage to the attention of the courts; that person had to be someone to whom the "unlawfulness" of the marriage gave some (material) offence.^31 This charge laid by another is what is referred to (but permanently uninterpretable without information now lost to us) in the sentence in Edward Ward's deposition: "And for the resydew of the article he thinks nowe to be trewe, but not then."^32

If we look at the Levitical degrees, the tables of consanguinity and affinity, we see how these already incorporate the idea of "offence caused." "Consanguinity" conforms broadly with what we might expect: a man may not marry his mother, his father's sister, or his mother's sister, his sister, his daughter, or the daughter of his own son or daughter.[33] The table of consanguinity prohibits marriages with close blood ties, in the generations in which it might plausibly occur (parent, sibling, offspring, grandchild). The table of affinity, by contrast, reflects unions which might produce conflicting inheritance claims.[34] A man might not marry his father's wife, his uncle's wife, his father's wife's daughter, his brother's wife, or his wife's sister, his son's wife, or his wife's daughter, nor the daughter of his wife's son or daughter. None of these are blood ties, but each creates complications over the *line*. In particular, the marriage of a widow to her dead husband's brother threatens the son's inheritance claim. The son is first in line, his father's brother second; the marriage of the dowager widow to the second in line threatens to overwhelm the claim of the legitimate heir.

Notoriously, Henry VIII's marriage to his dead brother Arthur's widow, Catherine of Aragon, was incestuous under the Levitican tables of affinity.[35] Since Claudius's marriage to Gertrude is, like Henry VIII's, a marriage to a dead brother's widow, there is no doubt in the play of the incest, and Hamlet states the case directly:

> Let me not think on't—Frailty thy name is woman—
> A little month, or ere those shoes were old
> With which she follow'd my poor father's body,
> Like Niobe, all tears—why, she—
> O God, a beast that wants discourse of reason
> Would have mourn'd longer—married with my uncle,
> My father's brother—but no more like my father
> Than I to Hercules. Within a month.
> Ere yet the salt of most unrighteous tears
> Had left the flushing in her galled eyes,
> She married—O most wicked speed! To post
> With such dexterity to incestuous sheets![36]

The ghost of Hamlet senior puts the case more forcefully still, but unlike Hamlet, gives the active part in the incest entirely to Claudius:

> Ay, that incestuous, that adulterate beast,
> With witchcraft of his wit, with traitorous gifts—
> O wicked wit, and gifts that have the power
> So to seduce!—won to his shameful lust
> The will of my most seeming-virtuous queen. . . .
> O horrible! O horrible! most horrible!
> If thou has nature in thee, bear it not,
> Let not the royal bed of Denmark be
> A couch for luxury and damned incest.[37]

An offence—incest—but (as in the case from the court records) some anxiety as to *who* has been materially offended. In kinship terms there is an offence. It goes unrecognised until someone claims it as such.

Kinship and inheritance are remarkably strong themes in the play from its opening moments.[38] Young Hamlet is heir to Old Hamlet, just as young Fortinbras is heir to Old Fortinbras: *he* comes at the head of an army to reclaim his inheritance.[39] Claudius's first entrance as King, with Hamlet as not-King (dressed in mourning black), immediately emphasises the alienation of the Hamlet line. Indeed, what is striking about this first entrance is that it is entirely *unexpected* in revealing to the audience *Claudius* as King (referred to throughout the play simply as "King"—here only as "Claudius King of Denmark"), sumptuously, with Hamlet in mourning black. Everything in the earlier scenes has prepared the audience for *Hamlet's* appearance as King. The prolonged mourning (an interesting topic itself in early modern history) insistently keeps the direct line, Old Hamlet/Young Hamlet present. And Claudius's opening words fix for the audience the *usurpation*:

> Though yet of Hamlet our dear brother's death
> The memory be green, and that it us befitted
> To bear our hearts in grief, and our whole kingdom
> To be contracted in one brow of woe,
> Yet so far hath discretion fought with nature
> That we with wisest sorrow think on him
> Together with remembrance of ourselves.
> Therefore our sometime sister, now our queen,
> Th'imperial jointress to this warlike state,
> Have we . . .
> Taken to wife.[40]

The first exchange of words between Claudius and Hamlet (somewhat late in the scene—it follows the "fatherly" exchange with Laertes) underlines the fact that the "unlawful" marriage has strengthened the line in Claudius's favour, and to Hamlet's detriment:

KING: But now, my cousin Hamlet, and my son—

HAMLET: A little more than kin, and less than kind.

KING: How is it that the clouds still hang on you?

HAMLET: Not so, my lord, I am too much in the
sun.[41]

If Hamlet is Claudius's cousin, Hamlet should be king; if Hamlet is Claudius's son, then he is confirmed as line-dependent on Claudius, who sits legitimately on the throne. I suggest that Act I in its entirety dwells deliberately on *incest* as a material offence committed against Hamlet.[42]

Claudius's unlawful marriage to Hamlet's mother, Gertrude, cuts Hamlet out of the line.[43] The offence is against Hamlet. But for a mother to connive in wronging her own blood-son (even if passively) makes her an *emotional* focus for the blame—not simply the unlawful marriage, but the unnatural treatment of a son.[44] She has indeed committed a sinful and unlawful act, on which Hamlet obsessively dwells. He does so as one to whom that act has caused harm, disturbing the conventional relationship between blood-bond and line-bond, so that his filial duty towards his mother is now at odds with his obligations towards his father and himself (the legitimate line). The act is sexual (as Hamlet insistently reminds us). Its consequences are *material* for the line, and Hamlet is equally insistent about that:

HAMLET: Now mother, what's the matter?

QUEEN: Hamlet, thou hast thy father much offended.[45]

HAMLET: Mother, you have my father much offended. . . . [46]

QUEEN: Have you forgot me?

HAMLET: No, by the rood, not so.
          You are the Queen, your husband's brother's wife,
          And, would it were not so, you are my mother. . . . [47]

QUEEN: What have I done, that thou dar'st wag thy tongue
          In noise so rude against me?

HAMLET: Such an act
          That blurs the grace and blush of modesty.[48]

Offence against Old Hamlet ("my father"); offensive behaviour towards Claudius ("thy father," because Gertrude is "[her] husband's brother's wife," and thus he her son's father). Hamlet is caught between the knowledge of an unlawful marriage, a crime committed (and perhaps two), to which the community turns a blind eye,[49] and a sense of personal outrage at a wrong perpetrated against himself, by his close kin, when to rectify that outrage would be to commit petty treason.[50]

Here, I suggest, we have an alternative account of "(the man) . . . dominated by an emotion which is inexpressible, because it is in *excess* of the facts as they appear"—one in which we can see quite clearly that in so far as Gertrude is supposed to have behaved monstrously and unnaturally towards her first husband *and* her son, her guilt—in direct contrast to Claudius's—is culturally constructed so as to represent her as responsible without allowing her agency.[51] In my version, the intensity of feeling, the sense of outrage on Hamlet's behalf is still there, but it is produced as a consequence of offences recognised within the early modern community (in which Gertrude is much more straightforwardly and specifically implicated). In *this* account, Gertrude has participated in the remarriage—has (literally) *alienated* her son, and Old Hamlet's name (and does not apparently accept Hamlet's urging to leave Claudius's bed, because that argument (his) does not effect *her*).

We have not, then, exonerated Gertrude, but we have recovered the guilt surrounding her as a condition of her oppression: she is required by the kinship rules of her community to remain faithful to her deceased husband; that same community deprives her of any but the proxy influence her remarriage gives her, over her son's future. Yet she is the emotional focus in the play's cultural construction of the guilt which taints the State of Denmark.

Let me end by reminding you of something I said at the start: that there are grave reasons why I have found myself pushed to look for evidence of such agency in history—this is by no means simply an urge to identify my own critical position as an end in itself. It is above all the consequences for women of thus shifting the focus from text and discourse to history and agency, which, for me, currently, "motivates the turn to history."[52] As a Shakespeare critic, I have become tired of having to listen to offensive critical discourses, for which the author need apparently take no responsibility, which excavate desire in discourse so as to "objectivate" the female subject— object of desire, object of blame, permanently victim.[53] After my initial reaction, which was one of anger (as some people will remember all too well),[54] it occurred to me that there must be something *wrong* with such accounts in relation to women, whether or not such critical enterprises were valuable in relation to men and patriarchy. For in history, women are *not* permanently in the object position, they are subjects. To be always object and victim is not the material reality of woman's existence, nor is it her lived experience. If we look at event, at agency in history, the inevitability of these accounts disappears. And we find that we are once again entitled to ask (as I have done in the case of Gertrude): Who, after all, has been wronged, and by whom?

Notes

1. *Hamlet*, III.ii.224–30. All references are to the Arden edition, ed. Harold Jenkins (London, 1982).

2. *Reading Shakespeare historically* (forthcoming).

3. I am particularly grateful to Annabel Patterson and Jean Howard, with whom I discussed that earlier draft at length, on that occasion, and to Bill Sherman, who couldn't be there, but who criticised the paper at length and in detail afterwards.

4. Simpson 1987–8.

5. *Ibid.*, 724–5. For another powerful argument which meshes with Simpson's doubts about the authenticity of discourse theorists' commitment to "history" see Montrose 1986.

6. "In particular, given the current popularity of discourse analysis, it seems likely that for many practitioners the historical method will remain founded in covertly idealist reconstructions" (*ibid.*).

7. Catherine Belsey, in her "Making histories then and now: Shakespeare from *Richard II* to *Henry V*," gives an elegant account of the ideological motivation for the privileging of a master-narrative version of history in criticism of Shakespeare's "history" plays. Unlike Simpson, however, she sees the possibility of a postmodernist deconstruction which "uncovers the differences *within* rationality, and thus writes of it *otherwise*," and which will thereby "activate the differences and promote political intervention." She proposes this as an alternative to both "the master-narrative of inexorable and teleological development" and "a (dis)continuous and fragmentary present, a world of infinite differences which are ultimately undifferentiated because they are all confined to the signifying surface of things."

8. For a challenging account of these developments in cultural history see Chartier 1988.

9. See, for instance, Geertz 1984; M. Rosaldo 1984; Shweder and Bourne 1984; Bruner 1986.

10. For a clear account of the way in which political commitment sharpens the focus of feminist historical work, see Jean Howard's "Towards a postmodern, politically committed, historical practice" in *Uses of History* (1991).

11. See most eloquently Davis 1987.

12. See Jardine 1990.

13. See first of all Geertz 1973, p. 51; then Greenblatt 1980, p. 3.

14. See Geertz 1973, pp. 15–16.

15. Geertz 1973, p. 13.

16. Greenblatt 1988, p. 1. I am grateful to Bill Sherman for making this helpful connection for me, and for his continued support for my efforts to get to grips with recent writings in social anthropology.

17. See Geertz 1973, p. 35:

The image of a constant human nature independent of time, place, and circumstance, of studies and professions, transient fashions and temporary opinions, may be an illusion, that what man is may be so entangled with where he is, who he is, and what he believes that it is inseparable from them. It is precisely the consideration of such a possibility that led to the rise of the concept of culture and the decline of the uniformitarian view of man. Whatever else modern anthropology asserts—and it seems to have asserted almost everything at one time or another—it is firm in the conviction that men unmodified by the customs of particular places do not in fact exist, have never existed, and most important, could not in the very nature of the case exist. There is, there can be, no backstage where we can catch a glimpse of Mascou's actors as "real persons" lounging about in street clothes, disengaged from their profession, displaying with artless candor their spontaneous desires and unprompted passions.

18. I leave aside here the issue of the disadvantaging of women *per se* in Lacanian theory, see Jardine 1989.

19. This coexistence is made easier by the fact that social anthropologists like Geertz have thoroughly absorbed psychoanalytical theory, and tend to assume the Freudian subject as the starting point for their discussions of the cultural construction of selfhood. See Geertz 1973; Rosaldo 1984.

20. See Neely 1988, pp. 5–18.

21. In our Symposium discussions it became clear, I think, that in this respect (and this respect *only*) feminist critics are currently at an advantage in the critical debate being

conducted around historicist and deconstructive critical approaches to text. Since they have a declared political objective, they are entitled to discard methodologies which fail to contribute constructively to it.

22. I concede, after many discussions on the subject, that taking Eliot as starting-point is in some sense a rhetorical device. But I find it striking that Eliot is fully aware of Freud, and thus that psychoanalytical reading of the play is established before psychoanalytical theory is explicitly introduced into literary studies.

23. Eliot 1932, pp. 144–5.

24. For a clear account of the consistent allocation of blame to the woman in psychoanalytical readings of *Hamlet* and *Measure for Measure* see Rose 1985.

25. *ibid.*, pp. 116–7. See also her very clear rehearsal of a series of psychoanalytical readings of *Hamlet* prompted by Eliot's essay.

26. Shell 1988, p. 24.

27. The same kind of account can be given of Ferdinand's "incestuous desire" for his sister, in *The Duchess of Malfi*. See Jardine 1983b.

28. Gibson 1730; Burn 1763.

29. Gibson 1730; Burn 1763.

30. Surtees Society 1845, p. 59. The "marks" made by both dependents indicates that they were illiterate (a fact which is confirmed within Edward Ward's deposition).

31. See Davis 1983 for a clear case in which an unlawful relationship goes unreported in the community until a charge is brought by an individual who regards the "marriage" as depriving him of something (land) due to him: "The new Martin was not only a husband, but also an heir, a nephew, and an important peasant proprietor in Artigat. It was in these roles that the trouble finally began" (p. 51).

32. In fact, the canons of 1603 were drawn up hastily upon Elizabeth's death, since at her death it was suddenly realised that there now was no body of valid ecclesiastical law (her own legislation having been specified as for the duration of her reign). Owing to an oversight, the 1603 canons did not go through Parliament until some three years later, when it was realised that the clergy was probably operating outside statute law, and the situation was rectified. Patrick Collinson has recently suggested to me that these canons in fact *never* went on to the statute book—that in fact the Tudor and Stuart governments left church law in a kind of deliberate limbo. All of this is really to suggest that (*a*) it was extraordinarily difficult to operate the various competing demands of common law, statute, and canon law, and (*b*) "moral" and "legal" demands might readily be perceived to be in opposition, the legal contrary to custom, or the moral dubious within the technical law.

33. There are exactly comparable tables of consanguinity and affinity for the woman.

34. Indeed, this is how theological dictionaries traditional describe the rules of affinity—as concerning *property*.

35. So was Henry's marriage to Ann Boleyn, since he had already had a relationship with her sister (Catholic propaganda, interestingly, claimed more obvious incest: that Ann was in fact Henry's daughter).

36. *Hamlet* I.ii.146–57. And see the Book of Common Prayer, cit. Jenkins, *Hamlet*, 319, n. 14. For another example of explicit affinity incest in the drama see Spurio's relationship with his stepmother in Tourneur's *The revenger's tragedy*. There, as here, the unlawfulness of the relationship is emphasised by the repeated formula from the tables of affinity: "*Spurio.* I would 'twere love, but 't 'as a fouler name/ Than lust; you are my father's wife, your Grace may guess now / What I call it" (I.ii.129–31). In *Cymbeline* Cymbeline tries both to force Imogen to divorce her true husband, Posthumous, and to enter into an incestuous marriage with her stepbrother, Cloten.

37. I.v.42–6; 80–3.

38. For extended discussion of the "elective" monarchy in Denmark, see Harold Jenkins's

discussion in the recent Arden edition. I point out for brevity that Scotland was an elective monarchy: the eldest son of the reigning monarch was removed at birth to the care of the Earl of Marr. In due course the clans were assembled, and he was "elected" her to his father.

39.   "Now sir, young Fortinbras, . . . [comes] to recover from us by strong hand . . . those foresaid lands / So by his father lost" (I.i.98–107).

40.   I.ii.1–14.

41.   I.ii.64–7, and then see 107–12: "You are the most immediate to our throne, / And with no less nobility of love / Than that which dearest father bears his son / Do I impart toward you."

42.   The offence is committed against Hamlet senior *and* Hamlet junior. See Greenblatt 1986, p. 219: "The ghost of Old Hamlet—'of life, of crown, of queen at once dispatched'— returns to his land to demand that his son take the life of the imposter who has seized his identity." There seems to be a useful notion here of "Hamlet" as an identity, a nexus of relations that Hamlet junior *ought* to occupy. See Girard 1986, 285–6: "This significance of twins and brothers . . . must be present . . . if we are to interpret correctly the scene in which Hamlet, holding in his hands the two portraits of his father and his uncle . . . tries to convince his mother that an enormous difference exists between the two. There would be no Hamlet 'problem' if the hero really believed what he says. It is also himself, therefore, that he is trying to convince."

43.   Had Hamlet an heir himself his position would be strengthened (the play stresses Gertrude's maturity). I have come to think that *this* is the emphasis which so insistently produces Ophelia as fallen woman—were she pregnant she would threaten the (new) line in Denmark.

44.   The intensity of the blame this occasions stands comparison with the blame which drives Ophelia insane—the murder of a father by the daughter's "husband" (an act of petty treason, carried out by a king's son). Early modern inheritance law consistently reflects anxiety as to whether mothers can be expected to act reliably on their male offspring's behalf, in the absence of a male head of household. See Jardine 1987, p. 9.

45.   That is, "been offensive to."

46.   That is, "committed an offence against."

47.   See Bullinger: "A woman maye not mary husbandes brother" (fol. xvir).

48.   III.iv.7–41.

49.   On this account the possible *murder* of the king is a secondary issue.

50.   On murder by wife or child as petty treason see Sharpe.

51.   It is because this particular cultural construction of female guilt is still current that it remains plausibly "real" to critics.

52.   The phrase comes from Howard 1986, p. 13, and is a question addressed to all those whose work has been called "New Historicist"—"What motivates the turn to history?" (p. 14).

53.   "Objectivate" is Chartier's term. See, for instance, Chartier 1988: "To combat [the] reduction of thoughts to objects or to 'objectivations' . . . a definition of history primarily sensitive to inequalities in the appropriation of common materials or practices has come into being" (p. 102).

54.   San Diego, 1984.

Works Cited

Belsey, Catherine (1991) "Making histories then and now: Shakespeare from *Richard II* to *Henry V*" in F. Barker *et al.* (eds.) *Uses of History: Marxism, Postmodernism, and the Renaissance*, Manchester.

Bruner, E. M. (1986) "Experience and its Expressions" in V. Turner and Bruner (eds.) *The Anthropology of Experience*, Urbana, Illinois.

Burn, R. (1963) *Ecclesiastical Law*.

Chartier, Roger (1988) *Cultural History: Between Practices and Representations*, trans. L. G. Cochrane, Cambridge.

Davis, Natalie Z. (1983) *The Return of Martin Guerre*, Cambridge, Mass.

——— (1987) *Fiction in the Archives: Pardon Tales and their Tellers in Sixteenth-Century France*, Stanford, California and Cambridge.

Eliot, T. S. (1932) *Selected Essays*, London.

Geertz, Clifford (1973) *The Interpretation of Cultures*, New York.

——— (1984) " 'From the Native's Point of View': on the Nature of Anthropological Understanding" in Shweder and LeVine (1984), pp. 123–36.

Gibson, Edward (1730) *Codex Iuris Ecclesiastica Anglicanae*.

Greenblatt, Stephen (1980) *Renaissance Self-fashioning: from More to Shakespeare*, Chicago.

——— (1988) *Shakespearean Negotiations: the Circulation of Social Energy in Renaissance England*, Oxford.

Howard, Jean (1986) "The New Historicism in Renaissance Studies," *English Literary Renaissance*, 16, pp. 13–43.

——— (1991) "Towards a postmodern politically committed, historical practice" in Barker *et al.* (eds.) *Uses of History: Marxism, Postmodernism and the Renaissance*, Manchester.

Jardine, Lisa (1983) *"The Duchess of Malfi:* A Case Study in the Representation of Women" in S. Kappeler and N. Bryson (eds.) *Teaching the Text*, London.

——— (1987) "Cultural Confusion and Shakespeare's Learned Heroines," *Shakespeare Quarterly*, 38, pp. 1–18.

——— (1990) " 'Why Should he call her Whore?': Defamation and Desdemona's Case," in M. Warner and M. Tudeau-Clayton (eds.) *Strategies of Interpretation: Essays in Honour of Frank Kermode*, London.

Neely, Carol Thomas (1988) "Constructing the Subject: Feminist Practice and the New Renaissance Discourses," *English Literary Renaissance*, 18, pp. 5–18.

Rosaldo, M. Z. (1984) "Towards an Anthropology of Self and Feeling" in Shweder and LeVine (1984), pp. 137–57.

Rose, Jacqueline (1985) "Sexuality and the Reading of Shakespeare" in J. Drakakis (ed.) *Alternative Shakespeares*, London.

Shweder, R. A. and E. J. Bourne (1984) "Does the Concept of the Person Vary Cross-culturally?" in Shweder and Levine (1984), pp. 158–99.

Shweder, R. A. and R. A. LeVine (eds.) (1984) *Culture Theory: Essays on Mind, Self and Emotion*, Cambridge.

Sharpe, J. A. (1984) *Crime in Early Modern England 1550–1750*, London.

Shell, Marc (1988) *The End of Kinship*, Stanford, California.

Simpson, David (1987–8) "Literary Criticism and the Return to 'History,' " *Critical Inquiry*, 14, pp. 721–47.

Surtees Society (1845) *Depositions and other Ecclesiastical Proceedings from the Courts of Durham, extending from the 1311 to the Rign of Elizabeth*, London.

Index

$\blacklozenge$